Bouchard obeyed the order, which was little short of suicide, went over the embankment, and was promptly shot down. Petty and others crawled forward to drag him to safety. The German mortar shells were bursting closer now, and the pent-up tension in the men was explosive. All it needed was a spark, and that spark was Sergeant McHugh. Leaping to his feet, the young Ranger brandished his submachine gun over his head and yelled, "Let's go get the bastards!" All the tension in the men suddenly released; they leapt to their feet and swept up the hill, snarling, cursing, yelling in blood lust.

Seeing the assaulting line of Rangers going forward with fixed bayonets and firing from the hip was an experience Sergeant Petty would never forget. "I know that I will never see a more brave and glorious sight," he recalled. "It was for me indeed a moment of being proud to be a Ranger."

D0348625

By Robert W. Black
Published by The Ballantine Publishing Group:

RANGERS IN KOREA
RANGERS IN WORLD WAR II

Books published by The Ballantine Publishing Group
are available at quantity discounts on bulk purchases
for premium, educational, fund-raising, and special
sales use. For details, please call 1-800-733-3000.

RANGERS IN WORLD WAR II

Robert W. Black

BALLANTINE BOOKS • NEW YORK

A Ballantine Book
Published by The Ballantine Publishing Group
Copyright © 1992 by Robert W. Black

All rights reserved under International and Pan-American Copyright Conventions. Published in the United States by The Ballantine Publishing Group, a division of Random House, Inc., New York, and simultaneously in Canada by Random House of Canada Limited, Toronto.

Ballantine is a registered trademark and the Ballantine colophon is a trademark of Random House, Inc.

www.ballantinebooks.com

Library of Congress Catalog Card Number: 91-93162

ISBN 0-8041-0565-0

Manufactured in the United States of America

First Edition: April 1992

10   9   8   7   6   5   4   3   2

FOR THE RANGERS

CONTENTS

ACKNOWLEDGMENTS

Centuries ago, John Donne wrote that "No man is an island." That is especially true when a writer sets forth to tell of an event. I am indebted to many people for their encouragement and assistance. My deep thanks to Rangers Jim Altieri and Lou Lisko; to Marcell Swank, Len Lomell, Bill Petty, and Herm Stein; to Colonel Roy Murray, General Ted Conway, and Colonels Herm Dammer and Dick Sullivan; and to Joe Fineberg, Joe Cain, Fran Coughlin, Ray Alm, Rex Sharp, and Jack McDeuitt. Thanks to all of the Rangers who gave of their time for interviews. The staff of the U.S. Army Military History Institute are old friends and were of great assistance. Thanks to the staffs of the National Archives at Suitland, Maryland, the Infantry Center Library at Fort Benning, Georgia, the Special Warfare Center Library at Fort Bragg, North Carolina, and the Military Personnel Center at St. Louis, Missouri.

A very special thanks to Carolyn Stansbury who took the rough-hewn product and polished it. Thanks to Al Hart of Fox Chase Agency and Owen Lock, Stephen Sterns, and the editorial staff of Ivy Books for making this dream a reality.

FOREWORD

I was twelve years old when the Japanese attacked Pearl Harbor on December 7, 1941, and I was ready for war. I had read Dumas's *The Three Musketeers*, Sabatini's *Captain Blood*, and the great Ranger classic *Northwest Passage* by Kenneth Roberts, and my ears had been filled with bugle calls and rolling drums, my thoughts centered on flashing swords and the rattle of musketry. From Dieppe in 1942 onward, I followed the exploits of the Rangers with a fervent adulation. But in 1945 when the war ended, the only shot I had heard was when I fired off the family shotgun to locally announce the unconditional surrender of the Japanese.

I cried bitter tears because I had missed my chance to go to war.

In 1950, I was serving with the 82d Airborne Division at Fort Bragg, North Carolina, when North Korea invaded South Korea. Soon a call went out for volunteer paratroopers to become Rangers. I volunteered and became one of America's first Airborne Rangers. As a member of the 8th Airborne Ranger Company, I fought in Korea and at last experienced the challenge, fear, hate, trust, and brotherly love a man knows in war.

I would never cry for war again.

Around 1960, I read a book titled *The Spearheaders* by Ranger James Altieri, a member of the 1st and 4th Ranger Battalions of World War II. Jim Altieri recounted the story of how a Commando instructor had told the members of the 1st Ranger Battalion to remember, "It is all in the heart and the mind." Having fought in combat as a Ranger, I knew the truth of these words.

On July 12, 1968, in Vietnam, I led three South Vietnamese

Regional Force companies in a day-long battle with a North Vietnamese Army (NVA) battalion. In late afternoon, under circumstances of great difficulty, I had reached the end of my physical and mental resources. At that moment, exhausted and drained and lying in the slime of a delta rice paddy, an inner voice said to me, "It is all in the heart and the mind. You can achieve anything. It is all in the mind and the heart."

From those words, from that spirit, came the strength and purpose to carry on and complete my mission.

That is the spirit of the American Ranger, a band of brothers that is uniquely American and has its roots buried three and a half centuries deep in American history.

This book is about that spirit—it is the story of the Ranger battalions of World War II. It is not a story of supermen or demigods. This is an account of men immersed in the outrage of war. In the battles that are recounted, there was courage and fear; men went beyond the call of duty and men functioned in shock or broke before the horror they encountered. They loved each other as men can love each other only during the time they are in battle. They fought not only the enemy but often among themselves. Some found solace in prayer, and some found it in a bottle. There was comradeship and jealousy, compassion and ruthlessness.

Above all, there was duty and the Ranger spirit, "It is all in the heart and the mind."

They prevailed.

CHAPTER 1

FOUNDING

The years 1939–1942 saw the cruel hand of war grasp much of the world. The Nazi war machine had swallowed up most of Europe; Czechoslovakia was absorbed, Poland crushed, and Belgium, Holland, and France lay prostrate under the German boot. The swastika flew over Norway, and the British had been driven back to their isolated little isle, losing most of their weapons and equipment and barely saving 338,226 Allied soldiers in the desperate evacuation of Dunkirk. By sending troops to Greece, British Prime Minister Winston Churchill had tried to save what he would call the "soft underbelly of Europe," but the resourceful Germans moved swiftly to crush his plans. Coming to the rescue of their posturing Italian ally, Benito Mussolini, they thrashed the nations of their southeastern flank and conquered Yugoslavia and Greece.

In search of *lebensraum* (living space), the Germans then turned hungry eyes eastward. The Soviet Union had taken advantage of German victories, using the pact between Hitler and Stalin to seize Estonia, Latvia, Lithuania, and parts of Poland and Romania. When it suited their purpose, the Nazis disregarded this pact of conquest and turned the might of Germany on Russia. Though Napoleon had failed to defeat the Russians, Hitler was certain he could succeed. As time would prove, the Soviet Union was a long way from being finished, but in the summer of 1942, the tracks of Hitler's panzers and the tramp of German hobnailed boots sounded at the gates of Moscow and deep into the Black Sea region.

The Japanese, seeking dominion under the guise of the title "Greater East Asia Co-Prosperity Sphere," had seized

Manchuria and invaded China. Puffed up by success, the Japanese then engaged themselves in one of the greatest tactical victories and simultaneously one of the most ill-advised strategic military moves of all time. On December 7, 1941, they attacked United States air, land, and naval forces at Pearl Harbor on the island of Oahu in the Hawaiian island chain.

Overnight, the United States was transformed from a squabbling divided citizenry, where many wanted no part of any war, to an angry, unified nation, totally committed to the support of its allies and the destruction of its enemies. Though raw, unprepared, and unaccustomed to the role thrust upon it, the United States was the most powerful nation in the world. In the times to come, the United States would play a major role in the defeat of Italy and Germany and carry by far the greatest burden in the victory over Japan. But the power of the United States needed time to develop. Much British Commonwealth, Russian, and American blood would be shed due to the American and British prewar, shortsighted, penny-pinching approach to military matters. Bataan, Guam, Wake, and Corregidor fell to the Japanese; Malaya was taken and Australia threatened, but from the moment America entered the war, the Axis was doomed.

Victory was far in the future, however, on a day in April 1942 when Col. Lucian King Truscott reported to the army chief of staff, Gen. George Marshall in Washington, D.C.

Truscott was a soldier's soldier. It was World War I that led the young teacher from Chatfield, Texas, to seek an army commission, and once in the army, he found it a home. Nineteen years a company-grade officer, Truscott was a fighting intellectual, well grounded in military basics, having spent years teaching military subjects. He was also keenly aware that he was a forty-seven-year-old soldier without combat experience.

Prior to his meeting with Marshall, Truscott passed before the scrutiny of Gen. Mark W. Clark of Headquarters Army Ground Forces and Gen. Dwight Eisenhower, chief of the War Department Operations Division. He knew that he was being selected to lead a group of American officers who would go to England to become a member of the staff of Lord Louis Mountbatten, head of Combined Operations. Mountbatten had charge of the Commandos, the daring hit-and-run raiders, who despite their small numbers, were giving the Germans migraine headaches and serving in the equally important role of providing the civilian populace of the United Kingdom with something to feel good about.

Truscott was thrilled that he would have the opportunity to serve with this highly trained fighting force, and his curiosity as to why he would be sent was quickly answered. General Marshall saw Germany as the greater threat and the Russian continuance in the war as vital.

Marshall believed it would be necessary for the Americans and British to make a cross-channel invasion, hopefully in 1943. To do this, American forces would be concentrated in England. Marshall had confidence in American training but recognized there was no substitute for battle experience. If some Americans had the opportunity to go into action with the Commandos, they could then be spread among the American units selected to lead the invasion and, as teachers and leaders, upgrade American capability.

On a trip to England from April 4 to April 19, 1942, Marshall discussed his views with Mountbatten and received agreement. The staff went to work. At an April 15 London meeting, British Maj. Gen. J. C. Haydon of Combined Operations Headquarters, the American Cols. A. C. Wedemeyer and J. E. Hull, and a Major Wilson worked out two tentative proposals.

The first was that a number of American officers, noncommissioned officers, and privates should be selected and trained with the British Commandos to form the nucleus or framework around which an American commando unit could be built up. The figure of twelve officers, twenty NCOs and forty enlisted men was suggested.

It was also decided that concurrently with the training of that group twenty other officers and forty NCOs should be trained with the intention of sending them back to the United States as instructors in commando methods.

Also on April 15, Mountbatten put forth his proposal for an American staff to work with his headquarters—eight officers from the U.S. Army, Navy, and Marines. One of the officers was to be an aviator, another a communications officer, and a third from intelligence. This team was to be headed by a senior officer with the suggested title of U.S. Adviser on Combined Operations. Mountbatten also passed on a document showing the composition of a British Commando unit (headquarters, seven officers and seventy-one other ranks, and six fighting troops each of three officers and sixty-two other ranks) as a guide for the formation of an American commando unit.

George Marshall selected Truscott to head the American effort. Joining Mountbatten's staff, Truscott would concentrate on American participation in commando training and operations and would spread the combat-experienced Americans among the units which were to conduct the cross-channel invasion.

After reporting to Marshall, Truscott received his detailed orders from Eisenhower. He was cautioned about keeping the formation of new organizations to a minimum. "If you do find it necessary to organize such units," Eisenhower further told Truscott, "I hope that you will find some other name than 'commandos,' for the glamor of that name will always remain—and properly so—British."

A week after leaving the United States, Truscott was in London. The American commanders and staff on the scene were not happy with his mission or his latitude, but there was little they could do but grumble. Truscott and his small team of American land, air, and naval officers got a friendlier reception at Combined Operations Headquarters where Lord Louis Mountbatten and his staff gathered to welcome the Americans.

Combined Operations Headquarters was born of the necessity to have a single headquarters combining air, ground, and naval forces to plan and conduct raiding operations.

The British, with their long experience in naval warfare, had established a combined operations development center at Portsmouth in 1936. The idea of combined operations to land raiding parties was put forth by several men, but the voice with power was that of soldier/writer/politician Prime Minister Winston S. Churchill. His support was based upon his personal experiencĕ and long study of war. Churchill was to prove a champion of the small, elite, and aggressive unit.

In the Norway campaign of April 1940, the British were employing "independent companies," and though trained for raiding, the necessities of combat required they fight more in the manner of line infantry. Nonetheless, these companies would be the forerunner of the Commandos.

In June 1940, Britain's feisty prime minister was looking at the German success using elite units called "storm troops." Churchill had to give considerable attention to defense during this stage of the war and was seeking twenty thousand storm troops, or "Leopards" as he called them, to form rapid-reaction forces that would "spring at the throat of any small landings or descents."

On June 6, 1940, Churchill was writing to British chief of staff Lord Ismay about organizing newly arriving Australian units in such manner that their missions could include the capability of "landing on the friendly coasts now held by the enemy." Churchill wanted highly trained troops of what he called the "hunter class" to spread terror up and down the German-occupied coasts of Europe. He referred to this tactic as "butcher and bolt," but saw it leading to the day when major coastal cities could be surprised and taken. The more territory the Germans occupied, the more spread out and vulnerable their forces became. Churchill was adamant about the need for offensive action and continued to press for "Striking Companies."

Lt. Col. D. W. Clarke of the British General Staff (who is credited with being the inspiration of the idea for the Commandos) had sent an early memorandum on the subject of raiding forces up the chain of command. He was now assigned the mission of preparing plans for such a force. Clarke's personal experience included service against Arab guerrillas in Palestine, and he had studied the history of small mobile and hard-hitting raiding forces in various wars. A prime example was the Boer War in South Africa (1899–1902) in which small bands of farmers of Dutch/German extraction organized into "commandos" had raised havoc with the mighty British Army. Clarke knew his subject and believed in his mission. He would be the first Commando wounded in action.

In the early stages of the war in 1940, British resources were strained to the limit. Every available army battalion was needed for the defense of the home island and the overseas empire. The sea duties of the Royal Navy absorbed the strength of the Royal Marines. Thus, starting with the Independent Companies, through the Special Services Battalions that followed, and on into the Commandos, there was a need to form new units, a need to take highly trained men who were skilled in amphibious operations, put them in self-contained and self-supporting units and organize them so that these units would fit in existing amphibious transport and landing craft.

Lieutenant Colonel Clarke prepared his plan and suggested the units be called "commandos." The word is widely credited to have originated with the Boers of South Africa, but it was used by British Gen. John Forbes in writing to Col. Henry Bouquet during the campaign against Fort Duquesne (present-day Pittsburgh) as early as June of 1758. Originally the word "commando" meant only the organization, but it has since come to encompass the men who served in it. In selecting the name Commando, Clarke must have been aware that Winston Churchill had gained national fame as an escaped prisoner during the Boer War. The name Commando was certain to touch memories of youth and glory in the prime minister.

The volunteers for the new Commandos came from every unit in the British Army and all walks of life and experience.

Combined operations training centers were established based on the "Jack-and-John" or "me-and-my-pal" teamwork principle of two men looking out for and assisting each other through the difficult training. Much emphasis was placed on individual initiative. The men were given funds but were responsible for their own billeting. When the men were dismissed after a long grueling day of training, they might be told that their next formation would be at a given point and time fifty miles away. They were not told how to get there.

Small raids began in June 1940 and spread from near Boulogne on the French coast to Guernsey in the Channel Islands to the Lofoten Islands near the Arctic Circle, then to the island of Vaagso in Norway and another raid on the Lofotens.

The greatest success was the raid on Saint-Nazaire where Commandos put out of commission the world's largest dry-dock, an 1100-foot-long facility critical to the battleships of the German Navy. To a nation as dependent on its sea-lanes as Britain, this raid was of enormous importance. These were followed by attacks at Dieppe, Madagascar, North Africa, Sicily, and Walcheren. The targets of the raids varied from the destruction of lighthouses, pipelines, mining equipment, shipping, and aircraft to shore reconnaissance and an unsuccessful attempt to kill or kidnap Gen. Erwin Rommel. Sometimes the Commandos failed. The raid on Guernsey was such a botched job that Churchill exploded, "Let there be no more Guernseys!"

Initially headed by Lt. Gen. Sir Alan Bourne, who was followed by Admiral of the Fleet Sir Roger Keyes, the Commandos came to reach their zenith under Louis Mountbatten, who assumed command in October 1941.

Throughout a time when Britain was forced on the defensive, it was the well-publicized attack spirit and daring of the Commandos that gave the hope, the promise of victory.

Through these long months, Churchill would not retreat from his belief in this raiding force. His views were expressed in a letter to Secretary of State for War Anthony Eden: "The defeat of France was accomplished by an incredibly small number of highly equipped elite, while the dull mass of the German Army came on behind, made good the conquest and occupied it."

This observation by Churchill was founded in fact. A December 1940 report by the German Army High Command pointed out that their May 1940 attacks succeeded largely by use of assault detachments. The German High Command chided its infantry in general for being too closely massed in attacks and lacking the necessary offensive drive.

Opposition to Commando units came quickly as the old guard of the British Army took offense. The same arguments used in America against the formation of Ranger units in Colonial and modern times were used by British officers in opposition to the Commandos. Such units could not do anything that regular units could not, robbed the army of its best men, and the organization of them was a slap in the face to the regular establishment. When reluctant officers were slow to carry out his wishes, Churchill wrote to Secretary Eden, suggesting that an example be made of "one or two," and pressed for the reports that would give him assurance his wishes were being carried out.

When the American Truscott arrived, he found the British headquarters and their system was a bewildering maze. Even the common language was a matter of separation. A promotion to brigadier general gave him prestige that helped his official relations with staff members. Weeks would pass before Truscott felt he understood the British system. But with that understanding came the recognition that the United States should form its own special operations units.

This belief was based upon three factors:

1. The American buildup of forces was in its infancy. There were only two U.S. Army divisions in Britain: the 34th Infantry Division and the 1st Armored Division.
2. The number of raids planned by Combined Operation Headquarters was limited in number, and most of those involved relatively small forces. There was a large pool of trained and eager Commandos from Britain and Canada waiting their turn for action. It was unlikely newly arrived Americans would go to the head of the combat line.
3. The British based the size of a Commando unit on the carrying capability of their landing craft. Because newly arrived American soldiers engaged in raiding would be using British landing craft, it seemed best to follow the example and form new American units rather than try to piecemeal existing American organizations, thus destroying their operational integrity.

But the idea remained that these units would serve as training vehicles, which men would leave when they gained sufficient combat experience to spread their knowledge throughout the assault elements of the planned cross-channel invasion force.

Work had gone forward on the Commando project prior to Truscott's arrival. Agreement had been reached with Combined Operation Headquarters to send two officers and two NCOs for a two-week orientation course with the Commandos. Preliminary plans had been laid for formation of a skeletonized commando of two troops including tentative tables of organization and a proposed request drafted to the War Department for grades and ratings.

Truscott acknowledged this preliminary work in a May 26 letter to General Bolte. He stated that with the increased number of American troops available in Northern Ireland, it was possible to form "a complete Commando of 5 or 6 troops" (400–500, total strength).

Truscott recommended that a complete commando be organized at the earliest practical time. He requested authority for the grades and ranks and for the tentative tables of organization and allowances to be completed by his officers. Truscott also decided to place Maj. (later general) Theodore Conway with the Commandos as his liaison. The result of these recommendations was the authorization from the War Department in late May 1942 to form a provisional organization.

With the highest level of authority behind him, Truscott then drafted a letter that was passed to Maj. Gen. James E. Chaney, commanding general of United States Army Forces British Isles. (Shortly thereafter, the headquarters' name became Headquarters European Theater Operations U.S. Army. [ETOUSA]) Chaney had not been enthused about Truscott's mission, but knowing the orders came from General Marshall, he set about the preparation of a letter to Gen. Russell P. Hartle, the man who would provide the forces.

Hartle commanded the 34th Infantry Division until the division arrived overseas. On arrival in Northern Ireland, Hartle assumed command of U.S. Army Northern Ireland forces (USANIF) and turned over command of the division to his assistant division commander. An advance party from U.S. V Corps headquarters was in Northern Ireland, and Hartle would soon assume command of that organization as commander of both USANIF and U.S. Army V Corps. Serving as aide to General Hartle was an energetic captain named William Orlando Darby.

As Truscott was not in Hartle's chain of command, the

letter dated June 1, 1942, classified SECRET and titled "Commando Organization," contained the authority line of BY COMMAND OF MAJOR GENERAL CHANEY. The letter contained instructions which became of considerable significance to the course of events.

The first paragraph of the letter opened with the sentence, "The War Department has directed the organization of a unit for training and demonstrations purposes." Paragraph 2-a, under the heading "Purpose" read as follows: "This unit is to be considered a training and demonstration unit, and will be trained and will participate in actual raids under British control. It is expected that after such training and experience, as many men as practicable will be returned to their organization and their places filled by other men."

The letter put forth the type of volunteer that was sought. Well-trained soldiers were needed who had good judgment, initiative, and common sense; were in good physical condition; and, if possible, possessed skills such as mountaineering, demolition, weaponry, and seamanship. There was no age limit. General Hartle was to choose the site of training. American methods, tactical doctrine, and equipment were to be used as much as possible. The 34th Division would handle the administration and supplies.

The volunteers were to come from U.S. Army V Corps, which had two divisions. The 34th Infantry Division was a National Guard division with roots in the states of Iowa, North and South Dakota, and Minnesota. Called to active service on February 10, 1941, the Red Bull Division (so named because its patch showed the head and horns of a red bull) was based at Camp Clairborne, Louisiana. Filled out with men from across the country, the 34th trained hard and later fought its way to an outstanding record.

The 34th had taken part in the famed Louisiana maneuvers of 1941 and sailed for Europe beginning January 15, 1942. They arrived in the Belfast, Northern Ireland, area on January 26, 1942, thus claiming for themselves the honor of being the first American ground combat forces to arrive on British soil in WWII.

The other half of V Corps was the 1st Armored Division, commanded by Gen. Orlando P. Ward, and was activated at

Fort Knox, Kentucky, on July 15, 1940. Staging through Fort Dix, New Jersey, most of the division sailed aboard the *Queen Mary* on May 10, 1942, arriving on the Clyde on May 16 for stationing in Northern Ireland.

Truscott personally communicated the instructions on the formation of the new unit to the commanders and staffs of the 34th Infantry and 1st Armored Divisions.

No commander is enthusiastic about having some of his most energetic men taken from him, but the orders to provide men for the new unit came at the direction of General Marshall, the army chief of staff. General Chaney's letter to General Hartle stressed that commanders should disregard the inconvenience. General Ward felt people trained to be armored soldiers ought to stay armored, but when it was pointed out to him from whence the instructions came, he naturally cooperated.

A top-notch officer was needed to command the fledgling unit. On a Sunday morning, General Hartle, his chief of staff Col. (later major general) Edmond Leavey, and Hartle's aide, Capt. William Darby, were driving to church in Belfast. Hartle turned to Leavey and said, "We can't get very far with this new job unless we have somebody good to put in charge of it—any ideas?"

Leavey knew that Captain Darby hated being an aide and felt Darby was being wasted in the job. He looked at the pleading expression on Darby's face and said to Hartle, "Why don't you give the job to Bill?"

Hartle grinned and asked Darby, "Bill, what do you say to that?" Darby leaped at the opportunity. When Bill Darby passed through the doors of church that Sunday morning, he must have felt that his prayers had been answered. He would command the new force.[1]

A June 7 letter from Hartle titled "Commando Organization" to those under his command opened with the words "In order to provide battle trained personnel in ALL units, the 1st Battalion consisting of a Headquarters Company (8 officers, 69 enlisted) and 6 companies (3 officers and 62 enlisted men) each for a total of 26 officers and 441 enlisted men, will be formed from troops in the USANIF, preferably from volunteers." (In comparison, a World War II American rifle battalion totaled 22 officers and 864 men.) The letter further stated that "the organization of the battalion will be completed within ten days."

For the newly forming volunteer unit, a 10 percent dropout/reject rate was calculated, so the search was on the 520 top-notch officers and men.

William O. Darby in time would be known affectionately as "El Darbo" by his men. His charismatic personality and flair for leadership set the tone from the beginning of the World War II Ranger experience.

Darby was born and raised in Fort Smith, Arkansas, a frontier town that was once the home of Judge Isaac C. Parker, "The Hanging Judge." Bill Darby was well liked. The words "handsome," "intelligent," "industrious," and "enthusiastic" were showered on him. His early life was middle-class. While growing up, he worked to help out his church-oriented family. The failures of others who had been nominated allowed him to enter the U.S. Military Academy in 1929. While at West Point, he was an average student but a strong leader. He played intramural soccer one year and was in the choir throughout his cadet days. Despite mediocre grades, his leadership ability resulted in him being selected for captain of Company I, a job he performed well.

After graduation as an artillery officer in 1933, Darby went on to the usual variety of company/battery-level assignments from reconnaissance to supply to executive officer to commander. In the army of the thirties, he worked with horses and mules as well as men and motors, thus gaining knowledge useful in mountain transport and tactics. He participated in the Louisiana maneuvers of 1940 and then went to Puerto Rico for amphibious operations.

Fate seems to have played a major role in Darby's life. From the need for two applicants nominated ahead of him to fail before he could make it into West Point to the sudden cancellation of orders to Hawaii and subsequent orders appointing him as Hartle's aide, there was a force working in William Darby's life that allowed him to be the right man at the right place at the right time. Fortune gave Darby opportunity; from it he would carve his niche in history.

The officers for the new battalion were selected by Darby and Colonel Hayford, a staff officer from V Corps headquarters. A wise choice was made by Darby in selecting tall, blond-haired Capt. Herman W. Dammer[2] as his executive officer. Dammer had been a cavalry lieutenant with the New York National Guard. Called to active duty in February 1941, he was serving in Northern Ireland as adjutant of an antiaircraft artillery unit when his chance came to volunteer. Dammer had never been to an antiaircraft school and felt his unit would probably spend the rest of the war guarding Belfast. Dammer wanted to be part of the war; he wanted to be an infantryman.

For reasons Dammer never knew, Darby selected him as executive officer and made him responsible to get the staff functioning and serve as plans-and-training officer.

The army separates itself into the castes of Regular Army, National Guard, and Reserve. The so-called "one army" is not a reality in assignment or promotion. This policy was particularly strong in the days prior to World War II. The selection of the National Guard's Dammer by the Regular Army's Darby says much good about both men.

Another key officer for the new unit was Capt. Roy A. Murray. Murray was a reserve officer, schooled at the University of California. Murray was thirty-three years old at the time of his selection, six months older than Darby, and the senior man in years among those chosen. Murray was an athlete and outdoorsman, a cross-country runner, whose hobbies included hiking and fishing. He had experience in civilian life in navigation and boat handling. Murray had keen analytical and good communicational skills. His recommendations were sound, and he was a strong leader who had a profound influence on subsequent Ranger activities.

The old toast, "To a bloody war and quick promotion," was suited to Darby. He was promoted to major on June 1, 1942, and on August 6 of the same year made lieutenant colonel.

In an October 27, 1944, speech to the Army Navy Staff College in Washington, D.C., Darby said the following: "My Rangers were formed up in a little town called Carrickfergus,

North Ireland, and were formed completely with volunteers from the V Corps. About 50 percent came out of the 34th Division, and about 40 percent came out of the 1st Armored Division, and the final 10 percent came out of the V Corps at large." A large percentage of the volunteers were already infantry. From the regiments of the 34th Infantry Division, the 133d Infantry provided seventy-five volunteers, the 135th Infantry sixty-nine, and the 168th Infantry sent seventy-one. The mix allowed for the great diversity of experience that such units attract.

Classified material is intended to only be shared with those who have a "need to know." If Darby knew that the secret instructions were to create "a training and demonstration unit" and that the instructions were "to return as many men as possible to their original units," he did not tell his subordinates. The men who volunteered for the 1st Ranger Battalion did not know it. They wanted at the Germans. They were volunteering to be part of an American commando unit. Forty-seven years later, Dammer said, "What sense would it make to take commando training back to an antiaircraft unit?"

Selected officers formed interview boards, consisting of two men, and visited all units in Northern Ireland, looking for volunteers. There were rigorous physical examinations: 20/20 vision was required, no eyeglasses, no movable dentures, or night blindness. The Commando's average age was twenty-five; that seemed to be a guide. The youngest American selected was eighteen, the oldest thirty-three. In-depth interviews in which a man's attitude and desire were revealed were a major factor in selection.

British Commando officers had on occasion required their candidates to report for interview naked, thus having a better opportunity to stress the man while observing his mental bearing and physical equipment. The Americans did not follow this practice.

The men chosen came from a wide variety of ethnic, social, and economic backgrounds, including salesmen, musicians, police officers, boxers, and singers. Cpl. Anthony Rada was from Flint, Michigan, where in prewar days he had worked on the General Motors assembly line and studied commercial art. T/5 Jim Altieri was a Pennsylvanian who had been a welder and a steelworker, yet felt comfortable with both a rifle and a pen. Pvt. George Creed was a former coal miner from West Virginia. Pfc. Carlo Contrera was Brooklyn born and madly in love with a girl back home. Sgt. Joe Dye had the blood of the American Indian in his veins as did a man whose name drew a great deal of attention, Pvt. Sampson P. Oneskunk.

The first group of enlisted volunteers (three hundred men) arrived from the 34th Division on June 11.

There is a heady sense of excitement in the beginnings of a new enterprise. One of the early questions to be answered was "what shall we call this outfit?"

There are several claimants as to whose idea it was to call the new organization "Rangers." The name had not been in the American military lexicon since the close of the Indian Wars, therefore, someone had done his historical homework or possibly been captivated by the popular prewar novel, *Northwest Passage*, by Kenneth Roberts. The *New York Times* in an August 20, 1942, article credited Capt. Anthony Levioro, a former reporter for the *Times*. Mountbatten later stated that he suggested the name. Maj. Ted Conway, who was a part of the proceedings, comes down clearly in favor of General Truscott. In his memoirs, Truscott wrote, "Many names were recommended, I selected Rangers."

It is clear from Truscott's writing that he viewed the name Ranger not as a hangover from the British colonial period but as an American experience.

A June 13 letter from Chancy to Hartle titled "Organization of the 1st Ranger Battalion" stated that "the designation of this unit will be the 1st Ranger Battalion."

On June 14, 1942, 1st Lt. Alfred H. Nelson penned a report to Truscott. Lieutenants Nelson and Lyle with Sergeants Woodarceak and Musgradd, all formerly of the 135th Infantry, had spent May 19 to June 12 on detached service with the Commandos. Their travels took them to Ardrossan, Scotland, to meet with Brigadier Laycock of the Commandos, then on to Achnacarry where they met Lieutenant Colonel Vaughn and spent several days in Commando training. Next they went to Dorlin House, Scotland, and training with

Number 9 Commando, then Inveraray, Scotland, for combined operations. Next they went to London for administrative detail, and then to Southampton to watch infantry units in combined training. Then, their exhausting travels at an end, they journeyed to Lurgan, Ireland. Along the way, they ran out of money and had to borrow it from British officers, thus creating an administrative nightmare. What the purpose was of sending two young lieutenants and two sergeants gallivanting around the countryside, being briefed by colonels and brigadiers, remains obscure. The trip report of the experience must have had Truscott shaking his head either in mirth or bewilderment. It is doubtful that Lieutenant Nelson surprised Truscott by concluding that "successful Commando units are completely trained infantry soldiers, who must be in the highest physical standard and kept that way by rigorous training."

Nelson then wrote: "Their esprit de corps must be kept at its peak by frequent allusions to their superiority to troops trained in ordinary ways." This statement resulted in a question mark being placed in the margin.

Lieutenant Nelson continued that "Their advanced training should be complete, and each man trained for the job he is to do." Then he delivered the chauvinistic finale: "We do believe that it is possible by use of some of the British methods, plus some that I am sure will be devised by our own commanders, to train American personnel to do a better job in any situation than that done by their British forerunners." No American commander could have wished for more zeal in a subordinate.

By June 15, the shakedown of the new unit was well under way. Two thousand men had volunteered; 575 of these had come to Carrickfergus, and 104 had already been returned to their former units. Darby organized six interview teams, each staffed with two officers, to go in search of more volunteers.

CHAPTER 2

TRAINING

The requirement to form within ten days was a spur to action. The June 11 group of volunteers from the 34th was followed on the 12th by the men from the 1st Armored Division. On the same day, the first rejected officer was returned to his parent unit. From the 13th to the 18th, more volunteers arrived. On the 15th, the companies were organized and assigned areas; 104 rejects returned to their old units, and nine quarter-ton vehicles (peeps) were received.

On June 19 by General Order No. 7, Headquarters US-ANIF and V Corps (Reinforced), the 1st Ranger Battalion was activated.

On the day of its activation, the 1st Ranger Battalion sent seven officers and twelve enlisted men to temporary duty with the 2d Canadian Division in Cowes on the Isle of Wight. This division was in preparation for a raid on Dieppe.

From the 20th to the 28th of June 1942 at Sunnyland Camp, Carrickfergus, the 1st Ranger Battalion formed for battle.

The initial tables of organization and basic allotments were worked up by Maj. Ted Conway. To prepare himself, Conway visited Commando units in Scotland and participated in some of their training exercises. His end product was a blend of British strength figures and American equipment. The instructions, typed out on letter-size paper, established the 1st Ranger Battalion with a headquarters company and six Ranger companies, designated A to F.

The battalion headquarters initially consisted of the following men:

Battalion Commander: Maj. William O. Darby
Executive Officer and Operations and Training Officer
  (S-3): Capt. Herman Dammer
Adjutant (S-1): 1st Lt. Howard W. Karbel
Supply Officer (S-4): 1st Lt. Axel W. Anderson
Medical Officer: 1st Lt. William A. Jarrett
Communications Officer: 1st Lt. George P. Sunshine

Headquarters Company had a communications platoon
and a staff platoon that was composed of three sections:

Administrative and personnel
Intelligence and operations
Supply and transportation

Each Ranger company consisted of three officers and
sixty-three enlisted men organized into a company headquarters and two platoons. Initial company commanders were:

Co. A: 1st Lt. Gordon Klefman
Co. B: 1st Lt. Alfred H. Nelson
Co. C: Capt. William Martin
Co. D: Capt. Alvah Miller
Co. E: 1st Lt. Max Schneider
Co. F: Capt. Roy Murray

The four-man company headquarters of a lettered company consisted of:

Company Commander—captain or lieutenant
First Sergeant—master sergeant
Company Clerk—corporal
Messenger—private

Each platoon consisted of a platoon headquarters, two assault sections and a mortar section:

Platoon Headquarters:
  Platoon Leader—lieutenant

Platoon Sergeant—technical sergeant
Messenger—private
Sniper—private

Eleven-man Assault Section (two per platoon):

Section Leader—staff sergeant
Asst. Section Leader—corporal
Browning Automatic Rifleman—corporal or T/5
Asst. Automatic Rifleman—private
Five Riflemen—privates
Two Scouts—privates

Weapons included .45 caliber pistol, M-1903 Springfield rifle with bayonet and grenade launcher, four A-4 light machine guns, four Thompson submachine guns, two 60mm mortars, two 2.36-inch rocket launchers, and eight Browning automatic rifles per rifle company. Headquarters Company had six 81mm mortars. Each company was authorized twelve brass knuckles.

Lead scouts were armed with the .45 caliber Thompson submachine gun. The riflemen were initially armed with the Springfield M-1903 rifle. These were replaced with M-1 rifles near Argyll, Scotland, in August of 1942 prior to the battalion leaving England for Africa.

Mortar sections were initially equipped with one 60mm mortar per platoon. The squad was organized as follows:

Mortar Section Sergeant (gunner)—staff sergeant
Asst. Section Sergeant (asst. gunner)—corporal
Three Ammunition Bearers—privates
(Riflemen often carried additional mortar ammunition.)

The table of organization of a Ranger infantry battalion was reasonably adequate, flexible, and adjusted as necessary. The initial thinking was that a mess section would not be necessary as these were raiders who could exist on a chocolate bar for the duration of their mission. In training areas, the Rangers would be attached to another unit for rations.

The table of organization and equipment would evolve over the course of the war, and the unit would at times add additional men and the weapons and equipment necessary for the task. (1944 tables of organization for a Ranger battalion and a Ranger company are shown at Appendix A.) Signal equipment authorized included semaphore flags, SCR-284 and SCR-536 radios and EE-8 telephones. For transportation, the battalion was authorized six motorcycles for Headquarters Company, nine quarter-ton trucks (peeps), a one-and-a-half-ton truck used by the S-4 section and to haul rations, and a station wagon for the commander's use. The station wagon did not arrive.

The British Commando "Sykes" knife (now a symbol of Rangers) was issued to the 1st Ranger Battalion at Achnacarry (other battalions were not issued this). Men wore the M-1917A1 steel helmet of World War I vintage until arrival at Dundee where the WWII model was issued. The 1st Ranger Battalion was authorized two pieces of British equipment: a quantity of six .55 caliber "Boys" antitank guns and the British Vibram boot for each individual. The 1st Ranger Battalion did not wear special boots. The standard canvas legging of the army was cut in half to facilitate marching and became a source of pride that was worn throughout the life of the battalion and also in the 3d and 4th Battalions. The 2d and 5th Battalions wore Corcoran Paratrooper jump boots.

Organization is but a single step on the road to a first-class fighting unit. The next step, indeed giant leap, was to prepare each man for battle. "We must remember that one man is much the same as another, and that he is best who is trained in the severest school," wrote Thucydides in his history of the Peloponnesian Wars. Those who have endured the severest school know well that it is attitude and desire that enables one to succeed in the rigors of hard training and combat. For the young and eager men of the 1st Ranger Battalion, the volunteer spirit was about to be put to the test.

In a quiet, green glen in Inverness, Scotland, stood Achnacarry, the ivy-covered castle domain of the Lord of the Camerons. This warrior clan, whose skirling bagpipes played "The Camerons are Coming" in many a battle, graciously and patriotically allowed the government of Great Britain the use of their holdings during World War II. It was at Achnacarry in February 1942 that a Commando training depot (one of several) was established. It was into this place that the 1st Ranger Battalion closed on July 1 and 2, 1942.

The undisputed master of Achnacarry was its large and determined commandant, Lt. Col. Charles E. Vaughn. Vaughn and Darby would get along well.

The instructors were men of the British SS (Special Services) Brigade and Commando commissioned and noncommissioned officers. Much of the instruction was done by one officer and two or more sergeants responsible for each Ranger company. On occasion, committee-type instruction was used. The training was performed simultaneously. One company might be involved in scouting and patrolling while another was on a speed march; they would then change off.

Ranger officers performed the same training as their men and were expected to be the first to face the challenge. Darby and Dammer took the training, alternating the companies with which they shared the experience. But the staff could not both train and perform their duties. Lieutenant Anderson, the S-4, was overheard to tell Darby, "I'll go on the march or I'll get your supplies. Which do you want?"

The men slept in teepee-shaped tents, eight men to a tent. A major hardship was subsisting off of English rations, such as fish and tea for breakfast. After many complaints, an American mess team was attached from the 34th Infantry Division. As one of the cooks arrived, he hurried off to pass a message from his mess sergeant to Captain Martin. Sgt. Peer Buck had known Martin and was asking for help in getting out of a unit that was resisting his release and into the Rangers. Buck, who was born in Copenhagen, Denmark, had come to the United States at age three, gaining American citizenship through his father. In 1928, while at the University of Minnesota School of Agriculture, he began boxing, fighting as a middleweight at 168 pounds. Buck was a strong man and had a series of adventures in the ring, including a memorable bout with a fellow called "Big Boy Peterson." Buck got his chance to serve the Rangers as a mess sergeant but that was not enough. He asked Darby several times to allow him to be a Ranger.

"You're a married man, aren't you?" Darby asked.

"Yes," Buck replied.

"Then what do you want to be a Ranger for?"

"Because that's the way I want to go," Buck responded.

Darby liked that spirit, but it was some time before he would agree.

The training was arduous from the start. Physical training was stressed, with emphasis on speed marches with pack and equipment and the overcoming of difficult obstacles. River and stream crossings (Ranger Lamont Hoctel drowned in one of these), swimming in ice-cold water, the high slide down ropes over streams, and cliff climbing were challenges that, when conquered, greatly increased a man's confidence. There were weapons and bayonet training, scouting and patrolling, small-unit tactics, hand-to-hand combat, map reading, and first aid. Amphibious training featured landings, often made using live ammunition. Under live fire, collapsible boats, Higgens boats (infantry landing craft), and British assault boats were used. Experience in night operations received emphasis. Daylight tactical training stressed fire and maneuver on closing with the enemy, one assault section moving while covered by the fire of the other section and that of the mortars.

Safety was secondary to realism in training. The live-fire exercises were especially dangerous. On one amphibious landing exercise, the fire shattered the paddles in the Rangers' hands; 1st Sgt. Donald Torbett of Company F was shot through the buttocks and temporarily evacuated while Captain Murray and the rest of the company continued on the mission. Torbett was not seriously injured and would survive the war without additional physical injury. Men find great humor in someone else being shot in the buttocks. Henceforth, First Sergeant Torbett would be known as "Butt."

The speed march was at the heart of the Ranger toughening process. Day after day, the marching feet pounded the earth. Men grew accustomed to walking through fatigue and pain. It was this training that many would credit with saving their lives.[1]

Throughout the training, discipline and a spirit of working together were dominant themes. Those who were found unfit were returned to their former units.

Changes were made to the table of organization. Initially, the assault sections had an M-1919A4 light machine gun. On the recommendation of Colonel Vaughn, who felt the added weight slowed down the assault section, the machine guns were pooled at battalion headquarters and replaced in the assault sections by Browning automatic rifles. Also at Colonel Vaughn's suggestion, the 60mm mortar sections were combined and became part of Ranger (rifle) company headquarters.

Throughout training at Achnacarry, the British cooks had prepared the food.[2] Peer Buck and his cooks had worked in the background, supplementing the British food with American rations. The cooks did not train, but Buck and his cooks made themselves useful, bringing boats to shore, doing odd jobs, and keeping trim by going on hikes. Darby liked that.

The rigorous training was also a weeding-out process. Officers and enlisted men who could not meet the high standards or were too greatly injured to continue were dropped from the rolls. Three men developed acute jaundice and were evacuated.

On July 13, 1942, another group of Americans assembled at Achnacarry to begin training. This detachment was intended to provide the trained instructors that had been envisioned in the London conference of April. A total of eighteen officers and fifty enlisted men under Lt. Col. D. H. Hudelson and Maj. A. M. Miller began training on July 15 and finished on the 30th.

After a month of Achnacarry training, most of the 1st Ranger Battalion moved by rail and motor on August 1 to Dorlin House, a Commando training center near Argyle on the western coast of Scotland. The battalion was separated with A and B Companies at Roshven, C and D at Glenborrodale, Companies E and F at Glencripesdale, and Headquarters at Salen and Shielbraige. Here, with pairs of companies working together, a wide variety of beach configurations enabled the Rangers to hone their amphibious landing skills. Coming in over deep water or shallow, through chop, wave, and surf over the level beach or cliff, they used a wide variety of small craft such as R boats, drifters, cobles, and cutters to make their way to shore.

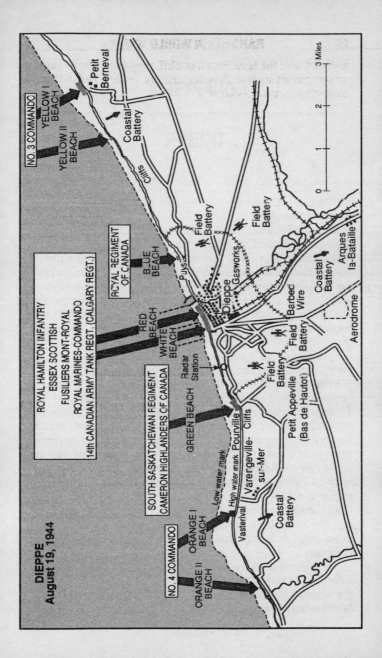

DIEPPE
August 19, 1944

NO. 3 COMMANDO

YELLOW I
BEACH

Petit
Berneval

YELLOW II
BEACH

Coastal
Battery

Cliffs

3 Miles

2

1

0

Field
Battery

Field
Battery

ROYAL REGIMENT OF CANADA

BLUE BEACH

Puys

Coastal
Battery

Arques
la-Bataille

ROYAL HAMILTON INFANTRY
ESSEX SCOTTISH
FUSILIERS MONT-ROYAL
ROYAL MARINES-COMMAND)
14th CANADIAN ARMY TANK REGT. (CALGARY REGT.)

Gasworks

Dieppe

Barbed
Wire

Aerodrome

Field
Battery

RED BEACH

WHITE
BEACH

Field
Battery

SOUTH SASKATCHEWAN REGIMENT
CAMERON HIGHLANDERS OF CANADA

Radar
Station

GREEN BEACH

Petit Appeville
(Bas de Hautot)

Field
Battery

Pourville

Varengeville-
su·-Mer

Cliffs

High water mark

Low-water-mark

Vasterival

Coastal
Battery

NO. 4 COMMANDO

ORANGE I
BEACH

ORANGE II BEACH

CHAPTER 3

DIEPPE

Dieppe is a quiet seaport on that portion of the coast of France frequently called "The Iron Coast." The terrain there is harsh and foreboding, a place of high chalk cliffs, occasionally penetrated by the mouths of rivers. Dieppe city is on the Arques River. It is a summer place for tourists, even though bathers are hindered by its flint-stone beaches, which are uncomfortable to lie on, difficult to cross, and as soldiers would learn, impossible to dig in. Anxious for income, the town fathers established gambling casinos, giving the town the reputation of being "the poor man's Monte Carlo." For centuries Dieppe has been a quaint and quiet rendezvous, but for nine hours on a day in August of 1942, Dieppe shed its sleepy mantle and became a place of hope and horror.[1]

In the spring of 1942, the British were anxious to conduct a large-scale raid on the German-occupied coast of France. There were several purposes to the raid: To gain the preinvasion experience of putting a large body of men and equipment, including tanks, ashore under air and sea covering fires; to test the enemy response; and to learn how fast he could rise to the challenge, and hopefully, give the appearance of helping the Russians by causing the Germans to worry about their western defense and draw off some forces from the Russian front. There was also concern about Allied morale. Something in the nature of offensive action needed to be done to bring ground war in Western Europe to the Germans.

The planning was initially a British effort of Mountbatten's Combined Operations Headquarters. Mountbatten thought the operation could succeed if battle-experienced Royal Marines and Commandos were used for the operation. These were not granted him. Other British ground forces were limited because much of the British Army was deployed overseas. Readily available, however, was the Canadian 2d Division, which had been in England since 1940.

The Canadians were superbly trained; some observers felt they were overtrained. They had worked long and hard to prepare for battle which did not come. The result was a lessening of discipline, and problems with the local populace were not uncommon. Anxious to have its men committed to action, the Canadian leaders saw the Dieppe raid as the perfect opportunity. This yearning for battle resulted in British acceptance of the Canadians, and their over-eager participation in planning would demonstrate serious gaps.

The British did not have a high opinion of the state of training that had been reached by the recently arrived Americans. However, on learning of the planned raid, President Roosevelt insisted that American forces take part. There is more to war than battle, and the master politician Roosevelt understood the favorable impact that American participation would have on the home front.

This resulted in seven officers and twelve enlisted men being detached from the 1st Ranger Battalion on the day of its activation to prepare to participate in the raid with the Canadians.

Code-named "Rutter," the raid was planned for July 4, 1942. The troops were loaded and ready to make the assault when bad weather, combined with an enemy air raid that damaged several ships, disrupted the timetable. The Dieppe operation was called off. On July 11, the seven officers and twelve enlisted men of the 1st Ranger Battalion, who had been detached to the 2d Canadian Division, were returned to Darby's command.

Officers at the Combined Operations Headquarters felt the need for the raid was still there. Despite the risk that the Germans might have learned what was afoot, the decision was made by Lord Mountbatten to resurrect the plan. Prime Minister Winston Churchill was convinced of the value of the Dieppe operation, and his support overwhelmed opposing voices.

Under the code name "Jubilee," the raid was rescheduled

for August 19. The main assault force would be an armored regiment and six infantry battalions of the 2d Canadian Division under Major General Roberts. Artillery and engineers were included. The plan was brutally simple. The Canadians would go in with a frontal assault over the beaches of Dieppe to seize the town. Throughout the course of the Dieppe raid planning, heavy naval fire-support was of a lower priority than the hope for surprising the enemy. A battleship was requested, but the British Navy refused to put one of its capital ships at risk in the narrow waters of the English Channel. The use of heavy bombers was planned but ruled out—the Royal Air Force doubted that even state-of-the-art bombing would take out the beach defenses and would probably result in much death and destruction to Dieppe and its people. Air support would be in large measure the machine guns from British Spitfire fighter aircraft, which would attack just prior to the landing. This would prove ineffective and served primarily to arouse the Germans. Airborne troops were also planned for, but their inability to jump in bad weather resulted in planners deciding against using them when the operation plan was concluded.

German coastal batteries, located on high ground to each side of the city, were in position to control the approaches and beaches of Dieppe. To the east (left) of Dieppe near the town of Berneval was a four-gun battery of six-inch guns (named the Goebbels Battery) located approximately 150 yards inshore. The mission of eliminating these guns was given to Number 3 Commando under Lieutenant Colonel Durnford-Slater.

The guns to the west (right) were near Varence-ville-Surmer and were a six-gun battery of 15cm guns with longer range than those at Berneval. These guns were to be taken out by Number 4 Commando under Lt. Col. Lord Lovat. The distance between the two batteries was approximately eleven miles, with Dieppe centered but slightly closer to Berneval.

Knowing only that it was a hazardous mission, Darby and Dammer volunteered for the mission, but both were turned down. All information was based upon "need to know," and it is questionable if Bill Darby knew the objective his men were destined for; Dammer did not. For the second attempt, new men were selected. This was probably because by August 1, the Rangers had completed Commando training at Achnacarry, and all were better prepared to serve alongside their Commando counterparts. In all, fifty Rangers (six officers and forty-four enlisted men) were chosen. The enlisted men were selected by their company commanders and represented each company of the First Ranger Battalion.

On August 1, Capt. Roy Murray of F Company led a detachment of four officers and thirty-six men from the 1st Ranger Battalion on a rail journey to London. There, the Americans split, with a detachment of thirty-six Rangers under Captain Murray boarding a train for Seaford, England, to report to Lt. Col. Durnford-Slater, the officer commanding Number 3 Commando. The other group consisting of four Rangers under the leadership of S Sgt. Kenneth D. Stempson caught a train to Portland, England, to report to Lt. Col. Lord Lovat, officer commanding Number 4 Commando.

On August 15, another order was published that sent five Rangers under Lt. Robert Flanagan to the Canadian forces. Leaving the Battalion on the 16th, these men went by rail through London to report to Farnham, England, to a Major Stockley, an officer who was involved with planning movements of 2d Canadian Division units.

The final distribution of Rangers was as follows.

Rangers with Number 3 Commando

With Hq. Troop (From F Co. 1st Ranger Battalion):	With #4 Troop (From C Co. 1st Ranger Battalion):
Captain Roy A. Murray	2d Lt. Charles M. Shunstrom
Sgt. Edwin C. Thompson	Sgt. John C. Knapp
Sgt. Tom Sorby	Sgt. Dick Sellers
Pfc. Howard W. Andre	T/5 John H. Smith
Pfc. Stanley Bush	Pfc. James O. Edwards
Pfc. Pete Preston	Pfc. Donald G. Johnson
Pvt. Don A. Earnwood	Pfc. Charles F. Grant

With #3 Troop
(From A Co. 1st Ranger
  Battalion):
  1st Lt. Leonard F. Dirks
  Sgt. Harold A. Adams
  Sgt. Mervin T. Heacock
  T/5 Joseph C. Phillips
  Pfc. Howard T. Hedenstad
  Pfc. James A. Mosely
  Pfc. Edwin J. Moger

With #4 Troop
(From E Co. 1st Ranger
  Battalion):
  S Sgt. Lester Kness
  Sgt. Theodore Q. Butts
  Pfc. Clare P. Beitel
  Pfc. Charles Reilly
  Pfc. Owen W. Sweazey
  Pfc. Charles R. Coy

With #3 Troop
(From D Co. 1st Ranger
  Battalion):
  Sgt. Marvin L. Kavanaugh
  Sgt. Gino Mercuriali
  T/5 Michael Kerecman
  T/5 William S. Brinkley
  Pfc. William S. Girdley
  Pvt. Jacque M. Nixon

With #6 Troop
(From B Co. 1st Ranger
  Battalion):
  2d Lt. Edwin V. Loustalot
  S Sgt. Merritt M. Bertholf
  Sgt. Albert T. Jacobson
  Pfc. Walter A. Bresnahan
  Pfc. William B. Lienhas
  Pfc. Donald L. Hayes
  Pfc. Edwin R. Furru

Rangers with Number 4 Commando
(All with "A" Troop)

From Headquarters Co. 1st
  Ranger Battalion:
  S Sgt. Kenneth D.
    Stempson

From C Co. 1st Ranger
  Battalion:
  Cpl. William R. Brady

From Headquarters Co. 1st
  Ranger Battalion:
  Sgt. Alex J. Szima

From D Co. 1st Ranger
  Battalion:
  Cpl. Franklin M. Koons

Rangers with Canadian Units

From E Co. 1st Ranger
  Battalion:
  1st Lt. Roberts Flanagan,
  South Saskatchewan
  Regiment

From C Co. 1st Ranger
  Battalion:
  2d Lt. Joseph H. Randall,
  Royal Hamilton Light
  Infantry

From A Co. 1st Ranger
  Battalion:

From D. Co. 1st Ranger
  Battalion:

Sgt. Lloyd N. Church,
Queen's Own Cameron
Highlanders

Sgt. Kenneth G. Kenyon,
Royal Regiment of Canada

From Headquarters Co. 1st
Ranger Battalion:
Sgt. Marcell G. Swank,
Queen's Own Cameron
Highlanders

From E Co. 1st Ranger
Battalion:
T/4 Howard M. Henry,
Essex Scottish Regiment

The officers planning the raid viewed American participation more as a favor to the Americans to give them combat
experience. Obviously, the busy staff officers had little time
for planning the activities of "tourists," as Ranger Marcell
Swank, who was with the Canadians, referred to the treatment of himself. The Rangers with the Canadians arrived but
a few hours before the operation began and were along for the
experience.

The six Rangers who were attached to the Canadians had a
particularly unusual experience. On the afternoon of August
17, 1942, they arrived at Farnham. On the 18th, Lieutenant
Flanagan reported as ordered to Major Stockley at East
Bridge House. This house was ostensibly a British Naval Rest
Center, but a look around convinced Flanagan that it was a
dispersal point for special troops. In addition to men of the
Royal Navy and Marines, there were French Commandos,
Sudeten Germans, a Russian, and a group that were referred
to as "The Phantoms." Flanagan observed that non-English-
speaking types were disguised as Canadians.

Stockley was surprised to hear that two officers were in the
party and told Flanagan to wait. Later in the day, he called
Flanagan back and told him the name of the craft that each
American was to report to; no other information was given.
Later, without briefing, the six Rangers were placed in a bus
with a British sergeant and driven by the assembly areas of
Canadian units. At each unit, one Ranger would be told to
dismount; Rangers Church and Swank were the only men
dropped off with the same unit. Swank remembers a field in
which Canadian troops were lying about and how uncomfortable the two American Rangers felt standing apart. It was
only a few hours from embarkation, yet the six Americans

had not been told what the mission was or what their part in it was to be.

The thirty-six Rangers who were attached to Number 3 Commando and the four who were with Number 4 Commando fared better. They had been trained with their British counterparts and were treated as equals by their Commando sections, given meaningful assignments, and in some cases were incorporated into the British Commando system of "Jack and John" with one Ranger working with one Commando. From August 2 to 10, Number 3 Commandos and Rangers practiced for the mission of going in over beach and cliff, through emplacements and obstacles to destroy heavy-gun positions. From August 11 to 18, they performed physical training, street fighting, cliff climbing, and range firing and practiced assault tactics. Those Rangers with Number 4 Commando were undergoing a similar experience. Commando leaders planned, organized, and conducted operations down to the last detail. The after-action reports of Capt. Roy Murray and other Rangers who participated with the Commandos in the Dieppe operation fairly sparkle with praise of the Commandos.

The Rangers were somewhat an object of envy as they had just been issued the Garand (M-1) rifle. Its eight-shot, semi-automatic capability was one of the military wonders of World War II.

A total of 6,086 officers and men composed the raiding force. Two hundred fifty-two ships of relatively small size traveled the seventy-mile stretch of channel, departing England at 1830 hours on the moonlit night of August 18 with the mission of effecting landing during that period just before the dawn when visibility is enhanced. This time is known as "before morning nautical twilight" (BMNT). On the morning of August 19 BMNT was at 0430 hours. The attack would be made at 0450; high tide would be at 0503.

The fleet included nine destroyers, one gunboat, nine landing ships, and seventy-three landing craft. There were no gunfire-support ships larger than a destroyer, one of which, HMS *Calpe*, was designated as the headquarters ship.

Each beach was color coded. Number 3 Commando had the mission of landing at Yellow Beach I near Berneval and

Yellow II near Belleville-sur-Mer. Lieutenant Colonel Durn-ford-Slater's plan was to land part of his force on each beach and envelop the gun positions. Durnford-Slater would lead the assault on Yellow Beach I while Maj. Peter Young would lead the Yellow Beach II party. Number 3 Commando departed Newhaven, England, in twenty landing craft personnel (LCP). These were wooden Higgins boats with a capability of carrying twenty men each. The boats were unarmed, unarmored, and uncomfortable, and their engines unreliable. In order for these small craft to make the long trip across the Channel, jerry cans of fuel had to be tied along the gunwales. This gasoline proved a considerable problem when boats came under fire.

Lieutenant Colonel Durnford-Slater was aboard the escort vessel, steam gunboat No. 5, along with a number of Commandos and Rangers. The Americans with Number 3 Commando wore denim or olive drab shirt and trousers; their faces were darkened, and steel helmets were covered with camouflage netting (Number 4 Commando wore woolen caps). American riflemen were carrying 176 rounds of .30 caliber ammunition. Commando riflemen were armed with bolt-action rifles and carried 100 rounds.

One of the planning mistakes was to place critical equipment for the operation in a single boat. The communications personnel were in one boat, and all the wire-cutting equipment in another. The loss of a single boat could and did hamper operations. When the LCP carrying the wire-cutting equipment was sunk, the German wire obstacles proved formidable.

Enroute to France, several of the LCPs developed engine trouble and had to turn back. Seven miles from the French coast, the raid went sour, when at 0347 hours the craft carrying Number 3 Commando encountered an alert German convoy of E-boats escorting a German tanker. While a chance meeting, the Germans were quick to engage. At least five German vessels turned their guns on the English steam gunboat, which, after a gallant fight, was put out of action. Rangers Stanley Bush, John J. Knapp, and Charles Reilly were aboard steam gunboat Number 5 and were wounded.

Helpless and without the protection of the gunboat, the Commandos and Rangers in the landing craft reeled under the whiplash of the fire from the German ships. Ranger Gino Mercuriali saw the German E-boat fire appearing as "flaming onions," that looked like they were aimed right between a man's eyes. On board steam gunboat Number 5, Ranger Les Kness saw wounded laying about the deck. Fire had broken out topside, and the British sailors had formed a bucket brigade, with the buckets coming up from the galley below. Kness joined the line and passed a galley bucket that no one recognized contained the British breakfast. A British sailor threw the contents on the fire and cried out in amazement and dismay, "Blimey, look at the fooking kippers!"

As dawn broke, all about him Mercuriali saw the chaos of battle as aircraft were shot from a smoke-darkened sky (106 Allied aircraft were lost). Parachutes oscillated to the water, while on shore and sea the guns hammered away. Mercuriali had to transfer to another craft, but the second one was also among those which could not make it to shore. Ranger Edwin Moger was wounded on one of these craft. Lieutenant Shunstrom reported he was on a flak ship (steam gunboat Number 5). When they got to the beach, the landing craft did not show up so they had to return. Four landing craft were sunk, one of which had Sgt. Merritt M. Bertholf on board. When his craft was blasted out of the water, Bertholf made it to shore. Weaponless and under fire, he was able to swim to another landing craft. Thirteen landing craft were badly shot up and/or driven off. One of the thirteen had Lt. Leonard Dirks on board. Driven off by enemy fire, his boat went to Dieppe to help with supporting fire until 1130. The remaining five or six landing craft pointed their bows to Yellow Beach I and continued on, landing twenty-five minutes late at 0515. These boats included among their occupants the B Company Rangers attached to Capt. R. L. Wills's #6 troop. Wills had a mixed lot of survivors from #2, #5, and #6 troops and four Americans. The Americans were Lt. Edward Loustalot and Rangers Albert Jacobsen, Walter Bresnahan, and Edwin Ferru. These four were the only Rangers with Number 3 Commando to cross the beach.

There was little opposition at the beach. Three gullies led

off to high ground. Wills chose the left gully and the party moved off. Their progress was slowed by the necessity to cut through the numerous barbed-wire entanglements that the Germans had erected. They continued by trail and reached high ground, where they proceeded in the direction of the German guns. Attacking through a built-up area inland about five hundred yards, Wills's men were taken under heavy fire and forced to withdraw. German positions to their rear had now been occupied by Wehrmacht soldiers. The Commandos and Rangers had to fight to get back to the beach. During this part of the action, Lieutenant Loustelot raced across a field of poppies, leading an attack on a German automatic weapons position. He died in the attempt. Ranger Bresnahan spent a moment beside Loustelot's body before battle action forced him to move on.

Wills's group fought their way to the beach, Wills being shot in the throat in the process. They fought back against German fire from the cliffs, and some found shelter in a cave. They wanted to break free, but there were no landing craft to extract them. The German infantry began to move down on the beach. Lt. William Wright of the Commandos was the only officer still effective. A battle-experienced man, Wright knew the effort was hopeless and surrendered the small group of British and Americans.

Among those taken prisoner were Rangers Albert T. Jacobson, Walter A. Bresnahan, and Edwin R. Furru. Furru was wounded when the German vehicle he was traveling in was strafed by a British fighter. As the first American ground force captives, Jacobson and Bresnahan were taken to Berlin for interrogation. The Ranger prisoners were then sent to the German prison camp known as Stalag VII-B.

Things went better for the eighteen men of Number 3 Commando who landed at Yellow Beach II. They were able to land undetected and move without serious mishap until relatively close to the guns. Shifting about under increasingly heavy fire, the Commandos were able to bring direct fire on the gun crews. Much discomfited, the Germans turned one of the large guns and lowered the tube to fire directly on the Commandos. Fortunately for the English, the gun barrel would not sufficiently depress, and the shells went screaming off into the French countryside. While unable to disable the guns, Maj. Peter Young and his Commandos were able to so distract the gun crews that the Berneval guns were not a significant factor to the raiding force.

On the western flank, the four Rangers with Lord Lovat's Number 4 Commando headed for Orange Beach. Number 4 Commando had a better crossing than Number 3, as they were aboard the more substantial landing ship, *Prince Albert*. Lord Lovat had also divided his force in two parties, with him leading the group that would go ashore on Orange Beach II and Major Mills-Roberts leading the men who would go ashore on Orange Beach I. Orange Beach I and II were approximately fourteen hundred yards apart. Sgt. Alex J. Szima of Headquarters Company, 1st Ranger Battalion and Cpl. Frank Koons of Company D were attached to A Troop of Number 4 Commando, with Szima being with the first section and Koons with the second. A troop was designated to land on Orange I Beach.

Szima, a Regular Army sergeant, had been appalled when Lord Louis Mountbatten made his farewell remarks to Number 4 Commando. They included the chill words, "We expect over 60 percent casualties . . . and to those of you that will die tomorrow, may God have mercy on your souls."

Szima did not accept that he would be one of those to die, but if he did, he wanted to go to his grave in an American uniform and wearing his American sergeant's stripes rather than Commando dress. Accordingly, he dressed for battle in U.S. garb.

S. Sgt. Kenneth D. Stempson of Headquarters Company, 1st Ranger Battalion, was the senior Ranger with Number 4 Commando. Stempson hailed from Russell, Minnesota, and had been a railroad worker. Accompanying him was the six-foot-four-inch William R. Brady of Grand Forks, North Dakota, and Company B.

Lovat's 252 men were a few minutes early. Transferring from the *Prince Albert* to twenty-four-man landing craft called ALC's, they were enroute to shore by 0430. As the boats headed for shore, the beaches lay quiet, waiting expectantly in the damp, gray light.

The landing went with clockwork precision. The Commandos and Rangers went ashore in an amphibious operation so smooth that Stempson would later say they did not get their feet wet. Supported by air strikes, Mills-Roberts's men blasted out barbed-wire entanglements, gained, and climbed the cliffs. They ran through a small French village. The guns were now firing, and each moment they did so meant greater danger to the convoy of the main assault force. Running through woods and underbrush, the men closed on the enemy position. The point of observation they sought was found at a small barn from which they had a clear view of the enemy battery.

The unsuspecting enemy gunners were a sniper's dream. On Mills-Roberts's order, a Commando sniper took deliberate aim and killed a German gun layer with a single shot.

The German gun crews stopped firing in astonishment and quickly became the target of Commando and Ranger weapons. Ranger Alex Szima was in the courtyard of the barn, while Ranger Franklin Koons found a firing position in a nearby stable. Szima saw the Germans about 150 yards distant and wearing white T-shirts and shiny black helmets. The Commando and Ranger fire was heavy and effective, with the surviving German gunners seeking shelter behind sandbags.

German infantry, probably of the 1st Battalion, 571st Infantry Regiment, began to search out the raiders with mortar and machine-gun fire. Their rifle fire was accurate, and Commandos began to fall, with several shot through the head. A 20mm gun in a flak tower opened fire, and Commandos McDonough and Davis returned fire using a .55 caliber Boys antitank gun. The two Commandos succeeded in jamming the revolving mechanism on the tower. Other Commandos set up a mortar and opened indirect fire on the German gun position. Under fire, Szima changed positions three times, the last being in a manure pile. From the stable, Koons had a clear and undisturbed field of fire on the gun positions and saw two Germans go down before his fire. He kept up a heavy volume of accurate rifle fire that did much to prevent the Germans from using the guns. Cpl. Franklin Koons was decorated by both the Americans and the British for being the first American ground soldier to kill a German in World War II.

German sniper fire increased and began to come from the

rear. Under orders, half of Mills-Roberts's force faced about and engaged that enemy. Ranger Szima was carrying armor-piercing ammunition in his rifle belt. He saw the shiny black helmet of a German on the opposite side of the road and emptied a clip at it. To the right, at a distance of two-hundred yards, Szima observed the shiny black helmet of a German firing from a rooftop; another eight rounds went that way.

The Commando mortar team quickly ranged their target and with the third round, accuracy combined with luck. The mortar shell landed in a stack of cordite, a smokeless high explosive in the shape of cord. The resultant explosion and fire ripped apart one of the German gun positions.

Meanwhile, the master of panache, Lord Shimi Lovat, attired in a gray cashmere sweater and slacks and carrying a light hunting rifle, had brought his men ashore on Orange Beach II. They were greeted by heavy German fire and wire obstacles. Ranger S. Sgt. Kenneth Stempson was part of a twelve-man group assigned to knock out enemy automatic weapons emplacements and clear the way for the demolition team. Four men went down, but the men threw netting over the barbed wire that allowed them to cross. Using tubular ladders, they then scaled a cliff of about thirty feet in height. Suffering more casualties, the raiders charged forward. Ranger Stempson and two Commandos closed on an obvious German pillbox, only to find it empty. The Germans had set up their machine gun about twenty yards away, but if the German move was designed to deceive, it worked against them. The route of their ammunition bearers was exposed and they became ready prey. "When you hit them, they rolled like jackrabbits," Stempson later told Szima. Finally, a red-headed Commando got close enough to silence the machine gun with a grenade.

Ranger Bill Brady[2] was the third man off the landing craft when his group hit Orange Beach II, running hard. Besides his personal weapon, Brady was carrying grenade pouch, Bren Gun clip, smoke grenades, a high-explosive mortar shell, and a section of scaling ladder. Brady's party had the mission of getting inland to block a key crossroad and prevent reinforcement of the German battery. As Brady's group scaled the cliffs, they encountered accurate German fire.

Brady's grenade pouch had broken loose. The time it took him to repair it made him number five in climbing the ladder. The man above was shot and fell upon Brady. Then a bullet creased his buttocks, and the man behind him was hit in the mouth. On top of the cliff, the men penetrated barbed-wire entanglements and proceeded up a ravine, under German sniper fire.

The telephone lines that provided German communication between the guns and an observation post in a lighthouse were nearby. As the assault boats were not within sight of guns, this communication was critical to the Germans. The stalwart Ranger Bill Brady stood by the pole while a Commando named Finney climbed up on his shoulders to cut the wire. The men were under fire, and bullets slapped into the pole while the wire was being cut. Finney received the British Military Medal for this action.

Continuing on, the small group of A Troop Commandos located the crossroads and established defensive positions on the crossroads. A ten-man German patrol came in view, with five men on each side of the road. When the Germans were within fifteen yards, Brady and Commandos opened fire, dropping three or four of the enemy and dispersing the rest. After the guns were destroyed, Brady and the men withdrew on order safely to the beach.

Lovat's party had difficulty going cross-country to reach their assault point. Flooded terrain and minefields were followed by woods and hedges. Behind schedule, they ran for approximately a mile and a half. Enroute they encountered a German platoon forming up, perhaps to strike at Mills-Roberts's force. Lovat's men fell upon the Germans, shooting them down to the last man. When in position, both Lovat's and Mills-Roberts's forces fixed bayonets and attacked. The final assault on the gun positions was bloody for both sides, but the Commandos quickly prevailed, and the guns were destroyed. The withdrawal to the beach was made under fire.

Ranger Alex Szima had fired all of his armor-piercing ammunition and removed the troublesome paper shields from around the ammunition in his bandoleers in preparation for the withdrawal. Ranger Szima had the additional duty on his way to the beach of serving as a rear guard and number two man to Commando McDonough on the long-barrelled Boys .55 caliber antitank rifle. Szima felt he owed this duty to his accurate shooting on the rifle range. When Mills-Roberts saw Szima put a tight group of shots into the target the first time he fired the M-1 rifle, Mills-Roberts had asked, "Sergeant, are you a member of the American rifle team?"

Szima replied, "No, sir, I'm just a bartender from Dayton, Ohio."

As the men of Number 4 Commando withdrew down a road to the beach, Ranger Szima and Commando McDonough covered the withdrawal in a preplanned and rehearsed pattern of positions and moves. There was a close call when Szima, believing that all friendly forces were behind him, heard the sound of approaching boots coming from behind a stone wall near a gate. Szima brought his rifle to his shoulder and had begun the trigger squeeze when he saw Ranger Franklin Koons walk through the gate into his sights.

Telling Koons to rejoin the main body, Szima and McDonough began their withdrawal. Their movement was expedited by the arrival of a truckload of German infantry at the spot they had just vacated. The Germans got out of the truck, looked over the Commando and German casualties, got back in the truck and drove toward the two raiders. McDonough fired the Boys antitank rifle, and Szima loosed a clip of rifle fire at the Germans. The two comrades-in-arms then grasped the ungainly weapon and began running side by side down the road toward the beach. McDonough was on the left and Szima on the right, with his M-1 in his left hand and the barrel of the antitank rifle in his right. As McDonough increased speed, Szima found himself running sideways. In a scene worthy of a Mack Sennett silent movie comedy, the two were tripped up by the long barrel of the antitank rifle and rolled over and over in the dust of the road. Regaining their weapons, if not their dignity, the two men rejoined the main body, where fortunately McDonough remembered the password.

Spitfires of the Royal Air Force provided covering fire and smoked the beach as Number 4 Commando withdrew through heavy rifle fire carrying wounded into neck-deep water to the boats. The flawless operation of Number 4 Commando was to be a bright spot of sun in a day of gloom.

The British Commandos and American Rangers were at Dieppe to support the main landing by Canadian forces. The greatest burden and loss of life at Dieppe fell upon the Canadians. They suffered a thousand dead and two thousand captured. The Canadians came ashore in a frontal attack into the teeth of well-prepared defenses, established by a German enemy who carried his own well-deserved reputation for being a courageous fighter. The 302d German Infantry Division was alert and ready. On August 19, 1942, the Canadians did all that flesh could do against fire, but as has been proven on battlefield after battlefield against an aroused entrenched enemy, courage is not a substitute for fire support.

For the Canadians, the raid was a disaster, 68 percent of the 4,963 Canadians who participated were casualties. Nine hundred thirteen Canadians were killed. On the bloody beaches of Dieppe, the 2d Canadian Division was rendered incapable of action. It would have to be rebuilt.

The Canadian forces were designated to land on four beaches:

On Green Beach at Pourville would land the South Saskatchewan Regiment and the Cameron Highlanders of Canada.

On White Beach, the main beach of the Dieppe raid, the Royal Hamilton Light Infantry would come ashore, as would the Fusilers Mont Royal, the Royal Marine Commando, and the 14th Canadian Tank Regiment of the Calgary Regiment.

Red Beach (to the left flank of White Beach) would be the landing site of the Essex Scottish, and on Blue Beach at Puys, the Royal Regiment of Canada would come ashore.

Infantrymen in war are close-knit, with family feeling toward their unit. Americans and Canadians are much alike, but to be thrust alone into a unit of another army on the eve of a man's first battle is a difficult adjustment.

For those six Rangers who went with the Canadian forces, there was not the feeling of being integrated into the Canadian units. No effort was made to give them a task. Ranger Kenneth Kenyon was with the Royal Regiment of Canada; the boat he was on did not land. Kenyon was then put aboard the HMS *Calpe* where he was wounded by strafing German aircraft. Lt. Joseph H. Randall was with the Royal Hamilton

Light Infantry. Strong and good looking, the twenty-three-year-old Randall claimed Washington, D.C., as his hometown and was the only child of a military family. He died on White Beach at the water's edge, probably the first American of the ground forces to die in Europe in World War II. T/4 Howard Henry was from Science Hill, Kentucky. Henry was a man who had planned to be an electrical engineer and was proud of his big black moustache. Ranger Henry was wounded at Dieppe and died in an English hospital.

Lt. Robert Flanagan had boarded the *Princess Beatrix*, a diesel-powered vessel of about a thousand tons, carrying men of the South Saskatchewan Regiment. He was told he would be an "observer," and a friendly officer informed him that the destination was Dieppe. They sailed at 1930 hours, August 18, and at midnight Flanagan went below to get some rest. At 0330, the *Beatrix* was rammed amidship by another vessel and began taking water. Key hatches were closed trapping him below decks. By the time Flanagan got to the deck, the landing craft were headed for the beach into shore-battery fire. The *Beatrix* crew made what repairs it could and began the trip back to England. Flanagan did not get ashore.

Sgt. Marcell G. Swank[3] and Sgt. Lloyd N. Church had been the last of the six Rangers to be dropped off with units of the 2d Canadian Division on August 18. The two Rangers found themselves with the Cameron Highlanders. Shortly after the Rangers arrived, trucks came. The Highlanders and the two Rangers were trucked to the port of Newhaven, where they were loaded on board Eureka landing boats and sailed at dusk. Well out into the English Channel, Rangers Swank and Church went to the Canadian lieutenant in charge and identified themselves. The lieutenant was astounded at their presence and did his best to brief the two Rangers, using a strip photo of the beach and a hooded flashlight. The lieutenant told them to follow a particular sergeant. Follow him, Swank thought, Hell, I can't even see him!

The Cameron Highlanders were the second wave to attack on Green Beach and came into an aroused German defense. The Camerons were riding in plywood landing craft. About one thousand yards off Green Beach, the craft formed in a single line and moved toward the beach. The sound and fury of hell began as German shore batteries, machine guns, and mortars opened fire. Above the angry roar of battle and the growl of racing engines came a sound that riveted the attention of Ranger Swank. On a small forward deck of the landing craft to Swank's right, Cameron piper Cpl. Alex Graham stood courageously playing "The One Hundred Pipers."

"He stood there," recalled Swank, "defiantly telling the world that the Camerons were coming. God what a glory." Inspired by their piper, the Camerons landed on Green Beach with courage and élan and swept forward, but success was not to be theirs that day. On landing, the two Americans were separated. They rejoined at the aid station, each thinking the other might be wounded. An overworked Canadian doctor pressed them into service as litter bearers. Later, Swank and Church were together on the Green Beach withdrawal, running toward a landing craft when Church was shot in the head. Ranger Swank dragged his friend to the seawall. Church would be taken prisoner by the Germans. Though he lived through the war, he never fully recovered and died in 1950. Swank remained with the Highlanders and during the withdrawal swam to a landing craft under fire. Wounded in the right forearm, Swank was taken by the landing craft to the HMS *Calpe* where he was helped aboard by Ranger Kenyon, who was himself wounded a few minutes later by strafing German aircraft.

Bill Darby was anxious to get his men back. Ranger Merritt Bertholf had heard Commandos received "survivors' leave" after an operation.

"When do I get *my* survivors' leave?" Bertholf asked Darby.

"After the war," Darby replied.

There were shortcomings in the planning for Dieppe that in hindsight seem so obvious they are appalling. The ground forces performed heroically, the Royal Navy and Royal Air Force fighter/reconnaissance squadrons that participated did a superb job, but the lack of strong fire support for a landing force making a frontal assault on prepared positions defies understanding. A few cruisers, a battleship, and/or carpet bombing may have saved hundreds of Allied lives and years of suffering by those troops shot up. Watching the attack from shipboard, Brigadier General Truscott was appalled at the insufficient naval gunfire support. He was told by British naval officers that cruisers could not be risked in such restricted water.

After the battle, the Canadians flew maple leaves from home to be strewn on the caskets of their dead. French Marshal Henri Petain, the chief of the Vichy French government, sent congratulations to the German High Command in France.

Argument may never be settled regarding the worth of the Dieppe raid. From a battlefield viewpoint, it was a bloody disaster. Lord Mountbatten was convinced that Dieppe was vital to the successful landing that would come at Normandy. The official view was that valuable lessons were learned for the future invasion of the Continent. The need for naval gunfire and bomber support, how better to control an amphibious operation, beach control, obstacle removal, and attacks on fortified positions were areas where training improved as a result of the Dieppe.

For the Rangers, Dieppe was special, for here they forged a bond in blood with the Commandos. They also received recognition. The American press took this new unit to its heart and gave the name "Ranger" a recognition it had deserved since Colonial times.

One result unexpected by the planners and participants was the power of the American press. General Eisenhower had insisted the number of Americans participating be kept secret and be referred to as "a detachment from a United States Ranger battalion." Anxious to put the best face on the circumstance, the British released a propaganda blitz that made Dieppe seem like a well-executed prelude to a full-scale invasion. Eisenhower had a public relations staff loaded with talent. They saw the event as the opportunity to blow the American trumpet and proceeded to do so with a flurry of releases. The *New York Times* of August 20, 1942, proclaimed, "for the first time United States troops took part in a raid on the Continent. The raiding force also included Canadians, British, and fighting French." Other American newspapers and magazines quickly followed suit with stories that made it seem that Dieppe was predominantly an American operation with some British and Canadian support. The press offices and governments of the Allies were upset, but the American press had only taken up their initial euphoria and added an American flavor. Soon, however, Allied complaint and the bad news from the beaches of Dieppe cooled the American propaganda machine.

Most disgraceful was the effort by some American journalists to enhance their own image by claiming to have been ashore at the side of the Rangers. One reporter claimed to be standing at the side of an American Ranger who shot a sniper and became the first American to kill a German in this war. The Ranger who was so identified was among those who did not make it ashore.

Though the public relations people overstepped the mark, the result was an American public that was cheering offensive action and wanting more. In that respect, the fifty Rangers who participated and the twelve Rangers who crossed the beaches of Dieppe were worth an army division to the American war effort. Later generations of American fighting men would learn to their sorrow how frustrating it is to fight a war without the support of the people at home. At Dieppe, the Rangers made America proud of its sons, and America cheered.

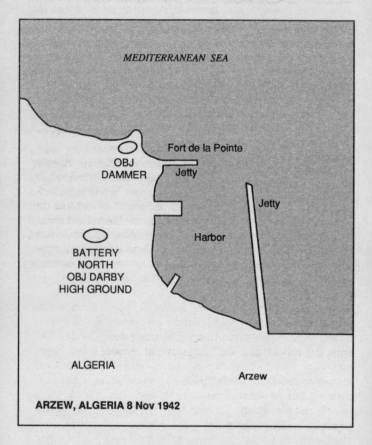

MEDITERRANEAN SEA

Fort de la Pointe

OBJ
DAMMER

Jetty

Jetty

Harbor

BATTERY
NORTH
OBJ DARBY
HIGH GROUND

ALGERIA

Arzew

ARZEW, ALGERIA 8 Nov 1942

CHAPTER 4

NORTH AFRICA

Filled with pride that brother Rangers had been the first Americans to cross a European beach in this great struggle, the men of the 1st Ranger Battalion welcomed home the participants. Training had an added impetus with the certainty that others would soon have their turn at the enemy.

With their training at Dorlin complete, the 1st Ranger Battalion moved to Dundee on the east coast of Scotland on September 3. Here they began training with Number 1 Commando, which had been organized in mid-1940 and had the experience of several small combat operations behind them. While with Lt. Col. T. Trevor and his Number 1 Commando at Dundee, the Rangers were being prepared to participate in raids on the Norwegian coast. Practice for combat took on realism as assaults were made on fortifications and gun positions.

On September 11, Ranger James R. Ruschkewicz was killed and Ranger Aaron M. Salkin was severely wounded in a land mine explosion at Barry rifle range near Dundee. Despite this misfortune, the Ranger life at Dundee was a happy one. Here they had the experience of being billeted at local homes and mixing with the friendly citizenry. There was hard training, but for young men there was also time for a drink, a dance, and a winsome Scottish lass. This opportunity for enjoyment brought about the need for military police. Peer Buck and his cooks and Rangers from throughout the battalion shared this duty.

Ranger Warren Evans was battalion sergeant major. A former football player, Evans was big, handsome, and could sing with a voice that led to the nickname "Bing," after Bing

Crosby. Bing Evans was better than a platoon of military police for keeping order.

The planned mission to raid the Norwegian coast in company with the Commandos was cancelled. There were no other missions pending that would fulfill the requirement to go into battle with the Commandos, who by this time had a considerable pool of Commando-trained British, Canadian, and French troops eagerly awaiting a shot at a German.

Fortunately, a combat opportunity for the Rangers was about to occur. An invasion of North Africa by primarily American assault forces was being planned. At Dieppe and other raids, amphibious landing and assault was followed by withdrawal. The new Ranger requirement would be to spearhead an invasion, take an objective, and hold it until relieved. Given the number and importance of amphibious invasions in World War II, this added dimension offered an opportunity for the perpetuation of the Ranger unit.

Moving to tents and mud fields at Corker Hill near Glasgow, the 1st Ranger Battalion was assigned to army II Corps on September 24, 1942. They were then attached to Maj. Gen. Terry Allen's 1st Infantry Division and further attached to the 18th Regimental Combat Team for administration and supply.

At Corker Hill, the 1st Ranger Battalion was given a combat mission. With these orders, the concept of the 1st Ranger Battalion becoming a training and demonstration unit under British tactical employment was set aside. Its first battle experience as a battalion would be as an American unit under American control.

There was an air of expectancy at battalion headquarters. The mission was an assault landing, one that in Bill Darby's view would require some strong fire support. Darby had been an artillery officer, and in the months ahead, his training and thinking led him to seek increased fire support for the Rangers. D Company was converted to a mortar company, using 81mm mortars. The D Company Rangers looked upon this as a challenge. Sgt. Robert Ehalt was a former blacksmith, and he and other enterprising Ranger mortarmen quickly adapted the light-weight, wheeled cart that was used by heavy weapons companies to transport water-cooled machine guns. This cart enabled the mortar crews to move much more rapidly than they could if trying to manhandle the weapon and to arrive fresher at the firing point. There are few places a man can go that a small cart cannot accompany. The use of the cart was a prime example that, in the Rangers, brains were more important than brawn.

New faces began to appear in the battalion area. Father Albert E. Basil, a Roman Catholic chaplain, was given orders attaching him to the 1st Ranger Battalion. Basil established a bond of caring that would endure through many trials ahead. Wearing his jaunty Commando green beret, Father Basil went with and among the Rangers and earned their respect and affection.

European Theater Command assigned two photographers to accompany the battalion. Phil Stern had worked for *LOOK* and *LIFE* magazines, and Henry Paluch was a movie photographer. Months later Darby would try to get the assignment of these photographers revoked, saying "They take up spaces that can be filled by riflemen." But time would prove the worth of Ranger photography. Paluch went on to other assignments, but Phil Stern remained with the battalion until wounded in Africa. Phil Stern's photographs and news reports would be of value in getting recognition of Ranger accomplishments.[1]

At Corker Hill, Peer Buck's mess team was now free to cook American style for the men. Buck was still trying to persuade Darby to let him have a combat role. Darby would not agree but his liking for Buck continued to grow. At Corker Hill, the mess team was absorbed into the battalion and one of the greatest difficulties of the young organization was solved.

At the completion of the training phase, the 1st Ranger Battalion was a finely honed fighting machine, lacking only the experience of combat. The men had been cross-trained in a wide variety of weapons, mines, and demolitions. One exception was the mortar. "We did not try to make everyone a mortarman," Dammer said. The 60mm mortar was left in the hands of the crews who, along with D Company and the 81mm mortars, stressed movement and going in and out of action. Much of the training was at night and over water.

There was good teamwork between the companies and the staff.

On October 13, 1942, the 1st Ranger Battalion moved by rail to Courock, Scotland, and embarked on the HMS *Royal Scotsman*, the HMS *Ulster Monarch*, and the HMS *Royal Ulsterman*. These ships would become home for the 1st Rangers until early November.

On September 30, 1942, European Theater of Operations (ETOUSA) sent a directive to II Corps (Gen. Mark Clark) to "organize the 2d Provisional Ranger Battalion from forces under your command." The directive stated that the general purpose of the new unit would be identical to that of the 1st Ranger Battalion. "It will be used as a training unit for a maximum number of selected officers and enlisted men of combat units to receive training experience in actual combat after which they will return to their organization." Like the 1st Ranger Battalion, the new unit would be attached to the Special Services Brigade (British) for training and tactical control.

General Clark turned to the 29th Infantry Division, a National Guard division from Maryland and Virginia, to provide the men for the new Ranger battalion.

Training continued for the 1st Ranger Battalion. From October 13 until October 20, they prepared for and participated in the preinvasion exercise called "Mosstrooper." Back at Clyde, they made final preparation for sailing and commitment to battle.

TORCH was the operation code name of the 1942 Anglo/American invasion of French North Africa. With the fall of France, the conquering Germans permitted a French collaboration government to be established at Vichy, France, which controlled the French forces in North Africa.

The decision to seize this French territory was made by the British and Americans in July 1942 after considerable and often heated debate. The Americans wanted an early invasion of the continent of Europe. The British felt it doubtful that the Allies could sustain such an invasion in 1943. They looked upon an effort in French North Africa as a desirable way to bring pressure to bear on Germany without the risk of disaster that a direct attack on Hitler's "fortress Europe" would bring.

The memory of the horrible bloodletting of World War I ran justifiably deep with the British. They favored a peripheral strategy. The Americans were opposed; they wanted to go for the Nazi jugular with a cross-channel invasion of Europe. The military argument that resulted became so fierce that senior Americans began to talk of transferring American priority to the Pacific Theater. The British view prevailed when President Roosevelt, persuaded by Prime Minister Churchill, ordered the American Joint Chiefs of Staff to support the operation. This was a monumental decision. Going into North Africa meant that a much longer time would be required to build up forces to invade Europe and strike at the heart of Nazi Germany. It would also lead to the invasion of Sicily and a bloody peripheral campaign in Italy.

On the plus side was the early committing of U.S. troops to battle, the attrition placed on the widespread German Army, and the protection this campaign offered to Gibraltar, the gateway to the Mediterranean.

TORCH was a far-flung operation involving three separate amphibious task force landings at three separate objectives in two countries. The eastern task force consisted of both British and American forces and would land in the vicinity of Algiers, Algeria. The center task force, made up of American ground forces transported by the Royal Navy, would land in the vicinity of Oran, Algeria, 260 miles west of Algiers. The western task force was made up of American forces sailing directly from the United States. These troops would go ashore in an area centered on Casablanca, Morocco.

The three-stage plan called for first getting a solid foothold in North Africa; second, moving outward to control all of French North Africa and, if necessary, Spanish Morocco; and third, moving east across Libya to hit from the rear the Germans and Italians who were fighting the British Eighth Army.

The invasion was set for the early morning hours of November 8, 1942.

For the undertaking, the 1st Ranger Battalion remained assigned to the U.S. Army II Corps under Maj. Gen. Lloyd

Fredendall, who would command the center task force. Fredendall continued his attachment of the Rangers to the feisty Terry Allen's 1st Infantry Division.

The mission of the center task force was to seize Oran, a substantial seaport of some 400,000 people. Terry Allen planned to do this using a double envelopment by the 1st Infantry Division and a wide encircling movement by Combat Command B of the 1st Armored Division. Allen planned for the bulk of his force to land at Arzew, a small seaport some twenty miles to the east of Oran. Allen organized his force with the 16th Infantry Regiment, reinforced, as Combat Team 16, the 18th Infantry Regiment as Combat Team 18, and Combat Command B of the 1st Armored Division as Task Force Red, to land at Arzew. The 26th Regiment and the remainder of Combat Command B would land on the opposite side of Oran. The separate task forces would then squeeze the big port city between them.

The capture of Oran was vital as it would give the sea-dependent Allies an excellent port and naval base.

The pregame feeling of eager concern rumbled in the pits of men's stomachs, but the Americans wanted the challenge they had trained for. There is something about being designated first that motivates men. The 1st Infantry Division wears a red numeral "1" on an olive drab background as a shoulder insignia. The informal motto of the division was "If you are going to be one, why not be a big red one?" This team of the 1st Infantry and 1st Armored Divisions and the 1st Ranger Battalion saw Arzew as the opportunity for three ace units to show their worth.

High ground dominated the port of Arzew. At the top of a steep, flat-faced hill, the French had built a battery General Allen called "North" and the French called *"Supérieur."* Consisting of four 105mm guns, the battery dominated the harbor, its approaches, and the town. The harbor had several moles (breakwaters) and was formed by two concrete jetties, reaching nearly a mile into the sea and closing to a narrow entrance. There was a harbor boom, which could be closed to prevent ships from entering. A lesser fort on the harbor point of land was appropriately named "Ford de La Pointe." Three 75mm guns pointed seaward from this location.

Both gun batteries, and in particular the one on the high ground, were so located that the mission of the center task force could not be accomplished until the guns were under American control. Only then could the harbor be seized and heavy equipment landed. The 1st Ranger Battalion was given the mission of making the landing ahead of the task force and eliminating the guns. Intelligence was good; Darby and Dammer spent hours studying the aerial photographs of the Arzew area. To keep the battalion intact in the seizure of either objective would arouse the other and give the enemy time to react. The two leaders came to the conclusion that only by splitting the battalion could they gain the advantage of surprise.

This meant that one force would have to go into the harbor of Arzew and, by stealth or assault, seize the lower fort. If that action did arouse the defenders on the high ground, it was hoped that their attention would be drawn away from the Rangers coming at them from the rear.

The seacoast around Arzew featured rocky waters running into cliffs. It offered little in the way of suitable landing sites. There was a scant stretch of beach so small as to scarcely warrant the name, and that beach was behind rocks and reef in such a way as to be a navigator's nightmare. The Royal Navy initially scoffed at the idea of taking men into wading distance of this shore. But having their own reputation for doing the impossible, the British became intrigued with the challenge.

The harbor boom presented another problem. There was no way of knowing if it would be open or closed at the time of the landing. If the boom was closed and the attacking force prevented from entering or was delayed, the whole operation could be jeopardized. Darby and Dammer decided to heavily weight the force that went after the high-ground battery as the taking of this objective could better insure the subsequent capture of the harbor fort.

There were other considerations. No one could be certain of how the French military would react to a landing in Africa. The shore batteries were manned by French naval personnel, men with reason to hate the British. At Oran in 1940, the English had destroyed the great ships of the French Navy to prevent them falling into German hands. French sailors died under British guns, and the memory still burned in the hearts of the French Navy. There was a question of whether troops could land from boats directly onto the mole. A British intelligence photo of a fisherman off-loading his catch directly from his rowboat onto the mole proved direct landing by troops was possible.

The final plan called for Major Dammer to lead Companies A and B against the harbor fort while Lieutenant Colonel Darby took Headquarters Company and C, D, E, and F Companies against the high-ground position.

On October 26, the convoy sailed from the Clyde. After stopping at Gibraltar on November 5 for oil and water, the ships moved on into the Mediterranean Sea. The deception plan was to make German intelligence think the convoy was bound for the eastern Mediterranean. The Germans were aware of the convoy and were planning to attack it later in its journey, but the deception plan worked, and the landing in North Africa took them by surprise.

In blackout, the convoy moved close to the Algerian shore. The French garrison was not alert. Lights could be seen burning at the end of the jetties; even the buoys were lit to assist navigation. Lowered down the sides of the HMS *Royal Scotsman* at midnight, Dammer's men headed for the harbor in eight of the quiet-running British LCA landing craft. Despite the harbor lights, the landing craft flotilla commander had difficulty finding his way into and about the harbor. First, the Royal Navy officer led the boats of Dammer's force in at the wrong angle, then back out and in again past the mole they were supposed to land on, then, as the garrison still slept, around again. Twice the mole was rammed noisily. Part of the confusion was due to large cargo ships blocking landing places and raftlike lighters that were moored beside the mole in groups, making it difficult for the landing craft to approach the mole.

Scrambling ashore at 0100 hours, thirty minutes before Darby's force, Company B Rangers established blocking positions to prevent reinforcements from reaching the fort, while Company A moved through to attack the fort and the gun positions. The months of preparation paid off as the men moved swiftly and accurately to positions they had studied on sand tables and rehearsed in practice assaults.

The fort was an ancient one, in decay yet formidable and capable of strong resistance. Ranger scouts Bruder and Lacosse were in the lead as the 1st Section, 1st Platoon of Company A closed on the gun positions. In the darkness, they came upon a sentry who challenged in French. A ranger, probably Lacosse, responded *"Nous sommes vos amis"* (We are your friends). The sentry passed the group on.

B Company's positions were on natural avenues of approach and so arranged that those who walked into the web would have difficulty getting out. B Company promptly began to garner prisoners. A Company, as the assault force, was split into two groups with the 2d Platoon going through the fort gate while the 1st Platoon moved farther along the wall, then up a grassy embankment that had three tiers of barbed wire, to get at the guns.

At the B Company positions, a Frenchman tried to flee and was fired upon. By this time, the Rangers from the 2d Platoon were inside the fort. Darby later was reported to have said they had followed in a French soldier carrying a basket of laundry on his head. 1st Platoon Rangers had just finished cutting the wire, when automatic weapons fired. French warning sirens went off, and from the fort gate 2d Platoon Rangers yelled the cry of the Lone Ranger of radio fame, "Hi Ho Silver!" The 1st Platoon Rangers responded with, "Away" and charged up the embankment, capturing the gun positions without a shot being fired.

At the fort, Ranger Murray Katzen armed with Thompson submachine gun and grenades attacked a French barracks and captured forty-two men. The commandant and a woman, probably not his wife, were captured in bed. From the time of landing, the harbor fort was taken in fifteen minutes with only one casualty, a French soldier killed. Company B was not so fortunate. Engaged by snipers, some of whom were believed to be firing from the rear of the Ranger positions, the Rangers had Lieutenant Carran shot through the shoulder and Ranger George W. Grisamer, who died after being shot in the stomach.

After capturing the harbor fort, Dammer made radio contact with Darby and sent men to secure the port facilities and link up with Darby. At 0215 Dammer fired the flares that told his seniors of success. On board his command ship, Gen. Terry Allen expressed his joy.

Darby's E, F, and Headquarters Companies were on the *Ulster Monarch* with C and D Companies on the *Royal Ulsterman*. As the landing craft were lowered to the water, a problem occurred with a davit, and one end of a boat lowered while the other did not. The result was that the Ranger occupants and equipment were spilled into the sea. Unfortunately, equipment lost included Darby's signal equipment, radios, and flares.

The small boats scurried around picking up Rangers who were swimming for their lives in the dark sea. In the process of milling around, the boat commanders became confused and lost their location.

"Have you the faintest idea where we are?" Darby asked the flotilla commander.

"I haven't the foggiest," replied the naval officer.

Seeing the confusion, the British captain of a larger ship directed that the small craft follow him and led them on the proper course for shore.

With the boats on course, the British seamen showed great skill and the plan began to work smoothly. The Rangers landed without incident at approximately 0130 hours, were challenged by an alert sentry (who they quickly captured), then moved up a coastal road toward the objective. A British support ship moved close to shore, and though blacked out, the bulk of her could be seen and was a comforting view to the climbing men. Darby set up his 81mm mortars in a defilade position five hundred yards from the objective, then with C, E, and F Companies on line began to close on the high-ground battery. Initially, they were undetected, but after having cut through half of the fourteen-foot-wide band of barbed wire that protected the fort, the French suddenly opened a heavy fire that stopped the Rangers. Darby was controlling his men with a small SCR-536 company radio but had good communications. He was able to withdraw his men somewhat and call for fire support from his mortars. The

French positions did not have overhead cover, and the fifty to sixty rounds of mortar fire were accurate. Between 0300 and 0400 hours, when Darby gave the command to assault, the resistance was ended. D Company could be justly proud of its gunnery. Though they kept the 81mm mortars throughout the Tunisian Campaign, Arzew was the first and last salvo of D Company as an 81mm mortar unit. They served well. The Rangers took over three hundred prisoners.

While the Rangers attacked the forts, the navy was waiting offshore to off-load the main body of the center task force troops. Darby was to signal his success to his seniors by means of a varied-color series of flares, flares that now rested on the bottom of the sea. All Darby had left was green flares, so he fired them one after another in hopes of getting his message across.

As the flares were not fired in the prearranged color combination of green and white, his efforts were not believed and the task force delayed landing the rest of the troops for two hours. Darby never forgot this lesson in the importance of shore-to-ship communications and paid particular attention to it in future operations.

With the dawn, French snipers harassed the landing forces. These were brought under fire and killed or captured. There was scattered resistance. The door to the French Foreign Legion fort was kicked in. Ranger Ed Dean[2] charged in with his submachine gun at the ready, but the drum magazine fell off in the process. Dean remembers the French soldiers standing there, grinning. Later, Dean turned in his submachine gun and armed himself with a dependable M-1 rifle. By noon, the Arzew mission was complete. The French commanders, having satisfied their honor, surrendered.

The invasion of North Africa was not a walkover. Gen. George Patton's western task force near Casablanca was heavily engaged. Major actions included a fierce battle between French and American warships that resulted in significant French losses.

The Ranger and 1st Division landing at Arzew was the easternmost of a trident-shaped landing by Fredendall's center task force. In the center of the attacks, a raiding force consisting of most of the 3d Battalion of the 6th Armored Infantry Battalion, carried in two British cutters, entered Oran harbor to seize the docks as the Rangers were doing at Arzew. The Oran raiding party did not achieve surprise; the ships were sunk; 189 Americans were killed, and 157 wounded and captured. Less than 50 of a 460 man raiding force emerged unscathed from the fire of the alert French defense. This demonstrated what the inefficient boat handling by the Royal Navy's landing craft flotilla commander could have cost the Rangers. Fortunately, surprise was achieved. With the Rangers at their throat, the French found it in their interest to surrender. Thus, Arzew was an excellent beginning for well-trained but untried troops. Gen. Terry Allen said "their initial mission was accomplished with great dash and vigor."

St. Cloud was a town of about 3,500 souls located in an open, agricultural area along the Oran–Arzew highway. It was a place of stone houses sitting in a wide, bowl-shaped depression with clear fields of fire for the defender and no cover or concealment for the attacker. St. Cloud was, as Terry Allen later called it, "a tough nut to crack." Allen gave the 18th Regimental Combat Team under Col. Frank Greer the mission of seizing St. Cloud as a stepping-stone to Oran. Greer committed his 1st Battalion, and it was stopped cold. He then added the 2d with the same result. A battalion of the French Foreign Legion and the 16th Tunisian Regiment were in the town, using machine guns, mortars, and artillery on Americans trying to advance over open terrain.

General Allen decided to contain the French in St. Cloud with one battalion of the 18th, while the other two passed around the town and continued to move on Oran. To help with the containment, he offered Colonel Greer Ranger assistance.

Company C, which for a day was given the mission of protecting 1st Division headquarters, found itself on the following day, November 9, 1942, attached to the 1st Battalion, 18th Infantry. The battalion commander ordered the Rangers to make a night march around the town of St. Cloud and block the road south to prevent the exit of enemy troops. Dawn found the Rangers in position and revealed a motor convoy stopped on the road. The Rangers promptly moved to the attack with Lt. Charles Shunstrom and the 2d Platoon on the left and the company commander, Gordon Klefman, and the 1st Platoon moving straight ahead. Immediately, the Rangers came under intense mortar, machine-gun, and 75mm artillery fire. The Rangers tried fire and maneuver but were pinned down. It soon became evident that the enemy artillery was emplaced near the convoy. The Rangers dug in and fought a pitched battle. It was not until Allen's force captured Oran that the senior French commander there ordered the St. Cloud forces to stop fighting. About 1500 hours, the French surrendered. Company C was hard hit. The 1st Ranger Battalion action report says "the company was badly shot up." Company commander Gordon L. Klefman and Rangers Elmer Eskola and Alder L. Nystron were killed and one officer and eight additional Rangers wounded.

Meanwhile on D-day, Company E moved by train for attachment to the 1st Battalion, 16th Infantry Regiment. Elements of the 16th Infantry had captured La Macta, a town that controlled a key bridge over an unfordable gorge. The 1st Division soldiers reported they were under heavy counterattack by French forces. Company E moved by rail, east along the coast, to Port-aux-Poules and was given the mission of clearing the road to La Macta. Moving forward, the Rangers came under fire, deployed, and used fire and maneuver to kill and wound "a number" of the enemy. A Frenchman, firing a Hotchkiss machine gun at long range, was pinning down a large number of the American infantry. Ranger scouts Ed Dean and Joe Dye mounted a half-track and set off after the French crew, who soon stopped firing.

Speedily accomplishing their mission, E Company entered the town. When the commander they were attached to felt the French threat had passed, E Company rode the train back to Arzew.

On November 10, the 1st Ranger Battalion was relieved of attachment to the 1st Infantry Division and placed in II Corps reserve, with duties of guarding prisoners, gun positions, and hospitals and providing town security. Terry Allen appointed Bill Darby to the interesting position of town mayor of Arzew. The appointment gave a new dimension to the Ranger commander and his men. Darby was now faced with the need to provide water and electricity to the city he had just attacked. There were questions on where the dead could be buried and could the local house of prostitution be reopened. Herm Dammer recalls that the need for local fishermen to go to sea to fish in a combat zone was a problem. Many of the difficulties were resolved by installing the mayor of Arzew in the office next door to Darby and letting the French system function under American control.

With combat experience behind them, the Rangers now had three months to hone their skills. Under the broiling sun and with great emphasis on night operations, the Rangers practiced and practiced their craft. Physical training, speed marches, amphibious landings, and tactical exercises were daily fare. Some of the men also made acquaintance with the local wine and women, and there were the usual discipline problems. Darby used some of his men to serve as military police. Often in the military, commanders play the role of the beloved leader while the executive officer serves as the hatchet man. It was not that way in the 1st Ranger Battalion. Dammer worked closely with his commander on keeping men in control and took action on his own when he deemed it necessary. When he so desired, Darby would have Sgt. Maj. Bing Evans bring the errant Ranger before him and take action. At times, the Rangers had their own stockade in the form of a barbed-wire enclosure. Those in custody would pitch their tents inside the wire.

Back in England on December 2, Headquarters European Theater (ETOUSA) recommended the organization of another Ranger battalion to the adjutant general of the War Department. The letter praised the accomplishments of the 1st Ranger Battalion, but stated that the 1st Battalion was now in the Mediterranean and would probably not return to England. ETOUSA wanted a second Ranger battalion promptly organized and trained within theater. The request stated: "Experience has proven that specially trained units of this character are invaluable in landing operations, for the reduction of coast defenses, and similar missions." The invasion of North Africa had drawn off American combat forces in England. ETOUSA asked that the bulk of the personnel for the new organization come from the United States. There was only one American combat division in the theater (the 29th Infantry Division), which had arrived understrength. ETOUSA was organizing a small provisional[3] Ranger battalion within that division, but stated that "this provisional battalion will be returned to the division upon completion of its training and will not be available for independent missions." ETOUSA wanted high-quality men and included proposed tables of organization in the request. It was noted that Lord Mountbatten was in favor of the plan and would provide Commando facilities. ETOUSA wanted authority to organize one company of the 2d Ranger Battalion from personnel in the United Kingdom to complete necessary preparatory work prior to the arrival of the rest of the battalion.

While awaiting action on the 2d Ranger Battalion, ETOUSA on December 20, 1942, put into effect its September 30 directive and began the formation of the Ranger battalion from and for the 29th Infantry Division. At Tidworth Barracks, volunteers were put through rigorous screening. Maj. Randolph Millholland, who had attended the British General Headquarters (GHQ) Battle School, was designated commanding officer. Millholland promptly began to put his men through preparatory training to ready them for Achnacarry and the Commandos.

On Christmas Eve in Africa, the 1st Rangers were presented with orders to prepare for a night raid on Italian radar, radio, and coastal emplacements on the island of Galita off the Tunisian coast. The Rangers were on board their assault ship HMS *Queen Emma* when the operation was canceled.

Once more preparation for battle was initiated. The 1st Ranger Battalion began a concentrated training program, stressing weapons, tactical, and physical training. Operations at night also received emphasis.

With the development of a Headquarters Fifth Army directed Invasion Training Center in January 1943, the 1st Rangers moved a short distance down the coast from Arzew to Port-aux-Poules, Algeria, and began demonstrating the techniques of live-fire amphibious landings.

The German high command had reacted speedily to the American and British North African invasion. It was obvious that such a force constituted a threat to the rear of German forces in North Africa. Field Marshal Rommel was retreating west through Libya before Montgomery's Eighth Army. When he reached Tunisia, Rommel needed space to effect a northward turn toward the sea; the Allied landings threatened this move. German aircraft began ferrying troops across the Mediterranean. A race for Tunisia developed.

While the Rangers trained hard, the use of specially trained assault forces was becoming grudgingly adapted by the U.S. military. In the United States, the Second United States Army commanded by Gen. Ben Lear had opened a two-week Ranger training course at Camp Forrest, Tennessee, based on Raider training being given by the Marines. The school had a successful but brief existence. The same arguments raised in the British Army about the Commandos were raised in the American Army. There is nothing these units can do that a rifle battalion trained for the mission could not do, cried the critics. They complained that the Ranger concept drew off men of leadership ability that were critically needed in other units. "We simply do not have enough men to afford the luxury of having these units sit out the fight between missions," huffed officers who seemed to be under the impression that infantry units never go into reserve, rest, and refit posture.

The American Rangers did not have a champion as Winston Churchill was for the British Commandos or a combined operation headquarters with a senior officer to stand up for them as Mountbatten did for his men.

Meanwhile, in Africa on January 26, 1943, the 1st Ranger Battalion welcomed Capt. Jack B. Street, five other officers, and one hundred enlisted men. The welcome for the replacements was tumultuous. As the trucks bearing the new arrivals entered the Ranger area, the Ranger veterans sprayed the area around and under the vehicles of the replacements with rifle and automatic weapons fire.

One of the new men was Lt. Robert F. Neal, who had been undergoing specialized amphibious training in the United States in the destruction of underwater obstacles when told he was going to the Rangers. On arrival in Africa, Darby gave Neal and the other new men a choice of joining the Rangers or not.

Some of the new arrivals immediately went to existing companies. As a temporary measure, the remainder of the new men were organized as Company G, under the command of Capt. Jack Street.

On January 27, there was an unusual casualty statistic when a Ranger was trampled by a bull.

Back in England on Monday, February 1, 1943, ten officers and 166 men of the 29th Infantry Division arrived at Achnacarry. The men were billeted in Nissen huts and some in tents. Everyone ate British rations. The British called this group the U.S. 2d Ranger Battalion, but the American Army referred to them as the 29th Ranger Battalion and, confirming the divisional tie, sent their mail through the divisional post office.

The 29th Rangers were formed into Headquarters Company and A and B Companies. The men wore Paratrooper boots and trained hard in the constant wet and mud of winter in Scotland. "They were never completely dry from one day to another," stated a report. The records show that they were a dedicated group of men, and the 29th Rangers complained when details took them away from training. They were also angry at themselves when being outdone by British instructors, who were specialists in their fields. On time off, many 29th Rangers worked on weapons assembly and disassembly on their own. All this rated high with the Commando instructors, who spoke favorably of the 29th Rangers.

The battalion commander, Lt. Col. Randy Millholland, was well respected. Small, feisty, and energetic, the thirty-six-year-old former cost accountant from Cumberland, Maryland, told his men to keep their eyes and ears open and their mouths shut. The men were very attentive to their instructors. They were fiercely proud of their unit. It was widely known that they did not want to be returned to the division or used as "school" troops. The men wanted their Ranger battalion to be as independent as the 1st Ranger Battalion was.

In North Africa with the 1st Battalion, there was little opportunity for their new volunteers to settle in. On February 3, the battalion was loaded on C-47 transport planes at Oran and flown to Tunisia as part of II Corps. Near the Tunisian city of Gafsa, the Rangers established a base camp.

Tunisia was bounded on the north and east by the Mediterranean Sea and on the south by the great Sahara Desert. The western part, which adjoined Algeria, consisted of a mix of desert, mountains, and fertile coastal areas.

The front was fluid. The wide frontage involved dictated a mobile defense, using scattered outposts and strong points with a rapid response reserve. The Germans opted to have their Italian allies man the outposts, while German forces would play the role of firemen responding to threats when and where needed. The Americans found it worthwhile to terrorize the Italians and tire the German reserves. Night raids by the Rangers were an ideal means of accomplishing the goal.

On February 9, Darby received orders from 1st Division to raid an enemy position located on rocky hills near Sened Station. This was a mountain cut that served as an avenue of approach to the flat Tunisian plains. Darby made a preliminary study of the objective and decided to use Companies A, E, and F to make the attack, with the 81mm mortars from Headquarters Company in support. These personnel with their equipment were loaded on trucks and moved on the night of February 10 to an assembly area approximately twelve miles from the enemy position. A night march over difficult terrain took them to a high-ground position approximately four miles from the objective. This place was close enough that enemy positions could be observed. Here the Rangers went to ground, covering themselves with shelter halves and brush to avoid enemy observation. Around noon, Darby and Dammer led a reconnaissance party, studying the Italian position. On their return, final plans for the attack were made, and company officers and noncommissioned officers were briefed.

As the desert sun slipped beneath the rim of the earth, the Rangers—with faces darkened, equipment taped down, and wearing woolen caps—arose from cover and began their approach march, keeping terrain features between them and the enemy, using folds in the earth and the night skills months of hard training had given them to move forward undetected. They moved to within one mile of the enemy, then waited until 2300 hours, a time just prior to the setting of the moon, before the approach was continued. As they neared the objective, company guides led the men to predesignated points approximately five hundred yards from the enemy positions. Here the three Ranger companies formed one line, with Company A on the left, Company E in the center, and Company F on the right. With fixed bayonets and on command, they moved forward. In the black of night, Ranger leaders were able to control the movements of their men by the use of hooded, colored flashlights. The leaders would briefly display their lights rearward, enabling the higher echelon to observe the location of the unit, then adjust its location by use of radio. By this method, Dammer and Darby were able to move the battalion into a line formation in complete darkness.

Italian automatic-weapons men became suspicious and began to loose bursts of fire over the Rangers' heads. The Rangers did not respond but continued climbing the slopes toward the Italian positions. More and more Italian weapons began firing, but the nervous gunners were firing high and their gun flashes served only to reveal their locations. Attacking with fixed bayonets, A, E, and F Companies hit the Italians hard. Meanwhile, the 81mm mortars fired on the rear of the Italian positions as the terrified Italians attempted to flee.

In less than thirty minutes, the Italians were driven from position, suffering an estimated seventy-five killed and the loss of five machine guns and a 50mm antitank weapon. Eleven men of the 10th Bersaglieri Regiment were taken. Ranger Elmer W. Garrison was killed, decapitated by an Italian shell, and twenty other Rangers were wounded. Hustling their prisoners along, the Rangers withdrew to Gafsa in several groups. Darby's orders were that on return there would be no delay and no waiting. Every man knew that if he could not make it, he would be sacrificed. What applied to the Americans applied to the prisoners. A Ranger sergeant through an Italian-speaking Ranger told a wounded Italian he must keep up the pace or die. The Italian fell behind. The Italian-speaking Ranger could not bear the prisoner's pleas and turned away. Another Ranger killed the Italian.

II Corps was jubilant over the success of the raid. A dozen

Rangers were decorated with the Silver Star,[4] and Bing Evans and Walter Wojcik received battlefield commissions. With the promotion of Bing Evans, former mess sergeant Peer Buck became the battalion sergeant major. The ceremonies that accompanied all this varied from the formal to the ludicrous. Robert Neal had been wounded in the leg by shrapnel. As he lay in the hospital, a man entered and asked curtly "You Lieutenant Neal?" When Neal acknowledged, the man said, "Here's your Purple Heart," and tossed the medal to him.

The raid at Sened Station was a brilliant success. After the night of February 12, 1942, Italian soldiers slept uneasily, their dreams haunted by specters of American Rangers.

In early February 1943, the German forces in North Africa were divided, with Colonel-General Von Arnim and his Fifth Panzer Army holding the line against the Allied forces that landed in TORCH and Field Marshal Rommel, with his Panzer Army Afrika, retreating before General Montgomery's Eighth Army. General Eisenhower wanted to seize Tunisia before the Germans could link up. The two German commanders perceived this danger but did not agree on how to prevent it. Rommel wanted an all-out tank thrust. Von Arnim was on the scene and knew the forces were not available to sustain such an effort. He sought offensive action but on a more limited scale. On February 14, Von Arnim sent the 10th and 21st Panzer Divisions, under strong air support, into the attack on American II Corps positions at the Faid Pass. The Germans began trouncing American units, with the American 1st Armored Division suffering heavy tank and personnel losses. The American II Corps withdrew, in some cases in chaos. That same day, the 1st Ranger Battalion was ordered from the vicinity of Gafsa, Tunisia, to a position near the town of Feriana. Companies D and G served as rear guard for Col. Fred Butler's 1st Division force.

The remainder of the 1st Ranger Battalion was being employed in a rear-guard action and, while covering the withdrawal, came under air attack by German Stuka dive bombers. Caught in the open, Ranger Bob Ehalt tried to outrun the bombs and machine guns of the aircraft. The German pilot missed him, but Ehalt would never forget the sound of the sirens on the Stuka's wings as it screamed downward.

During the corps retreat, the 1st Ranger Battalion was alone with only small arms and rudimentary infantry antitank weapons. The battalion's withdrawal was of necessity over open ground that was ideal tank country. The sound of German armor could be clearly heard, with the German columns paralleling the Rangers. It seemed only a matter of time before the Rangers and German tanks met. There was justifiable concern among officers and men. A good military leader has a feel for inspiration, even if bravado is necessary. Darby told his men, "If we get caught by the tanks, God help the tanks." It was a remark that would bring laughter from some, a curse from a man never heard to curse before, and instilled in others a pride that they would never forget. The bold withdrawal was accomplished without a battle with enemy armor. Ranger Jim Alticri remembers that the Rangers were angry about withdrawing. "We could not stomach the American Army retreating."

"We did not want to eat crow," added Ranger Gene "Koppy" Kopveiler.

The Rangers occupied high-ground positions to the left (east) of Feriana on February 15 but the next day were moved to dig in astride the Feriana–Tebessa road. On the 17th, the Rangers were ordered to hold Dernaia Pass and the critical road to Tebessa. The Rangers experienced no heavy combat here, but day and night patrols were active. A ten-man Ranger patrol was sent out, with the men distributed between a quarter-ton truck and a weapons carrier. The patrol proceeded into the mountains, then dismounted and were sent off in different directions to scout. Cpl. Paul Hermsen had a hand-held radio but, due to the mountainous terrain, could not establish communication. After a three- to four-hour scout, Hermsen returned to the assembly point to find the other men and the vehicles gone. While searching, Hermsen turned a corner of a mountain trail and encountered a patrol of approximately twenty Italians led by a German officer. Hermsen had two grenades, which he threw then went prone and opened fire with his rifle. Hermsen had killed three of the enemy including the German officer, but while reloading he was suddenly paralyzed. Another patrol had come up from his rear, and an enemy soldier had driven a bayonet thrust at Hermsen that caught the Ranger's cartridge belt and pinned it against his spine. He expected death, but American artillery began to land, and the enemy forces cleared the area, taking him prisoner. Thus began an odyssey that would take Hermsen to Germany, where he would both escape to and later from the Russians and eventually return to American lines in May 1945.

Elsewhere, Von Arnim's attack was met by American counterattack and stopped by February 17. German high command now gave overall command and Von Arnim's panzers to Rommel, who promptly attacked and by the 19th had reached the critical Kasserine Pass.

At Kasserine Pass, the Germans gave the untested Americans a bloody welcome to war. At Kasserine Pass the Americans lost the 168th Regimental Combat Team (the 168th was the former unit of many Rangers) and a tank battalion.

For the 1st Ranger Battalion, hunting was good along the Feriani–Tebessa highway. Around 0800 on February 20, two sedans, a truck, and a motorcycle approached the Ranger positions and were fired upon. The truck was destroyed and one of the sedans captured, while the other sedan and the motorcycle fled.

Seven Italians were captured and three killed. About 1500 the same day, another sedan approached. This time three Italians were killed and one wounded. The next day, it was the Germans' turn. A truck and two troop carriers were taken, and a number of German prisoners went into the bag. Many of the Germans and Italians were military police proceeding into what they thought was a safe zone. The enemy soon became aware of the Ranger location and began to shell them with artillery. American counterbattery fire silenced the enemy guns.

Lt. George Sunshine drove a jeep to a spot on high ground forward of the Ranger position. This location provided for excellent observation of German positions. Sunshine had an enjoyable time bringing artillery fire on the Germans, but the Germans were not amused. They sent out two heavily armed scout cars, who hotly pursued Lieutenant Sunshine back to Ranger lines.

On February 22, 1st Division commander Gen. Terry Allen wrote Darby that "There is a hell of a mess on our front." Allen asked for a reinforced company with a "hairy-chested company commander with big nuts." Lt. James B. Lyle and his Company C were sent to the 16th Infantry as a mobile reserve.

American and British forces beat off Rommel's attacks, and by the night of February 22, the Germans' bold gamble had failed.

Disputes between the German generals Rommel and Von Arnim had hindered the German cause. On February 23, Berlin gave Rommel overall authority in North Africa, but it came too late. The German offensive had lost its steam and the Allies were gearing up to go on the offensive themselves. Lieutenant Lyle's Company C was not committed, the crisis passed, and it was back with the battalion by the 24th.

Ranger patrols were active, reporting on enemy activity on the Kasserine–Feriana road, but for the Rangers, the period of February 25 to 28 was termed "comparatively inactive" in their action report.

In the cold of Achnacarry, on February 26, 1943, the 29th Rangers were introduced to senior officers and the press. A special train carried the dignitaries and journalists to view a day-long series of exercises that included physical training with logs, climbing, attack on strong points, bayonet drill, unarmed and knife combat, and me-and-my-pal reconnaissance in pairs. Prior to departure, the visitors had tea. British observers included Lord Mountbatten and Major General Haydon of Combined Operations. The American senior officers were Lt. Gen. Frank H. Andrews, commanding general of the European Theater; his deputy, Maj. Gen. Russell Hartle; and his chief liaison officer, Brig. Gen. Norman D. Cota.

On completion of their graduation show, the 29th Rangers moved near Winchester and were attached to Lord Lovat's Number 4 Commando. The relationship was a good one. The Americans began tactical training and beach and cliff training. A report to Cota stated, "There is a sharp contrast in their vigor and assurance now and last February when they arrived at Achnacarry." The unit still consisted of a Headquarters Company and two rifle companies but was expecting to grow.

In the United States, General Lear and his Second Army had the experience of operating a short-lived, two-week Ranger course at Camp Forrest, Tennessee. As a result, on March 11, 1943, the commanding officer 11th Detachment Special Troops at Camp Forrest was ordered to activate on April 1, 1943, the 2d Ranger Battalion. Nationwide, men were called upon to volunteer.

In North Africa on March 1, the 1st Ranger Battalion was relieved by the 60th Infantry and moved near La Kouif in II Corps reserve. On March 6, the United States Army II Corps received a new commander, Gen. George S. Patton. On March 9, the ailing Field Marshal Erwin Rommel left Africa. He would not return. Step by step the allies were hemming the Germans and Italians against the Mediterranean Sea.

On March 14, 1943, the 1st Rangers moved by truck to the vicinity of Dernaia, Tunisia, where they were once again attached to the 1st Infantry Division. The Ranger mission was to protect division artillery and maintain contact between the 16th and 18th Regimental Combat Teams. The 1st Division was moving to contact in Operation WOP, but there was little contact. Gafsa fell with ease. The 1st Ranger Battalion was placed on trucks and moved to near Gafsa, where it remained in 1st Division reserve.

The American II Corps now consisted of the 1st Armored Division and the 1st, 9th, and 34th Infantry Divisions, minus several detached regiments. The British General Alexander, feeling that American forces were not yet on a par with the Germans, used British forces to hammer the Germans, with Anderson's First Army attacking in the north and Montgomery's Eighth Army coming from the east. Situated between the two British forces, the American II Corps was assigned a support mission that included permission to reconnoiter toward Maknassy, a town approximately fifty miles from the Gulf of Gabes. True to his nature, Patton saw a reconnaissance as an opportunity to attack. Terry Allen's 1st Division was ordered to "take the commanding ground east of El-Guettar."

The terrain in Tunisia is dramatic. Plains flat as a billiard table lead to sharp, jutting mountains and narrow passes that are a defender's dream. Attached to the 1st Infantry Division, the Rangers were assigned on March 15 the mission of locating enemy forces. They moved forward to El-Guettar to find the enemy had fled. El-Guettar was an important road junction, a place where one key road led across the flats to Gabes and ran behind the German key defenses on their Mareth line. The other led through the tight mountain pass called Djebel El Ank toward Sfax (a djebel is a rocky outcropping). The contesting armies did not need to occupy El-Guettar to control the area. The mountain passes were key. It was at the pass of Djebal El Ank that the Rangers located the enemy positions.

The opposing force spread throughout the area was approximately six thousand members of the Italian Centauro Armored Division. At the pass, gun batteries were protected by automatic weapons and naturally defensible terrain in the shape of a funnel. American forces making a frontal attack would be poured into the wide mouth of the funnel and find themselves under heavy fire at the narrowing neck.

Gen. Terry Allen planned his attack with the 18th Infantry on the right, attacking toward Gabes, and the 26th attacking east toward Sfax. The 1st Ranger Battalion had the mission of attacking east along the mountain ridges of Djebal Orbata to protect the left (north) flank of the 26th Infantry.

Ranger reconnaissance patrols searched for a way to get behind the guns that threatened the 26th Infantry. The patrols were led by the Lt. Walter Wojcik, who had received a battlefield commission as a result of the Sened Station action. If Walt Wojcik had been one of King Arthur's knights, he would have been Sir Galahad. Wojcik was absolutely courageous. An Eagle Scout and a star athlete, he was a moral marvel. When it was his turn to be duty officer, he would go anywhere to check on the men except to cross the threshold of a house of prostitution.

By dint of skillful scouting, Wojcik and his men found the way to get above the enemy. On March 18 and 19, the Rangers endured enemy shelling while readying themselves for the attack.

On the 20th of March, with Wojcik showing the way, the Rangers made a tortuous six-mile march over terrain thought to be impassable by the enemy. Moving to high ground that overlooked the enemy positions at Djebel Ank Pass, the Rangers attacked at 0600 hours with a Ranger sounding charge on a bugle. Surprised and terrified, the Italians, whose heavy weapons were facing down the pass, put up a weak resistance and surrendered. Those who resisted were killed. The attached 4.2-inch mortar company came into position and began to engage Italian positions not yet reached. Pressing on, the Rangers were able to make full use of their Commando chaplain. Speaking in Italian, Father Basil called on the enemy to surrender. In all, the Rangers took some two hundred prisoners as a result of their action. The 26th Infantry had an easy passage, and over a thousand prisoners were garnered. There were no Rangers killed in the action and only one was wounded.

On the evening of the 21st, they returned to El-Guettar and moved into division reserve. The Germans sought to regain the lost ground by counterattacking with their 10th Panzer Division. By the 23d, the Rangers were back, face-to-face with the enemy. The Rangers' position was on line to the left of the 3d Battalion, 16th Infantry. This position was attacked by approximately sixty enemy tanks and a dismounted infantry battalion. The attack was broken up by artillery fire.

Still being used as an infantry battalion, on March 24 the Rangers moved to the right flank of the 18th Infantry, cleared the town of Jebel Berda of enemy, and blocked enemy forces from high-ground positions. On March 25, the 1st Ranger Battalion served as rear guard for the withdrawing 18th Infantry. On the 25th, Rangers Leonard H. Sporman, John J. Ball, and Nelson Trent, all of Company C, were killed. The battalion assumed defensive positions, preventing enemy infiltration until March 27, when they were relieved by 9th Infantry Division elements. The Rangers then reverted to 1st Division reserve in the vicinity of Gafsa.

On March 31, A and B Companies were sent by truck some twenty-five miles north of Gafsa to establish an early warning outpost in the event of an enemy breakthrough, but the Germans had shot their bolt. Companies rotated into outpost duty, and the remainder of the battalion, when not in the Gafsa bivouac, was reinforced with attached tank destroyers and combat engineers and occupied positions suited to delay possible enemy attack.

At Camp Forrest, Tennessee, the 2d Ranger Battalion was activated on April 1, 1943. As with the 1st Battalion, the 2d Rangers would have a headquarters company and six Ranger infantry companies designated A–F. These companies would have a strength of three officers and sixty-five enlisted men. Arms, equipment, and organization were in line with that of the 1st Battalion. Several members of the 1st Ranger Battalion under Capt. Dean H. Knudson had returned to assist in the organization of the 2d Battalion. The veteran rangers were of benefit in passing on "lessons learned."

In North Africa, the expected German attacks did not materialize. By April 10, 1943, all Ranger companies were reunited in the olive groves of Gafsa.

The African campaign was over for the Rangers, and by May 13 was over for the Axis forces. Over 32,000 men of the German and Italian armies were killed and several hundred thousand captured, including most of the men of the Herman Goering, 10th, and 21st Panzer Divisions, and other famed units of the Afrika Korps.

During the North African campaign, the 1st Ranger Battalion was not only called upon to conduct those operations normally associated with Ranger activities but used in the fireman role on missions more normally performed by infantry battalions.

The Rangers performed as spearheaders, civil administrators and police, raiders, recruiters, trainers, and line infantry and did it all well. The battalion was awarded the Presidential Unit Citation for the battle of El Guettar.

On April 14, Darby wrote through channels to General Eisenhower, who was commanding in Africa, a letter titled "Procurement of Personnel Necessary for Activation of Additional Ranger Battalions."

Working under the aggressive generals Terry Allen and George Patton, both of whom were Ranger enthusiasts, Darby

had been instructed to provide two additional Ranger battalions for operation HUSKY (the invasion of Sicily). In his letter,
Darby foresaw the need for approximately fifty-two additional officers and one thousand enlisted men. He discussed
the sources from which these additional volunteers might
come, including the combat organizations and replacement
depots. Among the combat troops, he included the battalion
of Ranger-trained troops in the United Kingdom (the 29th
Ranger Battalion). Darby wanted the 29th Rangers but could
not get them. He wrote, "Those troops in the United Kingdom undergoing Ranger-type training, of which there is a
battalion, constitute an excellent source, but are not available
at present because of other priority troop movements."

Attempting to draw volunteers from combat-experienced
units having their own replacement problems would raise a
firestorm of criticism. Darby concluded that the best available source for personnel was replacement centers.

Darby's request was passed through channels from Eisenhower to Marshall, who on April 19, 1943, granted authority to
activate the "3d and 4th Ranger Battalions." The feeling at the
War Department that Rangers were temporary was expressed
in the suggestion that "after need for these battalions is passed,
personnel therein might be returned to parent organizations so
that personnel might attain highest rating commensurate with
proven ability. This will also reduce replacement problem
which is critical here at this time and which it is estimated will
remain critical until summer."

This response which curiously expresses concern for personal promotion and one thousand men influencing the replacement stream was made at a time when the United States
Army numbered over six million men.

On April 22, Eisenhower's headquarters gave Darby the
written approval to proceed with recruiting visits to "any or
all replacement depots in this theater." Armed with this writ,
Darby with Murray, Shunstrom, and some senior noncommissioned officers as his recruiters went forth. They were
seeking true volunteers with a clean record who hopefully
had basic infantry training, were at least five feet, six inches
in height, in excellent condition, and not over thirty-five
years of age. To insure that Ranger veterans would be in lead-

ership positions, the volunteers who were not technicians would not be over the grade of private first class and transfers would be made in grade.

Though there were now to be three Ranger battalions in North Africa, no provision was made for an overall command headquarters, though Darby as senior battalion commander would properly assume the role. Less certain were the staff measures needed to control joint operations of the three battalions. Darby would remain as commander of the 1st Battalion and would use C and D Companies as his cadre. Maj. Herm Dammer would assume command of the 3d Ranger Battalion with Capt. Max Schneider as his executive officer and would use A and B Companies to cadre his unit.

Capt. Roy Murray, with Capt. Walter Nye as his executive officer, would command the 4th Battalion using E and F as the basis for his organization. Maj. William Martin would replace Dammer as executive officer of the 1st Battalion.

Murray's staff consisted of the three aces named Walter Nye as executive officer, the battlefield-commissioned Les Kness as operations officer, and Leilyn Young as intelligence officer. While Murray was pondering other assignments, two medical service corps officers arrived, in possession of a jeep from a replacement depot, and asked to sign on. Murray followed the principle of not asking silly questions if one did not want silly answers. He did not ask the two eager young volunteers where they got the jeep. Murray was reluctant to bring in medical types in slots he wanted filled by infantry officers but the fast-talking young officers plied his ears with unmodest estimates of their worth. Lt. James Lavin became the personnel officer of the 4th Rangers, and Lt. Joe Fineberg[5] became the supply officer. Murray never regretted the decision to bring them on the staff.

Training of the newly organized 1st, 3d, and 4th Ranger Battalions began promptly and was based on the training that had been received from the Commandos, with the added lessons learned in North Africa. The speed march was a key means of conditioning, and night and amphibious operations were practiced. The leadership of the battalions had considerable experience by this time, and training progressed rapidly. Though the hard core of veterans of the 1st Battalion was now dispersed, there was time to bring all three battalions to a high state of readiness. The Rangers were ready for the invasion of Sicily.

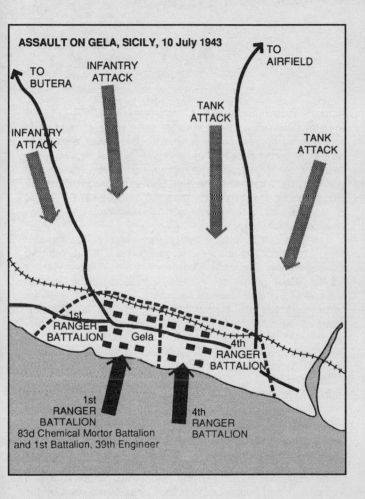

ASSAULT ON GELA, SICILY, 10 July 1943

TO BUTERA

INFANTRY ATTACK

TO AIRFIELD

INFANTRY ATTACK

TANK ATTACK

TANK ATTACK

1st RANGER BATTALION

Gela

4th RANGER BATTALION

1st RANGER BATTALION

83d Chemical Mortor Battalion and 1st Battalion, 39th Engineer

4th RANGER BATTALION

CHAPTER 5

SICILY

Sicily is a mountainous island approximately 140 miles long and 110 miles wide—roughly the size of Vermont. The southernmost part of Sicily is ninety miles from Africa; at its northeast, across the Strait of Messina, Sicily is but two miles from the toe of the Italian geographical boot. Strategically placed in the Mediterranean Sea, Sicily is a place of history: Rome and Carthage met in war on the island, and in 1943 the Americans and British would battle the Germans and Italians upon its ancient slopes.

The decision to invade Sicily was made at the January 1943 Casablanca meeting between President Roosevelt and Prime Minister Churchill. The decision was another victory for the British peripheral strategy of gnawing at the German flanks and irritated General Marshall, who wanted to strike across the English Channel for the German jugular. The Germans had to expect both. There was little to cheer in Germany in 1943. On the Russian front, Stalingrad was a disaster, and Montgomery's victory at El Alamein and the Allied success in North Africa caused the lights to burn late in the war rooms of Berlin.

Many Germans felt that Italy was more of a burden than an asset, but in his rise to power, Hitler had learned much from Mussolini, and Hitler felt Italy was important to his cause.

For the Italians, war was becoming a wearisome, increasingly frightening thing. These people, whose ancestors ruled the world, were far from the military glory of the Roman Empire. Lacking strong leadership, poorly equipped and armed, and concerned that they were being used by the Germans, they were the least effective of the Axis forces. What most Italians wanted was a graceful way out of the war.

Those with a vested interest also sought to preserve the Fascist system, but Roosevelt's call for unconditional surrender ended any hope of that. The Sicilians despised the Germans and had little more affection for the Italians, the feeling being best summed up by an old woman who would scream at a Ranger who spoke Italian: "What are you hitting us for. Go to Rome and hit the people who are responsible for this!"

Some Italian generals felt their country was a pawn of the Germans and sought the return of Italian forces fighting on the Russian front. Initially the Italians were uneasy about being reinforced by German divisions offered by Hitler. They feared the Germans would take charge. The Italians needed help and finally accepted it, but they retained overall command in Sicily.

Disposing a force of some ten Italian and three German divisions, Italian Gen. Alfred Guzzoni arranged his forces with six "coast" divisions and scattered lesser forces close to the shores, backed by a mobile reserve of the remaining divisions.

For the Allies, a victory in North Africa raised the question of what to do with the forces that would become available. The British felt an invasion of Sicily would bring a prompt German response, drawing off forces from the English Channel defenses of France and perhaps the Russian front. Few senior American officers thought an Italian campaign worthwhile. The idea of fighting up the long axis of Italy in mountain warfare that led to the Alps was deemed foolish. The British also hoped that a strike at Sicily would knock Italy out of the war and bring Turkey in on the side of the Allies. The Americans went along with that, but felt Sicily was to be the last stop before going across the channel to France.

The operation code name for the invasion of Sicily was HUSKY. It would be ostensibly under the command of General Eisenhower, but in practice the command structure would be a committee system, with the British exercising the most votes. The British Gen. Sir Harold R. L. G. Alexander, as commander of the Allied Army Group, exercised control over the invasion forces. Disputes in the joint American-British planning and operations staff (Force 141) were settled in favor of the British plan when the Tunisian campaign dragged out, making it unlikely that shipping and forces could be brought to England before the fall or winter of 1943. With the understanding that some forces could be diverted to the war against Japan, the Americans agreed to the British invasion plan. The British, who excelled at deception, put fake plans, detailing an invasion of Greece and Sardinia, on a corpse and floated it off the coast of Spain. Though the German generals knew Sicily would be the objective, Hitler took the bait and reinforced Greece and Sardinia.

Though the objective was settled, the method of seizing it was not. There were the usual staff battles and a powerful objection to the direction of planning from the British Gen. Bernard Montgomery.

What with the bickering, it was early May 1943 before the invasion plan was finalized. To the disgust of many Americans, Montgomery's Eighth Army was assigned the major role. Landing in southwest Sicily from Capo Passero north to Syracuse, the British were to attack northward. The obvious objective was the coastal city of Messina only two miles from the Italian mainland. The capture of Messina would shut off the Axis forces' primary escape route. To facilitate his part of the operation, Montgomery would have a road and port advantage over his allies. The Americans were assigned the role of protecting the Eighth Army's left flank. American forces would land to the west of the British on a seventy-mile front. The American Seventh Army would be born in battle, as its headquarters would become operational on landing. Commanded by Gen. George Patton, the principal force of the Seventh Army was Gen. Omar Bradley's II Corps. Going under the name Shark Force, II Corps would include Troy Middleton's 45th Infantry Division, reinforced. The 45th was on the American right and centered on Scoglitti. Also in Shark Force was Terry Allen's 1st Infantry Division, minus the 18th Infantry Regiment (in Seventh Army Reserve), and the 1st and 4th Ranger Battalions located in the center, going ashore at Gela. Meanwhile, the 504 and 505 Parachute Regiments of the 82d Airborne Division would drop inland between the 45th and 1st Division beachheads.

The second and smaller American force, called Joss Force,

consisted of Lucian Truscott's 3d Infantry Division, reinforced to include the 3d Ranger Battalion. This force would land on the American left (west) at Licata. In general terms, the missions were to establish the beachhead, seize airfields nearby, secure and operate the ports of Gela and Licata, and tie in with the British in preparation to press the attack.

Gela, a town of some thirty thousand people, was a sleepy fishing community. There was a wide plain to the rear of Gela and a pier that extended from the center of town some nine hundred feet into the water. The water close to the beaches was shallow, with intermittent sandbars that could ground landing craft. The invasion planners were concerned that landing forces would have to wade long distances to get ashore thus exposing them to a devastating enemy fire. The Gela area would be the objective of the 1st Infantry Division, reinforced. To seize the town, General Allen formed a provisional group he called Force X. Headed by Bill Darby, Force X would consist of the 1st and 4th Ranger Battalions, three companies of Rangers' old friends, the 4.2-inch mortar company, 83d Chemical Mortar Battalion[1]; and the 1st Battalion, 39th Engineers. Force X had the mission of going ashore at Gela to seize the high ground, eliminate enemy gun positions that dominated the area, and secure the town and additional objectives. Darby and Murray decided to make the landing with the two battalions abreast. The pier at Gela would be an easily observed dividing point during landing: The 1st Battalion, on the west, would land to the left of the pier and take the left half of Gela and the guns; the 4th Battalion, on the east, would go to the right of the pier and take the right half of the city. The 1st Battalion, 39th Engineers, would clear the beach of mines for follow-on forces and, in the tradition of combat engineers, be prepared to fight as infantry. The 83d Chemical Mortar Battalion would provide fire support.

In the 1st Ranger Battalion sector, three phase lines would be used to control the Ranger advance. (A phase line is an imaginary line on a map that is used to control the movement of troops. It might be a road or a stream, but it is linear and to the front of the objective. Units would report in upon reaching each phase line, and could be told to hold position or continue to advance, thus better coordinating the movement of large groups of men.) The first phase line was the beachfront buildings. Phase line two was the main street, and the third phase line the north end of Gela. On arrival at each phase line, commanders would establish contact with Force X headquarters and units to right and left.

The 1st Ranger Battalion would land in four waves with companies C, D, E, and F in the first wave; A and B in the second; engineers in the third; and mortars in the fourth. A submarine with a red light on its stern was to guide the assault craft to shore. The four companies of the first wave were to clear the beach and main street. Companies A and B would pass through and move up the main street to attack a coastal gun battery on the left (west) edge of town.

The 4th Ranger Battalion would land in two waves with A, B, C, and a headquarters detachment in the first wave, then D, E, and F. The 4th Rangers were to clear their area of responsibility of enemy and secure the southeast part of Gela.

Some twenty miles westward, Dammer, with his 3d Ranger Battalion, would be going ashore at Licata, a town similar in size to Gela. Licata lay at the mouth of the Salso River. It was a small hub town, offering port, rail, and road facilities. Licata sat on a seaside mound with a plain of about six miles at its back and dominating high ground rising up to sixteen hundred feet in the distance. An uncompleted airstrip lay two miles inland to the northwest. There was a beach and cliffs that faced eastward. General Truscott planned to land the infantry and support armor of his forty-five-thousand-man force as expeditiously as possible and employ a pincer movement to seize Licata. There were four beaches available to him, and Truscott planned to use all. The left and right pincers each consisted of two separate forces, each with an inner and outer force. Herm Dammer's 3d Ranger Battalion was part of the inner force of the left (west) pincer. Dammer's mission was to land on Green Beach, some three miles west of Licata, then attack on a line of direction through Mount Sole, mass, and attack Licata from the west. The 2d Battalion, 15th Infantry, would follow.

Since organizing into three battalions in early May, the 1st, 3d, and 4th Rangers had undergone six weeks of intensive training in the Atlas Mountains near Nemours, Algeria. In June 1943, the Ranger battalions moved to join their divisions. The 1st and 4th Battalions moved near Zeralda, about twenty miles from Algiers, for attachment to Allen's 1st Division. The 3d Ranger Battalion moved to Bizerte, Tunisia, to join Truscott's 3d Infantry Division.

Bill Darby and Roy Murray led the 1st and 4th Ranger Battalions in an intensive program of preparation for the invasion. Mock-ups of Gela objectives were built, and two live-fire rehearsals, timed to invasion schedules, were conducted with the U.S. Navy, complete with barbed-wire entanglements. The Rangers and sailors, who were to put them ashore, worked together to the point that the boat crews and passengers functioned as a team. The communication and coordination lessons learned at Arzew were practiced over and over. A source of great concern to Darby and Murray was that the submarine that was to lead the landing craft to shore was not part of the rehearsals. This failure to allow face-to-face coordination boded ill.

On the Tunisian coast near Bizerte, Dammer's Rangers of the 3d Battalion participated in training similar to that of the 1st and 4th Battalions.

On June 19th, the anniversary of the activation of the 1st Ranger Battalion, the 1st and 4th Battalions held a birthday celebration. The two battalions passed in review with Major General Allen as reviewing officer. The cooks prepared a cake with "1 Year" written on the top—Darby and Allen held it, with Allen steadying an oversized candle while Roy Murray cut the cake with a Sykes knife.

Elsewhere in the world, the men of two other Ranger battalions trained hard—the 29th Ranger Battalion in England and the 2nd Ranger Battalion at Camp Forrest, Tennessee. On June 30, 1943, Maj. James E. Rudder[2] assumed command of the 2d Ranger Battalion. Rudder was firm but fair, and he looked after the welfare of the men. Training included the long-distance speed march, the morning run, weapons training, map reading, communications, and hand-to-hand combat. The men were learning that the Ranger is the ultimate infantryman, trained in the same infantry skills as a line soldier but in a much more intense and demanding school.

On the day that Major Rudder assumed command of the 2d Ranger Battalion, the 1st and 4th Ranger Battalions and other Force X components loaded on ships at Algiers harbor. From Algiers, the convoy moved to Bizerte where it joined the convoy carrying the 3d Infantry Division forces, including the 3d Ranger Battalion. The operation of the convoys involved great coordination. The American forces staged from ports that reached from Algiers to Bizerte. British Eighth Army ports were from Sfax to Syria.

On the evening of July 9, a fierce storm battered the convoys, equipment was damaged, and soldiers and sailors became violently seasick. A few gray hairs were added to General Patton's pate, but his weatherman had the gumption to predict fair weather for battle, and he was right. Though the sea swells continued, the storm eased.

The stage was set. The defending Axis forces numbered approximately 350,000 and the invading Allies nearly 500,000. Allied air power pummeled Sicilian airfields and raised havoc about the island, while providing deception raids elsewhere in the Mediterranean. Studying intelligence reports, the Italian General Guzzoni correctly interpreted the Allied intentions and warned his forces of imminent attack. Guzzoni ordered installations destroyed to prevent their use—including the port at Licata and later the pier at Gela. On the evening of July 9, 1943, German and Italian soldiers waited, knowing the blow was coming and wondering where it would fall. The bad weather comforted some, the enemy soldiers thinking a landing in such weather unlikely.

Meanwhile, the British and American Airborne forces that were to land in front of their respective armies flew through the gathering darkness. Each aircraft was a study in tension. Rough air, navigational difficulties, and troop-carrier pilots who were lacking sufficient night training and making their first combat drop made a fiasco of the air drop. Men were dropped in the sea or scattered over southeast Sicily. A tragedy occurred near Gela when transport aircraft carrying

Paratroopers flew over a naval task force that had just been bombed by German planes. Twenty-three of the aircraft carrying men of the 82d Airborne were shot down by American guns. The surviving paratroopers pressed on. Though seldom landing on their assigned objectives, small groups of American paratroopers roamed about the Sicilian countryside, tearing up communications and attacking anything within their capability. General Guzzoni, while somewhat confused by all these reports, at least knew the attack was coming in southeastern Sicily. Guzzoni began to move his mobile forces to the threatened areas. The reconstituted German Herman Goering Division was ordered to Gela.

At San Mollarella, three miles west of Licata, the 3d Ranger Battalion scheduled to land at 0300 went ashore on Green Beach at 0255.

Dammer's Rangers landed with six companies abreast. Dammer, with Companies A, B, and C, landed to the left of Rocca Mollarella, while Alvah Miller, the executive officer, led D, E, and F Companies to the right of the rock. On the extreme left, Company A blew the wire at the base of Mount Polisca and climbed the steep slopes to clear the high ground of enemy. B Company, with a platoon from Company C, was temporarily delayed by machine-gun fire but rapidly cleared the beach, moved east of Mount Polisca, and eliminated the Italian positions from the west of the basin between the high ground. Part of Company C, 3d Rangers, used rocks at surfside as a position to establish a base of fire. Other C Company Rangers climbed the rock face by using the Italian barbed-wire obstacles as handholds. The C Company Rangers were in the enemy positions while the Italians were still trying to occupy them. One by one, the Italian positions were captured or destroyed. D Company went after Italian mortar positions behind the high ground and eliminated them. Moving swiftly across the beach, E and F Companies cut their way through barbed-wire obstacles and knocked out two enemy machine guns on high ground fifteen hundred yards east of the beach. In training, the Rangers had pinpointed Italian gun positions by studying aerial photos. Though the guns were often concealed, their protective barbed wire was clearly visible. The

Rangers found this method of pinpointing gun locations to be accurate within a few feet.

Careful preparation and aggressive action paid off. The men of the 3d Ranger Battalion had the satisfaction of watching the 2d Battalion, 15th Infantry, come ashore and pass through to their objectives. All of Truscott's invasion objectives were being met.

By 1500 hours on D-day, July 10, the 3d Ranger Battalion's mission was accomplished, and they were placed in division reserve, with the task of guarding the port of Licata. For the next fifteen hours, the battalion found reserve to be more dangerous than attack. German aircraft were strafing and bombing the harbor, and American antiaircraft fire was equally dangerous. The 3d Rangers suffered three times more casualties in reserve than it did in the assault.

At Gela, the Rangers left the USS *Dickman* and the HMS *Albert and Charles*. Loading into landing craft, the men gripped their weapons and peered shoreward through a night made eerie by the fires started by air strikes. As the Ranger boats pulled away from the *Dickman*, someone with a spark of inspiration began to play Glenn Miller's "American Patrol" over the ship's loudspeaker system. The Rangers felt pride and battle lust rise within them.

Circling, the boats carrying the Rangers found Darby's concern justified. The submarine that was supposed to guide them to shore did not materialize. Critical time was passing, time that would cost lives. A navy officer, bringing up third-wave boats, knew his job and, with Darby's assistance, began to put the boats into position and lead them ashore. Men remember Darby's boat coming through the night, with Darby calling, "Follow me."

It was a scene worthy of Dante. Italian searchlights flicked on and began to illuminate the boats. The American Navy response was quick and accurate. Naval gunfire-support ships including the destroyer *Shubrick* and cruiser *Savannah* shot out the Italians' lights. The Italians then blew up the Gela pier with a tremendous roar. Machine guns and mortars lashed the Ranger boats. The Rangers fired back from the craft, engaging enemy machine guns with 2.36-inch rocket launchers.

One landing craft hit a sand bar and began to capsize. Thinking they were in shallow water, the Rangers jumped off. Dragged down in deep water by the weight of their equipment, Lt. Joseph Zagata and sixteen men of Company E drowned. Other boats stopped to help, which created a situation where elements of the second wave landed before the first.

Between 0300 and 0305, the 1st Ranger Battalion came ashore.

The beach was a maze of wire obstacles and antipersonnel and antitank mine fields. In the 4th Battalion zone, the courageous Lieutenant Wojcik died at the head of D Company, when his rush exploded a mine. Other Rangers were badly wounded, and in Wojcik's company all the officers were casualties. The quiet, soft-spoken, 1st Sgt. Randall Harris led the men on while wounded and holding his protruding intestines in place with his cartridge belt. A native of San Diego, California, the twenty-nine-year-old Harris ignored his wounds and, in two hours of battle, led his Rangers to complete their mission. Harris would receive the Distinguished Service Cross and a battlefield commission.

Fighting their way through enemy beach defenses, the Rangers swept into Gela, fighting house to house. Roy Murray's 4th Battalion seized the town square. Some Italians tried to fight it out, using the cathedral as a position; they died, some falling around the altar. The 1st Battalion landed in two waves, with Companies C, D, E, and F to the west of the wrecked pier. These companies secured their section of beach and established a line from the northwest edge of town to the center, destroying several machine-gun nests and experiencing moderate street fighting enroute. A and B Companies landed at 0305, with the mission of destroying two naval-gun batteries and a mortar battery at the northwest edge of Gela. Lt. James Lyle commanded the joint force of A and B Companies and had told his men to shoot everything that moved if they expected to be alive the following day. Companies A and B moved through town, with columns on each side of the street, covering each other. There were many Italian soldiers in Gela, and as they ran from the houses, they were shot down. The A Company first sergeant saw four men running into a bunker that formed a roadblock. As the last man tried to close the door, the sergeant kicked it open and fired bursts of submachine-gun fire, then followed with a grenade. Two heavy machine guns and a 47mm antitank gun were neutralized. The Rangers swept on.

Due to a radio being dropped in the sea, the 4.2-inch mortar support Lyle expected was not available. One Ranger section moved up a ditch, blew the protective wire, and went in among the guns with grenades and small arms. An enemy mortar platoon was taken out by grenades. The Rangers had captured three 77mm field pieces whose sights had been removed. The varied backgrounds and cross training of the Rangers was immediately put to use. Three gun crews were formed and spent two hours in gun drill. Lyle's position was astride Highway 115, and the innovative move would prove worthwhile.

At 0730 a group of enemy barricaded in a schoolhouse fired on 1st Ranger Battalion headquarters, and a sharp fight ensued. Going up against automatic-weapons' fire, Darby detected a quiver in his driver, Carlo Contrera.

"What are you shaking for?" Darby asked. "Are you scared?"

"No, sir," Contrera responded, "I'm just shaking with patriotism."

When the Rangers prevailed, they found themselves with a bag of fifty-two Italian officers. These people were fortunate to be captured. There were many Italian bodies scattered throughout the streets of Gela.

The suffering of combat touched all sides. German aircraft were bombing and strafing indiscriminately. With first light had come a single German plane, which accurately bombed a landing ship carrying men and equipment of the 33d Field Artillery Battalion. Ammunition and gasoline began to explode, and many American soldiers were horribly burned and died screaming.

First Battalion, 39th Engineers, had come ashore immediately behind the Rangers and began clearing the beach of mines and obstacles. By 0800, the Rangers had consolidated their objectives and established defensive positions at the outskirts of Gela and tied in with 1st Division troops. Murray's 4th Battalion was on the right, and Darby's 1st on the left. The 4.2-inch mortars were ashore and in position.

The Italian General Guzzoni made strenuous efforts to throw the Americans back into the sea. Reinforcing his coastal troops, Guzzoni planned a counterattack against the beachhead, using General Chirieleison's Livorno Division, much of General Conrath's Herman Goering Division, and assorted Italian mobile units. But the enemy communications and movement were hindered by air strikes and the actions of American paratroopers, and the counterattack was uncoordinated. An Italian tank–infantry team of reinforced company size came south down Highway 17 toward Gela, but naval gunfire disrupted their advance, and some tanks were knocked out. When the remaining Italian tanks moved forward, the infantry did not accompany them.

Around 0900, Lyle's men reported nine enemy light tanks of the Renault type approaching from the north. Four tanks stopped at a grove of trees at about five-thousand-yards range. The remaining five of these Italian tanks entered Gela. They were about to learn a deadly lesson. Unprotected by infantry, the Italian tankers found themselves in a built-up area, confronted by determined American Rangers, who attacked the tanks from basement windows and rooftops, using bazookas, sticky grenades (see Appendix D), and satchel charges. Men, including Lieutenant Colonel Darby, climbed on the tanks, trying to open the hatches so that grenades could be dropped into the crew compartment. Capt. Jack Street dropped fifteen-pound explosive charges from the roof of a building on the tanks. As the surviving tanks moved deeper into town, Darby and Chuck Shunstrom brought up a 37mm antitank gun by jeep, positioned it in the square, and with Darby as gunner and Shunstrom as loader, destroyed a tank. The surviving Italian tankers were badly beaten up and hurriedly withdrew under fire.

At Captain Lyle's direction, the four tanks that had remained in the grove were taken under 4.2-inch mortar fire. One tank was left smoking; the others fled.

Shortly thereafter, the Italian tanks reappeared, and Lyle began to use his captured artillery. Without the sights, the Ranger gunners sighted along the tubes. They had a Ranger in an observation post on the gun–target line. The first round from the Ranger artillery landed on the observation post. The Ranger who was in the position was shaken up but not wounded. Naturally perturbed, he became quite vocal, and the elevation of the guns was raised. The Ranger artillery then forced the withdrawal of the tanks and scattered a nest of some two hundred enemy from their concealment in and about a farmhouse.

Throughout the night of July 10, action continued. Both sides knew the dawn would bring a desperate battle, and there were constant patrols by both sides.

All along the beachhead, 1st Division forces were coming ashore through surf and shallows to push toward their objectives.

Often in heavy fighting, the Americans struggled to get their armor and heavy antitank weapons ashore while being pounded by German aircraft. Increasingly heavy tank attacks had to be met with naval gunfire and the limited resources ashore. The heaviest American casualties of the Sicilian campaign were suffered in the fighting in and around Gela.

The German General Conrath, commanding the Herman Goering Panzer Division, was having coordination problems getting his infantry and tanks together. He was supposed to attack at the same time as the Italians but was late. Conrath was faced with a hard choice—attack the beachhead with fast-moving armor or wait until a separate armored, infantry-heavy column could come up and support the tanks. Probably aware through aerial reconnaissance that American armor was not yet ashore, Conrath decided to attack with unsupported tanks.

Meanwhile, in the early morning hours of July 11, the 3d Ranger Battalion was relieved from their Licata mission and marched to a bivouac area[3] south of San Oliva.

If things were temporarily quiet for the 3d Battalion, they were not for the 1st and 4th: action was hot around Gela. Early on the 11th, German armor began to swarm around

American positions, and the fighting was vicious. In the 1st Division area, the Germans penetrated the 26th Infantry's positions. German tanks were so close to the beach that naval gunfire could not be employed, and the Germans were reporting victory.

Further to the east, a battalion of Italian infantry from the Livorno Division moved southeast along the Butera–Gela road. The Livorno Infantry Battalion came marching in formation, in a manner more in keeping with the Napoleonic wars than World War II. This attack was directed toward the area of Gela defended by A and B Companies.

Darby and the remainder of the Rangers were involved with the German tanks attacking Gela. Darby told Lyle to fight with what he had—some 120 Rangers. Lyle rounded up some engineer and quartermaster troops and formed a perimeter.

Artillery and 4.2-inch mortars were engaging the oncoming enemy but were not stopping them. The enemy was responding with counterfire, and Lyle loosened his helmet chin strap to avoid a concussion. A voice behind him said, "Captain, your chin strap is unbuckled." It was the Seventh Army commander, Gen. George S. Patton. Lyle buckled the errant strap and briefed Patton on the grim situation. As Patton was leaving, he said to Lyle, "Kill every one of the goddamn bastards."

A more solid form of inspiration came a few minutes later in the person of a naval gunfire observer from the cruiser *Savannah*. "Having trouble, soldier?" asked the navy man. In a few minutes, fire from the ship's six-inch guns, with variable time fuses set to explode just above the ground, was falling on the enemy line of march. The *Savannah* fired five hundred rounds on the hapless Italians. When the dust and smoke cleared, the surviving Italians could be seen staggering around in shock. Lyle promptly led his Rangers in the attack. Not a shot was necessary—over four hundred Italians were taken prisoner. Men said that bodies were hanging from trees and blown to bits by the *Savannah*'s guns.

About noon on the 11th, Gela was attacked by eighteen German tanks, sweeping across the plain. The Rangers pounded the Germans with naval gunfire, 4.2-inch mortars, and artillery. The attack was beaten off, with twelve tanks destroyed. In the sky, German aircraft continued their attacks with more success. In the Gela harbor, a Liberty ship carrying ammunition was bombed and exploded.

To the east, the German attack was furious, but American infantry and artillery beat them. The American artillery that was ashore cranked down the tubes and fired directly at the attackers. When the Germans tried to withdraw, they came under the big guns of the American Navy, who butchered them.

One of the hallmarks of the Ranger experience of World War II was the training that allowed leaders to call upon and effectively use supporting fire. The power of each Ranger was thus magnified. In Sicily, this lesson was clearly demonstrated.

Beaten by the magnificent blend of raw courage, training, and enormous firepower, the enemy withdrew and left Gela to the Americans. German tank losses at the beachhead were so severe that when supporting infantry did arrive, the German attack could not be sustained. General Conrath was not accustomed to seeing German troops running in panic, falling victim to rumor and fear. In a July 12 message to his troops, he wrote: "withdrawal without orders and cowardice are to be punished on the spot and if necessary by the use of weapons." Conrath promised death sentences in serious cases.

The 45th Infantry Division was seeking a new commander for its 180th Infantry Regiment. On July 12 General Patton awarded Bill Darby the Distinguished Service Cross and offered him the command of the 180th. The move would have resulted in promotion to full colonel, but Darby declined in order to stay with his Rangers. This was the second time he declined a promotion that required a transfer.

The 1st Ranger Battalion next received orders to seize Monte Lapa and Monte Zai, the high ground on the Gela–Butera road. This was ground known to be held by the enemy. Darby planned his attack using Companies D and F to seize the high ground to the right of the road, while he sent the 1st Battalion, 41st Armored Infantry, minus one company, to attack the fortification of San Nicola. The engineers would fight as infantry as needed, and the 4.2-inch mortars would be in support. Making a night march, the force attacked the enemy positions at 0430 on July 12, 1943. The Rangers were on the right flank, attacking high ground to the right of the road, while the 1st Battalion, 41st Armored Infantry, was on the left, attempting to seize a potent enemy fortification. The enemy was strongly entrenched and subjecting the Rangers to heavy machine-gun fire, but Companies D and F reached their objective. Less accustomed to night attacks, the infantry had difficulty finding the route to its objective. When dawn came, they were caught in the open and had to pull back under machine-gun, heavy mortar, and the artillery fire of five batteries. Captain Colby, company commander of D Company, could observe the enemy batteries from his high-ground position, and called on a navy forward observer at Darby's command post. With Colby directing the adjustments, the guns of the *Savannah* began to fire over a seven-mile range on the enemy batteries, blasting them out of existence. Darby brought up the 1st Battalion, 39th Engineers, and sent them and the 1st Battalion, 41st Infantry, to attack the high-ground positions to the left of the road. By 1400 hours, the resistance had ceased. The navy, and in particular the *Savannah*, received the praise and appreciation of both the infantry and engineers. Company C later moved from Gela and rejoined the battalion. Ranger patrols went forward during the night and ambushed a German mine-and-reconnaissance party along the Gela–Butera road, killing eleven Germans and wounding four.

On the morning of July 13, the 1st and 4th Ranger Battalions, with the 83d Chemical Weapons Battalion, were attached to the newly landed 2nd Armored Division. The Rangers preferred being with the 1st Division. The association with Terry Allen's 1st Infantry Division was one of the high points of the Ranger experience. Like George Patton, Lucian Truscott, and Norman Cota, Terry Allen was a strong supporter of the Ranger philosophy. His views were demonstrated when Allen established Ranger platoons within his infantry battalions.

There was one battle at Gela the Rangers did not win. For the purpose of battle honors, it shall be known as the Battle of the Bakery. The participants were the hungry women of Gela, a Polish baker, and a young Ranger sergeant named Marcell Swank. With the fight for Gela concluded, the tommy-gun-carrying Ranger Swank had been assigned the mission of guarding a bakery, where the skilled Pole was baking fresh bread for the troops. The women of Gela were ragged, hungry, and had families to feed. The women protested their need to no avail and then gathered across the street from the bakery, muttering among themselves. Suddenly they advanced in a solid, determined phalanx. Ranger Swank reacted by firing a burst in the air. The women recoiled to the far side of the street in fear, where they cursed Swank and made obscene gestures. Finally gathering their courage, the women again advanced. In desperation, Swank fired in the air again. The women retreated to the middle of the street, but they knew they had him. The next charge came home with vigor. Ranger Swank and the Polish baker fled.

At 0800 on July 14, 1943, Dammer's 3d Ranger Battalion foot-marched to Campobello, arriving about 2000 hours. From there, the Rangers had a thirty-minute ride by truck to Naro. At midnight, the 3d Rangers began an approach march along the Naro–Favara railroad: Their objective was Hill 313 and the adjoining high ground located about one thousand yards east of Favara, which they reached by 0530 hours on July 15. There was no contact with the enemy. About 1000 hours, Dammer led a company into Favara, and shortly after noon, battalion patrols made contact with elements of the 7th U.S. Infantry Regiment.

While the 3d Rangers were moving to the attack on the 14th, the 1st and 4th Ranger Battalions were facing what seemed an impossible task.

There are times when a military objective seems so impregnable that it challenges professional pride and the imagination. Perched like an eagle's nest high above the Sicilian Plain, the ancient fortress town of Butera glowered down on the road to Enna. Eight miles inland at an elevation of nearly four thousand feet, Butera was protected by razor-backed ridges and steep cliffs. Access to this fortress was by a climbing, twisted, snakelike road that was heavily wired, and bordered with mine fields covered by automatic and antitank weapons. For centuries, those who had sought to conquer Sicily had bypassed Butera. But bypass was not advisable in World War II, for Butera was a forward observer's dream. From this mountain aerie the defenders could observe the movement of American forces for miles and bring artillery fire and air strikes to bear upon that movement. Butera had to be taken, and the Rangers were given the mission.

Once again, Darby skillfully employed artillery and naval gunfire to pound the fortress by day. Darby decided to make his attack at night, testing the waters with one company moving to surprise the enemy, while the remainder of the Ranger force was prepared to commit to battle if the opportunity was there. Darby called upon Capt. Charles "Chuck" Shunstrom and the Rangers of E Company, 1st Ranger Battalion. Shunstrom was a man at home in war. He liked close combat and was said to have killed with his knife.

Moving after dark, Shunstrom and his two platoons began a three-mile approach march. Enroute, Shunstrom periodically kept in radio contact with Darby, who had supporting fire ready when needed. Reaching the mountain's base, the Rangers climbed for several hours and then infiltrated enemy positions until fired upon by a machine gun. A platoon leader and his radio operator were wounded. A scout, armed with a submachine gun, killed seven Italians at the machine-gun nest, allowing the Rangers to move on.

Sgt. Francis P. Padrucco took over the platoon. While artillery men waited with their hands on their lanyards, Shunstrom sent out a flanking platoon that reported the opportunity existed to press on. The Rangers moved into the assault, using marching fire, then closed with bayonet and hand-to-hand combat.

In the flanking platoon, Rangers John Constantine and John See crept up on a large group of Italians with German officers. Constantine spoke Italian and yelled at the Italians to surrender.

The German officers tried to get the Italians to fight, but the soldiers had had enough. After a brief scuffle, the Germans looked to their own safety and fled while the Italians surrendered. The two platoons of Company E swept into the town, and the green flares of victory soared skyward. A fortress deemed impregnable had fallen before an imaginative night attack by less than fifty Rangers. The Germans and Italians who escaped fled toward Mazzarino where another Italian defensive position had been established. Their arrival in panic caused the defenders of that position to flee. The area was in an uproar of confusion for the Germans and Italians, some of whom were captured by Americans when they walked into positions they thought secure. The history of the 1st Infantry Division refers to the Ranger assault on Butera as "one of the most brilliant actions of the war."

The dynamic Seventh Army commander, George S. Patton, was not content to play a supporting role to any army commander and certainly not the equally arrogant British Gen. Bernard Montgomery. Stretching the latitude of his orders to the maximum, Patton ordered a reconnaissance in force in the Agrigento area. This was only a stepping-stone. If things went well, Patton meant to grab the north-coast city of Palermo.

At 1730 hours on the 15th, Dammer's 3d Rangers were attached to the 7th Infantry for the Agrigento reconnaissance. Dammer was ordered to move down Highway 122 toward Agrigento, bypass the town and capture Montaperto, then move south and seize Porto Empedocle, some twenty-five miles west of Licata. The seizure of the port facilities at Porto Empedocle would greatly facilitate Patton's logistics and give a boost to his move on Palermo. The Ranger mission called for independent action while moving through enemy-held territory.

At 1900 hours, the 3d Rangers began a night march in a column of companies, A through F, in sequence. Sporadic and inaccurate artillery fire was encountered, as well as a blown bridge over a deep ravine that precluded the assistance of American armor should the need arise.

At 0030 hours, enemy forces at a roadblock opened fire on the Rangers. Enemy riflemen were on high ground to the right of the road, and a machine gun and small caliber cannon were firing from positions on each side of the road about thirty yards from the roadblock.

Dammer sent A Company attacking along the road, and the Rangers eliminated the gun positions with grenades and small arms. Simultaneously, D Company deployed and attacked the riflemen on the high ground. These Rangers held their fire until they closed with the enemy. A withering blast of fire silenced the opposition. Company C deployed and passed through D to occupy the top of the hill.

An hour from the first shot the action was over. The 165 surviving Italians were taken under guard to Favera and presented to the 7th Infantry.

About 0600 hours on the 16th, Dammer's Rangers began moving toward Montaperto. The enemy began to use air-burst artillery, but the rounds exploded too high to be effective. As the Rangers reached Highway 118, an enemy motor convoy came speeding around a bend. Ten sidecar-type motorcycles and two trucks came in view at a range of five hundred yards and closing. Most of the 3d Ranger Battalion was on the hillside overlooking the road. Quickly taking cover behind rocks, the Rangers waited. When the enemy were directly to the front, four Ranger companies opened fire. The devastating hail of bullets ripped into the enemy column. Vehicles with dead drivers spun off the road and crashed. Enemy corpses littered the highway. All the vehicles were destroyed, and the surviving forty enemy soldiers taken prisoner.

Continuing forward, the 3d Rangers climbed the high hill to Montaperto and took their first objective without incident. Four batteries of enemy artillery could be seen in the valley below them. Using automatic weapons, rifles, and the ten 60mm mortars in the companies, the Rangers opened fire: in a few minutes smoke and flame rose from the enemy gun positions as ammunition exploded. Some Italians escaped, but most died or came up the hill with their hands in the air.

South of Montaperto was a high, long, and sheer-faced hill that dominated the area. Protected by one-hundred-foot cliffs, the enemy had constructed an installation believed to be a coastal-defense-control radio station.

Dammer gave Company C of his 3d Rangers the mission to destroy the enemy facility. The remainder of the battalion would bypass the hill and continue on the approach to Porto Empedocle.

Deployed at the base of the cliff, with two platoons abreast, ten yards between men, Company C crossed a field of wheat stubble toward the trail junction. The company's 60mm mortars were set up to provide on-call supporting fire.

As the Rangers came within three hundred yards of the cliff, an Italian soldier appeared at the top and began shouting. A Ranger who could speak Italian told the company commander that the man was calling, "Turn back or we fire!" Dammer was informed, and C Company continued moving forward. The Italian soldier disappeared from view.

Near the base of the cliffs was a jumble of large boulders. The Rangers took cover and surveyed the quiet scene. In the cliff face was an opening, inviting yet threatening. Taking one section, the company commander went forward. Inside the tunnel was a stairway cut into the rock. With senses straining, the Rangers began to climb—to their relief, the stairway was clear. The company commander sent a messenger down to tell the remainder of the company to fix bayonets and come fast.

Peering from the tunnel, the company commander saw that the tents and buildings of the outpost appeared deserted. A low wall about fifteen yards to the front would provide cover for the attacking Rangers, who went forward, snarling and screaming to terrify the enemy.

Scarcely had the first men cleared the tunnel when Italians began coming out of foxholes, windows, and doors with their hands in the air. A sniper fired on a Ranger and was promptly killed. The prisoners were the command group of the Arigento area. Twenty officers and sixteen enlisted men were captured, including the colonel commanding.

Three men escaped down the south slope, carrying a machine gun. Their route intersected that of the remainder of the 3d Rangers. An immediate attempt was made to radio the information to Dammer. Before contact could be made, the machine gun opened fire.

An F Company platoon went after the machine gun. At about four hundred yards range, the platoon leader, Lt. Raymond F. Campbell, was killed. When the Rangers closed on the gun, the crew surrendered.

By 1400 hours, Company C had rejoined the 3d Battalion. At 1420 Dammer's Rangers moved to the attack.

The seacoast town of Porto Empedocle was located on high hills and cliffs, and a deep ravine divided the town. Dammer decided to lead A, B, and C Companies to attack the area east of the ravine while D, E, and F Companies under Capt. Alvah Miller would attack to the west of the ravine. The mortar sections were set up six hundred yards north of Porto Empedocle. The prisoners and their guards would be kept in the vicinity of the mortars until they were told to follow on.

About six hundred yards north of the objective, Dammer and Miller's groups deployed and went into the attack. A machine gun that opened fire on Company A was eliminated. Another crew was taken while trying to set up their gun. Against light resistance, Dammer's men went forward, shooting the door off a pillbox and capturing the three soldiers within.

Miller's D, E, and F Companies had heavier going. Small arms and antiaircraft weapons from in and around a walled cemetery lashed out at the Rangers. E Company went after this position, trapped, and captured the occupants. Those who escaped and those who occupied positions in the town were taken care of in house-to-house fighting, with grenades and small-arms fire.

By 1600 hours, it was over. The captured enemy machine guns were in place in a perimeter defense established by B, C, D, and E Companies on the edge of Porto Empedocle. Company A was occupied in building a makeshift prisoner-of-war compound. A compound was necessary as the 3d Ranger Battalion had captured 91 Germans and 675 Italians that day alone.

Entitled to a rest, the Rangers instead got shellfire. A float-type spotter plane for a U.S. warship circled the town, and naval gunfire began to land in a draw close by the C Company position. Much inspired, the Rangers made strenuous efforts to identify themselves. After another salvo and more effort at identification, the spotter plane flew out to sea. The spotter aircraft soon returned, in company with another plane and flying a sheet from the wing strut. Landing outside the harbor, the plane carefully taxied past the jetty into the dock where Dammer was waiting.

Dammer was then flown to the cruiser *Philadelphia*, where he radioed the capture of Porto Empedocle to General Truscott.

But the action was not over for the 3d Ranger Battalion. In darkness, fifteen Italian light tanks (Renault type), wearing a death's head device, came upon a Ranger radio patrol, consisting of the battalion signal officer and two enlisted men, who were accompanying a motorized patrol of the 3d Reconnaissance Troop, 3d Infantry Division. The Americans were stopped at a blown bridge when the Italian tanks attacked. Men were wounded, but the engagement did not go well for the tanks. The Ranger communications sergeant, Robert H. Haliday, thrust a grenade through a port in the lead tank. With its crew dead or wounded, the tank plunged down an embankment. In the darkness, two tank crews abandoned their tanks and were captured.

At 1900 hours on July 17, Maj. Herm Dammer's 3d Ranger Battalion received orders to return to Montaperto.

The dream operation of the 3d Ranger Battalion was concluded. Operating independently ahead of friendly forces, the battalion skillfully employed firepower and aggressive action to take enemy positions. The information provided was of significant value to higher command in the development of a fluid situation.

On July 17, General Alexander gave Patton approval for a drive on Palermo. Patton put together a provisional (temporary) corps, consisting of the 3d Infantry, 2d Armored, and 82d Airborne Divisions under the command of Maj. Gen. Geoffrey Keyes, and began the attack. Keyes formed the 1st and 4th Ranger Battalions, the 39th Infantry Regimental Combat Team, and the 1st Battalion of the 77th Field Artillery into Task Force X and gave the command to Darby. The drive toward Palermo was made in record time. The 3d Infantry Division used the "Truscott trot"[4] to cover one hundred miles in four days. The 3d Ranger Battalion was a part of the lead force. At Calmonica they outposted the 3d Division's left flank and maintained contact with the 82d Airborne Division to the left.

Darby and Force X did a superb job of assisting the 3d Infantry Division and covering the flank of the 2nd Armored. The hectic pace made several shifts of command necessary. On July 20, the 3d Ranger Battalion was attached to the 82d Airborne Division, relieved from attachment to the 82d Airborne Division and attached to Task Force X, and then relieved from Task Force X and attached to the Provisional Corps.

Ranger companies were used to guard prisoner-of-war camps and as road guides for the 2d Armored Division that Patton had selected to bear him into Palermo, which surrendered on July 22. On the 23d, George Patton and the 2d Armored arrived to find the 3d Infantry Division controlling the streets of Palermo. Task Force X captured Marsala on July 24. On July 25, Benito Mussolini was thrown out of office as Italian leader and replaced by Marshal Badoglio. The next day the Combined Chiefs of Staff ordered General Eisenhower to begin planning for an invasion of the Italian mainland at Salerno. On the German side, Hitler foresaw the collapse of his Italian allies. The Germans moved additional forces to northern Italy and made plans to disarm the Italians.

In Sicily, coping with Italian prisoners was a problem. An example of the prisoner situation was contained in a July 25 message from Lt. Col. John Toffey of the 39th Infantry to Darby. Lieutenant Colonel Toffey stated that he had turned over to the 3d Ranger Battalion 4,356 prisoners and had 2,500 more being turned over that date. Toffey wanted Seventh Army Headquarters to know that neither the 39th Infantry nor the 3d Ranger Battalion had the transportation, messing, or other basic facilities to deal with that many prisoners.

Roy Murray and his jeep driver set the example for prisoner transportation and feeding. Murray and his driver were in a jeep, mounted with a .50 caliber machine gun, checking on coastal patrols. Taking a turn down a side road, the two men came upon an airfield where there were some 150 Italians and a few Germans under an Italian general. The aircraft on the field had been rendered unserviceable, and the Italians were ready to surrender. Murray and his driver kept a close eye on the Germans while he considered ways to bring home his prisoners. The Italians had a large truck available. Murray ordered them to load all weapons and rations on the truck. Murray's driver walked in front, followed by the prisoners and the truck, while Murray brought up the rear in his machine-gun–mounted jeep.

The Italians were eager to surrender. They feared reprisal from both the Germans, who thought them quitters, and the Sicilians, who were furious at the destruction that was being visited on them. The Italians would hide in the hills and hurry down at the sight of Americans, hoping for the chance to surrender. Men of Ranger units, moving forward rapidly, sometimes told them to "bug off" and surrender to someone else.

The desperation of the Italians was evidenced by the experience of the 3d Ranger Battalion's Italian-speaking Jake Gilardi. Gilardi and another Ranger were driving a jeep and trailer loaded with ammunition to resupply the battalion, when they stopped by the roadside to answer the call of nature. Sounds coming from a nearby barn aroused their curiosity. Gilardi and his companion stepped into the barn, where they were immediately surrounded by heavily armed Italian soldiers, who pointed their weapons menacingly at the Rangers. An Italian major stepped forward and put the muzzle of his pistol to Gilardi's forehead. "I am your prisoner," the Italian hissed.

On July 25, the 39th Infantry and 1st Battalion, 77th Artillery, were ordered to II Corps. Task Force X now consisted of the 1st, 3d, and 4th Ranger Battalions, all of whom were involved in guarding prisoners and stores.

Senior commanders on both sides knew that Messina was the key to Sicily. It appeared to General Guzzoni that the greatest threat to that city was the British Eighth Army fighting its way up the coast, so Guzzoni put his best forces, including the Herman Goering Division, in front of the British and stalled their attack. Hitler was also reinforcing his Italian allies with the 29th Panzer Grenadier Division and elements of the 1st Parachute Division.

With Montgomery stalled, General Alexander gave Patton approval to attack east from Palermo to Messina. With characteristic fervor, Patton launched the 1st, 3d, and 45th Infantry Divisions in the attack. Resistance became increasingly stiff.

Montgomery tried an end run, and both Montgomery and Patton tried amphibious operations behind the Axis forces; neither had great success. The German General Hube fought a skillful delaying action. Hube had the advantage of terrain. Rugged mountains left only a bitterly contested coast road as a means of rapid advance to Messina.

The 1st, less one company, and 4th Ranger Battalions were encamped near Corleone and did not participate in this drive, but the 3d Infantry Division made full use of the 3d Ranger Battalion in rooting out pockets of enemy resistance. Dammer's Rangers traversed over one hundred miles of tortuous mountains. In doing so, they were resupplied by a pack-mule train of fifty animals that allowed them to operate in a largely self-sufficient manner. Darby organized this mule train, and Captain Worth's company of the 1st Battalion were the mule skinners. Once again, El Darbo's experience was useful. His prewar service with 75mm pack-howitzer units had given Darby experience with both the mule and the pack howitzer, and that knowledge was of great help to the 3d Battalion on their drive.

At the conclusion of the push to Messina, the 3d Rangers moved to Corleone and joined the 1st and 4th. Darby exercised command over the three battalions that were unofficially called "Ranger Force." Replacements were secured, and training was resumed, with emphasis on night operations.

On August 10, 1943, two men widely separated by distance yet linked by philosophy addressed letters attempting to clarify the future status of the Rangers.

From Sicily, the letter written by Lt. Col. William Darby was titled "Status of Ranger Battalions" and addressed through General Patton as commander of the Seventh Army to General Eisenhower as commander in chief of Allied Forces.

Darby reviewed the history of the Ranger battalions, beginning with the formation of the 1st Ranger Battalion on June 19, 1942. His review indicates that he had no knowledge that the 1st Rangers were formed as a "training and demonstration unit." Darby wrote that the "organization was patterned after the British Commandos and it was evidently the intent that we operate in a similar manner as we became attached for training and operations to the Special Services Brigade (British)."

Darby also wrote of the participation of the 1st Ranger Battalion in the African campaign, and the formation of additional Ranger battalions for the invasion of Sicily. He reviewed his earlier request that a Ranger Force headquarters be approved to accomplish training, operations, and administration of the three battalions and noted that his request had been disapproved.

He stated that despite the existence of Ranger units since June of 1942, no assurance had been received that this type organization was considered permanent by the War Department. In fact, Darby concluded, indications were that the organizations were considered to be of a transient nature and to have no permanent place in army organization.

Darby sought a review of Ranger unit performance, and if the reports of action proved their operational value, that the previous decision be reconsidered and the Ranger battalions formed into a permanent organization assigned as Corps, Army, or GHQ troops.

The intensity of Darby's feeling was expressed by his request that if the Ranger battalions were not granted permanent status, they should be disbanded and re-formed along the lines of a regularly approved organization.

If permanent status was not granted, Darby felt the Ranger battalions could be re-formed into a reconnaissance regiment.

The frustration of this gallant officer is clearly evident in this letter. Bill Darby was a career officer, a man who had twice turned down promotion to stay with his Rangers. This is not the action of a self-seeker. As Robert Rogers tried unsuccessfully in the 1700s, Bill Darby was trying to take away the perceived stigma of Rangers being "bastard" units. That he was willing to see his beloved Rangers be transformed into a reconnaissance regiment rather than remain as they were demonstrates the intensity of his belief in the Rangers.

Bill Darby was the only Ranger officer who at that moment in time had the necessary stature to even hope to bring permanency to American Ranger units. His willingness to forgo for this cause the opportunity to climb rapidly to general officer rank is an everlasting tribute to his character.

General Patton loved a fighter and wholeheartedly endorsed Darby's request. Patton wanted a Ranger regiment, headed by Darby and assigned to Seventh Army.

The other letter dated August 10, 1943 was written in England by Brig. Gen. Norman S. Cota, Combined Operations G-3 Section. Cota's letter was titled "Need for Ranger Battalions in ETOUSA" and sent through the G-3 to the commanding general of European Theater of Operations United States Army (ETOUSA).

Cota wrote that experience in North Africa and Sicily had demonstrated that Ranger battalions were vitally necessary. He continued that Ranger battalions were needed for operations being contemplated in the European theater. Cota wrote of the type of individual required and the training necessary for Rangers and pointed out that there was only one understrength Ranger battalion in ETOUSA (the 29th Ranger Battalion). He also noted that there was no long-range plan of training or development in the European theater to remedy the lack of sufficient Ranger battalions.

Cota discussed the three Ranger battalions in Sicily and wrote enthusiastically about Bill Darby. Cota called Darby "the foremost Ranger expert," and "the ideal leader for this type of unique military effort." Cota sought immediate consolidation of all previous information about Ranger training and experience and specifically recommended that the European theater immediately develop a Ranger training program, with Bill Darby and a cadre of Ranger officers and enlisted men brought from Sicily to develop the program. In putting forth this proposal, Norman Cota stressed that "a specific and peculiar type of leadership is required." In Cota's view, Bill Darby best exemplified that type of officer and he compared Darby with Knute Rockne, the famous football coach of Notre Dame.

While both letters made their way through the administrative process, the German Army was demonstrating efficiency in defeat.

In Sicily, the Americans and British won the terrain, but during the period August 3–17, 1943, the Germans and Italians skillfully ferried over one hundred thousand men and ten thousand vehicles, including tanks, to the Italian mainland. With ridiculously low losses, the Germans ferried three tough divisions back to Italy. When Messina fell on August 17, American and British fighting men knew they had not seen the last of the Herman Goering Division.

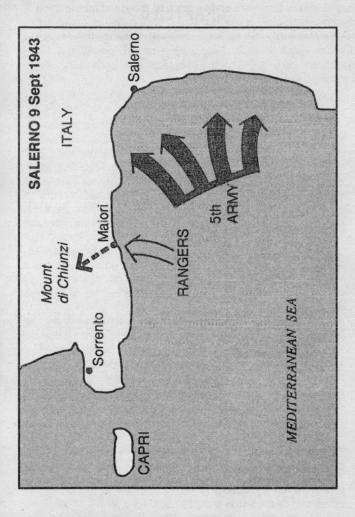

SALERNO 9 Sept 1943

ITALY

Salerno

Mount di Chiunzi

Maiori

Sorrento

RANGERS

5th ARMY

CAPRI

MEDITERRANEAN SEA

CHAPTER 6

ITALY

While proving themselves in combat, the Rangers were constantly beset by the problem of legitimacy. The army was a parent that turned hot and cold. "We need you, we want you, but we don't recognize you," was the theme. Maj. Gilbert W. Embury of Combined Operations G-3 (European Theater of Operations) waged an unrelenting effort to establish a planning office to plan and provide for a Ranger division. This organization was intended to be similar to the British Special Services Brigade (the Commandos). Some staff officers wanted volunteers taken from a division, given Ranger training, then returned to that division as a division task force. There was a school of thought that all American infantrymen should receive Ranger training. None of this thinking would become doctrine in World War II.

September 1943 opened with a new member joining the Ranger family. On September 1, the 5th Ranger Battalion was activated at Camp Forrest, Tennessee. The 5th came alive with 34 officers and 563 enlisted men. Among the requirements for joining the new unit was the ability to meet the physical capabilities of a parachutist, to qualify in all arms the battalion possessed, and to have been part of a unit which had experienced a division-size maneuver.

On the other side of the Atlantic, a smaller Ranger birth was occurring. The memories of the tank attacks at Gela were fresh. Looking for additional firepower, on September 1, 1943, Darby organized from within the 1st Ranger Battalion a provisional antitank platoon. The unit was put under the command of the battle-hungry Capt. Charles M. Shunstrom. Artillerymen and volunteers were transferred into the platoon from throughout the battalion. The platoon quickly be-

came known among the rangers as cannon company. Four
M-3 half-tracks (75mm gun motor carriages) were secured, and
the Ranger gunners began to practice. The four half-tracks
were named *Ace of Diamonds*, *Ace of Hearts*, *Ace of Spades*,
and *Ace of Clubs*. Shunstrom's jeep was called "the Joker."

In the United Kingdom on September 2, the 29th Ranger
Battalion (HQ and four Ranger companies) moved to Dorlin
House for advanced assault training. The 29th Rangers were
building a great reputation with the Commando officers, who
praised them highly. Two 29th Rangers went on a Commando
raid on an island off the coast of France. One of the men covered the withdrawal of his group to the boats and in the
process, killed three Germans and wounded others.

Despite proven ability, the 29th Rangers were kept in a
provisional status. A report on Ranger activity contained
the following words regarding the 29th Rangers. "It is a bastard outfit having no official existence, no approved T/O, no
nothing to be exact. Yet it is training and while differently
composed (HQ detachment and four line companies) as con-
trasted with the 1st Ranger Battalion . . . one cannot simply
say that the unit does not exist because it has no official
birth."

Rangers on both sides of the Atlantic were anxious for
battle. The Allied war machine was now geared up. Beset on
several fronts, the Germans waited for the next blow—they
would not have long to wait. With Sicily in the bag, the
Americans and British turned operational eyes elsewhere.

Even though the battle for Sicily was over, the behind-the-
scenes battle between the military chiefs was still raging.
Marshall wanted the cross-channel invasion, the U.S. Navy
wanted its ships in the Pacific, and the British wanted more
peripheral action in the Mediterranean—Italy if possible or
through the Balkans. A compromise was reached, with Marshall and the British prevailing. Marshall won agreement that
the cross-channel invasion of Europe would be the highest
priority and would take place in 1944. The British got a limited invasion of Italy that would complement the cross-
channel effort by drawing off German divisions. Under the
code name, AVALANCHE, planning for the Italian campaign

was put under Gen. Mark Clark, commander of the U.S. Fifth
Army, with the goal of seizing Naples as a base for future operations. At the same time, secret negotiations were going on
with Badoglio's Italian government to take the Italians out of
the war, thus, hopefully, complicating life for the Germans.
Hitler's men were prepared for this and ready to disarm the
Italians and treat them as a conquered people. Toward the end
of the Sicilian campaign, the U.S. Army lost a fighting commander when General Patton was relieved for slapping a hospitalized patient who had no visible wound.

On September 3, 1943, the British 5th and Canadian 1st
Divisions crossed the Strait of Messina from Sicily and
landed at the toe of the boot of Italy. Resistance was light, but
the hope of drawing German forces south into a trap did not
succeed. September 3–7 saw Allied convoys bringing Mark
Clark's invasion forces together. The 36th Infantry Division
was coming from Oran. This untested National Guard division would join the U.S. 45th Infantry Division and the
British 46th and 56th Infantry Divisions in the invasion force.
The U.S. 3d and 34th Infantry Divisions and the British 7th
Armored would quickly join the fight.

While events were heating up in Italy, the temperature also
took a turn for the warmer for the men of the 2d Ranger Battalion. On September 4, the battalion departed Camp Forrest,
Tennessee, by train. The destination was Fort Pierce, Florida,
and the U.S. Navy Scout and Raiders School. Eleven days of
training began on September 6. This training was geared to
prepare the Rangers for amphibious operations. Landing
nets, rubber boats, and the Landing Craft Assault (LCA) were
used. Over and over, by night and by day, the 2d Rangers
practiced assault landings from the sea, the stings of mosqui-
toes and jellyfish leaving lasting memories.

On September 8, the Italians announced their surrender.
Though some Italians fought back, the Germans quickly
seized key facilities and disarmed Italian units. The German
plan was well formed and executed, but it took time and tied
down troops to disarm the Italians, and German forces in the
south of Italy were left at a bare minimum. The British were

benefactors of this German weakness when they successfully dispatched a force from Africa to capture the Italian naval base at Taranto in the heel of the Italian boot.

The area of Salerno now became the Allied amphibious objective. The area is shaped much like a human hand, with the thumb extended. The tip of the first finger represents Naples, with Mount Vesuvius and Pompeii below it. The thumb represents the Sorrento Peninsula. At the base of the thumb, just below the knuckle, are Amalfi and Maiori, and directly inward, the Nocera defile and the critical Route 18 which ran to Pompeii and Naples. On down the wrist would be Salerno.

At 0330 on September 9, General Clark's Fifth Army began to come ashore at Salerno. The British X Corps (including the Ranger Force) would land in the north of the sector while the American VI Corps would go ashore to the south. But the Germans could read a map as well as anyone and made their plans accordingly. Initially, the Germans had only the 16th Panzer Division to contest the area. The officers of the 16th Panzers calculated that the Salerno beaches were a likely place for invasion and prepared well. When the landings came, the German 16th Panzer Division fought a superb defense. The U.S. VI Corps sent the men of the 36th Infantry Division ashore without air or naval support in the hopes of achieving surprise. The Germans were ready and badly shot up the initial waves before withdrawing. German valor, plus a lack of aggressiveness in Fifth Army, began to turn the landing into a bloody and slow-moving operation.

Expectation is a dangerous thing, and hopes were too high of the benefits of an Italian surrender. As the Allied command moved slowly, German units, who had completed their mission against the Italians, began to move south. The 16th Panzer Division gave ground grudgingly.

On the north flank of the invasion, however, things were going better. Several miles above Salerno was the small seacoast town of Maiori. The pebbled beach at this mountainous village was overlooked by the Germans and undefended. This error would cost the Germans dearly for the beach was ideal for a Ranger landing. The Ranger Force now consisted of the 1st, 3d, and 4th Ranger Battalions with Number 2 and

Number 41 British Commando and Companies C and D of the 83d Chemical Battalion (4.2-inch mortar).

The Ranger Force mission was to land at Maiori and move inland some six miles to seize high ground commanding the plains and road network that led north to Naples. Successful accomplishment of the mission would secure General Clark's left flank and threaten the German lines of communication with Naples.

Loading on September 7, the Ranger Force sailed from Sicily in Landing Craft Infantry (LCI) in the early morning hours of the 8th. The convoy was detected by German aircraft during the afternoon and came under repeated air attack well into the night. As they approached the Italian coast, the LCIs bearing the Rangers and Commandos and their escorts left the main convoy and put their bows toward Maiori. At 0310 hours on the 9th, the 4th Ranger Battalion landed and led the way over the beaches of Maiori. Murray's Rangers had the mission of establishing a beachhead and securing the right and left flanks for the Ranger Force. Surprise was complete and the beach was not mined. To the south, the Rangers could hear heavy firing as a fierce battle raged along the beaches.

Forty-five minutes after the 4th Battalion landed, the 1st came ashore, and fifteen minutes later at 0400 the 3d Rangers landed. The Rangers' use of colored flashlights as a means of identification was well developed. Leaders down to section level carried flashlights with red lenses, and the letter *R* was flashed in Morse code to establish identification.

While the 4th Battalion came ashore, Numbers 2 and 41 Commandos were landing to the right of the Rangers to seize Salerno. Companies B, C, D, and E of the 4th Ranger Battalion cleared Maiori and occupied the high ground overlooking the town. Company A of the 4th moved along the coast road to the west, occupied high ground, and set up a roadblock, where an unwary German driver lost his life and his vehicle to the Rangers.

Company F moved on the coast road toward Salerno. Fox Company had the mission of eliminating two enemy observation posts and a machine gun. A mile and a half down the road, the Rangers captured a German NCO, two other enlisted men, and a sidecar-type motorcycle. Next came a fortified observation post, which they shot up, killing one Italian and wounding another. A half mile on near Lanterna, another fortified post was engaged, and two Rangers were wounded. Four Italians were killed and one wounded. Mission accomplished, the men of F Company, 4th Ranger Battalion, set up a roadblock and awaited orders.

The 1st Battalion moved along the Maiori–Vaccaro road with F Company in the lead followed by E, D, B, and A. Company C was in battalion reserve. The 1st reached its objective, the high ground at Mount St. Angelo, at 0800 hours, after overcoming enemy reconnaissance parties and destroying an armored vehicle. The 3d Battalion moved in on the left of the 1st. The 3d Rangers had the mission of seizing high ground in the vicinity of Pagani. The 3d made the move to Mount di Chiunzi without incident; by 0900 hours, the battalion had a company south of the pass, three more companies occupied the ridge north of the pass, and two companies were in reserve. At 1700 hours, Companies A and B of the 1st Rangers were attached to the 3d Ranger Battalion, and Company C of the 1st joined its remaining sister companies on the line.

Perched like eagles high in the Sorentine Mountains, the Rangers were in a superb position. In control of the high ground and outposting (the spurs leading to it), the Rangers controlled the critical Chiunzi pass and the Nocera defile. The Rangers also overlooked Highway 18, the main supply route for the Germans, and possession of this key terrain was a grip on the German throat. The weighty 4.2-inch mortars were carried to the top of the mountains, where they wreaked havoc with German logistical routes. The mortarmen of the 83d Chemical performed brilliantly, often firing at two thousand yards beyond the rated range for the weapon.

Darby's artillery background stood him in good stead here. In addition to the devastating fire of the 83d Chemical Battalion's 4.2-inch mortars and Shunstrom's Cannon Company, Darby requested and got two naval forward observer parties, one of which was British. With the big-gun fire of the British battleship *Howe* and other Allied cruisers supporting, the Rangers began to harass German installations and resupply efforts. In the hours of darkness, interdictory fire[1] and Ranger combat patrols disrupted the Germans and caused them to withdraw troops critically needed from the battle south of Salerno to attack the Rangers.

Predictably, the German reaction was prompt and violent. Unable to dislodge the Rangers by frontal assault, the Germans pounded them constantly with artillery and mortars, while searching for a weak spot where advantage could be gained. The long-barreled German 88mm guns whiplashed the Rangers. One deadly portion of the Chiunzi pass was known as "88 Junction."

The Ranger position on the high ground soon became even more important. On September 10, the Germans began to move most of their force northward to hold the Naples area. A German platoon-size combat patrol encountered Rangers of the 3d Battalion on Mount di Chiunzi; one Ranger and three Germans were killed. A squad-size force of Rangers, moving forward to protect an artillery observation post, encountered another German force. The men of the 3d Rangers killed twelve Germans at the loss of one American.

On September 11, the 4th Rangers moved north above Amalfi, then inland. Three companies were sent to take the towering Mount Pendola, which dominated German positions near Gregnano, while two other companies moved up the coast road and seized a critical piece of high ground that would block the Sorrento Peninsula. The 3d Rangers captured a captain and an enlisted man of the Herman Goering Division. On the 12th, Company C of the 4th Ranger Battalion moved to high ground overlooking German positions in the town of Castellammare. A patrol went into the town to test German strength and found it—well-guarded German artillery was in the town. In the ensuing fight, twelve Germans were killed or wounded before the patrol had to withdraw with one Ranger officer and one enlisted man wounded. Ranger scouts remained behind to map enemy positions, then passed through enemy lines with the information.

A and D Companies of the 4th Rangers with H Company, 504th Parachute Infantry attached attacked a German position at Gregnano and ran into concentrated automatic-weapons and artillery fire. The Americans were forced to withdraw to Mount Pendola, with a loss of one man killed and two missing. At 1600 hours on the 12th, the 3d Rangers intercepted a three-man German reconnaissance patrol, killing the leader. He was identified as coming from a parachute regiment with the Herman Goering Division—two hundred Germans of that division had begun moving onto a ridge near the Rangers. The Rangers put six 60mm mortars into action with devastating effect. The Germans fled, leaving nine bodies, and blood-soaked bandages and abandoned equipment showed that many more had been killed or wounded.

One after the other, small-unit actions reaped their bloody harvest on both sides. Both American and German artillery fire was constant and severe, and the shrapnel took its toll. The 3d Ranger Battalion medical officer, Capt. Emil Schuster, had established his aid station in a clearly visible, stone house that stood up under enemy high explosive. Known as "Fort Schuster," the sturdy building seemed to represent the Ranger spirit.

The Rangers were pounding Italian towns held or used by the Germans. War is hard on soldier and civilian alike, and the mayor of the town of Angri wrote a letter on September 13 that a brave messenger brought through the fighting to Roy Murray.

The Mayor of Angri wrote in his plea:

Excuse me if I communicate to you that is many days that your batteries let come on our city a shower of projectiles that makes a great destruction of houses and men, children, women and so on. All the population of this city (ANGRI) more than 20,000 inhabitants, are sudden fear for the men wounded and death. Will you please change the position of your cannon and do not shot on our city. This is an appeal that all population of Angri does to you. Commander save our children, save old men, save our women, save the population, please. God bless you.

Regrettably, the Germans were running supplies through the town, and the suffering continued until the enemy was driven out.

The Americans and British poured in reinforcements to support the Ranger force positions. Relieved at Mount Pendola by men of the 504th Airborne, the 4th Ranger Battalion rejoined the 1st and 3d Rangers on September 14 and took up positions on the high ground northwest of Polvico. Darby's command reached 8,500 troops, including the British 23d Armored Brigade.

Allied efforts to drive inland were bitterly contested by the Germans. It was not until September 15 that the beachhead was considered safe.

Back in the States at Fort Pierce, Florida, the 2d Rangers completed amphibious training and threw a party that was just short of open warfare. On the 17th with the best, indeed, the fervent wishes of the Fort Pierce community for a speedy departure, Rudder's Rangers left for Fort Dix, New Jersey. At Fort Dix and Camp Shanks, the men of the 2d Rangers received advanced training in preparation for overseas movement.

In Italy on the 17th, elements of the 4th Rangers relieved the 3d Ranger Battalion which moved into a bivouac area one-half mile west of Polvica.

The fighting the Rangers experienced was vicious. There was constant cold. There was never sufficient water and ammunition. Men dug deep in the earth, yet were shaken like rag dolls by the violence of high explosives. There was sickness and constant tension. Not surprisingly, some men in foxholes began to grumble that this was not a proper employment for Rangers.

Meanwhile, Chuck Shunstrom was having a great time with Cannon Company. Ranger Joe Cain was on *Ace of Diamonds* and remembers the half-track–mounted 75mm guns hiding in the pass with Shunstrom forward in "the Joker," peering through field glasses looking for targets. When Shunstrom saw a chance to shoot, he would signal forward one or more of the tracks and unload a hail of shells on the Germans then crank up the engines and scoot back into the pass. This technique angered the Germans greatly and they would respond with salvos of artillery. Cannon Company was gone by the time the Germans responded, but the men in the foxholes caught the German ire. Ed Dean remembers that more than once, the Rangers in the foxholes crouched under German high explosives and cursed Shunstrom and his cannons with passion.

On September 18, the 1st Ranger Battalion was relieved by the 2d Battalion, 325 Glider Infantry. The 1st Rangers had been under constant artillery fire for nine days and nights and had beaten off seven attacks by German infantry. The 1st and 3d Ranger Battalions were attached to the 82d Airborne Division and placed in division reserve.

Meanwhile, the 4th Rangers were still getting constant action. This was infantry war that required the highest skill to survive and accomplish the mission. This was patrolling. Small bands of American Rangers and elite German troops kept up continuous efforts to reconnoiter and conduct combat operations against their opponents. Both sides used mortars and artillery with terrible effect. There was nothing grand about this action—it was a small dirty fight in a dark alley with no rules save to kill the enemy.

Lt. Joe Fineberg was the supply officer for the 4th Ranger Battalion. Fineberg had responded to Murray's question, "Why do you want to be in the Rangers?" with the words, "I can make sure you are equipped." Fineberg was a Ranger hustler. He got two sniper rifles for every company, Springfield 03s with telescopes. He was an honest officer, who only lied to get more rations for the men. Ranging about with his jeep named "Matzoh Ball" and trailer, Fineberg took a special delight in getting all-wool British socks or a hot meal for the men of the 4th.

Fineberg's audacity occasionally brought him to near disaster. On one occasion, he secured a landing craft and went to a supply ship, returning to the 4th Rangers with some eight hundred cartons of cigarettes and other items. It turned out that Fineberg had secured the cigarette rations for the entire Ranger force. Darby was furious and made a personal visit to Murray, wanting Fineberg's scalp. It took some fast talking to convince El Darbo that it was all some kind of mistake.

Fineberg often heard the church bells just prior to the crash of German artillery. He made the connection, and an investigation was begun. German troops dressed as monks were occupying churches—without any military equipment and often speaking Italian, they were believed to be churchmen. When they saw Allied forces approaching points on which the Germans had planned artillery concentrations, these Germans would ring the bells a certain number of times. Other German-occupied churches would relay the signal until their batteries got the message. The Rangers took the matter up with local Church authorities and the Germans were rooted out.

The Allied forces were now ready to make their attack to seize Naples. The Germans could no longer sustain operations in southernmost Italy. Beginning September 18, German forces withdrew from the islands of Sardinia and Corsica.

On the 18th, D Company of the 4th moved from Chiunzi down the road toward Sala to reconnoiter for roadblocks, mines, and prepared demolitions. The Germans fought fiercely. The company commander and five Rangers were wounded; three more Rangers were missing in action. The Rangers counted sixteen German casualties.

The reconnaissance was the prelude to a Ranger Force attack on Sala. The 4th Battalion remained in position and provided guides through the mountains, while the 1st and 3d Rangers launched their attack.

The attack was made without incident. The Germans had withdrawn north toward Naples, where they began to destroy the dock facilities. The Rangers remained in the Sala–Polvico–Pigno area, protecting the flank of the British 46th Division until September 29. On the 29th, 1st and 3d Rangers marched approximately ten miles to Castellammare and bivouacked near town. There they were joined by the 4th Battalion.

During the month of September, the Rangers lost twenty-two men killed in action, eight who died of wounds, nine who were missing in action, and seventy-three men who were wounded. Without army acceptance as a permanent force, there was no vehicle to provide trained replacements. The Rangers, though designed to be a small hard-hitting force to raid or spearhead, were being used in the manner of line infantry. They performed the job well but the loss of men who were Ranger-trained hurt the special capability of the Rangers. Still, new men were brought in. Don Clark, an eighteen-year-old from Iowa, was one of the men who volunteered at this time. "It was unique training," Clark said, "they took you into German territory." Trained on-line in battle, the new Rangers learned patrolling on patrol. It was a bloody and wasteful school. "One thing you could be sure of," Clark said, "you were going to be engaged." John Prochek also became a Ranger in Italy, joining the 3d Battalion. "You were not allowed to wear the Ranger patch until you proved yourself," Prochek recalled. "What a proud day it was when I was granted that right."

The constant digging of foxholes had given the Rangers a working knowledge of agronomy, but their education was to be broadened. On October 1, Naples fell to Allied forces. On October 3, the Ranger Force moved by truck from bivouac near Castellammare to the Botanical Gardens and buildings of the Napoli Institute of Botany at Naples. On October 8, 1943, the Ranger Force was detached from the 82d Airborne Division and went into Fifth Army Reserve. Murray's 4th Ranger Battalion was attached to VI Corps. The study of botany was short, and on October 10 the 1st and 3d Rangers moved by truck some fifty miles to a former school building at San Lazzaro near Amalfi, Italy. The 4th Rangers also moved south. On October 14, the 4th Rangers loaded trucks at 0805 hours and drove to Sorrento, arriving at 1030. All the battalions were busy. More replacements were coming in. The constant process of training consumed the attention of the men.

The Germans were determined to delay south of Rome as long as possible. The German General Kesselring decided to refuse ground above the Volturno River until after mid-October. This would give him time to prepare a winter line position. The terrain and weather favored defense and delay. Once they crossed the Volturno, the Allied forces faced one hundred miles of high mountains and deep ravines. The rivers and streams were flooded with heavy autumn rains, bridges were washed out, and mud was a tenacious foe, and the Germans intended that before the Allied forces reached the eternal city of Rome, they would pay the price of passage in blood. On October 12, Fifth Army attacked. The long, fighting trek north began.

* * *

In England, the downside of September seemed to offer combat hope for the 29th Rangers. On September 20, a company of the 29th moved to Dover to be used in a raid on the Continent. The Ranger effort was to be the preliminary part of a larger assault. Once again, the men faced disappointment when the raid was canceled.

On October 18, 1943, Headquarters, 29th Infantry Division, published General Orders Number 27, and the men of the 29th Ranger Battalion saw their hopes and dreams dashed. The order carried out the direction of a September 30 letter of Headquarters European Theater of Operations. The 29th Ranger Battalion was disbanded effective October 18, 1943.

The men of the 29th Rangers were volunteers to a man. Their spirit and their accomplishments received fulsome praise from their British instructors. They distinguished themselves on maneuvers, performed well in the limited combat operations allowed them. Then it was over. The 99th Separate Battalion (Norwegian) was to receive Commando training and two battalions of Rangers were training in the United States. The War Department made the decision that the overall troop basis of the army only allowed for three Ranger battalions in the Western Atlantic and two in the United Kingdom. The judgment was made that the battalions trained in the United States were better trained than those who had been trained by the Commandos, although there was no valid basis for that judgment.

A staff report included the following words: "But the life of the unit was coming to an unnatural end. It was to be returned to its basic units . . . because 'War Department felt they could bring over better trained ranger-type units from the states.' What a lot of waste has gone into this. These men, while benefiting tremendously from their training as Rangers, are no longer a striking force. Their experience will probably not be put to use in the division if past conduct of the division is any criterion. The men themselves are terribly broken up over the fate of their unit. AWOL's have already started, a thing which is rare indeed in Ranger or Commando units."

Frustrated and angry, some of the 29th Rangers turned their tommy guns loose on their cantonment area and made sieves of the Quonset huts.

The 29th Division did not keep these Rangers together as a fighting force. Men often went back to the same jobs they had left. Individually, the men distinguished themselves in heavy fighting from D-day until the Germans were defeated. Some fought still wearing their Ranger insignia. To receive such aggressive training and then to be put among men who have not had similar training is to make death or injury probable. Many of the 29th Rangers paid that price.

While the 29th Rangers were being disbanded, in Italy war raged on. By the beginning of November, General Alexander's 15th Army Group stretched from the Gulf of Gaeta to the Adriatic Sea. General Clark's Fifth Army held the left (south) of the line, with General Montgomery's Eighth Army in the center, and General Knightly's Commonwealth V Corps on the right (north). The Allies were faced by some six infantry, three mechanized infantry, and three Panzer divisions of the German Tenth Army.

In the American sector, the German main line was called the Gustav line. The forward defenses were known as the Winter Line.

Approximately thirty-six miles north of Naples, Fifth Army faced the enemy. It was to the area near the Volturno River and the town of Venafro that the 4th Ranger Battalion moved on November 1, 1942. Leaving the Sorrento area at 0800 hours, the 4th Rangers moved seventy miles by truck to a bivouac area near Caiazzo. The Mignano Valley was narrowed and contained Route 6, the main highway to Rome. American infantry was having rough going moving on this axis. The mission of the 4th Rangers was to make a night infiltration of German high-ground positions in the area, then seize positions that dominated a key juncture of the Mignano Valley and Route 6.

At 1715 hours on November 3, the 4th Ranger Battalion left their Sesto Campano bivouac area, crossed the Volturno River at a ford, then began a grueling twelve-mile climb over rough terrain. Ranger reconnaissance had made contact with friendly Italians, who showed them a little-used trail. Moving on this trail, the Rangers reached Hill 620 where they established a radio-relay station to communicate with higher headquarters.

Continuing their climb, the 4th Rangers moved to a point north of Hill 861 and its adjacent ridgeline. It was now 0615 the morning of the 4th. Despite the grueling climb, there was no time for rest. German patrols were active. Companies A, B, and C tangled with two six-man patrols and one patrol of twenty-two men. The Germans were hit hard with sixteen killed and four taken prisoner. There were no Ranger casualties.

The remainder of the morning, recon patrols went south and southwest. At 1430 hours, Capt. Walter Nye led Companies D, E, and F to the top of Mount Cavalle. From this excellent point of observation, the Rangers saw a German column consisting of twelve mules and fifty men. This group was soon joined by twelve to fifteen German soldiers with a wire-stringing party.

The Germans saw the Ranger scouts and promptly attacked. E Company met this force in a head-on attack, while D Company swung south to hit the Germans in the flank. Company F remained in position to guard the Ranger back door. E Company drove the Germans rearward into the rifle and mortar fire of D Company. The attack continued until it reached well–dug-in German emplacements on Hill 689. The route to the German positions was over open ground. German mortar and artillery fire began to deliver a hail of shrapnel. Some of the artillery was firing direct fire on the Rangers, and one platoon of E Company was temporarily pinned down. Heavily pounded, the Rangers withdrew with a loss of two killed, seven wounded, and nine missing. They had killed twenty-four Germans and taken two German prisoners. F Company added to the prisoner bag when they captured four men from a German patrol.

As night came, the 4th Ranger Battalion regrouped and established outposts and listening posts. Roy Murray made plans to again attack the estimated two hundred Germans on Hill 689. During the night, a small German patrol attacked the radio-relay position. Two Germans were killed, with no injury to the Rangers.

On the morning of November 5, B Company was detached to evacuate the wounded. The remainder of the battalion moved to attack positions. C Company would make the assault and concealed itself in a draw below Hill 689. Companies D and F moved to high ground where they could give direct fire support to Company C. Company A was in reserve, with orders to follow C once Hill 689 was taken. Company E guarded the left and rear flank.

At 1130 hours the attack kicked off, and the alert Germans met the Rangers with automatic-weapons, mortar, and artillery fire. A German reinforced platoon moved onto the hill, increasing the German strength, and the Germans were getting intense and accurate fire support. The Rangers had only the weapons they had at hand. Artillery support requested of 3d Division was not received. The Ranger attack was beaten off with a loss of five killed, eight wounded, and six missing. This was the type of situation where men do not count enemy dead. Under the cover of darkness Ranger patrols searched for the wounded and missing.

At 2000 hours, an E Company patrol made contact with elements of the U.S. 15th Infantry Regiment, 3d Infantry Division. In classic fashion the Rangers had infiltrated enemy lines, operating over terrain so cruel as to be an enemy in itself. Even though they were fighting in mountain terrain in winter, due to the nature of the mission, the Rangers had only lightweight, tanker jackets and haversacks with C rations and a single ground sheet. The weather was bitterly cold with rain and sleet. Men shivered and struggled for relief from the cold that cramped them. They tried putting two men with ground sheets together in the hope that body warmth would help—it did not. There was no respite from the cold. There was also no resupply of ammunition, rations, or water provided to the Rangers. To care for the wounded and see to their evacuation was a major effort in itself. To stay behind enemy lines any longer would have been foolhardy, indeed, suicidal. Seven Rangers had been killed, nineteen wounded and evacuated, and twenty-two were missing. Forty-two Germans were known to have been killed and ten captured.

On November 5, Murray requested the G-3 of VI corps to relieve the Rangers of the mission. Companies C and D moved to Sesto Compano for food and water.

On the same day the 4th Rangers were undergoing this

ordeal, the men of the 5th Rangers left Camp Forrest, Tennessee, enroute to the amphibious training base at Fort Pierce, Florida—two weeks of specialized training lay ahead.

On the 6th at 0630 hours, the rest of the 4th Ranger Battalion was granted relief, came down from the hills, and reassembled at Sesto Campano.

On November 8, the 1st Ranger Battalion was attached to 45th Infantry Division. The 1st Rangers were given the mission of relieving the 180th Infantry in the Venafro sector. This was followed by a similar attachment of the 4th Ranger Battalion on the 9th. The Fifth Army had moved forward slowly. The 45th Division was now in the foothills of the mountains above Venafro. The Germans still held the heights which dominated the roads and valleys and behind them towered the peak of Mount Cassino.

The 4th Ranger Battalion was given the mission of linking the left flank of the 45th Division and the right flank of the 3d Division. This entailed taking a high-ground position and establishing a roadblock on the Ceppagna–San Pietro road. On November 9, the 1st Ranger Battalion moved on line beside the 4th. Companies A, B, E, and F relieved companies of the 180th on line, and C and D Companies were held in reserve. On the 10th the 509th Parachute Infantry Battalion was added to Darby's command. Swift German ME-109 fighter aircraft swept over the Ranger position twice, dropping five-hundred-pound bombs.

On the morning of the 10th, the 4th Rangers sent out reconnaissance patrols to Hills 560 and 670. Hill 670 contained a German force that was well dug in. Hill 570 was free of the enemy and was promptly occupied by Company A. On the 11th, E Company relieved Company A.

Commanders and operations officers tend to associate the terms "company" and "battalion" with a certain strength. This often works to the disadvantage of Ranger units that are used in line-infantry circumstances. At full strength, Ranger units are considerably smaller than their line counterparts. In combat, the losses often further serve to make the term "company" not an accurate reflection of strength. On Hill 570, Company A, 4th Ranger Battalion consisted of three officers and forty-three enlisted men, about the size of a rifle platoon. E Company had but one officer and thirty-four enlisted men. All the other Ranger companies were at comparable strength.

At 0430 hours on the morning of November 11, F Company moved to an attack position on the slope of Hill 570. B Company followed F. Behind close artillery and 4.2-inch mortar fire, F Company attacked and captured Hill 670 at 1200 hours. Five Germans were captured; one Ranger was killed and three wounded. The Germans dug in on the reverse slope and made two small counterattacks that were beaten off. The Germans then contented themselves with sniper and machine-gun fire from their reverse-slope positions and the adjoining Hill 630.

On the 11th and 12th, the 1st Rangers were in a defensive posture, patrolling and backing up a 509th Parachute Infantry Battalion advance. Two prisoners were taken, one from the 29th Panzer Regiment.

At 0430 on November 12, Companies A and D of the 4th Rangers moved to join Company F on Hill 570. Once again artillery and the 4.2-inch mortars of the 83d Chemical Battalion blasted the German positions, with the Rangers of Company A, 4th Battalion, attacking along the ridgeline to Hill 630. Three Germans were killed; five officers and forty enlisted men captured. Another thirty Germans escaped. Meanwhile the 1st Rangers had seen German soldiers standing in the doorways of the town of Concacassalo—the Rangers worked the town over with artillery, and the Germans replied in kind.

The 4th Ranger Battalion now had four platoon-size companies covering a front of over 1500 yards. Enemy mortars and artillery kept firing on the Rangers throughout the night. At 0600 on November 13, German gunners began a forty-five-minute concentrated pounding of the Ranger positions. This was followed by an attack by a battalion-size German force. The Germans used three rifle companies on line, with their mortars and machine guns following close and giving effective support. The Ranger left and right flanks were rolled back, but the center held. By 0715 the Rangers were in dire straits. Every man was committed, cooks were carrying litters and drivers carrying ammunition. The 4.2-inch mortar fire was pulled tight against the Ranger front, and artillery was used to hammer German reinforcements. The 180th Infantry was called for assistance. The situation was desperate, but the men fought on. At 1100 hours, the Germans had enough and ceased their attack.

Now the Rangers had the advantage: the Germans were caught in the open, and the Rangers picked off man after man. The Germans tried white flags as a ruse to cover their escape, but the Rangers saw the enemy withdrawing and pounded them with artillery and mortars, causing heavy casualties. At 1330 hours, Company K of the 180th Infantry arrived and moved into position. Through the night the Germans searched for their wounded and withdrew.

During the attack, the 4th Ranger Battalion lost five men killed, thirty-six wounded and evacuated, and three missing in action. When graves registration[2] moved in on Hill 630, they found twenty-one dead Germans shot above the waist, and on the reverse slope lay the bodies of eighty more German soldiers. The enemy dead on the right flank was not counted, and there were no prisoners.

At 0300 on the 14th, the 180th Infantry relieved the 4th Rangers. Maj. Roy Murray's men then were attached to the 1st Ranger Battalion and moved into a battle position that was also a bivouac. While resting, they were guarding the right flank of the 180th Infantry and the left flank of the 1st Ranger Battalion.

A 1st Ranger patrol from F Company engaged a German patrol at 1500 hours on the 14th. Two Germans were killed; the survivors fled.

On the 16th and 17th, German artillery of a large caliber pounded the 1st Ranger positions. On the 18th German patrols probed the Ranger lines and were driven off by rifle fire.

The patrols were a prelude to a German attack on the 1st Rangers that struck the positions of C and D Companies at 1800 hours on the 19th. Company B reinforced its sister companies. Employing small arms and mortars effectively, the Rangers broke up the German attacks. Mines were a constant danger: on the 19th, the 4th Ranger Battalion ambulance was blown up while trying to pick up wounded men. The Germans used the cover of darkness and storms to plant Teller mines or dynamite sticks with percussion caps in tire ruts.

On the 20th, Company D flushed a German patrol that had come within one hundred yards of the 1st Rangers' lines and killed two. The Germans responded by constant sniping and intense artillery fire throughout the night. The shellfire was unrelenting and casualties constantly climbing. On the 21st, the Germans drove off a B Company patrol that was trying to drop Molotov cocktails (bottles filled with gasoline and a lighted wick) into a German-occupied cave. Company E briefly occupied an enemy ridge but did not have the strength to hold the position. On the 22d and 23d, both sides patrolled and pounded each other with mortar and artillery fire. At 1415 hours, the Germans launched an attack on the 1st Rangers' left flank. Company D was committed to assist, and the Germans were beaten back.

Stroke and counterstroke, the action continued in this manner for the remainder of November. Each day the casualty list mounted. Darby's superiors had no understanding of the capabilities and limitations of a Ranger unit. The knowledge and experience of the Rangers was being shot to pieces in line combat.

In the high, craggy mountains, men huddled behind boulders, scratching against the steep, rocky surfaces to prepare positions. The enemy was difficult to detect, and often the opponents were within hand-grenade range of each other.

On one November night, Lt. Warren "Bing" Evans, commanding F Company of the 3d Rangers, made a night reconnaissance to a piece of commanding terrain and found it unoccupied. On reporting to battalion, Evans was given instructions to occupy the hill.

With the light of a foggy dawn came the recognition that the Rangers were not alone. There was not one but two tops to this rocky hill, close together but divided by a deep ravine. The Rangers held one top, the Germans the other. Though the ravine was a considerable obstacle, the straight line distance between the hilltops was close enough that conversation could be carried on.

"Does anybody over there speak English?" Evans called.

"Yes, I can," a German replied, "I am the non-commissioned officer in charge."

"Let's declare a truce," Evans said. "I have a beautiful Red Cross girl over here who would like to meet you."

"No, thank you," the German said.

"Well, why don't you and your men come over and surrender, and we'll give you a steak dinner," Evans said.

The German laughed. "No," he replied, "I couldn't do that."

"You speak very good English," Evans said.

"I was educated at Michigan State, studying hotel management," the German said.

Thus began an unusual relationship. Neither side could dislodge the other. Each day around 1400, the two groups would stop shooting and grenading each other, and Bing Evans and the German NCO named Hans would talk back and forth. Souvenirs were tossed back and forth; these included photographs, knives, and even cameras.

One of the anomalies of war is that given the chance to know the man you are trying to kill, sometimes you find you have more in common with him than you do with some of your own countrymen.

Hans was the only member of the German force who spoke English. As their conversations became friendlier, Hans told Bing Evans that his parents owned a hotel near Leipzig. While a student at Michigan State, he went home to Germany on leave, and the German Army inducted him.

During one such quiet period, a lieutenant colonel of the 82d Airborne visited Evans and questioned why both peaks had not been occupied. Evans replied that the Germans were on the other peak and holding on to it with determination. The discussion became somewhat heated, the officer stating loudly and forcibly that there were no Germans there. To prove his point, the colonel climbed to the top of a boulder and looked over to the other peak. There but a short distance away was Hans, pointing a Schmeisser machine pistol at him. Though Hans could have killed the officer, he held his fire and called over to Bing Evans. "He hasn't been here long."

That evening the orders came to take the other hilltop. Moving off their position, the Rangers moved quietly down and around the opposite peak, approaching the German position from the rear. In sudden attack, the Rangers swept up and over the Germans. In the short furious fight, the Rangers prevailed. Among the dead was the good soldier Hans.

Until November 27, the 4th Battalion remained in fighting bivouac, running patrols and experiencing intermittent shelling. The winter war had racked men's bodies, and thoughts of home and comfort were often with them. Thanksgiving brought a real Thanksgiving dinner of hot turkey, potatoes, and gravy. The men were appreciative of the hot meal that the cooks had worked hard to prepare. On the 26th, an Austrian deserter identified himself as coming from the 29th Panzer Grenadier Division, old acquaintances of the Rangers. At 1200 on the 27th, the 4th Rangers were relieved by the 180th Infantry and moved to a bivouac area at Caiazzo to rest and reorganize.

On the 28th, Major Murray[1] took the morally courageous course of writing through channels to the commander-in-chief of the ground forces of the United States Army. Murray addressed the need for "a clear-cut directive." He sought official recognition of the Rangers as a permanent force. Murray wrote about the lack of trained replacements and the difficulties of taking men from overseas replacement depots and training them in combat to be Rangers. Murray asked that one hundred graduates a month be sent from the Camp Forrest Ranger Training Center. If this were done, Murray wrote "our replacement problem would no longer exist, and we would continue to be an effective fighting force without interruption."

Murray wrote of the advisability of taking battle-experienced Ranger officers from the battalions already in combat and placing them in command of newly formed Ranger battalions. This would provide the oncoming Ranger units with experienced leadership and give outstanding Ranger officers a chance to move up to higher command. Murray also recommended that Ranger officers, disabled physically or by wounds, could be well placed as training personnel at the Camp Forrest training center. Thus their experience would not be lost.

Finally, Murray wrote about the need for a force headquarters patterned after the British Combined Operations

Staff. This organization could, Murray wrote, "handle administrative problems, intelligence, long-range planning, the allocation of assignments to the various battalions, and, most important, decide if the assignment is a proper one for Rangers."

Major Murray recommended Lt. Col. William O. Darby, the senior battalion commander of the Rangers, as the best-fitted man to head up such a Ranger staff.

The wisdom of Roy Murray's observations would be proven again and again in future Ranger experience.

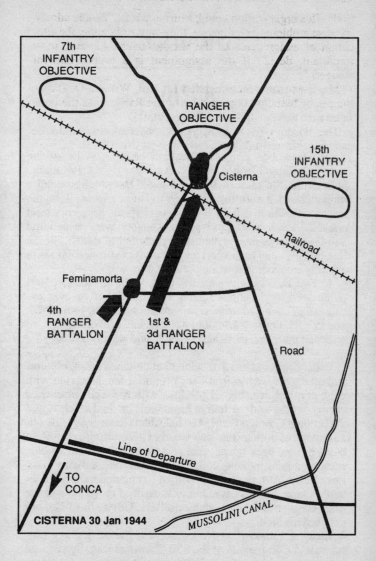

7th
INFANTRY
OBJECTIVE

RANGER
OBJECTIVE

15th
INFANTRY
OBJECTIVE

Cisterna

Railroad

Feminamorta

4th
RANGER
BATTALION

1st & 3d RANGER
BATTALION

Road

Line of Departure

TO CONCA

CISTERNA 30 Jan 1944

MUSSOLINI CANAL

CHAPTER 7

ANZIO

On December 1, 1943, England once again heard the sound of Ranger boots. Happy to be free of their military-police role, the men of the 2d Ranger Battalion boarded a train and took a nighttime journey to Bude, Cornwall, on the west coast of England. At Bude were cliffs the Rangers would come to know well, and some Rangers were issued the Browning Automatic Rifle and all learned to use it. The 2d Rangers also had the experience of living in private homes in a family environment while preparing for war.

At Fort Dix, New Jersey, the men of the 5th Ranger Battalion were undergoing final preparations before overseas shipment. They had arrived in New Jersey on November 20, and Lt. Col. Owen Carter and his men had been training hard on speed marches, tactical problems, and weapons firing.

In Italy, the cold hand of December clutched the mountains, and mud gave way to iron-hard ground. Men, shivering with cold, climbed ever higher to close with the well-entrenched enemy. Winter and the Italian mountains favored defense, and the brilliant German Field Marshal Albert Kesselring took full advantage of both terrain and weather. Kesselring's men were being pushed back but at great cost to the Allies—each ridge, each mountain took its toll. Faced with long casualty lists, grim-faced American and British commanders peered at battle maps. Success was being measured in yards, and the main German defensive positions, "The Gustav line," had not yet been reached.

Leaving Caiazzo on November 29, the 3d Ranger Battalion and Company B of the 83d Chemical Battalion moved by truck on a five-and-one-half hour ride to Venafro. II Corps wanted a limited reconnaissance of the area approaching the village of San Pietro. E Company drew the mission and sent several patrols forward within fifteen hundred yards of the village. The Germans were not there and the patrols moved to the vicinity of Ceppagna.

On December 4, Bing Evans's Company F made a reconnaissance along the northern slopes of Mount Sammucro. The key terrain in this area was Hill 950, part of a sawtooth ridge that overlooked San Pietro.

The 3d Ranger Battalion was now attached to the 36th Infantry Division. At 1200 hours the battalion moved from its base near Venafro to an assembly area 1000 yards southeast of Venafro. At 1800 hours the battalion moved west through Ceppagna, then north out of the village along the lower slope of ridge running northwest to Hill 950. About one thousand yards short of the objective, fire from two German machine guns engaged the Ranger scouts. The Rangers eliminated the guns and pressed forward, with E and F Companies in the assault. By 0600 hours December 8, the objective was taken.

The Americans did not hold the position long. At daylight, German machine guns, firing from the slopes of Mount Sammucro, made the hilltop untenable. Company B of the 83d Chemical laid down a screen of smoke for the Rangers. Hard hit, E and F Company were withdrawn to Hill 773. The 4.2 inch mortars came under heavy counterbattery fire. One platoon of Company B suffered 50 percent casualties. Meanwhile, a Ranger patrol located an enemy strong point and destroyed it by using small arms and artillery.

Again the order came down to take Hill 950. Under a heavy barrage of artillery that began at 0530, the Rangers swept up the slopes and Hill 950 was back in Ranger hands by 0600. Three German prisoners were taken. The withdrawing Germans contented themselves with pounding their lost position with artillery. Small German patrols probed the Ranger positions on December 10 but they were driven off. In the dark hours between December 10 and 11, the relief of the 3d Ranger Battalion by the 3d Battalion, 504 Parachute Infantry Regiment, began. The relief was completed by 0100 hours December 14. The 3d Rangers then withdrew by stages through Ceppagna and Vairano to an area near Pozzuoli.

The battles of the Venafro were different than the amphibious assaults and night reconnaissance the Rangers had trained for. At Venafro the Rangers experienced the strain of constant battle. Men who endure prolonged combat often suffer its many effects. Dr. Sheldon "Charlie" Sommers of the 1st Ranger Battalion found brave men suffering from battle burnout. Noncommissioned officers, who had distinguished themselves in battle, would come to Dr. Sommers and say, "Doc, I can't take it any more." Sommers would keep these men in the medical area about two hundred to five hundred yards behind the rifle pits. The battle-weary men would make coffee and perform chores. After a week or so of rest, they recovered their stability and went back to their units.

The Rangers were experienced soldiers and knew the tricks of reducing casualties from small-arms fire. Artillery, however, was another matter. Dr. Sommers found that the overwhelming number of casualties he treated were from shell fragment wounds, especially from the German 88mm gun. The much maligned steel helmet proved its worth; Dr. Sommers did not encounter any helmet penetration, though he did treat several men with scalp creases from deflected bullets or shrapnel.

On December 14, the 1st and 4th Ranger Battalions departed the Venafro area and moved to Lucrino Station in the vicinity of Naples. On the 20th, the 3d Battalion moved to join its sister battalions. This began a period of rejuvenation. Darby set aside some days in which men, worn down from a year and a half of stress and combat, could enjoy a movie, a swim, or an Italian woman.

While at Lucrino, the Rangers were visited by their old friend, Father Basil, who held Sunday morning services. The deep affection the Rangers felt for the man they considered the "Ranger Chaplain" was shown in a collection plate filled to the overflowing.

The officers of the 1st Ranger Battalion had a special treat when they met the nurses of the 225th Station Hospital. The occasion resulted in a great party at a castle south of Naples. An observer reported seeing Bill Darby and the head nurse looking at each other "like two eagles." It was a lively party with wine and music, and at least one marriage resulted.

Lucrino was also a lively place for Maj. Roy Murray. He was promoted to lieutenant colonel on December 30. It was at Lucrino that Murray, in an effort to give his battalion some distinction, allowed the men of the 4th to grow mustaches. The 4th Rangers responded with a will. When Bill Darby saw this happy band of hirsute Rangers, his West Point eyes went into a spin. Darby visited Murray and decreed that the mustaches had to go. Murray stood up for the unique gesture he had given his men. Most of the officers in the Rangers were from the Army Reserve or National Guard, and they would frequently joke with Darby, telling him that he couldn't run the Rangers if it was not for the Reserve and Guard. Darby would reply by thanking God that it only took one Regular to keep this unruly bunch of citizen-soldiers in line. The 4th Battalion was Roy Murray's command. Though Darby did not much like the mustaches, he did not require their removal.

Murray's next adventure occurred during a trip to Naples. His jeep was stolen. When the military police recovered the vehicle, they found that Murray had left a map of Italy inside the glove compartment. The map was unmarked. Maps of Italy were in profusion, and at the time, this map probably had less military value than a roll of toilet paper. But to the officers of the Criminal Investigation Corps, Murray's map was the opportunity to prove their worth. The investigators descended upon Lieutenant Colonel Murray, lectured him, and demanded he apologize. Murray gave the investigators his views on a variety of subjects, but he would not apologize.

The result was a January 5, 1944, written administrative reprimand filled with shock, grief, and paternal outrage. It was what old soldiers call a "horseshit and gunsmoke" paper. The document was addressed to Murray and signed by M. F. Grant, an administrative colonel of the Fifth Army headquarters. Having done their duty, the CIC went back to their usual business, and an unchastened Roy Murray went back to the war.

The rest period did not last long. Once again the recruiting of new volunteers and the hard training process began. Over and over the Rangers practiced night amphibious landings. Another major operation was in the wind.

While the men of the 1st, 3d, and 4th were receiving a well-earned rest, the 2d Ranger Battalion moved on December 27 and 28 to Titchfield, Hampshire County, on the south coast of England. Combat seemed close now.

On January 9, the great ocean liner HMS *Mauritania* sailed from New York harbor, bearing among its troop contingent the 5th Ranger Battalion. Nine days later the *Mauritania* docked at Liverpool, England, and the 5th Rangers moved by train to Leominster, England. Training began immediately.

Since the birth of the 3d and 4th Ranger Battalions at Nemours in Africa, these battalions had operated independently or under Darby as "senior battalion commander." The disadvantages of trying to control three battalions without a headquarters and staff were obvious, but the War Department would not permit a permanent command structure such as the birth of a Ranger regiment. The substitute was to allow the formation of a temporary unit known as the 6615th Ranger Force (Provisional). The Headquarters Company of the 6615th would consist of ten officers and one hundred enlisted men.

Bill Darby was promoted to colonel, with Lt. Gen. Mark Clark doing the honors. On January 16, the 6615th Ranger Force (Provisional) came into being.

With Darby in command, Herman Dammer became executive officer and S-3 (operations officer) of the 6615th. The S-1 (personnel officer) was Capt. Howard Karbel, the S-2 (intelligence officer) was Maj. William Martin, and the S-4 (supply officer) was Capt. Frederick Saams. A West Point classmate of Darby's named Jack Dobson was brought in to command the 1st Battalion. Maj. Alvah Miller who had been a Ranger since Achnacarry and Dammer's executive officer in the 3d, now became commander of the 3d Battalion. Roy Murray remained in command of the 4th Battalion.

The British General Alexander's 15th Army Group, with its main forces of the American Fifth and the British Eighth Armies, was having hard going in the high mountains of Italy. Kesselring's Southwest Army Group hung on to terrain grimly. The situation was intensely disturbing to Prime Minister Winston Churchill. Churchill knew the political benefits to the capture of Rome would be enormous: Axis pride would be badly shaken by the loss of one of the most famous cities in the world. Churchill pressed for an amphibious envelopment—a landing to the rear of the German Army that would jeopardize the German positions, trap large numbers of the enemy, and effect a speedy capture of Rome. Churchill wanted a "wild cat," thrown on shore. What he got was "Shingle."

Operation SHINGLE became a plan of attack along the Gustav line, with a simultaneous amphibious envelopment at Anzio, a seacoast town but forty miles from Rome. General Lucas with his VI Corps was given the mission of a night landing on beaches in the vicinity of Anzio to seize and secure the beachhead and then advance in the direction of the Colli Laziali (the Alban Hills). Located some seventeen miles from Anzio, the Colli Laziali is a large and dominant hill mass, possession of which controlled the roads to Rome.

The Allied Mediterranean forces were headed by the British Gen. Maitland Wilson and consisted of layers of British and American command. There were three key players on the Allied side. The British General Alexander commanded 15th Army Group which controlled Allied forces in Italy. One of the armies of 15th Army Group was the American Fifth Army under the direction of the Gen. Mark Clark. To execute Operation SHINGLE, General Clark chose the American VI Corps commanded by Gen. John P. Lucas. These three commanders had an uneasy relationship.

In the battles of priority between the British and American staffs, the great fight continued to be over the importance of Mediterranean or "soft underbelly"—Churchill's peripheral operations—as opposed to direct cross-channel assault as desired by the Americans. The Americans had given way to Churchill several times on this issue and were adamant. Operation OVERLORD, the cross-channel invasion of Europe, had to move to the top of the list. The Mediterranean under British control was left with the mission of drawing off and tying down German forces. Churchill and his generals delayed, argued, and cajoled to the best of their considerable abilities to keep forces in the Mediterranean. Churchill wanted Rome with a lover's ardor—he was determined to have it.

Faced with preparations for OVERLORD and fighting in the broad reaches of the Pacific Ocean, the United States Navy kept up an unrelenting struggle to draw off landing craft from the Mediterranean. Their success hurt operation SHINGLE.

The loss of shipping greatly reduced the amount of men and material that could be put on the Italian shore in the first wave of the landing—there was only sufficient transport to move two divisions. Then the convoys would have to return to Naples and embark the follow-on force. Several days would pass before additional muscle, including the armored division, could be landed.

The American VI Corps commander, John P. Lucas, was not in favor of the plan and compared it to Winston Churchill's disastrous Gallipoli campaign in World War I. At this stage of his military life, John Lucas was in a bad mental state for a commander. He was opposed to the operation he was leading, pessimistic, concerned, and indeed fearful that his forces would be trapped and annihilated.[1]

While Generals Alexander and Clark, as commanders above corps level, were expressing great optimism about an aggressive move on Rome, they were approving a Lucas plan that was geared to securing of the beachhead with infantry divisions followed by cautious movement forward.

General Lucas would land with his 1st Division (British) on the left (north) on Peter Beach. The Ranger Force would be in the center at Anzio, and the 3d Infantry Division (U.S.) would land on X-ray Beaches to the right (south). The 504th Parachute Infantry Regiment would make an airborne assault, beginning one hour before the beach landing, to seize the high ground north of Anzio and establish roadblocks to prevent German reinforcement and harass the enemy.

The fire support plan was rather curious. Supposedly in the interest of effecting a surprise landing, the navy was instructed not to fire prior to the troops landing. The exception to this was three rocket ships. One rocket ship was allocated to fire on each one of the beaches from H minus 16 to H minus 5. Surprise and rocket ships are an unlikely combination. Rocket ships were more noted for the terror their noise and enormous firepower generated than for stealth and accuracy.

On January 15, 1944, VI Corps sent the Ranger Force its mission orders. The Ranger Force consisted of the 1st, 3d, and 4th Ranger Battalions, the 509th Parachute Infantry Battalion, the 83d Chemical Battalion (4.2-inch mortar), and Company H of the 36th Engineers.

The Ranger Force had the mission of landing at 0200 hours D-day (January 22) at Anzio. In priority the mission on landing was:

1. Seize port facilities in Anzio and protect them from sabotage.
2. Destroy any existing defense batteries in the vicinity of Anzio.
3. Clear beach area between Anzio and Nettuno.
4. Secure and establish beachhead.
5. Contact 1st Infantry Division on the left, contact 3d Infantry Division on the right, and contact 504 Parachute Infantry Regiment in the north.

On contact with the 3d Infantry Division, the Ranger Force would be attached to it.

The ships assigned to lift the Ranger Force were old friends, HMS *Royal Ulsterman*, the *Princess Beatrix*, and the *Winchester Castle*. Landing Ship Tank 410 and LCT 542 and 551 completed the Ranger fleet. There were insufficient craft to bring the Rangers in on one wave. The first wave would have to unload, then the landing craft would return to the mother ships to pick up the second wave.

The Ranger Force Administrative Order for Operation SHINGLE contains an example of passing on instructions from higher headquarters that men in battle ignore. In reference to prisoners of war, the report states: "Any personal effects taken from prisoners must be receipted for by an officer, receipt countersigned by the prisoner, and copy given to the prisoner." The statement is proof positive that there is humor in war.

On January 20, the Ranger Force completed loading at Baia, Italy, to the north of Naples. On the 21st at 1200 hours, the ships weighed anchor and sailed from Pozzouli Bay.

Through the afternoon and into the long night the quiet prebattle contemplation occupied the time and minds of men.

Uncertainty is often more dangerous than reality; the imagination can be the worst of enemies. At 2230 hours, the men were formed for disembarkation. The process of waiting and wondering intensified. By 0001 hours on January 22, the ships were anchored off the Anzio shore and landing craft lowered. The Germans expected a seaborne landing but thought it would come further north. In the objective area they were unprepared. From the boats, men could see lights on shore and the twisting, weaving headlights of random vehicles driving along the coastal road.

At 0145 hours, the rocket ship allocated to X-ray Beach opened the assault with the rush and roar of fire. In two minutes, the ship expended nearly eight hundred high-explosive rockets and fired the red and green flares that indicated "mission complete." At 0150 hours, the rocket ship supporting Peter Beach unleashed its fire. All was quiet in the Ranger area. The fire-support ship allocated to fire on the Ranger Yellow Beach from H minus 10 to H minus 9 minutes was off course. The guide boats and landing craft rendezvoused and proceeded toward shore. The landing was made with precision at 0200 hours.

By 0202 the DUKWs (an amphibious vehicle, often called a "duck") carrying the 4.2-inch mortars, their crews, and the engineers were formed up. At 0210 they proceeded toward shore. One of the DUKWs was carrying three 57-mm anti-tank guns. This DUKW had motor trouble and shipped so much water that it had to be abandoned. The rocket support ship was now in position, but the Rangers were already ashore. The ship commander signaled Ranger Force that it was too late for him to fire.

By now, minor artillery fire was coming from Germans in the X-ray Beach sector, and there was heavy firing in the British Peter Beach area.

Ranger Force first wave landed at Anzio Yellow Beach at 0200 with the 1st Rangers (minus A Company) and 4th Rangers (minus F Company) abreast. The 1st Ranger Battalion was on the left and the 4th on the right. H Company, 36th Engineers, provided detachments of one officer and eight enlisted men to both Ranger battalions. The landing was uneventful for the Rangers and accomplished in text-book fashion. Two Germans were killed by 1st Rangers east of the beach. At the center of the beach area was the Anzio casino. In training, Darby, partially in jest, told the navy he wanted to be landed at the door of the casino and the navy put him within a few feet of it. General Lucas had every reason to be delighted. Later Lucas would confide to his diary, "I sent the Rangers in on Yellow Beach primarily to save that harbor. Everything was prepared by the enemy for its demolition, great holes dug in the mole and in the sides of all the build-ings, all filled with explosive materials, but they had time to blow very few of them."

While the Rangers fanned out to clear the beachhead, the engineer detachments set up beach lights and began clearing a number of mines from the beach. At 0300 the 83d Chemical Battalion minus C and D Companies, came ashore.

The 57mm antitank guns were needed ashore to blast open a roadblock at the east end of the beach. Fortunately, an as-sault landing craft found the abandoned DUKW and towed it to land. The guns were manhandled into position against the roadblock and destroyed it.

At 0330 men of the 1st Ranger Battalion reported en-gaging a German armored car to the rear of the casino. After a cat-and-mouse game, the Germans were killed. The vehicle, a wheeled personnel carrier, was taken. Ten minutes later Roy Murray reported that the 4th Rangers were on their initial phase line.

At 0345 the second wave, consisting of headquarters and five companies of the 3d Rangers and Company A of the 1st landed. The 3d Rangers had the mission of passing through the 4th to clean the town of enemy and to protect the port facilities. All three of the Ranger battalions were told to be prepared to advance north on order.

At 0350 Murray reported some small resistance at a foot-bridge just north of the railroad line; fire was coming from small arms, backed up by a machine gun. This action began to heat up. Elsewhere, two Germans were killed and their radio-equipped Volkswagen captured. At 0420 a pesky German gun position was located, and Rangers moved to take it out. The Germans in the area were confused and unable to coordinate their actions. The Ranger log states "German troops scattered all over hell with no uniformity."

The Ranger Force command post was established in the Anzio casino. Darby used the SCR-300 radio to communicate to the *Ulster Monarch* to keep informed of the progress in unloading; the SCR-536 radio and messengers were the means of communication with the battalions.

At 0445 two reinforced companies of Lieutenant Colonel Yarborough's 509th Parachute Infantry Battalion, Company F of the 4th Battalion, and additional men of H Company, 36th Engineers, were landed. The 509th mission was to clear the beach area between Anzio and Nettuno and attack Nettuno on Ranger Force order.

With minimal fighting, phase lines were being reached and objectives secured. By 0600 reserve ammunition, the signal section, and surgical equipment were on shore. The Rangers were among the most experienced American veterans of amphibious landings. They had learned the importance of having critical supplies on shore early. Even men in the first wave carried additional mortar rounds and boxes and bandoleers of ammunition. Coming ashore, men of the first wave would drop the extra ammunition above the water line. The ammunition could be gathered later; the important thing was that it was on shore.

At 0620 more DUKWs landed, carrying 4.2-inch mortar ammunition and additional men of the 83d Chemical Battalion.

By 0700 all Ranger Force personnel had cleared the ships. The 1st, 3d, and 4th Ranger Battalions were all on the second phase line. By 0805 the 4th Rangers had killed the enemy force at the bridge while the 3d Rangers overran a four-gun enemy battery of 100mm guns at the west end of Anzio. At 0815 Darby ordered the 509th Parachute Infantry Battalion to move on Nettuno.

Midmorning saw increasing German artillery and air action—the Germans sweeping in over the 3d Division beaches, bombing and strafing. By 0912 Yarborough's paratroopers were two-thirds of the way to their objective, having killed six to eight Germans. German tanks were being reported coming on the main road to Anzio. Engineer parties found the harbor and its facilities mined and wired for demolition, but the charges had not been connected.

As the morning wore on, enemy scout cars were observed, and another air attack struck the 3d Division beach. By 1040 the Ranger Force had captured twenty-four German prisoners and five Russians that the Germans were using in a labor gang. Nine German vehicles were captured.

Four German tanks began firing at the 1st Ranger Battalion positions, but the tanks were firing at long range and were not accurate. The 509th reported a prisoner from the 29th Panzer Grenadiers. The British informed Ranger Force that British tanks were on shore. At 1413, the 3d and 4th Ranger Battalions and the 509th were given orders to move forward. The 1st Ranger Battalion remained in location in reserve. By 1630 hours, supply ships were bringing in additional men and equipment and unloading them in the harbor. The 3d Rangers made contact with the Scots Guards of the British 1st Infantry Division.

The day ended with a lone German gun firing on the harbor and port. The road to Rome beckoned, but the orders from VI Corps called for consolidation. General Lucas expected a prompt German counterattack.

This was, however, a moment of opportunity: Lucas was unaware that the Germans had but a few battalions between the beachhead and Rome. A swift dash forward by an armored column and the Eternal City would have fallen like a ripe plum. With the forces already on shore, Cisterna and the high ground of the Alban Hills could have been in Allied hands. But the fast-moving armored column that was called for was not available to exploit the successful landing. Due to the shortage of landing craft and the troop configuration of the landing plan, the American 1st Armored Division armor was still sitting on the docks of Naples. Even the infantry was not unleashed. Fearful of disaster, General Lucas created just that by consolidating on a low-ground beachhead. At a time of success and opportunity like few commanders ever knew, Gen. John Lucas confided to his diary, "The strain of a thing like this is a terrible burden. Who the hell wants to be a general."

The afternoon of January 23, Ranger contact was made

with the 2d Battalion, 7th Infantry Regiment, of the 3d Infantry Division.

On the 24th, the 509th Parachute Infantry Battalion moved to fill the gap between the Rangers and the 7th Infantry. Enemy activity was building up as German forces recovered from the surprise, and the Germans were increasing patrolling and artillery fire, while German armor was seen operating on the roads to the northeast of Carroceto. The Germans were blowing bridges and mining roads. The British reported that a prisoner claimed a German Panzer division was enroute to the beachhead.

Rumor is a constant foe in war: There was a report of German parachutists dropping on Anzio, and the Rangers prepared for a stiff fight, only to find it was the crew of a shot-down German plane that had parachuted to earth. The best way for a commander to separate rumor from fact is to see for himself. Bill Darby did just that by making a personal reconnaissance on a motorcycle.

On the 24th, an LST (landing ship tank) carrying C and D Companies of the 83d Chemical Battalion hit a mine and blew up. Survivors were transferred to another ship which also hit a mine. Nearly three hundred men of the Rangers' favorite support unit were killed or wounded.

The Rangers were now under 3d Division (General Truscott commanding) control. The 3d Division ordered the Rangers to cover the 1st Division (British) left flank as the British moved forward to take Carroceto. The 4th Rangers and the 509th Paras, with a platoon from the 601st Tank Destroyers, drew the mission.

The attack kicked off on the 25th, with the 4th Rangers and 509th passing through 1st and 3d Ranger lines and meeting little resistance. The 83d Chemical displaced forward to support the lead battalions while 1st and 3d Rangers went into reserve. Patrols maintained contact with the British on the left and the 7th Infantry on the right. Truscott did not feel the situation at the beachhead was static; his men were fighting hard, and he felt an all-out 3d Division attack to seize Cisterna would succeed. General Lucas denied the request to advance as he wanted to wait until American armor was on shore.

Action on January 26 was relatively light. Positions were improved, and although a German counterattack on the British spilled over to the 4th Ranger location, it was contained.

The Ranger Force command post displaced forward. More troops were coming ashore, but enemy resistance was stiffening. German artillery, believed to be of the self-propelled type, was bringing increasing fire to bear on the beachhead.

Offense and defense, the cycle of war continued. On the 26th, the Rangers were instructed to prepare their portion of a main line of resistance, site machine guns and mortars, prepare wire obstacles, and mine avenues of approach.

These orders were followed by instruction to move forward at dawn on the 27th. The 3d and 4th Rangers and the 509th Paras kicked off in the attack. Lt. Randall Harris, commanding officer of F Company, 4th Rangers, led his men in an attack on a well-defended road junction. The Germans were concealed in and protected by thick-walled stone farmhouses. Harris and his executive officer, Howard Andre, charged the objective with the newly arrived Lt. Edwin Case's 1st platoon. Under heavy fire, Harris brought in Lt. Edward Haerger's second platoon from the flank. Sergeant Hildabrant and Private First Class Bosika were killed and six other Rangers wounded but the Germans were routed. Lt. Howard Andre was killed in the attack by German gunfire. Andre had participated in all five amphibious operations including Dieppe. The loss of his leadership was a heavy blow. Lt. Edwin Haerger crawled under fire and killed the remaining Germans with a grenade. The attack continued, and by noon the Rangers had reached their objectives. The fighting was growing more intense. The Germans were making excellent use of the stout Italian farmhouses as strong points by siting machine guns and self-propelled artillery in and around them. On the left, the British were catching the main thrust of the German counterattacks. In the confusion of battle, there was misunderstanding over the boundary, and two of the Ranger battalions temporarily moved into British territory. When the boundary problem was cleared up, the Rangers once again received instructions to go on the defensive. A heavy-weapons company, Company H of the 179th Infantry, was attached to provide additional fire support.

On the morning of the 28th, numerous German patrols began to probe Ranger positions. The German artillery stepped up its fire, using variable time fuses to burst their rounds overhead. Lt. Hubbel Powell, commanding officer of Company A, 4th Rangers, was killed and First Sergeant Seigo was wounded by the bombardment.

Around 1600 orders came down from 3d Division that the Ranger Force would be relieved by the British 1st Reconnaissance Regiment. Something was in the wind, and the Rangers were required. During the night of January 28, the Rangers were relieved and moved to a wooded assembly area closing on their new location by 0700 on the 29th. The 509th Parachute Infantry Battalion and Company H of the 179th Infantry passed from attachment to the Rangers to assume other duties.

From the man in the foxhole to the highest command there was recognition that the Allied forces were stalled on low ground. The Americans and British were steadily being hemmed in by ever-increasing German forces, who controlled the key terrain.

In hindsight, General Lucas who commanded VI Corps (and was later relieved) has been much criticized for being overly cautious and slow in moving inland from the beaches of Anzio. Curiously, Lucas's seniors, General Alexander and Gen. Mark Clark, seem to have escaped the censure of history. As a British soldier, General Alexander would have placed himself in a touchy situation by relieving the American Lucas. General Clark, however, had both the authority and the responsibility to insure his subordinate performed as he desired. Alexander and Clark visited Anzio after the troops were on shore, and neither general expressed dissatisfaction. Lucas was left under the impression his dispositions were approved.

The Germans were delighted at the slow pace of Allied movement. Kesselring had anticipated an Allied landing, and the Germans had strong forces in Italy that they were convinced could annihilate a landing force. Indeed, the Germans welcomed the opportunity. The destruction of an Allied landing force in Italy might well cause the Allies to discard plans of a cross-channel invasion.

To prepare for the amphibious end run, German rapid-reaction forces had been designated and placed on an alert, but the constant strain of alert waiting had taken its toll on the German soldiers. To give them rest, Kesselring had ordered a stand-down. In a stroke of good fortune, the German stand-down had coincided with the Allied invasion.

The Germans were caught totally by surprise. Unflappable, their reaction was superb. Kesselring immediately began moving every available unit to seal off the beachhead. The perception that Germans were rigid in their thinking and could not innovate was dispelled when a diverse mix of units were quickly welded into a task force. A battalion here, a company or platoon there, from one unit or another, the mix of Germans blended together. Kesselring placed General Schlemmer, commander of the 1st Para Corps, in charge of organizing the German structure. Schlemmer drew heavily on German antiaircraft units that employed the famed 88mm gun, and a screen of 88s used as antitank and field artillery was quickly established around the beachhead. Other artillery units, including big railroad guns, were moved forward.

Whatever hope the Allies had of moving quickly inland was shattered. Within two days the Germans were confident they could hold and were planning their death-stroke counter-attack. The caution displayed by General Lucas was much appreciated by the Germans, but even the German generals remained divided in opinion as to whether Lucas had the option of moving rapidly forward successfully. In the first forty-eight hours, a fast-moving Allied column could have reached Rome, but holding it was another matter. It is possible that the defeat Lucas feared by a quick attack toward Rome could have been a real threat. Kesselring was a fighting commander, and a precipitous German retreat before the two infantry divisions Lucas could muster was unlikely. The choice of consolidating the beachhead may not have been the overcaution of a tired and sick man (as Lucas has been portrayed and as his diary seems to affirm) but rather a reasonable decision based on the information he had that the Germans would have been able to cut off and trap the meager forces he had available had they moved pell-mell on Rome. General Truscott felt an effort to seize even the Colli Laziali would have been a disaster. Field Marshal Kesselring believed he could have and would have destroyed such an endeavor. As for General Clark, if he did not approve of General Lucas's decision, it would have taken only a single order from him to get it changed.

If Cisterna and the high ground could have been promptly taken by Lucas, what was obtainable on January 20 or 21 was beyond achievement less than a week after the landing. The Germans quickly occupied the Colli Laziali, and their position was such that by January 28 Kesselring was ready to counterattack. Fortunately for the men on the beaches, the wily German field marshal could not bring it off. Allied airpower played a major role in disrupting his plans and delaying the Germans.

The attack was also delayed by the Germans biting on the bare hook of a false landing. The Allies had prepared fake plans for another amphibious assault at Civitavecchia on the coast north of Rome. Like all good deception, the plan was a credible threat. On January 28, German High Command passed the information to Kesselring's Southwest Army Group and to Mackensen's Fourteenth Army. The result was that German troops that were needed for an Anzio counterattack were withdrawn and sent north.

Meanwhile, General Alexander's troops were beating themselves bloody against stiff resistance at Mount Cassino, and the British general was willing to take the chance of German reaction at Anzio. Alexander wanted a combined attack on the Germans from both the Anzio and the southern front. Strong pressure by Alexander at Army Group was put, through Clark at Fifth Army, on Lucas at VI Corps to move inland. Feeling the heat, Lucas planned a two-pronged attack in the direction of the Colli Laziali on the morning of January 29. The main attack was to be made by the British and Americans on the left.

The British 1st Infantry Division and the newly arrived Combat Command A of General Harmon's American 1st Armored were to take the most direct route inland, the Albano road. On the left of the beachhead, the British were to advance toward the Colli Laziali from the southwest. To the far left, the rest of the 1st Armored Division would make a flanking movement and approach the Colli Laziali from the west.

The attack on the right would be made by the 3d Infantry Division along with the 6615th Ranger Force and the 504th Parachute Infantry Regiment. The mission of General Truscott's 3d Division was to advance and seize Cisterna di Latina and prepare to continue the advance to seize the high ground vicinity of Cori, a town southeast of the Colli Laziali. Cori would provide the 3d Infantry Division an elevated attack route to the Colli Laziali, while the possession of the Cisterna and Highway 7 juncture would endanger the German left flank and place the 3d Division in position to use Highway 7 to attack the Colli Laziali.

Truscott's 3d Division was up against the Herman Goering Division, an all-German, all-volunteer unit of the German *Luftwaffe*. If they had been fighting for the Allies, these men would have been called well-motivated and courageous; as they were the enemy, they were described as fanatical.

Intelligence reports were that the Germans were planning to fight a delaying action back to the high ground. It was believed that the German forward units were spread out, using a system of spaced strong points supported by mobile reserves. Truscott wanted to place American units in the enemy rear to disrupt the Germans' position and isolate the forward defenses. The in-depth, fire-interlocked, and interdependent German defense would be thrown into disarray by the sudden appearance of Americans among them, disturbing their fire support and striking their reinforcements. Innovation was essential as the American attack would have to be made over terrain that was primarily flat and open—a killing ground.

The small but important road and railroad center of Cisterna lay to the front of the 3d Infantry Division. Passing through Cisterna was the high-speed Highway 7, the famed Appian Way. Highway 7 led northeast to Velletri at the foothills of the Colli Laziali, then on to Rome. The known dispositions of the Germans seemed to indicate a forward, delay-oriented defense-in-depth in front of Cisterna that had sufficient open space for smaller American forces to penetrate.

Truscott planned to infiltrate units through German positions as a prelude to his main attack. The Rangers would lead this effort and would seize the important road communications center of Cisterna. Darby's men were to move rapidly by infiltration a distance of about four miles to Cisterna, destroy enemy forces there, then hold the Cisterna area until relieved. Though hampered by the loss of experienced men wounded or killed in the Anzio line battles, the Rangers offered the best hope of making a successful infiltration attack.

But infiltration was not limited to the Rangers. The 7th Infantry Regiment on the left of the Rangers and the 15th Infantry on the right each had one battalion infiltrating to assist their regimental missions of cutting Highway 7 above and below Cisterna. All infiltrating forces—the Rangers, the 7th Infantry, and 15th Infantry—would begin moving an hour before the main attack commenced. Both infantry regiments had tanks from the 751st Tank Battalion and tank destroyers from the 601st Tank Destroyer Battalion attached. The 751st Tank Battalion was told to have the remainder of its tanks ready to support the 7th and 15th Infantry attacks with a secondary mission of destroying any enemy force encountered along the Conca–Feminamorta road. The 504th Parachute Infantry Regiment had the mission of screening the 7th Infantry to the line of departure, then acting as 3d Division reserve. Truscott planned for all the attacks to have the support of tanks, tank destroyers, and 3d Division artillery.

Truscott consulted Lucas about his infiltration plan, and both concurred that it was a good use of the Rangers. According to Truscott, Darby also agreed, although a number of surviving Rangers insist that while Darby agreed and accepted his orders with a determination to carry them out, he was not in favor of the plan. The relationship between a commander and his driver often gives the driver insight into his commander's feelings: Carlo Contrera, Darby's driver, later told friends that Darby was angry at the orders and remarked, "The men are too tired for another raid." Contrera said that Darby was concerned about the limited amount of time for reconnaissance for the attack—most of the reconnaissance information the Rangers had to rely on had been done by other units. Lieutenant Porter, communications officer of the 4th, told fellow Rangers he had overheard Darby asking for more time to conduct reconnaissance and evaluate the "current situation." Les Kness, S-3 of the 4th Rangers, recalls hearing Darby say, "It is not my plan."

While the Americans and British were preparing to attack, the Germans had not been idle. Right or wrong, the cautious movement of Clark and his subordinate Lucas enabled the Germans ample opportunity to continue to bring in forces. To understand Anzio, one must appreciate that no part of the beachhead was free of the constant pounding of German artillery. Men burrowed like animals to escape a steady hail of shrapnel from the 88s, the 170s, and the monster railroad gun known as Anzio Annie. As his strength increased, the skilled German commander continued his plan to launch an attack that would destroy the beachhead and drive the Allies into the sea.

Though the German attack was delayed, German reinforcement units were still available for the Anzio area. In fact the German force now outnumbered the Allies. As the German units moved in, they found defensive positions that were ideal. Having the benefit of long experience in fighting on myriad fronts, the Germans had become extraordinarily skillful in the preparation of defensive positions. Dug in behind mine fields and skillfully camouflaged in stone houses, silos, and outdoor ovens, the Germans were ready. The Allies were ill-informed about the location of the German main line, thinking it was in the Colli Laziali foothills. On January 29, the 3d Division G-2 estimate of the situation stated that the German main line of resistance would "undoubtedly be found on true high ground both east and west of Velletri." But the Germans, intent on pinning the Allies against the sea, had their defenses six miles farther forward on a line between Campoleone and Cisterna. The American infiltrating units were going directly into the teeth of the German defense. Estimating enemy strength and disposition is a difficult business, and the 3d Division G-2 estimate on the 29th was not a good one. It described the German attitude as "entirely defensive," and said the German stock of tanks and artillery was "not good." The estimate also identified some newly arrived

German reconnaissance battalions, including the 26th Panzer Grenadiers, some or all of which might (along with other units) be earmarked for the Anzio–Nettuno beachhead. G-2 believed that air reconnaissance and civilian or prisoner reports would identify newly arrived German divisions before they could counterattack.

General Lucas was deeply worried about the outcome, but under heavy pressure from Alexander and Clark, Lucas and his command made ready to attack on January 29. Fate, however, had a way of playing with even the best-laid plans. The British 1st Division planned to seize their line of departure using the Grenadier Guards, but enroute to a briefing on the operation, the Guards' officers ran into a German position and were shot down. Lucas reported in his diary that the Guards' commander, second-in-command, and all company commanders were either killed, wounded, or captured. The loss was so significant that the British requested and received a twenty-four-hour delay in the attack. This also resulted in a twenty-four-hour postponement of the American advance.

During that twenty-four-hour period, more German soldiers arrived on the battlefield. In the stone farmhouses around Cisterna, men of the Herman Goering Division watched as a newly arrived Panzer unit dug in their guns and sealed the gaps in the German line. This was not the battalion-size 26th Panzer Grenadiers intelligence said was earmarked for the Anzio beachhead—this was the 26th Panzer Division, and they were waiting for the Rangers.

At 1300 hours on January 29, 1944, Colonel Darby visited Truscott's command post, where all regimental and attached commanders were briefed on the plan of action. Back at Ranger Force headquarters, Darby at 1800 hours briefed his battalion commanders. The 1st Ranger Battalion was ordered to cross the line of departure at 0100 hours on January 30, and advance by infiltration along previously reconnoitered routes to Cisterna, destroy enemy forces there, and prepare for counterattack. At daylight, the 1st Rangers were to send a patrol to the northeast to contact the 7th Infantry.

The 3d Ranger Battalion, with a platoon of 4.2-inch mortars attached, was ordered to cross the line of departure fifteen minutes after the 1st Battalion had cleared, follow the 1st, and assist the 1st in its mission. The 3d Rangers were ordered to engage any enemy force that attempted to interfere with the 1st. On arrival at Cisterna, the 3d Rangers were to occupy the ground to the northeast and prepare to meet an enemy counterattack. At dawn, the 3d Rangers were to send a patrol to contact the 15th Infantry.

The Ranger attack would cross an area shaped like a triangle. At the apex of the triangle was the objective, Cisterna. At the base of the left edge was the town of Conca. Between Conca and Cisterna—about two miles from Cisterna—was the hamlet of Feminamorta (Italian for "dead woman"), also called Isola Bella. At the right edge was the town of Sessano. The left edge of the triangle was the Conca–Feminamorta–Cisterna road. This was the axis along which the 4th Rangers would attack. To the right of the 4th Rangers, at an initial distance of approximately one-half mile, would move the 1st, then the 3d Rangers. To the right of the 1st and 3d Rangers and forming the right edge of the triangle was Highway 7. From Sessano, Highway 7 ran to Cisterna then on to Rome. Initially the 1st and 3d Rangers would follow an irrigation ditch (the Pontano Ditch), but as the ditch expired, the 1st and 3d would parallel the Feminamorta–Cisterna road.

Outlining his plan of action, Darby stressed the importance of the 1st and 3d Rangers reaching their objective by infiltration and avoiding enemy contact enroute if possible. The 4th Battalion, with an eight-man mine-sweeping party attached, was ordered to cross the line of departure at 0200 hours on January 30 and advance the four miles to Cisterna via the Conca–Feminamorta–Cisterna road, clearing the road of mines and enemy. On arrival at Cisterna, the 4th would become the force reserve. Cannon Company and a platoon from the 601st Tank Destroyer Battalion were in reserve, with orders to be prepared to move on Cisterna via the Conca–Feminamorta–Cisterna road. The designation of a cannon company as a reserve was unusual, but the order seems to signify its intended use as a supporting force.

In his memoirs, Truscott states the 4th Ranger Battalion attack was tank supported, but the 3d Division operations order shows no tanks being attached to the Ranger Force. However, a secondary mission of the few tanks that comprised the "remainder" of the 751st Tank Battalion was to destroy any enemy force encountered along the Conca–Feminamorta road. That order did not provide tank coverage from Feminamorta to Cisterna. The Ranger Force operations order contains no mention of American tanks. In the action that followed, the limited effort of American tanks and the ineffectiveness of artillery support is evident. The Allied air forces had air superiority and had a plan to support the attack, but the air cover was planned to support the movement of armor, not the infiltration forces.

About 1930 hours on January 29, Gordon Jackson, the Red Cross field director, brought a truckload of mail into the Ranger bivouac area. The tie with home could not have come at a better time. Thirty minutes later, the 1st, 3d, and 4th Ranger Battalions moved from their assembly areas to the line of departure. The sky was moonless and cloud-filled. Men had to reckon with both cold and mud, for though the temperature was chilly, underneath the crust the ground was not frozen. At midnight, Darby and his battalion commanders met at a road junction for a communications check and last-minute coordination, including the password which was "bittersweet." The identification plan included the use of colored flashlights flashing the letter R. On arrival at Cisterna, if no other communications were available, the 1st and 3d Battalions were to fire a series of red Very flares.

The ground was too soft for the 4.2-inch mortar platoon to accompany the 3d Rangers cross-country, so Darby sent it along with the mortars accompanying the 4th Battalion. The Force command post was established in a farmhouse, and wire and radio communication established with the 4th Battalion and 3d Infantry Division. Radio silence was in effect for the 1st and 3d Ranger Battalions until a phase line was reached.

Patrols from the 15th Infantry had reported that the houses along the route of the 4th Battalion were clear of enemy for some distance. Based on this information, the 4th did not expect it would have to fight before it reached Feminamorta. The patrol report proved erroneous. The Germans were in the fields, the houses, and entrenched behind minefields. In truth, the Germans were at Anzio in force: the number of Germans at Anzio now exceeded 71,000, at least 10,000 more men than the attacking Allies could field.

The 4th Rangers crossed the line of departure in approach-march formation (with scouts and flankers to warn of enemy contact), then divided into two groups. Companies C, D, A, and B moved three hundred yards east of the road and then proceeded north, paralleling the road. Murray, Les Kness, the S-3 (operations officer), and the radio operators were with this element. Companies E, F, and the remainder of the head-quarters under the S-2 (intelligence officer) moved in the ditches beside the road. Force headquarters elements followed E and F on the road.

The terrain was devoid of cover: a flat field interlaced with irrigation ditches that were some twelve inches deep. The 4th Rangers had moved forward approximately eight hundred yards by 0300 when the alert Germans opened fire. Machine guns, mortars, and small-arms fire raked the 4th Rangers. The Germans were dug in, well-camouflaged, and had a rifle pit about every ten yards, with machine guns spaced every hundred yards. Interlocking fire at about one-foot height made movement on the flat suicidal. In the lead, Lt. George Nunnelly's Company C took the initial brunt of the fire. In the next fifteen minutes, Company C deployed left while Company D deployed right. Neither could make headway. Then, trying to flank the Germans, Companies A and B moved to the right of Company D and attacked. Both A and B companies were immediately pinned down by the heavy enemy fire, and communication with the E and F Companies was lost. Lieutenant Nunnelly was among those killed. The wounding or death of Ranger leaders and the loss of their radios created significant problems in command and control.

By 0600, the 4th Rangers were forced to dig in where they were. They pounded the Germans with artillery and mortar fire, but the Germans were not moving. The 83d Chemical Battalion tried valiantly to support with the 4.2-inch mortars, but their base plates shattered on frozen ground.

Six to eight American tanks (the remainder of the 751st Tank Battalion) soon arrived in the vicinity of Darby's command post. Under the cover of the tanks, a German roadblock of damaged vehicles was removed; however, in the darkness, the tanks did not move to support the 4th Rangers.

The infiltration attacks by the battalions of the 7th and 15th Infantry Regiments were stopped cold by the Germans. The 1st Battalion of the 7th Infantry was badly shot up and by midmorning had gained less than one thousand yards; the 15th had even less success.

The 1st and 3d Ranger Battalions were well to the right of the 4th, moving north, parallel to the Feminamorta–Cisterna road. The route of advance was in a deep irrigation ditch which offered some protection from enemy observation, and the movement progressed satisfactorily through enemy positions. Moving as silently as they could, the Rangers worked their way through the German forward positions. They soon passed close by German mortar crews and artillery positions, where the Germans could be clearly heard giving fire commands. The Rangers could have destroyed these units, but the mission was Cisterna.

While the Rangers were moving, the Germans were attacking Anzio harbor with air and artillery. Several large explosions turned the night sky to daylight. This illumination along with German flares slowed movement forward. Daylight was coming, and the Rangers had to make Cisterna under cover of darkness.

Emerging from the ditch, the 1st and 3d Rangers began moving along the Feminamorta–Cisterna road. In the dim visibility of before morning twilight, Ranger Robert Ehalt, sergeant major of the 1st Ranger Battalion, saw a lone German paralleling the Ranger route of advance. The German was obviously puzzled by the force moving toward Cisterna. He stayed clear by a hundred yards and would stand and watch, then move forward again. The actions of this German were those of a man suspicious but uncertain. As the German neared a barn, he disappeared. Shortly thereafter, a German vehicle moved rapidly from the barn area, heading for the German rear.

Maj. Jack Dobson, commanding 1st Ranger Battalion, was in a dilemma. Communications had been lost with Ranger Force headquarters. This was a devastating loss. Dobson could hear the sound of heavy firing to his left and right rear, and it was clear that the forces assigned to attack on both flanks were being held up. The 1st and 3d Rangers were deep in enemy territory with the 4th Battalion some two miles distant. Dobson could turn and attack the German artillery units he had passed, driving to link up with the 4th, but that was not the mission. Knowing full well the seriousness of his situation, Major Dobson pressed on toward Cisterna.

The route, however, was now barred by a German bivouac area. Ranger scouts moved to knife the German sentries. Though an often-used scene in Hollywood war movies, the silent disposal of a sentry is rare and one of the most difficult feats a soldier can perform. Lt. James Fowler was expert at the task and killed several sentries, but his good fortune did not last. Ranger Don Clark remembers that one German died noisily, screaming and flopping about as his throat was cut. In death, he provided the alarm, and the German camp came alive. The Rangers swept in among the startled enemy shooting and bayoneting them: an estimated company of Germans died. But surprise was lost, daylight was at hand, and the Rangers had not reached Cisterna. The battle-experienced Germans began to quickly bring fire to bear on the Rangers. Eight hundred yards short of Cisterna, in daylight and in the open, the Rangers found themselves in the midst of an aroused German defense.

Ranger Sgt. Carl Key of the 3d Ranger medical detachment later reported that the 3d Ranger Battalion was moving in a column of companies at dawn and had crossed Highway 7 and was moving north toward Cisterna in a stream bed, when they were fired upon by Germans fortified in houses to their right. Other German troops began to advance toward the battalion. Major Miller ordered three companies forward toward Cisterna while three others took up defensive positions to cover the movement. The Cisterna mission was foremost, and platoons were leapfrogged to the head of the column to continue forward progress while being covered by fire. The German attack was halted, but Maj. Alvah Miller, commander of the 3d Ranger Battalion, was killed by German artillery. Shortly thereafter, German light tanks came down Highway 7 from Cisterna and opened fire directly into the backs of the Rangers who were in the stream bed. Sgt. Frank Mattivi rushed a German tank with a grenade, leaping on the tank just as it was hit by a Ranger bazooka. Though bounced up in the air, Mattivi came down unhurt. Opening the tank hatch, he threw the grenade inside. While Mattivi was so occupied, his friend, Sgt. Tom Fergen, was attaching a sticky grenade to the side of the tank. One tank crewman appeared and Fergen shot him. This tank was destroyed, but others were causing heavy casualties. Busy with his duties as a medic, Sergeant Key lost track of the battle action until he found himself looking into the guns of a German squad and was captured.

Around 0700, Darby reestablished radio communication with Major Dobson by SCR-610. Dobson reported that he was located about eight hundred yards south of Cisterna and that three German self-propelled guns were giving him a good deal of trouble. He also reported that the 3d Battalion was to his east and that Major Miller had been killed. Just before communication was again lost, Dobson radioed that he was wounded but that progress was being made toward Cisterna. The 1st Battalion fought hard to gain a low ridge to the front of Cisterna, then to get a foothold in the town near the railroad station.

Darby ordered E and F Companies of the 4th Rangers to attack along the left side of the Feminamorta–Cisterna road. There was progress for a few hundred yards, then the two companies were pinned down. Casualties were heavy. Lt. Orin Taylor, commander of E Company, was killed, along with Lieutenant Case, the F Company platoon leader, who had just joined the Rangers.

Darby ordered Lt. Otis Davey, who had replaced Captain Shunstrom as the commander of Cannon Company, to take two half-tracks and two tank destroyers and try to break through the Germans holding up the 4th. The courageous Davey asked for volunteers and led off in an M-10 tank destroyer. The Ranger 75mm-cannon-mounted half-track *Ace of Diamonds* was directly behind him.

Passing the 4th Battalion, Joe Cain, who was on *Ace of Diamonds*, saw Germans in emplacements and lying in drainage ditches along the road. Cain was trying to bring the .30 caliber machine gun to fire on these Germans when the lead tank destroyer hit a mine. Undeterred, Lieutenant Davey jumped from the burning vehicle and climbed aboard *Ace of Diamonds*. In the confusion of battle, Cain was trying to swing the .30 caliber to fire and the traverse was blocked by Davey's body as he ordered the driver forward. *Ace of Diamonds* had gone but a short distance when it, too, hit a mine. Cain does not remember any German armor in this action, but a German 88 also hit *Ace of Diamonds*. The other American vehicles withdrew. Davey, Cain, and the remaining survivors tried to make it back to friendly positions. Cain was shot in the head, but other Rangers were able to help him return.

The 4th Battalion attack was completely stalled. Backed by accurate artillery and mortar fire and fighting from farm houses, buildings, and emplacements, the Germans were beating off the 4th Ranger mortar-supported attacks. At dawn the 4th was unable to make a penetration and had not gained contact with the 1st and 3d Battalions.

Around 0800 Ranger Force headquarters reestablished radio communications with the 1st Battalion. The 1st reported that it was fighting to gain a foothold in the outskirts of town and in the vicinity of the railroad station. Artillery fire was requested on the northern and western portion of town. Observation of the effects of the fire was reported as "impossible," so the fire was discontinued. Throughout the action, the absence of American artillery support for the 1st and 3d Battalions was devastating, though communications failure and intense enemy fire contributed to the difficulty in using artillery. There are indications that when leaders were hit, subordinates, many of whom were new to the Rangers, did not have the skill to call for and adjust artillery.

The Germans, meanwhile, were blanketing the Ranger attack with their own artillery fire. The Ranger Force command post also came under fire. Maj. Bill Martin, the Ranger Force intelligence officer, and Darby's clerk, Cpl. Presley Stroud, were killed.

As the German forces converged on the Rangers with tanks and flak wagons, the men of the 1st and 3d Battalions were increasingly scattered and less able to fight as a unified force. First Sgt. Donald McCullem of Company B, 3d Battalion, led an attack to seize a German-held farmhouse then beat off a determined German counterattack. There were numerous occurrences of individual heroism. There are also reports that some of those newly arrived and ill-trained troops promptly surrendered.

A German tank-infantry team advanced toward the remnants of Dobson's 1st Battalion, pulling surrendering Rangers from the ditches and forcing them to move in front of the column with their hands over their heads as they moved forward. When they could pick their targets, Dobson and his men opened fire on the Germans. The German infantry then began to shoot and bayonet the prisoners. The survivors were herded forward.

Around noon, the report was received that the 1st and 3d had been badly shot up and were surrounded. Enemy tanks and self-propelled guns were causing great damage. Shortly after noon, the report was received that the Rangers had been scattered and were being taken prisoner in small groups. Darby had intermittent radio communication with Sgt. Maj. Robert Ehalt of the 3d Battalion. Darby's intense frustration came through in an exhortation, a pleading to keep fighting and await help. Placing his hope on his veterans, Darby said, "Get the old men together and lam for it." Holed up in a farmhouse, with but ten men left to fight and ammunition nearing exhaustion, Ehalt continued to give battle, but the end was near. Two German tanks closed on the farmhouse and fired high-explosive rounds into the roof. An English-speaking German officer called upon the men to surrender or be killed. Around 1230, Ehalt radioed Darby that the battle was over and he was destroying the radio. Darby said, "Ehalt, I leave everything in your hands. Tell the men I am with them to the end."

At the farmhouse headquarters of Ranger Force, stunned officers and men looked numbly at each other. Trying to hold back tears, Darby asked his men to give him some time alone. For a few minutes Bill Darby gave himself over to grief. Then, recovering his composure, Darby moved to the field telephone and reported the loss of two of his battalions to 3d Division.

Near Cisterna, the Germans rounded up their captives. A German ordered the medical officer of the 3d Rangers to join a group of prisoners. The American doctor protested that his place was with the wounded. The German raised his pistol and shot the medical officer through the face, killing him.

Throughout the morning, 4th Battalion had continued to try to come to the aid of the 1st and 3d but was unable to penetrate the German defense.

Company E of the 4th had destroyed two enemy machine-gun positions and captured a building which overlooked the enemy main line of resistance[2] at a distance of about 150 yards. Throughout the night of the 30th, the 4th held its position, with intermittent exchanges of fire with the Germans. A, B, and E Companies were forward, with D Company serving as a reserve for A and B; C and F Companies were placed in battalion reserve.

Darby now ordered the 4th Battalion to attack at 1100 hours January 31 to seize two fortified houses near Feminamorta along the Conca–Feminamorta–Cisterna road. The mission of leading the attack was given to F Company of the 4th Rangers. With Howard Andre dead and Randall Harris wounded, Lt. Jim Altieri[3] was transferred from Company C to be the company commander of Company F. Jim Altieri—like Bing Evans, Ed Dean, Les Kness, Peer Buck, and other men who had earned battlefield promotion—had begun his career with the Rangers as an enlisted man. Starting as a T/5 (a technician corporal), Altieri had risen through the ranks to serve as a first sergeant and, on commissioning, a platoon leader.

Altieri received his orders in a meeting with Lt. Col. Roy Murray; Maj. Walter Nye, 4th Battalion executive officer; and Lt. Les Kness, the 4th Battalion operations officer.

Altieri decided to lead his men along the limited protection offered by an irrigation ditch. The bodies of dead Rangers from Altieri's platoon in Company C were still in the ditch—a silent testimony to the German machine gun that covered this approach. Altieri knew of the machine gun and planned to eliminate it with 60mm mortar fire; 4.2-inch mortars would bring fire onto the German positions in the farm houses. Two tanks and two 75mm guns of the Ranger Cannon Company would support the attack.

Shortly before 1100, Lt. Otis Davey came forward with the

tracked vehicles. As he opened the hatch and raised his head to talk with Major Nye, a German sniper killed Davey with a single shot in the temple.

At 1058, the supporting mortar fire began. At 1100 hours, Altieri led the way up the ditch. The Germans responded with heavy mortar, artillery, and machine-gun fire, but the F Company mortars did their job silencing the machine gun that covered the ditch. Though men were hit, the Rangers continued forward. As they neared the objective, F Company, with Company C in close support, used fire and maneuver to attack the two German positions. The combat was now hand-to-hand, but both houses were taken in heavy fighting. With these German positions eliminated, a mine-sweeping party was able to move forward and quickly clear the German mines, many of which were merely laid on top of the road.

Major Nye led the tracked vehicles forward, firing a .50 caliber machine gun in support of the F Company attack. Twenty German prisoners were taken, nineteen Germans were killed, and thirteen were wounded. Supported by two tanks and Company A, D Company of the 4th took several more farm houses. Company A took eleven prisoners and D Company eight. Behind the Rangers came the 3d Battalion, 15th Infantry, with tank support. German infantry began to rise from their positions and surrender. Approximately 150 more German prisoners were taken.

In the afternoon, the 15th Infantry passed through the 4th Rangers. The Rangers were then given the mission of guarding the Conca–Feminamorte–Cisterna road.

General Clark blamed the loss of the two Ranger battalions on General Truscott, saying that Rangers were unsuitable for such missions. Truscott responded that he had been responsible for organizing the Rangers and knew better than others what they were capable of. Truscott said both he and Darby felt the mission was proper for the Rangers, though Truscott accepted responsibility. Lucas also informed Clark that he had approved the plan and that he, too, accepted responsibility. Nonetheless, Clark was concerned about adverse publicity and ordered an investigation to fix responsibility, but with the men of the 1st and 3d Rangers in German POW camps, the investigation was a paper exercise that served no useful purpose save to delay criticism of events in Fifth Army.

From February 1 to 4, the Ranger Force and 4th Ranger Battalion remained in position, though the 4th Rangers were relieved of attachment to the 6615th Ranger Force and instead attached to the 504th Parachute Infantry Regiment on February 1. The 83d Chemical Battalion was relieved from attachment to the Rangers and attached to the 45th Infantry Division.

Later, a prisoner of war (a Polish private) stated that the attack on Cisterna was expected by the Germans. A newly arrived paratroop regiment had been moved into the area south of town. The prisoner claimed that the infiltration movement of the 1st and 3d Ranger Battalions had been detected early on and the destruction of the two units was caused by closing in on the triangle of roads south of Cisterna. The prisoner stated that some troops had made their way into town, but he did not know anything further of them. Some historians have used the report of this prisoner to characterize the action as the Rangers walking into an ambush.

That the Germans expected an attack on Cisterna is likely—naturally they would consider such a possibility; that the Germans knew the Rangers would infiltrate and set a trap is unlikely. It stretches the imagination to believe that German commanders would share their plans with a Polish private soldier impressed into German service. Prisoners often tell what they think their captors want to hear. The Germans won the battle honors that day, but they do not deserve the credit of having knowingly set a trap for the Rangers. It would be uncharacteristic of them to allow the Rangers to move close to artillery positions that the Rangers could have attacked, cut sentries' throats, and destroy a company of infantry in the hope that the Rangers would then walk into a trap.

American intelligence was not accurate concerning the location of the German main line of resistance. The Germans, building their forces for their own attack, had moved in units the Americans did not expect to be there. These German forces had skillfully prepared a defense in depth, and their leaders were aggressive and experienced. The Rangers did penetrate the German forward defenses, but delays prevented them from reaching Cisterna under the cover of darkness. When the Germans discovered the Rangers, the German re-action was timely and efficient. Caught in open fields in day-light by a numerically superior force of experienced German infantry with tanks and self-propelled artillery at hand, the result was inevitable. The comments of the men reflect vary-ing views:

"It was that screaming of that sentry," Ranger Don Clark later said.

"If we only would have had one more hour of darkness," was Ranger Robert Ehalt's comment.

Other contributing factors worthy of consideration include the loss of experience that was bled out of the Rangers in the Salerno campaign. This loss may have harmed the Rangers in the infiltration phase: during the night movement there were breaks in the column that delayed the advance. While training reduces this type of problem, it does not eliminate it. Only those who have led a column of men in night infiltration during war can truly appreciate the sneeze, the stumble, the noisy fall, or the exhausted soldier who falls asleep during a pause that can break the line of men moving through the night. It happens even in well-trained units. Sometimes it goes unnoticed by the enemy; sometimes it doesn't and the price is dear. That some untested men quickly surrendered during the battle at Cisterna points up the lack of proper training.

There have been numerous times in twentieth-century warfare when trapped units have used firepower to pin down the enemy while they break contact. At Cisterna there was a breakdown in fire support; air support was available to cover the armor advance but was not given to the Rangers. The ab-sence of American artillery in the final battle of the 1st and 3d Ranger Battalions was commented on by numerous sur-vivors. Faulty communications certainly played a role in this, and as the Germans closed in among the Rangers, the oppor-tunity to break contact through fire support was lost.

Even had the two Ranger Battalions succeeded in getting into Cisterna, the results would probably have been unchanged. Success depended upon the supporting attacks, and friendly forces could not break through.

A thirtieth anniversary report to the Ranger Battalions Association put the statistics of 1st and 3d Ranger Battalion Cisterna losses at 12 killed, 36 wounded, and 743 captured. At Anzio the same report listed 4th Ranger Battalion casualties at fifty-eight wounded and thirty killed. Most of the 4th's casualties were taken trying to break through to their sister battalions. Before taking them to prison camps in Germany, the Germans paraded the captured Rangers through the streets of Rome. Making full use of their triumph, the Germans insured their guards were large and well uniformed. The Italian reaction was mixed. Some men remember bitterly that youthful fascists threw garbage at them. Other men recall Italians trying to give water and making signs of support.

The Allied attacks at Anzio and at the Gustav line on the southern front were both failures. By February 3, VI Corps was on the defensive. In turn, the Germans attacked and were stopped. Then began the long stalemate, the prolonging of the agony of Anzio. It would not be until May 25, 1944, that Cisterna would fall to the Allies.

At Anzio there was grief and frustration at the loss of the 1st and 3d Ranger Battalions. The 4th Battalion guarded the road lines of communication from February 1 to 3. Murray's men then moved into a forward bivouac area where they remained under intermittent artillery fire until February 10. After five days of illness, Roy Murray was hospitalized with jaundice. Walter Nye took command of the battalion.

On the 10th, the 4th Rangers were attached to the 504th Parachute Infantry Regiment and placed in reserve. This was unlike reserve duty as most units knew it. Dug in near the Mussolini Canal on positions that covered Highway 7, the Rangers waged daily battle in a war of small-arms, mortar, and tank fire. Company A held a secondary line, with a mission of being prepared to counterattack. B and C Companies were on an outpost line, with a secondary counterattack mission. D and E Companies were guarding a bridge on the main line of resistance. F Company was in support of E and also had a counterattack mission.

From February 12 to 16, there was a series of combat patrols to contact the enemy and, if possible, bring back prisoners. The Germans were not biting; both sides were building up their strength. Artillery and air attacks continued from both sides.

On February 17, General Lucas appointed Col. William Darby as commander of the 179th Infantry Regiment, 45th Infantry Division. Arriving when the 179th was under attack, Darby characteristically went forward. Under Darby's strong leadership, the 179th held its ground and went on to build a distinguished record.

Ranger patrols continued on the 18th. The Germans were some five hundred yards distant, so it was not a long walk to find a fight. Both sides continued to pound each other with mortars and artillery. Ranger reports reflect great pride in the effectiveness of American counterbattery fire.

German patrols were also active, backed up by flak wagons and by self-propelled guns that were demonstrating great daring. A cat-and-mouse game was going on between American tank destroyers and a pesky German self-propelled gun. The German would move up to within seven hundred yards of the Ranger position and would hide behind buildings. Suddenly the gun would rumble into view and fire, at what seemed like point-blank range. Ten to twenty rounds would be fired, and the German would head for cover from counterbattery fire. The American tank destroyers would fire back, trying to root him out.

On the 25th, a Ranger patrol, under heavy fire, came back with a man unaccounted for. Patrols and counterbattery fire continued from the 26th through the 29th. Both the Rangers and the Germans were well dug in and with considerable firepower. In addition to their normal armament, the 4th Rangers had on line three .50 caliber machine guns, six heavy and thirty light machine guns. All bridges leading in had been blown and antitank and antipersonnel mine fields laid. This was all backed by 60mm and 81mm mortars, 4.2-inch mortars, artillery, tank destroyers, and tanks.

The Germans tried several attacks on areas adjacent to the Rangers. They used a miniature unmanned tank filled with high explosives to clear a path—it did not work well, and neither did the German attacks.

Through February and into March, the 4th Ranger Battalion remained attached to the 504th Parachute Infantry Regiment. With the beachhead at stalemate, the 4th Battalion spent much of its time on line in an aggressive defensive posture.

An overtone to the battle was the constant use of artillery. The Rangers could engage machine guns, tanks, and mortars, but the German 170mm artillery was out of reach. Any movement observed on either side brought a rain of shrapnel. In this environment, men on patrol moved in darkness across the shell-pocked ground, the pop and hiss of flares oscillating to earth giving an eerie aspect to the night sky. Freezing in position until the flare extinguished, the men moved on. There was barbed wire to penetrate, and both sides hung tin cans filled with small stones on the wire. These rattle cans were designed to give early warning. The barbed wire was covered by fire, tied in with the sometimes concealed mine fields. The incessant artillery fire cut telephone wires, and small parties of wiremen hurriedly traced wire, looking for the breaks.

The days of March saw three men of the 4th Rangers killed in action. Three more died of wounds and eighteen others were wounded in action.

At 2400 hours on March 22, the 4th Ranger Battalion was relieved from the 504th Parachute Infantry Regiment and attached to the 1st Special Service Force. The 4th Battalion remained in position until March 25, when it was relieved of all assignments to Fifth Army. Outpost positions were relieved by the 158th Infantry at 2000 hours and the 3d Regiment, 1st Special Service Force, relieved the Ranger companies on line.

Then on the 25th, the 4th Rangers moved to a bivouac area, where on the 26th they were separated into two groups. Men designated as veteran personnel from the battalion and Ranger Force headquarters were to be returned to the United States. This group totaled 19 officers and 134 enlisted men. The remainder of the men who had not accrued sufficient overseas and battle time to be considered for return home were transferred to the 1st Special Service Force.

On March 27, 1944, at 1030 hours, Lt. Col. Roy A. Murray,

Jr.'s 4th Ranger Battalion, consisting of 19 officers and 134 men, left the Anzio beachhead and sailed for Naples, enroute home to the U.S.A.

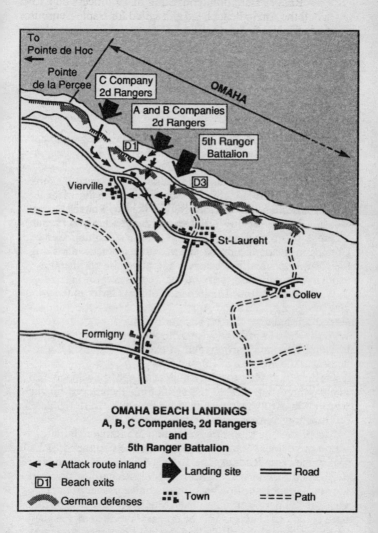

OMAHA BEACH LANDINGS
A, B, C Companies, 2d Rangers
and
5th Ranger Battalion

◄─ ◄ Attack route inland   ◆ Landing site   ══ Road

D1 Beach exits   ░░ Town   ==== Path

▨ German defenses

CHAPTER 8

D-DAY PLANNING

On April 1, 1944, the 2d Ranger Battalion was one year old. The battalion celebrated with a birthday party that included skits and spoofs that spared no one.

On the 2d, the 5th Ranger Battalion began travel by foot, boat, and rail from Tignabruich, Scotland, and on the 3d the 2d Ranger Battalion moved from Bude—the two Ranger Battalions met in Braunton in North Devonshire, England, and began a course of instruction at the U.S. Assault Training Center. Coming in on amphibious landings, the men practiced making their way over fortified beaches and attacking fortifications, using live ammunition, demolitions, and flamethrowers.

While at Braunton, Lieutenant Colonel Carter received a new assignment. Around April 17, Maj. Max Schneider assumed command of the 5th Ranger Battalion.

At the end of April, the 2d and 5th Ranger Battalions moved to Dorchester and participated in exercise "Fabius 1," a rehearsal of the invasion of Europe.

On the 6th of May, the 5th Rangers moved to Swanage, England, where they honed their climbing techniques on the steep cliffs. At Swanage, light machine guns were replaced by Browning automatic rifles.

May 9 saw the union of the 2d and 5th Ranger Battalions into a provisional Ranger group under the command of Lt. Col. James Earl Rudder. The Ranger Group was attached to the United States Army V Corps. Maj. Richard Sullivan of the 5th Ranger Battalion became executive officer of the Provisional Ranger Group, and the group staff was drawn from both battalions. The months of preparation, the emphasis on amphibious assault, cliff climbing, and violent action was now coming to fruition.

* * *

In the history of man's endeavors, few rival the scope, the magnitude of the World War II cross-channel invasion of Europe which began June 6, 1944. Planning for the assault began within six months after the United States entered the war and was pressed forward rapidly to help relieve pressure against the Soviet Union.

In 1942 the Germans were on the offense in Russia and the Soviet republics, killing millions and devastating the countryside. Stalin desperately needed Allied action in Western Europe to draw off German divisions that were hammering his army. With the great manpower and material potential of the United States entering the war, the Russians were clamoring for a second front. But even by 1942, the British had not forgotten the horror of the loss of a generation in the trenches of World War I. A cross-channel invasion could be but a prelude to another such murderous stalemate. Well into 1943, Churchill and his generals pursued a peripheral attack strategy. The astute Churchill also looked farther to the future. Churchill knew that Stalin's Russia was no friend of democracy: Joseph Stalin was ruler of a totalitarian state, a butcher of his own people, and a repressive dictator, who had cooperated with Hitler in the seizure of Europe until his own country was attacked in a falling-out of territorial thieves. Churchill was not inclined to trust such a man.

President Roosevelt and the Americans were single-minded about the defeat of Hitler. Roosevelt felt he could deal with Stalin. The Americans had the optimism and the naivete of the unbloodied. Though treated to Communist scorn and the theft of its technology, the United States would provide an incredible amount of war material to Russia, material that included over seven thousand tanks. In Asia, the Soviets were content to sit on the sidelines in the war with Japan until the moment of victory, while in Europe the Russians were suffering enormous casualties and tying down the bulk of the German Army. They fully expected America and Britain to open a second front against the Germans.

Not content to let the totalitarian states of Germany and Russia tear each other apart, the feeling in Washington was to get on with it: Germany was the enemy, the objective. General Marshall wanted to strike for the Nazi jugular.

In mid-1942, under pressure from the Americans and Russians, planning for the invasion began under a joint staff headed by the British Lt. Gen. Sir Frederick E. Morgan. In May 1943, at a Washington meeting with their staffs, Churchill and Roosevelt decided to launch a cross-channel invasion in 1944.

Meanwhile in Berlin, Adolph Hitler and his generals were poring over their maps. Nineteen forty-three was a year of dramatic change of German fortunes: more and more the Germans were being forced onto the defensive. Hitler had long boasted of his impenetrable "Atlantic Wall," but that was mostly propaganda. The French coast was weakly defended, stripped of troops for use in Russia. In November 1943, faced with the probability of invasion, Hitler ordered the improvement of defenses along the English Channel coast. To inspect the coastal defenses, Hitler sent a man the Allies feared, Field Marshal Erwin Rommel. Rommel's report was grim; the Germans were not prepared.

In the debates that followed, two strategies emerged. One view, which became personified by tank expert Field Marshal Gerd von Rundstedt (commander in the west), held that it was impossible to defend all the shoreline. Von Rundstedt's adherents wanted to hold strong mobile forces back from the coast. Wherever the Allies choose to come ashore, powerful rapid-reaction forces would move quickly to annihilate the beachhead.

The opposing view was represented by Field Marshal Rommel (who commanded Army Group B). Understanding Allied airpower, Rommel did not believe German mobile forces would have freedom of maneuver. When the invasion force came, Rommel believed it must be destroyed by shore defense forces as it landed or pinned down until close-in mobile reserves could come forward to complete the job.

At the outbreak of World War II, the German military machine was a model of efficiency, and the principal of unity of command had carried them far. The command structure broke down, however, and bickering between commanders and Hitler's meddling created military fiefdoms. Of the ten Panzer divisions available, Hitler kept four under his direct control, three went to General Blaskowitz whose Army Group G was in the South of France, and three went to Rommel's Army Group B. Though a tank expert and ostensibly the commander in the west, von Rundstedt was left without a tank division.

Rommel got his beachhead defense and the 2d and 21st Panzer Divisions and the 12th SS-Panzer Division, but the Panzer divisions were kept farther to the rear than he desired, and the commitment of them had to be cleared by Adolph Hitler.

"When and where will it come?" was the German question. "When and where should it go?" was the question of the Allies. Around the clock, day after day, month after month, thousands of men and women worked to develop the answers.

Both sides knew that in order for the Allied attack to succeed, it would have to be accomplished in three phases: lodgment, buildup, and breakout. Starting late, the Germans hurried to make a study of possible Allied landing sites. In Normandy, Rommel's shoreline defense took advantage of the steep cliffs where there were few places that provided an exit from the beach. The German plan was to secure these exit areas with fortified emplacements.

Work was in full swing by April 1944, with thousands of laborers and soldiers involved. Shortages of concrete and steel hampered the German effort, but the result was formidable. Tidal flats and beach shingles were sewn with irregularly shaped lines of obstacles. Landing craft and tank obstacles included an iron frame shaped like a gate but supported to fend off a landing craft. There was a line of heavy wooden beams sunk in the earth, pointing at the invader. There were steel beams welded at cross angles in such a manner that they would tear the hull of a landing craft. These obstacles often had powerful mines attached to them. Minefields and concertina wire[1] covered by machine guns were interspersed to hold infantry in place while they were shot down. Concrete emplacements for guns and troop shelters for infantry were often connected by communications trenches and tunnels and could support each other by fire. Where possible, the German weapons were sited to provide enfilade[2] fire down the line of the attacking troops, and effort was made to use grazing (low level) fire. It being better to shoot your enemy in the legs than shoot over his head, the Germans made strenuous effort to site their machine guns so they would fire no higher than two feet above the earth.

Machine guns, light and heavy artillery, and mortars filled the emplacements. Weapons have no national loyalty. Many of the artillery pieces used in the German defense had been captured from the French, the Poles, and the Russians.

The Allied intelligence gathering effort was relentless. The German manpower shortage required much of the construction of beach defenses to be done by slave or local labor. Underground resistance units provided a wealth of information on the burgeoning German defenses. In an incredible feat of daring one French contractor was able to hide and smuggle out a blueprint of a complete section of beach defenses. Aerial reconnaissance and visits by Commando parties also contributed valuable information. As the Atlantic Wall became reality, the Allies were well informed. In reviewing the Allied options, Hitler began to believe the landing would come in the Pas-de-Calais area northeast of the Seine River. There were good ports there, and the Germans reasoned the Allies would want to use the shortest route across the channel, one that would allow them to reach Germany in the most rapid manner.

The Allies were tempted to use the Pas-de-Calais area, but seeing the German buildup there, they opted for Normandy. An elaborate and successful deception plan played to the German belief that the Pas-de-Calais area was the objective. Even while the landings were occurring in Normandy, many of the best German divisions were held from battle, expecting the Pas-de-Calais landing that never came.

Among the many worthwhile features of a western Normandy landing was that it had excellent beaches within the range of Allied air cover. Thumblike, the Cotentin Peninsula juts into the English Channel. To land at the base of the thumb would put the Allies within striking distance of the great port of Cherbourg. The Allied planners also looked upon the ports of Le Havre and Brest with hungry eyes. Getting ashore was only a beginning: to succeed, an enormous quantity of men and material had to quickly pass through the funnel of the beachhead and spread over western Europe. Within four months of the decision to invade, the location was determined. In August 1943, the planners had their orders. The invasion site would be over forty miles in length. Stretching from the Orne River to beyond the Vire estuary, the invasion area included good beaches interspersed with steep and formidable cliffs.

Six months after landing site selection, in January 1944, General Eisenhower arrived from North Africa to assume command of the operation. Though the invasion plans were already on course, Eisenhower brought much to the effort, including increasing the number of assault divisions from five to nine. Often underrated as a strategist and tactician, Eisenhower has been better known for his knack of getting men of diverse nations and temperaments to work together toward their common goal. Given the prima-donna personalities of commanders Eisenhower dealt with, his success was beyond an accomplishment, it bordered on a miracle.

The British got the lion's share of command. Allied ground forces would be led by the feisty General Montgomery. Naval operations would be under the control of Adm. Sir Bertram H. Ramsay. Allied air forces would be directed by Air Chief Marshal Sir Trafford L. Leigh-Mallory. Among the greatest of burdens of the invasion preparation was the one carried by the American Lt. Gen. John C. H. Lee. Lee's Services of Supply was charged with the buildup of the largest and most comprehensive collection of war material in history.

The Allied force numbered 2,876,000 men. Over four thousand hulls would cleave the waters of the English Channel as the two great seapowers of the world combined forces. Twelve thousand Allied aircraft would take to the sky and forty-five divisions were ready for battle.

Allied air power was first into action. Through 1943 and into 1944, American and British airmen paid the high price to wrest control of the air from the Germans. Enemy aircraft factories and airfields were bombed repeatedly. To delay or preclude German ground reinforcement, railroad centers with their marshaling yards and rolling stock were laid to waste. The price was high, but Goering's vaunted *Luftwaffe* was beaten. The Allied air victory had a major impact on German operations in Russia. As the invasion date approached, Allied fighters and bombers made Herman Goering's name a curse on German lips.

Master of the set-piece battle, General Montgomery methodically planned his assault. Two armies consisting of nine divisions would make the initial assault. Three divisions of the British 2d Army would land on the Allied left, going in over three beaches, code-named Gold, Sword, and Juno. General Omar Bradley's American First Army would land on the right.

Consisting of V and VII Corps, U.S. First Army planned to enter Europe by day, employing the two corps abreast on two beaches designated Omaha and Utah.

Due to tide changes, the VII Corps would land first, coming ashore twenty minutes earlier on the east coast of the Cotentin Peninsula at Utah Beach. VII Corps would make the amphibious assault with the 4th Infantry Division. The 82d and 101st Airborne Divisions would make an airborne assault inland behind the German coastal defenses in the VII Corps area.

Given the code name Omaha, the six-thousand-yard beach between Vierville and Colleville was to be the main landing area for the American forces. The V Corps of the United States First Army, which included the 1st and 29th Infantry Divisions, would make this assault. The landing area was initially only sufficient to hold a reinforced division, but the plan called for an immediate expansion from Omaha Beach on a two-division front.

Thus, the assault plan called for a task force configuration. Task Force O under the command of Maj. Gen. Clarence Huebner, commanding general of the 1st Infantry Division, would make the Omaha Beach landing. On the left (east) would be the 16th Regimental Combat Team of the 1st Division. On the right, with the mission of making the assault on the western Omaha beaches and pushing inland in the direction of Grandcamp and Isigny, would be the 116th Regimental Combat Team of the 29th Infantry Division. Each of the attacking regiments would have two battalions in the attack with a third in support. Brigadier General Wyman, assistant division commander of the 1st Division, would be the senior man on Omaha Beach. Assisting him in the area of the 116th Regimental Combat Team was Brig. Gen. Norman Cota, assistant division commander of the 29th Infantry Division.

When Task Force O had completed its landing, Task Force B, consisting of the remainder of the 1st and 29th Infantry Divisions (reinforced), would make follow-on landings under the command of Major General Gerhardt of the 29th Division. The follow-on regiments of the 1st and 29th would join their divisions, and the two-division front would move inland, joining with flanking British and American forces to exploit the landing.

The statistical scope of the invasion can be misleading. In the nature of large military efforts, a relatively small number of men would make the first-wave landings. At Omaha Beach, the infantry element consisted of eight rifle companies (four each from the 16th and 116th Infantry Regiments) and Company C of the 2d Ranger Battalion.

Key terrain in the American sector was Pointe du Hoc. This natural fortress was a jutting point of land, a dagger point thrusting toward England. Here the flat farmland of Normandy ended in sheer and often overhanging cliffs eighty-three to one hundred feet high. Beneath these foreboding cliffs was a narrow, rocky, surf-pounded beach. Pointe du Hoc dominated Omaha and Utah, the two beaches on which the Americans were to land.

The Germans were quick to grasp the importance of Pointe du Hoc in their defensive scheme. Masters of the use of artillery fire, the Germans positioned a battery of six 155mm guns, captured from the French, on top of the cliff. Able to fire at ranges up to 25,000 yards, the guns could sweep both Omaha and Utah Beaches and cover the approach lanes almost from the point where the landing craft would cast off from the troop-carrying ships.

Strong natural positions, however, have a tendency to make the defender overconfident. Intelligence reported that the area of the Ranger assault was defended by troops of the German 726th Infantry Regiment of the 716th Infantry Division. Gen. Wilhelm Richter's 716th had been in the Normandy area since May 1941. Many of the men of the division were considered old for infantry combat. By 1944, the 716th had a high percentage of non-Germans pressed into its units. Intelligence did not consider the 716th a top-line German fighting unit. The German battery of artillery was guarded by an under-strength infantry company of approximately 125 men.

A reinforced-concrete observation post was placed well forward on the point. From here the German forward ob-servers could oversee both beaches and the sea, and direct the fire of the guns located to their rear. Primary positions for the guns were two casemates and four open emplacements. As workmen and material came available, the Germans intended to place all the guns in casemates.

Rommel's officers considered an assault up the cliffs un-likely, but they took precautions nonetheless. Barbed wire was emplaced along the top of the cliffs, and artillery shells were suspended in such a manner as to be exploded in the face of a cliff climber or dropped to explode on the beach. On top, a series of interlocking trenches and dugouts contained firing positions for machine guns and antiaircraft guns.

Of great concern to Allied intelligence was the German 352d Infantry Division, thought to be in training and reserve around St. Lo. Initially formed in October 1943, the 352d had a cadre of combat-hardened, experienced officers and non-commissioned officers from the Russian front. In January 1944, the 352d moved to the Cotentin Peninsula.

Gen. Dietrich Kraiss, commander of the 352d, was a fight-ing general and had to be. The German High Command often lived in a world of self-delusion, congratulating themselves when a new division was formed at the stroke of a pen; get-ting that division manned, equipped, and trained for combat was a matter for underlings. Kraiss struggled with his chain of command to get the weapons and equipment his men needed, and when the supplies were forthcoming, he trained them well.

In March 1944, the 352d was moved forward into the coastal defense, including the Omaha Beach area. By June, the German High Command considered the 352d Infantry Division among its best units.

Pointe du Hoc was the lock on the door to Europe. What was needed was a key, and the Allied planners tried several.

Air bombardment was an obvious choice. On April 15 and 25, May 22, and June 4, a rain of bombs fell upon the Pointe.

Aerial photographs showed severe damage to the cliff-top positions, including at least two of the emplacements. The Allied planners would like to have bombed this critical area incessantly, but to do so could tip their hand. It was decided to use air bombardment and naval gunfire to the maximum just prior to the landing. Heavy bombers of the RAF and the fourteen-inch guns of the battleship *Texas* gave the Pointe a workover on June 5 and 6, and American medium bombers made a last pass twenty minutes before H hour.

The planning staff understood that, while air and naval support could cause great damage, only men on the ground could insure control.

The mission was extraordinary; to accomplish it, motivated men must be trained in an extraordinary manner. To eliminate the guns of Pointe du Hoc, the planners directed the organization of a Ranger group, consisting of the 2d and 5th Ranger Battalions. Lt. Col. James Rudder, commander of the 2d Ranger Battalion, would lead the operation against the guns of Pointe du Hoc. Lt. Col. Max Schneider,[3] commander of the 5th Ranger Battalion, would serve as second-in-command.

The elimination of these guns on Pointe du Hoc was the primary mission of the Ranger group on D-day. In planning, all of the 2d Ranger Battalion (except for Company C) and all of the 5th Ranger Battalion were earmarked for the task.

There is evidence that, prior to the landing, senior officers of the 2d Rangers believed the guns had been moved from their forward positions. At least one intelligence map showed the notation "guns removed." This may have compounded the planning problem for Rudder but did not diminish the necessity of the mission. Guns that have been moved from a position can be returned to it or placed in an alternate position. It was critical to the invasion that German artillery not be allowed to fire from Pointe du Hoc.

To accomplish his overall mission, Colonel Rudder planned to use three elements designated Force A, B, and C. Force A would land three companies of the 2d Ranger Battalion simultaneously. E and F Companies would land on the eastern (left) side of Pointe du Hoc, and D Company would land on the west. While the assault companies were climbing the cliffs, seizing the Pointe, and eliminating the guns, Lieutenant Colonel Schneider with Force C (the 5th Ranger Battalion and Companies A and B of the 2d) were to stand off-shore, prepared to follow the three assault companies by thirty minutes.

In Force A, each of the ten boatloads of men in the three assault companies had a specific mission of top priority, the eliminating of the guns. When the Pointe was taken, Force C, the remaining eight Ranger companies, would land. The Ranger group would then move rapidly to the south. The second mission was to close a blacktop road that connected Vierville and Grandcamp. Blocking this road, the Rangers would hold position until linkup with the 116th Infantry of the 29th Infantry Division.

If Rudder's group failed to take Pointe du Hoc, Schneider was to land A and B Companies of the 2d Ranger Battalion at H plus 60 minutes and the 5th Ranger Battalion at H plus 65 minutes in the Eighth and Ninth waves going in on Omaha Dog Green Beach behind Company A of the 116th and Company C of the 2d Ranger Battalion. Schneider would then lead the 5th and A and B Company of the 2d in an overland attack to seize Pointe du Hoc.

To help insure the success of the primary plan, a twelve-man, fire-support group from the United States Navy and a forward observer from the 58th Armored Field Artillery Battalion would accompany Colonel Rudder's headquarters.

The third Ranger Force was Force B, consisting of Company C of the 2d Rangers, commanded by Capt. Ralph Goranson.[4] Company C Rangers had a unique mission. Omaha Charlie Beach on the extreme right of the 116th Infantry was the Ranger company landing site. The plan here called for Company B of the 743d Tank Battalion to come ashore in amphibious tanks at H plus 5 minutes to establish a base of fire. Company A of the 116th Infantry would follow the tanks at H plus 1 minute. At H plus 3 minutes Company C of the 2d Rangers would land to the right of Company A of the 116th. This landing would place the Company C Rangers west of Vierville at Pointe de la Percee, some three miles to the east (left) of where D, E, and F Companies were to land at Pointe du Hoc.

After landing, Goranson's company was to climb the cliffs at Pointe de la Percee, move east in the direction of Pointe du Hoc, seize the high ground, and eliminate enemy emplacements. These emplacements were located to provide a deadly flanking fire on the forces landing on Omaha Beach. When the emplacements at Pointe de la Percee were destroyed, Company C was to move westward along the cliffs to Pointe du Hoc, destroying any enemy positions they encountered until linkup with the 2d Rangers.

To prepare themselves for their mission, cliff climbing was a major vehicle of training. They were not taught cliff climbing by British or American experts. In the beginning, cliff, rope, and man were introduced to each other by trial and error. In May 1944, the men honed their self-developed skills on the steep cliffs of Swanage, Dorset, and other points along the English coast.

Innovative means had to be used to get the Rangers to the cliff tops. Various types of ropes and ladders were used. Rocket-fired, grapnel-equipped ropes were the primary tools of ascent. The three assault companies of Force A would be coming ashore in ten LCA landing craft, each carrying around twenty-two men. Each of the LCAs was equipped with grapnel-tipped rockets, mounted in pairs, at the bow, amidship, and stern. Behind the rocket was a box containing the coiled ropes. The pairs of rocket-launched ropes could be fired by one man, and each rope set was different. One rope set consisted of three-quarter-inch ropes, and another set of ropes had short rounded pieces of wood called "toggles" inserted approximately every four feet. The final pair consisted of rope ladders made of half-inch rope. In each LCA were two portable rockets with light-weight ropes. These could be carried ashore and fired from the beach. Ladders of several types were included in the planning. Four-foot-long sections of tubular steel ladders, each weighing four pounds, could be handed up and added to the top as the climb progressed. In the realm of the bizarre were four DUKWs equipped with extension ladders of the type used by fire departments. The DUKWs were to come out of the water, cross the beach, and lay their ladders on the cliff. These ladders, when fully extended, could reach to a height of one hundred feet. At the top of each ladder was a pair of Oerlikon machine guns.[5] One can only imagine what the reaction of a man would be when told his D-day mission was to fire machine guns while totally exposed, clinging to the top of a hundred-foot ladder.

The Rangers would wear fatigue uniforms, and some commented that they were dressed for summer while the Germans were in winter garb. Those men designated to be first to climb the ropes were to carry as little extra weight as possible. Some climbers favored the light-weight carbine but most stayed with the M-1 rifle or the Ranger firepower weapons: the Browning automatic rifle (BAR) or the Thompson submachine gun (the tommy gun).

In addition to ammunition, most of the men carried cast-iron-cased fragmentation grenades. Thermite grenades[6] were distributed among each company, and demolitions men carried a roll of C-2 explosive around their necks. 60mm mortars and 81mm mortars would follow the assault wave to shore. Food and even water were of lesser consideration. Each man was provided with a single food bar called a D bar. The plan was that when the man's pack came ashore in the accompanying supply craft, additional rations would be in the pack.

On June 1, the Ranger group moved from Marshaling Area D-5 in Dorchester, England, by motor to Weymouth for embarkation. Companies A, B, and C, with Colonel Rudder's command element, boarded HMS *Prince Charles*. Company D with the 2d Platoon of E Company went aboard HMS *Amsterdam*, while Company F, the 1st Platoon of E Company, and headquarters personnel were on HMS *Ben Machree*. Colonel Schneider's 5th Battalion boarded HMS *Prince Charles* and the Belgian ships HMS *Leopold* and HMS *Prince Baudouin*.

From June 2 to 5 was a time for final briefings. These briefings were very detailed, using sand tables and models, aerial maps and photos, and reports of the latest intelligence. Care of weapons and equipment, cards and contemplation, and an occasional shipboard movie passed the time.

On June 3, the men were informed that D-day would be June 5, H hour 0610. Bad weather caused a postponement.

On the 4th, the men were informed H hour was planned for 0630 on June 6, 1944.

At 0415 hours on June 5, General Eisenhower made the decision that, despite bad weather, he would launch the invasion. At 1630 hours on June 5, 1944, the Rangers sailed for France.

Much of the cross-channel trip was rough but uneventful. At 0200 there was an air-raid alert without result. To breakfast or not was a man's choice. Hot coffee, hot cakes, and seasickness pills served as breakfast for many.

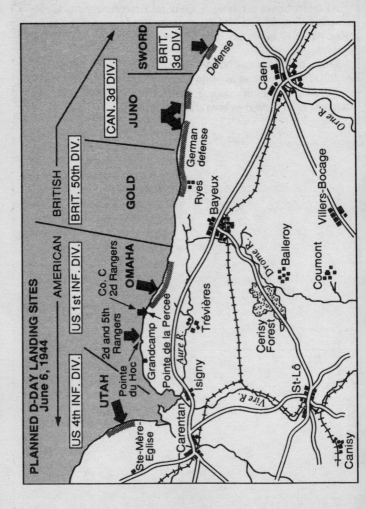

PLANNED D-DAY LANDING SITES
June 6, 1944

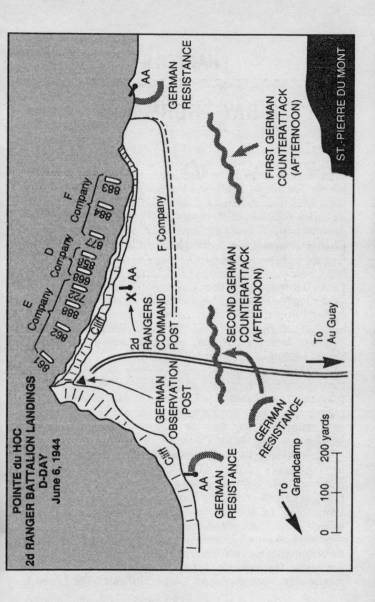

POINTE du HOC
2d RANGER BATTALION LANDINGS
D-DAY
June 6, 1944

E Company

D Company

F Company

Cliff

2d → X ⟶ AA
RANGERS COMMAND POST

F Company

AA
GERMAN RESISTANCE

ST.-PIERRE DU MONT

FIRST GERMAN COUNTERATTACK (AFTERNOON)

SECOND GERMAN COUNTERATTACK (AFTERNOON)

GERMAN OBSERVATION POST

Cliff

GERMAN RESISTANCE

AA
GERMAN RESISTANCE

To Au Guay

To Grandcamp

0   100   200 yards

CHAPTER 9

D-DAY—NORMANDY

In the dark hours of the morning of June 6, 1944, ten miles off the Normandy coast, the Ranger missions began. Lowering away from the *Prince Charles* at 0430, the three officers and sixty-five men of Company C (Force B) moved to rendezvous with the boats of Company A of the 116th Infantry. Charlie Company was divided between LCA 418, containing Captain Goranson and Lt. Bill Moody's 1st Platoon, and LCA 1038 with Lt. Sid Salomon's[1] 2d Platoon. One of the men on LCA 418 was Sgt. Walter Geldon of Bethlehem, Pennsylvania; June 6, 1944, was his third wedding anniversary.

The run into shore was made through heavy seas, and many of the men were violently sick. Ahead, piercing the darkness, were the red glare of rocket ships and flashes of bombs landing on the Normandy coast.

At 0445, the Landing Ships Infantry *Ben Machree* and *Amsterdam* unloaded their cargo of D, E, and F Company Rangers of the 2d Battalion (Force A) into the assault landing craft for the hour trip to shore. The seas were rough—a four-foot chop so strong that the Germans did not believe a landing was possible.

The cold spray soaked men to the skin, and the constant toss and heave of the small boats made stomachs queasy. Water began to fill the bottoms of the boats, and when pumps failed in several craft, men had to bail with their helmets. At about 0530, LCA 860 carrying Captain Slater and twenty men of D Company foundered.

Some men drowned. Rescue craft moved in and pulled the survivors from the cold waters. Taken to England, they would not rejoin the battalion for nineteen days. Several of the supply craft were also experiencing difficulty. The D and E

Company packs were jettisoned to lighten the load. One supply craft sank, with but a lone survivor.

The remaining nine landing craft and supply boats of Rudder's Force A moved toward shore in a double column. The intent was that those in the rear would speed up to form an assault line as the beach was approached.

At 0545 the landing craft containing Col. Max Schneider's Force C cast off from the mother ships and began the run toward shore.

Sunrise was at 0558. In the dim light of early morning, Captain Goranson and the men of Company C could see the landing craft that preceded them making progress toward Omaha Charlie Beach.

Omaha Charlie was the right flank (west) of the four sectors of Omaha Beach. This was the site of one of the four exits along Omaha Beach that would enable rapid access inland, called by the Allies "Exit D-1," and was the only one of the four that had a hard-surface road. Both the Allies and the Germans understood the critical nature of this area and planned their attack and defense accordingly.

The plan was that the initial landings on Omaha Beach were to be made by tanks fitted out to operate on land or water. Launched six thousand yards from shore, the tanks would swim to the beach, take up firing positions along the water's edge and support the infantry.

On Omaha Charlie, the plan was that the men of Company B, 743d Tank Battalion, would be first ashore, landing at 0625 hours. At 0631, Company A of the 116th Infantry would land, and at 0633, men of the 146th Engineer Combat Battalion and Company C of the 2d Ranger Battalion were to land. Then succeeding waves would land at five- to ten-minute intervals.

In the eastern (16th Infantry) sector of Omaha Beach, the amphibious tanks were launched in the heavy seas with disastrous results. Most sank on the way to shore, and only five reached the beach.

Courageous naval officers in the 116th Infantry zone brought their tank landing craft through a hail of fire that caused several sinkings. Steering onto the beach, these gallant men unloaded thirty-two tanks of the 743d Tank Battalion.

Though supporting naval artillery was heavy, the Germans took the leading craft at Omaha Charlie under a withering fire. Due to sunken landing craft, only eight of the sixteen tanks in Company B of the 743d Tank Battalion made it to shore. With most of their officers dead or wounded, the tankers laid down supporting fire from the edge of the beach.

At about 0636, the men of Company A, 116th, landed on Omaha Charlie. The company, which had been under heavy fire on the way in, found itself in the jaws of hell. One boat had foundered and another was ripped apart by the German fire, which beat on all the landing craft. When the ramps went down, the men in the lead were mowed down as they left the boats. Trying to escape the horror, heavily equipped men jumped over the side into water that was frequently over their heads. In one boat, all thirty-two occupants were killed. All officers and most of the noncommissioned officers of Company A, 116th, were casualties. Beaten down, the survivors would not cross the beach and tried to find shelter behind obstacles or in the water. The Germans picked them off.

Confusion on the part of other units contributed to the suffering of Company A, 116th. G Company, which was to land to the left of Company A, drifted left (east) and landed about one thousand yards away. In their sector of the beach, the remaining tanks of Company B of the 743d Tank Battalion and Company A, 116th Infantry, received all the initial attention of the German defenders.

Around 0645, nine minutes after the ramps dropped for Company A of the 116th, Company C of the 2d Rangers came ashore into the meat grinder of Omaha Charlie.

German machine guns, mortars, and artillery tore into the small Ranger company. LCA 418 with Captain Goranson and Lieutenant Moody's 1st Platoon was hit by enemy mortar or direct artillery fire on the ramp. Two other explosions ripped the craft, and men tried to escape over the side. Heavily laden men fought to keep from drowning in deep water.

As the ramps dropped, other Rangers struggled ashore. Some fell beneath the fire of a German machine gun firing directly into the boat, but the men kept moving. This was not the flamboyant charge so frequently depicted in war films: chilled, seasick, and numb with the horror they found on the beach, the Rangers struggled through soft, wet sand that mired their feet. There are times in battle when exhaustion is so great that even the sight of men dying about you and machine-gun bullets kicking up the earth at your feet are not sufficient to inspire rapid movement. So it was for the Rangers at Omaha Charlie.

The Rangers were not supermen, but they were volunteers and trained to a higher degree. That extra motivation and training enabled them to do what the brave men of Company A of the 116th had been unable to do—keep moving inland.

Of the 68 Rangers in Company C of the 2d Ranger Battalion, nineteen were killed, including Sergeant Geldon, who died on his third wedding anniversary. Thirteen Rangers were seriously wounded and five were lightly wounded in crossing the almost three hundred yards of exposed beach. Those who survived kept moving and crossed the beach. The wounded crawled behind them.

Blasted off his feet by concussion and lying facedown in the sand, Lt. Sid Salomon, platoon leader of 2d Platoon, thought his life had come to an end. Salomon tried to take his operations map from his assault jacket to pass it on to Sergeant Kennedy, Salomon's platoon sergeant, but as sand began kicking up in his face from bullets playing about him, Salomon felt a surge of the lust for life, got up, and moved forward.

Now the surviving Rangers had reached the base of a cliff, approximately ninety feet high. Lieutenant Moody, Sgt. Richard Garrett, Sgt. Julius Belcher, and Pfc. Otto Stephens found a crevice in which they could climb by using bayonets. Others followed. Lieutenant Moody and Stephens then moved along the cliff top, shouting directions to the remainder of the company. With the aid of toggle ropes, the men of Company C began to climb. No unit has a better claim to being first on the high ground at Omaha Beach than Company C of the 2d Ranger Battalion.

Though few in numbers, Ranger patrols set about reconnoitering the cliff top. On the high ground to the left of the Rangers was a stone house, badly beaten up by naval gunfire. Ranger reconnaissance patrols found that this farmhouse was tied in with German strongpoints protecting the exit from Omaha Beach to Vierville. The Germans were firing down the length of Omaha Beach. Lieutenant Moody and the six other Rangers cleared the stone house, Moody killing a German officer in the process. Though driven out several times, the Germans continued to infiltrate back to their fighting positions.

On top of the cliff, Lieutenants Moody and Salomon shared a shell hole while peering over the rim to examine the battlefield. As the two men poked their heads above the hole, Bill Moody was hit by a German bullet. Shot through the forehead, the brave officer died instantly. Sergeants Belcher and Morrow had meanwhile located a German machine-gun position placing enfilade fire on the beach. It was pay-back time. Belcher kicked open the rear door of the German position and threw a white-phosphorus grenade inside. As the badly burned Germans poured out of the position, Belcher killed them.

Meanwhile Rudder's Force A had not yet landed. Coming into shore behind a small British guide boat and two escorting gunboats, the Rangers found themselves confronted with an additional problem.

As daylight revealed the shoreline, several Rangers recognized that the cliff point they were headed for was not the objective. The British guide craft was leading the three companies of Rangers in Rudder's Force A toward Pointe de la Percee, some three miles to the east of Pointe du Hoc.

Tidal current played a major factor in navigation during the D-day landing. The pull was so strong that supporting destroyers, standing close inshore, were required to steam into the current to maintain station. At least one guide boat in Omaha Charlie drifted off station. Currents, battle smoke, morning haze, and the tension and confusion of battle all contributed to the fact that many units along Omaha Beach were landed to the east of their planned objectives.

Colonel Rudder, who was riding in LCA 888, the lead landing craft, ordered the coxswain to change course. After a brief protest, the correction was made. By now the landing craft were close to shore. Turning for the westward run, the boats came under fire from the shore. One DUKW was hit; five men aboard were casualties.

Supporting naval forces were keeping watch over the Ranger landing craft and moved to their aid. The British destroyer *Talybont* stood close inshore and took the German positions under fire, while the American destroyer *Satterlee* opened fire on German units who were moving into defensive positions.

Though Rudder's Force A Rangers were now headed for Pointe du Hoc, valuable time had been lost. The naval supporting fire had been timed to lift at 0625, five minutes before the planned Ranger touchdown. The error in direction made Force A over thirty minutes late, thirty minutes in which the Germans could reorganize and man their defenses. With the Force A landing craft coming in on the east flank of Pointe du Hoc instead of approaching the tip from the front, the original plan to land on both sides was no longer realistic. Rather than have D Company, which due to a sunken boat was now short twenty Rangers, and its company commander attempt to do a U-turn in landing craft, Rudder made the decision that the three companies would go on line and all land on the east flank of the Pointe.

At the same time, landing craft containing Col. Max Schneider with the 5th Ranger Battalion and A and B Companies of the 2d Rangers were embarked and moving toward shore in heavy seas. Scheduled to follow in at 0700, Schneider was waiting for a radio message or the sight of mortar-fired flares from Pointe du Hoc, which would signal him to make the follow-on landing.

On top of the cliffs near Omaha Charlie, Captain Goranson saw a boat carrying men of Company B of the 116th coming ashore in the fourth wave. Sending a messenger to them, he was soon joined by some twenty men of the 116th, who also came up the ropes.

Though not on his assigned objective, Goranson and his men were in a vital spot. The strongpoint that Company C was now in position to engage was a key point in the German defense scheme covering the D-1 exit to Vierville. Though few in number, officers and noncommissioned officers in

Company C led their men into the German trenches and began a series of small, very personal actions that disrupted the German defense. Using concealed routes of approach, the Germans reinforced from Vierville and fought hard to hang on to their strongpoint. Though not of sufficient strength to dislodge the enemy, Goranson's party, including the twenty men of Company B 116th, kept patrolling the trenches picking off German troops and destroying their mortar and machine-gun positions.

At 0700 hours, Rudder's Force A landing craft were approaching the east side of Pointe du Hoc. The assault plan had called for Schneider, with the eight follow-on Ranger companies, to wait until 0700 for the signal to come in behind Rudder's force. If no signal was received by 0700, Schneider was to land at Omaha Charlie Beach and move overland to destroy the guns of Pointe du Hoc. Knowing how critical reinforcement could be to the three assault companies, at 0700 Schneider delayed ordering his flotilla to lay-to offshore. Schneider waited beyond 0700, anxiously hoping for the signal that a successful landing had been made. The communication plan for the Ranger assault on Pointe du Hoc was the work of Lt. James W. "Ike" Eikner,[2] communications officer for Rudder's 2d Ranger Battalion. Eikner had alternate means of communication, including radio, visual signals, and carrier pigeons. The plan included mortar flares to be fired from the top of the cliffs as a signal for Schneider to close on the beach, and a series of radio code words Eikner developed. This was a generation of young men who had grown up playing pinball machines. When the machine was improperly jostled during the game, the machine would stop play and flash the signal "tilt." Thus, if Force A plans went astray, the word "tilt" was selected as the radio signal for Schneider to take his force to Omaha Charlie Beach.

As they moved closer to shore, the Force A landing craft began to peel off into position to land along a strip of rocky beach approximately five hundred yards long and thirty yards wide. On the right flank, landing from right to left were LCAs 861, 862, 888, and 722. These four boats carried Company E and Rudder's command element. D Company, with LCAs 668 and 858, was in the center, and the three LCAs numbered 887, 884, and 883 carrying Company F were on the Ranger left.

The first craft to land was LCA 888, carrying Colonel Rudder and much of his command element, plus men of Company E and four men of headquarters. Touchdown was between 0705 and 0708. The Germans could be seen on the cliff top. Sergeant Boggetto opened fire with his BAR and shot a German soldier, whose body fell from the cliff. The remainder of the Germans disappeared from view. As with other boat teams, Rudder's party embarked into deep shell holes, whose clay sides were slick and difficult to escape from. Under fire, Rudder's command group made it to the cliff wall, where the command post was established in a small cave.

On the extreme right, in LCA 861, Lt. Ted Lapres's craft came in near the tip of Pointe du Hoc. A small party of Germans were standing on the cliff top, trying to fire down into the boat. As Rangers leaped from the front of the craft, men in the rear fired on the Germans, driving them from sight.

As the LCAs closed the beach, cratering, enemy fire, and wet ropes created problems. The preliminary bombing and shelling had torn the landscape apart. Great chunks of cliff had been blown away, boulders hurled into the sea impeded the landing of some craft, and deep shell holes underwater became underwater traps. German artillery and mortars were not a significant factor during the landing phase of Pointe du Hoc: Automatic-weapon fire was received from the flanks, and small parties of German infantry appeared at the cliff's edge, trying to fire down into the D Company boats or shower them with grenades, but Rangers firing from landing craft and supporting gunfire from the USS *Satterlee* suppressed this action.

During the landing and climb, fifteen men were wounded and one killed. Suppressive fire on the cliff top and the audacity of the operation contributed to a relatively low initial casualty rate.

Pfc. John Sillmon of Company E on LCA 722 had every reason to feel like a fugitive from the law of averages. Sillmon was wounded three times on the run to shore and twice during landing. Despite five wounds, Sillmon survived.

Lt. Col. Thomas Trevor of the British Commandos served with the Rangers as British liaison and adviser on the Commando experience. The six-foot–six-inch–tall British officer took a head wound through his helmet as he landed. Bloodied and cursing the Germans, Trevor walked up and down the beach encouraging the men.

Military leadership is an art, dealing with human emotion and conflict, and it comes in many forms. One such example was 1st Sgt. Len Lomell[3] of Company D. Lomell was a young, aggressive man who needed the pay rank provided to support his aged parents. His ability and his need resulted in a rapid climb to first sergeant. Not a man to shy from discipline, Lomell had taken action against a subordinate sergeant during the training phase. In anger, the man had said words to the effect that they would soon be in combat and sometimes officers and noncommissioned officers got shot by their own men.

As he struggled to shore from LCA 668 carrying his weapons, a box of rope, and a hand projector rocket, Lomell was shot in the side, the force of the bullet spinning him around. Behind him was the man whom he had disciplined. Furious at what he thought was an attack on his life, Lomell went after the man, who angrily denied the charge. Another Ranger pulled Lomell away, saying he had seen the German who fired the shot. Probably the only man on the Pointe du Hoc climb whose range of emotion included embarrassment, Lomell apologized and went about his duties. The two men would later become close friends.

Automatic weapons firing from the east (left) and sited to enfilade the beach was the worst problem during the landings. One German machine gun was particularly effective.

Another problem was that the heavy seas had wetted down the climbing ropes, greatly increasing their weight. All six boat-mounted, rocket-propelled ropes of LCA 861 were fired without success. Then the hand-fired rockets were fired, and two grapnels caught. LCA 862 was the second landing craft from the left in landing. Two of the six ropes fired from this craft caught and held. In LCA 888, third from the left, none of the wet ropes reached the cliff top. Next from the left was

LCA 722; two ropes supported weight here. The right-hand craft for Company D was LCA 668; three of the six ropes held. In LCA 858, only one of the six ropes caught. In the F Company landing area, LCA 887 on the company right saw their first two ropes fall short. With the skilled steering of a cool-headed British coxswain, Lt. Robert Arman, the Ranger boat team commander, and his men wrestled the other four boat-mounted rockets, their ropes, and grapnels to shore. Set up on shore, the rockets could not be fired due to a missing lead wire. In one of the memorable events of the F Company D-day experience, Sgt. John Cripps stood close to the rockets, joining hot wires and exploding the rockets in turn. Men remember seeing bullets kicking up around Cripps's feet and mud and sand flying from the rocket explosions. The four ropes caught and held.

Next in line was LCA 884. Lt. Jacob Hill's boat team saw four of their ropes catch and hold, but each rope lay in a position clearly exposed to German fire. Three men were wounded getting ashore.

The extreme left landing craft and last to reach shore was LCA 883, carrying F Company commander Capt. Otto Masny, platoon leader Lt. Richard Wintz, and his boat team. Masny and his men were fortunate that a jutting portion of the cliff shielded this boat team from German enfilade fire. Masny had observed coxswains on some other boats dropping ramps and firing the rope rockets before touchdown. Masny ordered the boat landed before the rockets were fired. Pointing his pistol at the coxswain, Lieutenant Wintz restated the order in graphic terms. The combined result of these events was that LCA 883 made a dry landing, and five boat-fired ropes held.

The medical section of the 2d Rangers was led by Capt. Walter Block, M.D. Two medical enlisted personnel were with Dr. Block in LCA 722, and three aidmen were distributed among other landing craft. The aidmen were carrying seventy-five-pound packs of medical supplies. These were tied to fifty feet of rope. If the beach was under heavy fire, the medic could drop his pack, then, when he reached the shelter of the cliff, pull it after him. In a protected spot under the cliff, Block set up his aid station and a Red Cross flag.

By 0713 Lieutenant Eikner and his communications team of Rangers Lou Lisko,[4] C. S. Parker, and Stephen Liscinsky, had set up the heavy SCR-284 radio and were trying to establish communications by means of the SCR-284 and the SCR-300 radio. About 0725 Eikner radioed the code "tilt" to Schneider's force and received an acknowledgment.

Who acknowledged is unclear. On Schneider's part, there is no indication that the message was received. Unable to establish contact by SCR-300, Schneider's communications personnel set up their SCR-284 on board the headquarters LCA without success. Guide-craft radios were inoperable, and even the loud hailer failed. At 0715 Schneider's force received an unintelligible message. The only word that could be understood was "Charlie."

Schneider's Force C was close to shore off Omaha Charlie. The tide was coming in. Mine-tipped obstacles, which had been visible to the coxswains of the first wave, were now more difficult to locate. Landing craft were being pounded by artillery and machine-gun fire and blowing up from striking the mine-tipped obstacles.

While Schneider's Force C was coming into shore, Rudder's Force A climbed the cliffs of Pointe du Hoc. The climb was difficult; the wet and slippery ropes offered little grip. Some ropes were cut by German defenders, other ropes had their grapnels fail to catch hold, and still others were covered by German fire. In places, the bombing and shelling had collapsed the cliff faces, and mounds of clay and stone as high as twenty feet made a platform to climb the remainder of the cliff.

As the men reached the top of the cliffs, a sight of incredible destruction unfolded before their eyes. The preparatory bombing and shelling had created a surrealistic battlefield. All the study of maps and aerial photographs, all the hours spent poring over sand tables and mock-ups had given the Rangers a knowledge of every position, trench, and path—now none of it was recognizable.

Though the climbing of the cliffs has captured the imagination of the public, it was the manner in which the Rangers conducted themselves on reaching the top that best shows their uniqueness. From the first man up the rope, the Rangers' aggressive spirit was demonstrated. There was no hesitancy, no waiting until all the men of their squad, platoon, or company reached the summit: as small groups came up the ropes, they went over the edge and moved out. Some estimates run as high as twenty separate parties of Rangers quickly assembling at the top of the cliff and moving out toward objectives. The individual initiative and leadership of the junior noncommissioned officers demonstrated there is a shining example of what first-class infantry can accomplish.

This initiative on the part of the Rangers compounded the problems of the German defense. The Rangers were attacking everywhere, though not haphazardly. Each man was trying to accomplish what he knew had to be done. As the small groups encountered one another, they flowed together as raindrops become rivulets then streams.

The elimination of the observation post and the guns was the priority mission. Company D had the task of eliminating guns number four, five, and six on the western portion of the point. Company E was assigned the observation post and gun number three. Company F was to destroy guns number one and two on the east and the antiaircraft position near the east edge of the cliff.

When the initial objectives were accomplished, the companies were to move inland, coordinating their passage to a phase line south of the Pointe's fortified area. From there, D, E, and F Companies would move about one thousand yards inland, cross the coastal highway between Grandcamp–Isigny and Vierville and set up a blocking position. The headquarters group, with one platoon of Company E as security, would remain on the Pointe.

Under harassing fire from the observation post and some German positions on the west, the small parties of Rangers searched out their objectives only to find the casemate and the open emplacements destroyed and the guns missing.

At the tip of the point, E Company men engaged the observation post, which was firing at them with a machine gun and small arms. Sergeant Denbo and Private First Class Roberts crawled into a trench within grenade range of the OP and threw four grenades, three of which made it through the observation and firing slits. The machine gun stopped firing, but small arms continued, with Denbo receiving a head wound. Lieutenant Lapres came up with four men, including Sergeant Yardley who was carrying a rocket launcher. Yardley's second shot went into the observation post. As the German fire ceased, Yardley was left to guard the front of the OP while the rest went around the rear.

Meanwhile, without knowing of each other's presence, another element of Company E was attacking the observation post from the opposite side. Lieutenant Leagans, Sergeant Cleaves, Technician Fifth Class Thompson, Private, First Class Bellows, and Corporal Aguzzi were in this group. They had succeeded in driving under cover a German who had been throwing grenades over the cliff, and had shot the radio antenna off the top of the OP. Sergeant Cleaves was wounded by a mine, Lieutenant Leagans and Technician Fifth Class Thompson went on their mission, with Bellows covering, and Aguzzi remained to cover the rear entrance to the OP. No demolitions having come up the cliffs, the Rangers guarded the front and rear of the OP and waited for the Germans to come out.

E Company's Sergeants Smith and Robey reached the top of the cliff and saw some six Germans nearer the point throwing grenades down on the climbing Rangers. Robey dropped into a depression and fired two twenty-round magazines from his BAR. Three of the Germans went down. The remainder fled into shelters. Joined by Private, First Class Peterson, the three Rangers continued on their mission.

Coming into the left (east) of the E Company boats, the men of D Company, 2d Rangers, were met by fire and the deep, water-filled shell holes. Due to the cliff overhang and the position and wetness of the ropes that reached the cliff top, the ascent was slowed. When the ropes proved too slippery, Lomell directed the use of the four-foot sections of extension ladders. A few men used a toggle rope, but most used the ladders to reach an advantageous slope to the cliff. At the top, Lomell moved off with about twenty-two men of his 2d Platoon. Lt. George Kerchner's D Company 1st Platoon were in the second D Company boat team. Most of Kerchner's platoon went up a single rope. As they reached the top, small groups went after the guns. Within fifteen minutes of landing, the D Company Rangers had climbed the cliff and were moving on their assignment.

The three F Company boat teams were to the east of D Company. Facing automatic weapons fire and the deep craters, the men made their way to shore. Sgt. William "L-Rod" Petty[5] was some thirty feet up a rope, when the grapnel pulled loose. Fortunately the grapnel dragged, slowing his descent. The ropes fired by Sergeant Cripps helped the section greatly. The other two boat teams, led by Captain Masny and Lieutenant Hill, used the perfectly fired ropes of Masny's boat to reach the top.

Thirty minutes from touchdown, all Force A Rangers except some headquarters and mortar personnel had reached the top. Captain Block, the battalion medical officer, had his aid station functioning at the base of the cliff. In civilian life, Block was a pediatrician. In battle he remained a devoted father, who wrote fairy tales to his children.

That most of the rope rockets had functioned was the key to the success of the Rangers' aggressive assault. Less fortunate were the ladder-equipped DUKWs. The deep shell holes hindered them in gaining a footing on the beach. A greater problem was the small stones which covered the beach to a depth of several feet. One Ranger described movement on this beach as trying to gain traction on a deep pile of roller bearings. Forced to remain in the water, the DUKWs were buffeted by the surf and their ladders were ineffective. Sgt. William Stivison climbed to the top of one of these ladders to attempt firing the machine guns mounted at the top. Eighty feet in the air, trying to fire from a ladder swaying back and forth like a metronome, Stivison saw German tracers whipping about him in proof of the old adage that "a moving target attracts the eye."

The audacity of the assault up the cliffs had paid great dividends. Not expecting an attack over such an obstacle, the Germans had prepared their strongest defenses against an attack from inland.

As the small groups of Rangers moved to their assigned

objectives, they found the badly battered gun positions empty of artillery. The Germans had removed the guns before the invasion. Resistance was light and consisted primarily of fire from the western flank. An antiaircraft gun created the most significant problem and was attacked by Lt. Ted Lapres and his platoon from Company E.

Scarcely pausing, the Rangers now pressed on into the second phase of their mission, that of moving inland to block the Vierville–Grandcamp coastal road and destroy German communications.

Those last up the ropes hurried to join their companies. As groups merged, the movement inland began to develop along two axes, with D and E Company elements moving from the point to the highway and men of F Company moving parallel and east of D and E Companies.

At 0745 Colonel Rudder moved his command post from the base of the cliffs at Pointe du Hoc to a shell crater at the top.

Dr. Block moved his aid station to the top of the cliff, with medic Private, First Class Korb remaining on the beach to care for the seriously wounded who could not be taken to the top. Attempts to evacuate the wounded were broken up by enemy fire. Nothing could be done but give the wounded battlefield care.

Despite the slaughter on Omaha Charlie, succeeding waves of infantry and engineers had continued to land. Men of the 146th, 149th, and 121st Engineers valiantly tried to clear paths through the obstacles and were shot down in large numbers. Coming in behind Company A of the 116th and Company C of the 2d Rangers, the men of B and D Companies of the 116th Infantry were gunned down as the ramps dropped. The situation was chaos, compounded by fire-induced shock. While some men struggled to fight, others tried vainly to hide in the water or behind any object that seemed to offer protection.

Seeing the carnage of Omaha Charlie Beach, Colonel Schneider observed that Omaha Dog White to the left of Charlie was comparatively quiet. By hand and arm signals, Schneider ordered the remainder of his flotilla to steer to a landing point on the left of the carnage.

This change of direction by Colonel Schneider was one of the key tactical decisions of the invasion. It would place the right unit at the right place at the right time. The point of landing for Force C now included the left edge of Omaha Charlie Beach and Omaha Dog White.

The LCAs carrying the men of A, B, and some headquarters personnel of the 2d Ranger Battalion were on the right. For these men, the point of landing was on the attackers' left portion of Omaha Charlie approximately one thousand yards east of the beach exit.

The first wave consisted of six LCAs. From left to right these were: Two craft carrying Company A, 2d Rangers, the Ranger Group headquarters LCA, a 2d Ranger Battalion headquarters LCA, and two Company B, 2d Ranger Battalion, LCAs. Ramps went down at 0740, and the killing commenced.

The LCA carrying the 2d Platoon of B Company, 2d Rangers, hit a mine that blew off the bow landing ramp. Lieutenant Fitzsimmons was knocked unconscious by the explosion. The 2d Platoon LCA sank, throwing most of the men into deep water, most of whom made it to shore but lost their weapons and equipment. The 1st Platoon boat dropped its ramp, and the men started ashore. Lt. Robert Brice of the 1st Platoon of B Company was killed as he signaled his men forward. M. Sgt. Robert Lemin, the 2d Battalion sergeant major, was also killed. The Germans fired directly into the landing craft as the ramps dropped, then increased the enfilade fire of automatic weapons as the men reached shore.

Somehow the surviving Rangers continued to struggle inland. Captain Rafferty, company commander, and 1st Sgt. Edward Sowa of Company A 2d Rangers were both killed. Ranger Clyde Pattison took a burst of machine-gun fire through his right arm, ripping it to the consistency of hamburger. Pattison kept going and made it across the beach. The few surviving medics were busy elsewhere, so Pattison bandaged his own wounds; it would be three days before he reached a hospital.

With every minute, the number of casualties increased. Ranger chaplain Joseph Lacy[6] roamed the beach, binding wounds and comforting the dying. The surviving Rangers kept pressing on. First as individuals, then as teams, the Rangers crossed the beach.

Ranger William Clark was a medical aidman from Headquarters Company, 2d Ranger Battalion. Coming off the landing craft in cold water up to his waist, Clark could see a burning landing craft to his left and bullets hitting the water about him.

The beach was a charnel house of dead and dying. Clark passed a man whose face had been flattened by concussion, leaving his head looking curiously like a lollipop. One of the first wounds medic Clark had to treat was a sucking chest wound. Clark had heard about these wounds but never had seen one until now. Clark used sulfa powder on the wound, then found a gas mask floating in the water and cut a piece of rubber from it to cover the wound. Cries for medical assistance came from all parts of the beach, and the surviving medics did the best they could. Unable to evacuate the wounded, they treated men under fire and left them in position. The dead were strewn about or lying in rows where they had fallen. Clark could tell the Ranger dead by the bloused boots. There was no shortage of medical supplies. The beach was littered with equipment, including the aid kits of dead medical personnel.

On Pointe du Hoc, D, E, and F Companies, 2d Rangers, were moving inland. As the Rangers advanced, German resistance began to stiffen, and high explosives from German artillery began to fall around D and E Company. German small-arms fire came from the left front, and a machine gun opened up from the right. Sniper fire was coming from a group of farmhouses to the front of the Rangers. The fighting was increasingly costly. Five men of D Company were killed and two from Company E; eight men were wounded.

Despite the fire and casualties, the men of D and E Companies kept moving forward. As the Rangers reached the farm buildings, the Germans withdrew. Both German and American artillery was falling in the area. The American artillery was having a tendency to fall to the rear of the Rangers. While not directly effective against the Germans, it was a marvelous inspiration to keep moving inland.

Beyond the farm was a flat open space, some forty yards in width, terminating in a communications trench. Though under fire, the Rangers rushed the trench, running across the open area singly or in small scattered groups. A concrete roadblock provided temporary shelter for some Germans, but Ranger fire drove them off, and the advance continued to the next farm. Though some men were temporarily pinned down by fire, movement progressed and the road was soon reached.

From the east of D and E came Sgt. William Petty and some F Company men who had come ashore on LCA 887. The F Company Rangers moved inland, moving from crater to crater in short rapid bounds, then single file through a mine field. Enroute, the men were joined by Lt. Robert Arman. Continuing inland, the F Company Rangers were joined by four E Company men, who had moved to the flank to be clear of the German artillery falling on D and E. The main body of the F Company, consisting of about eighteen Rangers, oriented their movement on a country lane that led to the blacktop road.

Closer to the cliff, other men of the 2d Rangers were finding themselves confronted by German infantry. The German positions were connected by trenches and, in some cases, by underground passages. These allowed the German soldiers to move unobserved into areas the initial Ranger parties had passed. From the right of the Rangers (west) an antiaircraft gun began to be troublesome. A party of eight to twelve 1st Platoon, D Company, Rangers, moving on gun position six, came under heavy fire from artillery and mortars. As they spread out to escape the shrapnel, they were taken under fire by German infantry, who hunted them through the trenches and shell holes. Only one Ranger of this group avoided death or capture.

Capt. Otto Masny of F company was given the job of collecting any men nearby to organize a defense of Rudder's command post. The area was cleared again and again. There were times of quiet, but that quiet was often shattered by German fire and Ranger response. The troublesome German antiaircraft gun was eliminated by naval gunfire.

Actions involving small independent groups of men were occurring across the battle area.

At the point of Pointe du Hoc, the Germans at the observation post still held on. Satchel charges thrown inside ended the resistance. Eight Germans surrendered.

Lt. Jacob Hill and two men from F Company met a similar size group which included Pfc. William E. Anderson, a man who in the days and months ahead would demonstrate that his military rank did not reflect his superb initiative and ability to lead by personal example. Anderson and his companions were after a machine gun that was firing from the right of the Rangers, about 250 yards from the edge of the cliff.

Moving along hedgerows, Lieutenant Hill and his five men leapfrogged forward, with one element advancing while covered by the other. In this process, two men became separated. Crossing an open field under fire and capturing a prisoner, the remaining four men continued on. The German machine-gun crew was not aware of the threat coming from the flank. Covered by the other two Rangers, Lieutenant Hill and Private, First Class Anderson crawled to an embankment across the road from the German gun, while the Germans were firing in another direction. Lieutenant Hill stood up to pinpoint the location of the gun. Caught up in the excitement of battle, Lieutenant Hill stood a few yards from the Germans, loosing a string of profanity at them. Among his milder sentiments were "son of a bitch, you couldn't hit a bull in the ass with a bass fiddle."

It is doubtful that the Germans understood Hill's precise meaning, but he caught their attention, and they began to swing the machine gun in Hill's direction. Hill dropped behind the embankment, and Anderson tossed Hill a fragmentation grenade. Hill's throw was accurate, and the machine gun was eliminated.

On Omaha Charlie, A and B Companies of the 2d Rangers were taking a walk in hell. One hundred yards in from the water, there was a rock pile that provided a temporary haven from direct fire, beyond which was a seawall about four feet in height. It was to this area that the surviving Rangers made their way.

Fire support was forthcoming at a critical time. The tanks of the first wave 743d Tank Battalion had been hammered by

German antitank fire, but those tanks that still functioned were on the beach doing good service in bringing fire on the enemy. An enemy pillbox on the bluff was giving great difficulty— the big guns of the battleship *Texas* tore it apart.

Crossing the seawall, Rangers of Company A eliminated a machine gun that was killing their men.

Meanwhile Max Schneider was leading his 5th Ranger Battalion ashore on Omaha Dog White Beach. The sequence remains a matter of opinion. The narrative history of the 2d Ranger Battalion states that A and B Company preceded the 5th Battalion to shore, and when Schneider saw the difficulties being encountered by these companies, he altered the direction of the landing to Omaha Dog White (a minimal change). Maj. Richard Sullivan, who was executive officer of the Ranger Group that day, believes the men of A and B Company of the 2d and the 5th Ranger Battalion landed almost simultaneously.

In comparison with Dog Green, Omaha Dog White Beach was a garden spot. Company C of the 743d Tank Battalion had been first ashore here. Company G of the 116th had been scheduled to immediately follow but had landed considerably to the east. In trying to move laterally to its objective area, this unit became fragmented.

Company C of the 116th Infantry had originally been scheduled to land at H plus 50 minutes on Omaha Dog Green as the sixth wave on that beach. This unit came in on Dog White arriving at 0710. Relatively unscathed, the men crossed the beach and took shelter behind the seawall, some seventy-five yards in from the edge of the water.

Between 0730 and 0740, the regimental command group of the 116th Infantry landed on Omaha Dog White. This group included Brig. Gen. Norman Cota, assistant division commander of the 29th Division and senior officer on the western portion of Omaha Beach.

Around 0740 the men of the 5th Ranger Battalion came ashore in two waves. Companies A, B, and E and Schneider's command element were in the first wave. Immediately following were Companies C, D, and F and the remainder of Headquarters Company. One F Company boat had been swamped and its men picked up by an LCT and landed later.

In all, thirteen of the fourteen landing craft made it safely to shore.

Though subjected to fire while crossing the beach, the 5th Rangers casualties numbered no more than six. Some 450 of the 5th Rangers were moving into position behind the seawall.

It was now 0745. As Schneider's men crossed Dog White Beach, about 1100 yards west (to the right) of Omaha Dog Green Beach, Captain Goranson and his survivors, including the twenty men of the 116th Infantry, were all on top of the cliff and continuing to attack German positions.

On Dog White, Colonel Schneider had no communication with Company C and therefore no knowledge of the situation at Pointe du Hoc. Schneider's mission was to get overland to attack the guns of Pointe du Hoc. How to best accomplish that occupied his thoughts.

General Cota had the goal of getting the men off the beach and inland. Because of Colonel Schneider's decision to land to the east of his original landing site, General Cota now had sufficient force at hand to make what the War Department official history termed: "the most important penetration on the western beaches."

Though not a killing ground like Omaha Dog Green, Omaha Dog White Beach was still a dangerous place. Despite the danger, General Cota moved along Omaha Dog White Beach encouraging the men to move inland. Ranger Herb Epstein, who was intelligence sergeant for the 5th Ranger Battalion, recalls seeing Cota "sauntering" along the beach.

Ranger Epstein recalls Cota coming up to the 5th Ranger command group, who were under fire and prone while Schneider weighed his next move. Cota remained standing, and Max Schneider stood upright to converse with the general. Epstein recalls Cota saying, "We're counting on you Rangers to lead the way."

Ranger Mike Rehm who was nearby recalled Cota approaching and saying: "What outfit is this?" When given the reply "Rangers," Cota responded, "Well, goddamn it, if you're Rangers, get up and lead the way!" It was at this time that the motto *"Rangers lead the way"* was born.

Colonel Schneider and Maj. (later colonel) Richard Sullivan began to direct the men in a straightforward assault on the bluffs. Men of Company B, 5th Ranger Battalion, exploded bangalore torpedos under barbed-wire obstacles, clearing a path. Cota's encouragement was not only directed at the Rangers. Company C of the 116th was also on the move and fighting well. Who crossed the road first is impossible to determine and immaterial save for academic argument. Both units had demolition teams at work. In places the men of Company C, 116th, became intermixed with the larger force of Rangers.

Beyond the scawall was a lateral road that on its inshore side was laced with barbed-wire entanglements. These entanglements were covered by frontal and flanking fire. Beyond the wire lay a stretch of flat, open land about 150 yards in length. From the flat, the ground sloped steeply upward in open bluffs. The bluffs were covered with high grass and contained gullies and depressions. On the crest were the German foxholes and trenches. This was not a German strong point protecting a beach exit; therefore, the German defenses behind Omaha Dog White were not as formidable as those on Dog Green. But this was not known to the men facing the bluffs; they had only the knowledge that the attack had to be made over open ground. In a stroke of good fortune for the attackers, the dried grass was burning, and the smoke that blew eastward along bluffs helped conceal the men from German fire.

At about 0750, men of the 5th Rangers and Company C of the 116th Infantry began to cross the road, blow the wire, and cross the flat. At the base of the bluffs, the pace slowed. The heavy smoke caused some men to put on gas masks, an error they quickly regretted as the smoke penetrated and was trapped in the masks. Near the top of the bluff, the smoke cleared, and German mortar and automatic-weapons fire became heavy. A platoon from Company D of the 5th Rangers, led by Lt. Francis Dawson, eliminated a key German position. The attack continued.

During the attack on the high ground, seven men of Company A went up the bluffs to their front and were joined by six men from the 2d Platoon of Company B. This group tied in with the 5th Rangers. The survivors of Company A were being led by noncommissioned officers as all officers were casualties. Throughout the assault Technician Fifth Class Ray, a Browning automatic rifleman, distinguished himself with accurate hip fire on the Germans. Capt. Edgar Arnold of Company B led his 1st Platoon along the beach road in the direction of beach exit D-1. Supported by tank fire, the Rangers fought the Germans among beach houses. The B Company Rangers were unable to break through and returned to the landing area and moved up the bluff to join Company A and the 5th Rangers.

Omaha Dog Green took a heavy toll of the Rangers. Casualties among the 136 Rangers of A and B Companies and the headquarters personnel were 31 killed, 66 wounded, and 5 missing in action. The 2d Ranger medical detachment had performed yeoman service on the beach, and the medics frequently took up rifles and weapons to help root out the snipers, who spared no one.

In light of their heavy casualties, Colonel Schneider placed A and B Companies, 2d Rangers, in Force C Reserve, where Capt. Edgar Arnold reorganized the survivors into a composite company.

With the German outer crust penetrated, the 5th Rangers, with the new composite company of the 2d Rangers following, now began to move toward Vierville enroute to Pointe du Hoc.

German minefields were thick, necessitating the 5th Ranger Battalion moving in a column of companies. German infantry in well-concealed rifle pits contested the advance with heavy small-arms and automatic-weapons fire. With B Company, 5th Rangers, in the lead, Schneider's battalion moved toward Vierville. Attacking south, Company E ran into heavy German fire, including accurate artillery, and the attack was repulsed.

On crossing the seawall, Lt. Charles Parker and the 1st Platoon of Company A, 5th Rangers, became separated from the battalion. Busy with its own actions and out of communications with company or battalion headquarters, the 1st Platoon of Company A, 5th Rangers, pushed on toward Pointe du Hoc.

The platoon of 5th Rangers from F Company whose boat had been swamped were landed near St. Laurent, came under heavy German fire and could not rejoin the 5th Battalion.

Meanwhile on the high-ground position of Company C, 2d Rangers, the fighting was diminishing. Forced from their defenses, the Germans retreated, leaving behind sixty-nine of their bodies. During this phase of the fighting, Company C suffered two casualties.

At Pointe du Hoc, F Company Rangers, with Sgt. William Petty scouting, reached the juncture of the lane and highway. It was now 0805. In roughly an hour from landing, the 2d Rangers had reached their second geographical objective. Turning west and paralleling the blacktop, the F Company men encountered ineffective machine-gun fire near the hamlet of Auguay. Rangers Petty and McHugh flanked a farmhouse. In the backyard Petty was startled to see two effectively camouflaged Germans rise from the ground to his front. Petty dived forward, firing his BAR, but he was so close that the barrel of his rifle was between the two Germans. The experience was nonetheless unnerving for the Germans, who shouted *"Kamerad"* and surrendered. "Hell, L-Rod," commented McHugh, "that's a good way to save ammunition—just scare 'em to death."

Lead elements of D, E, and F Companies reached the highway and took up blocking positions to prevent German movement on the Vierville–Grandcamp highway and prevent the Germans from regaining control of the point.

D Company 1st Sgt. Len Lomell, with approximately twenty men, covered the western flank of the Ranger blocking position. Lomell established an outpost with a BAR man and six riflemen at the western edge of his position. Running south from the D Company position was a lane flanked by hedgerows. Leaders have a responsibility to know the area in which their troops are disposed, and First Sergeant Lomell and platoon sergeant Jack Kuhn were men who understood their responsibilities. About 0830 hours, the two noncommissioned officers walked down a lane that had the faint tracks of previous usage. About 250 yards down the lane, Lomell and Kuhn found the guns of Pointe du Hoc.

There were five powerful guns in the battery, disposed so as to fire toward Utah Beach but capable of being quickly reversed to cover Omaha. Ammunition was stacked nearby, the points were on the shells, and the firing charges ready. The most feared German battery of the invasion stood waiting but silent—the gun crews were missing.

Scarcely able to believe their good fortune, the two Ranger leaders went into action. Lomell had two thermite grenades with him. While Sergeant Kuhn kept watch, First Sergeant Lomell placed a grenade in the recoil mechanism of two of the guns and ignited them. He smashed the sights of the remaining guns with the butt of his tommy gun. The two Rangers then hurried back some seventy-five yards to their men to secure more grenades. Lomell and Kuhn then returned and rendered the remaining guns inoperative.

Probably the greatest mystery of D-day is why these guns were unmanned. The relationship between artillerymen and their guns is so close, so personal, that many times in battle the gunners have fought opposing forces in hand-to-hand combat rather than relinquish their guns. The theory has been advanced that the Germans were driven to shelter by the heavy bombardment and had not returned from their places of hiding, but this theory is not valid. The guns were in a location that did not suffer from bombardment, and even if they had been under fire, over thirty minutes had passed since the pre-invasion bombardment had been lifted, more than sufficient time for the German gunners to return from deep shelter.

The experience of Company F, 2d Rangers, offers a possible solution of the mystery of the missing gun crews. Sergeant Petty, with members of an F Company assault squad, caught eight enemy soldiers, obviously not infantry, fleeing from the area in front of D Company. This could have been one of the gun crews. F Company Rangers also took under fire a group of six to eight Germans, peddling furiously on bicycles, and shortly later a two-horse wagon with Germans emerged from a farmhouse complex approximately two hundred yards from the guns. Both groups of Germans were moving away from the area as fast as possible. Some or all of these Germans might have been the gun crews. Reinforcing this theory is Sergeant Petty's remembrance that "sounds of excitement" were coming from the D Company area while the first group of enemy soldiers were being captured.

German infantry obviously assumed the guns were secure. Initial historical reports taken soon after the operation state, "Not a German was in sight, and the only opposition was from occasional sniper fire some distance away." Lomell reported seeing seventy-five to one hundred Germans in an orchard some one hundred yards away. The Germans were formed up, receiving instructions. These men did not move to the guns when the guns and the ammunition were being destroyed. During the morning, a force of fifty to sixty well-armed German infantry, led by scouts, had approached D Company. The German force was too large for the twelve D Company Rangers to engage, so the D Company men maintained fire and camouflage discipline. The Germans passed, unaware they were under Ranger sights.

Meanwhile, a five-man patrol from Company E under Sergeant Rupinski came across the fields and found the main ammunition supply for the German battery. The E Company Rangers set fire to the powder bags, and a thunderous explosion occurred. The two Ranger parties quickly withdrew. Though the estimated 130 Germans nearby heavily outnumbered the twelve D Company Rangers in the blocking position at 0800, the Germans did not launch an attack until after darkness.

The German gun positions on Pointe du Hoc were still a nuisance. Rudder requested a destroyer to stand in close to the coast and go after the bothersome German position. Lieutenant Eikner was having good success in communicating with the navy by the use of signal lamps and relayed the corrections of gunfire as made by Lieutenant Johnson of the 58th Artillery Battalion, who was part of the naval shore-fire control team. With Johnson and Eikner working together, the British destroyer fired seven salvos from its main battery and blasted away that portion of the cliff where the German position was located. Radio communication was not very effective, and the problem was compounded by the Rangers having an incorrect Signal Operating Instruction (SOI).[7] This error probably stemmed from the attachment to the 116th Infantry who, being unaccustomed to having the Rangers attached, forgot to inform them of the change of SOI. Rudder went in harm's way once too often and around 1000 hours was shot in the thigh. Thereafter, his movement was greatly hindered.

The hallmark of the D-day Ranger experience continued to be the aggressive initiative displayed by individuals and small groups. In late morning, Lt. Jacob Hill and Pvt. J. Bacho went looking for Germans. Hill heard a German machine gun firing toward the point, and the two men moved in that direction. Bacho heard sounds and peered over a hedgerow. About a dozen Germans were lying on the ground talking. Though there were only two Rangers, Hill decided to grenade the Germans. Both Rangers threw fragmentation grenades over the top and dived for a ditch. The usually reliable American fragmentation grenades failed to fire. German potato-masher grenades came sailing back over the hedge, and a firefight developed, with the German numbers deciding the issue. Lieutenant Hill was shot in the chest by a machine pistol and died. Wounded in the hand, Bacho fell over Hill's body, placed his face on Hill's bleeding wound and feigned death. The Germans looked over the hedgerow and believed both Rangers were dead. At dark, Bacho made it back to the Pointe.

Putting in the blocking position, the 2d Battalion Rangers established an outposted perimeter defense, using previously prepared German positions where possible. By noon there were about sixty-five Rangers in the defense. Three paratroopers of the 101st Airborne had come overland and joined the Rangers. E and F Company had particularly good positions, overlooking a valley. The ground sloped away to a stream about three hundred yards to the front, offering a good field of fire.

Ranger patrols were active, yet no organized German defense or positions were found. The German soldiers who were bypassed were disorganized, fragmented, and now trying to rejoin their units. The route of travel for a number of these Germans took them across the valley. This brought them under the direct fire of the E and F Company Rangers.

On the left of the Ranger perimeter, Sergeant L-Rod Petty

Weapons used by early Ranger units: (L to R) 60mm mortar (partly obscured), "Boys" antitank gun (magazine on top), Springfield 03 rifle with bayonet in scabbard, .30 caliber machine gun on tripod with ammo, white phosphorous and fragmentation grenades with .45 caliber pistol, British Enfield rifle, Browning Automatic Rifle on bipod, and 81mm Mortar with ammo. 1st Ranger Battalion during training in northern Scotland. Ranger is wearing WW I–style helmet and carrying a .45 caliber Thompson submachine gun. Photo credit: James Altieri Collection, US Army Military History Institute (USAMHI).

1st Ranger Battalion training, northern Scotland: Crossing under barbed-wire obstacles. Photo credit: James Altieri Collection, USAMHI.

The 1st Rangers make a practice beach landing and assault during their training in northern Scotland. Photo credit: James Altieri Collection, USAMHI.

1st Ranger Battalion training in northern Scotland. Photo credit: James Altieri Collection, USAMHI.

A British Commando lights the cigarette of Ranger Alex Zcema after the raid on Dieppe. Ranger Bill Brady can be seen smiling (center). Photo credit: James Altieri Collection, USAMHI.

Officers and men of 4th Rangers being decorated in North Africa. Photo credit: Roy Murray Collection.

Typical terrain and town in North Africa during the Rangers time there. Photo credit: James Altieri Collection.

Prisoners of war captured by the Rangers in North Africa. Photo credit: James Altieri Collection.

German prisoners of war taken in the North Africa campaign dismounting from a truck. Photo credit: James Altieri Collection.

On board the British ship *Queen Emma,* for an aborted raid, December, 1942. (L to R) Walter F. Nye, 1st Platoon, F Company; Leilyn Young, 2d Platoon, F Company; Roy A. Murray, Commander of F Company — all from 1st Ranger Battalion. Each man later joined the 4th Rangers. Murray became commander of the 4th Ranger Battalion. Photo credit: Roy Murray Collection.

Life Magazine photo of a tank battle on the plains of Sicily, August 2, 1943. Photo credit: Bob Landry, © Time, Inc. From the James Altieri Collection.

Happy Thanksgiving—the 4th Rangers "enjoy" Thanksgiving dinner in the hills near Veafro and Monte Cassino in south-central Italy, November 25, 1943. (L to R) Two unidentified Rangers of the 4th Battalion, Captain Nye, executive officer, and Maj. Roy Murray, commanding officer, 4th Ranger Battalion. Photo credit: Roy Murray Collection.

Pointe du Hoc, Normandy, was the objective of the 2d Ranger Battalion on D day, June 6, 1944. Just to the right of the "point," the German observation post can be seen. On the other side of the Pointe was a small pebble beach where the Rangers made their landing. The cliffs were the same height and ruggedness as seen here. Photo credit: James Altieri Collection, USAMHI.

The 2d Ranger Battalion headed home from Europe in the Fall of 1945. Photo credit: Roy Murray Collection.

Fall, 1945: The surviving "charter" members of the 2d Ranger Battalion just before leaving for home. Photo credit: Roy Murray Collection.

of F company had found a shooter's heaven. Outposted with about nine F Company Rangers, Petty had a clear field of fire for his beloved BAR. As the unknowing enemy tried to pass in front of his position, Petty picked them off. His comrades have insisted that Petty brought down thirty of the enemy during the course of the D-day operation. Petty knew he "killed some people and wounded some," but as to specific numbers, his comment was "who counts in such situations."

Surviving Germans were rounded up; some forty prisoners would go into the bag.

On Omaha Beach, the Rangers of Company C had played an important role in clearing the way for the use of the Vierville beach exit. But the fighting in the German beach defenses had prevented Company C from reaching their original objective.

About 1430 Captain Goranson took a patrol west to reconnoiter Pointe de la Percee. As they arrived in a position to observe the point, they saw a destroyer standing close inshore eliminate the German positions. Another destroyer saw the Rangers and, mistaking them for the enemy, opened fire. A forward observer on the beach saw the error and called off the naval gunfire. Two Rangers were wounded and another concussed so badly that he had to be stopped from walking off the cliffs and accused a colonel of the 29th Division of stealing his rifle, when the rifle was slung from his shoulder.

Small parties of Germans attempted to attack F Company, 2d Ranger Battalion, positions but were beaten off by rifle fire. A second and more serious attack began around 1600. The number of men involved on each side was small, but the outcome was significant. Squad-size, machine-gun equipped German elements began moving in the direction of the command post. T/5 Herman Stein[8] and Ranger Manning fired from the German flank and dropped several at a range of forty yards. The Germans hesitated and took cover in shell holes. Sergeant Elder was nearby with a 60mm mortar, and he opened fire at close range. As the shells began to burst around them, the Germans tried to flee. Stein's BAR, the small arms of the other Rangers, and Elder's mortar took a toll that Stein described as "a turkey shoot." The mortar fire flushed another group of Germans with similar result.

With the cliffs and beach exit in friendly hands, the remaining twenty-eight men of Charlie Company, 2d Rangers, moved down to the Vierville draw. Here they made contact with a patrol from Force C that had returned to the beach to secure ammunition, and moved to join Colonel Schneider and his men, reaching them about 2200 hours.

The 5th Ranger Battalion fought its way through Vierville, but on the western edge of town, German resistance stiffened. Darkness began to settle. The 5th Rangers together with A, B, and C Companies of the 2d Rangers, Company C of the 116th Infantry, and elements of the 743d Tank Battalion set up a perimeter defense.

At Pointe du Hoc, Lt. Charles Parker and twenty-two men of the 1st Platoon of Company A, 5th Rangers, came through the dusk to join Rudder's Force A. Parker had led his platoon to the prearranged assembly area near Vierville. Slowed by heavy fighting, the remainder of the battalion did not arrive, so Parker set out overland. The platoon engaged in several firefights along the way and at one point had nearly forty German prisoners, most of whom escaped during a heavy action. When Parker arrived at around 2100 hours, he believed the remainder of the 5th Battalion was close behind him. Parker's platoon was assigned defensive positions, a welcome reinforcement to the men of the 2d Rangers.

With the coming of night, Rudder maintained his dispositions, with some eighty men of D, E, and F still forward of the Vierville–Grandcamp highway. F Company was on the left, E Company in the center, and D Company on the right. There was a risk of this small force being cut off, but the block was important. While German activity was increasing as they recovered from the opening shock of the invasion, no major counterattack had developed. Short of ammunition, the Rangers tightened up their lines and waited.

Lt. George Kerchner, platoon leader of 1st Platoon, D Company, had observed enemy activity southwest of the angle where D and E Company joined. There was a three-quarter moon, but night still changed the landscape: visibility that had been good during the daytime was difficult among the shadows of hedgerows and orchards. Shortly before midnight, Ranger outposts in front of the juncture of D and E Companies received German fire. Probably German patrols were probing in an effort to draw Ranger fire and determine their positions.

Around 0100 hours, the main German thrust materialized. German infantry had managed to move within one hundred yards of the Ranger positions. The Germans opened with whistles and shouting the names of their men, either as a means of location or to build morale. All the clamor was followed by machine-gun and small-arms fire, often heavily in tracer ammunition. German mortar fire was heavy but inaccurate. German infantry came forward, using marching fire as they moved.

Some of the Germans came in on the F Company area, but Sergeants Petty and Robey did good work with the BAR. The Germans had to be content with standoff fire. The main German thrust was near the juncture of D and E Companies, with the Company E platoon at this location being hardest hit. In the darkness, men fought as individuals and small groups. There was the usual night-battle confusion as to the location of both friends and enemy. The Germans overran the E Company positions, killing Lieutenant Leagans and killing or capturing nineteen Rangers of Company E.

No one could tell the strength of the German forces or the configuration of the remaining Ranger positions. A man ran into the F Company positions saying that D Company had been wiped out. Feeling they were left alone or had been bypassed, men were pulling out of position. All the burden of a prolonged day of battle was telling on them. Men were tired, and many were fighting with wounds. For most, the single D bar had been their only sustenance. Weapons fouled with heavy usage were jamming, and, short of ammunition, some Rangers were using German weapons and grenades. While effective, the distinctive sounds of the German weapons added to the confusion.

Believing they were outnumbered by the Germans in front and possibly infiltrated to their rear, the small group of 2d and 5th Rangers began to pull back to the Pointe. The withdrawal was normal for this type of circumstance: it was disorganized and men ran for their lives under the protective fires of several key people, in this instance, Petty and Robey covering with their BARs.

On reaching the blacktop and finding they were not pursued, a reorganization was made and efforts made to determine who was missing. Learning that Sergeant Petty was covering the withdrawal, Sergeant Alexander voluntarily went back to assist. As Alexander neared Petty's position, he was captured. With the immediate danger past for the rest of the men, the inevitable happened: men felt embarrassed and accused each other of pulling out. Men of the 5th Rangers felt they had been left to fend for themselves, and men of the 2d thought the 5th Rangers had pulled out. Men also felt anger toward others of their own units. They had not yet learned that uncertainty and confusion is magnified in a night battle.

Around 0400 some forty-eight men reached the Pointe and were placed in a defensive line that stretched from the former German gun positions three to five. Rudder was told the rest of the force had been destroyed.

But men had been left behind. Four were left in the F Company area, including Sergeant Petty, who created confusion among the Germans by opening fire when in their midst, then quickly moving in the darkness to a new position. D Company had two 1st Platoon Rangers killed in the German attack and two captured, but some fourteen D Company men were still occupying their original positions at the roadblock.

These men were not heavily engaged. They were unaware that a withdrawal had taken place until there was too much daylight for them to move. The Germans were not aware of their location. The Rangers left behind stayed under cover and maintained fire discipline. Their salvation was staying hidden.

The morning light revealed a grim situation at Pointe du Hoc. The remnants of the three Ranger companies numbered between ninety and one hundred men, with fifty-one wounded. Ammunition was seriously low. The Ranger position consisted of a strip on the Pointe that was some two hundred yards deep. There was no indication of relief. Rudder's request for reinforcement had resulted in a message that "all Rangers have been landed." A message sent to the 116th Infantry failed to gain permission for the 5th Rangers and the remainder of the 2d to push on to link up.

A relief force had been planned, but there were several disruptions. The 116th Infantry of the 29th Division had suffered 341 officers and men killed during the day. A German counterattack early in the morning of June 7 caused General Gerhardt of the 29th to pull off four Ranger companies of the 5th Battalion and tanks to protect Vierville, the beach exit, and the 29th Division command post.

At 0800 on June 7, a relief force moved to break through to the Rangers on Pointe du Hoc. The force was smaller than planned and was built around the remnants of A, B, and C Companies, 2d Rangers, under the superb leadership of Captain Arnold; C and D Companies of the 5th Rangers; 10 Sherman tanks; and some 250 men of Lt. Col. John Metcalf's 1st Battalion, 116th Infantry.

By 1100 hours, the column was within a thousand yards of Pointe du Hoc, nearing the lateral road that led to the Pointe. At this location, German resistance stiffened. Snipers and machine guns opened on Company A of the 2d Rangers, which was the point unit. The tanks came under heavy fire and withdrew. A heavy concentration of German artillery rained down on the men, causing numerous casualties and breaking up the attack. Lacking sufficient force to penetrate, the relief column withdrew to the town of St. Pierre and dug in for the night.

On Pointe du Hoc, the grim situation was greatly alleviated by the timely arrival of supplies. Maj. Jack Street—who had joined the Rangers at Nemours, commanded Company G of the 1st Battalion, and served so well in Sicily—was now a staff officer with Admiral Hall. Learning of the difficult circumstances of the Rangers on Pointe du Hoc, Major Street organized a relief party that included two landing craft with some thirty reinforcements, ammunition, water, and food. The seriously wounded were extracted.

As darkness fell on June 7, the men of D, E, and F Companies, 2d Ranger Battalion, held on grimly to the point of Pointe du Hoc. Meanwhile, the 29th Division made plans to press the relief in the morning. For the new effort, the 29th committed all three battalions of the 116th Infantry.

Tragedy occurred when the 3d Battalion, 116th Infantry, approaching from the south, heard the sound of German weapons being fired from Pointe du Hoc. Unaware that Rangers on the Pointe were using German weapons, the 3d Battalion opened fire on the Rangers with machine guns, tanks, artillery, and mortars. A recognition flare was fired and the American flag displayed, but the so-called "friendly fire" killed one Ranger and seriously wounded others.

When the error was corrected, the linkup was accomplished and German resistance reduced. By noon on June 8, the situation was well in hand. The attacking American forces pressed on, supported by the guns of the British cruiser *Glasgow*. By nightfall, the Germans had lost Grandcamp and the battle.

Despite the commitment of vast numbers of men and staggering quantities of material, the success of the invasion of Europe depended upon the relatively small number of men who made the initial landings.

The Rangers contributed greatly to this historic victory.

No Ranger unit engaged in the invasion of Europe suffered as heavily as the men of Company C, 2d Ranger Battalion. No one has a better claim to having been the first of the invasion force to reach high ground. The action the men of Company C, 2d Ranger Battalion, fought on top of the cliffs, assisted by men of Company B, 116th Infantry, was of significant help to the men caught in the hellfires of Omaha Beach.

A and B Companies of the 2d Rangers endured that hell on Omaha Dog Green yet continued to attack and seized the bluffs to their front.

The men of the 5th Ranger Battalion had a rendezvous with history on Omaha Beach. At precisely the right moment in time, they were in position and possessed the strength to lift the invasion beyond the beaches.

The men of D, E, and F of the 2d Rangers accomplished their mission: The guns of Pointe du Hoc were destroyed. While it could fire at either beach, this heavy artillery was pointed at Utah Beach. The 4th Infantry Division landed at Utah Beach with comparative ease. They were not under heavy fire from the Germans. The lead regiments of the 4th Division suffered only twelve fatalities prior to noon on D-day. The 4th Division's casualties on land for D-day were 137. Had the guns of Pointe du Hoc not been destroyed, the sands of Utah Beach may well have been soaked with the blood of American youth.

CHAPTER 10

BREST

While the 5th Rangers pressed the attack on Grandcamp, the survivors of the 2d Ranger Battalion took several hours to reorganize, determine the extent of their losses, and make a thorough search of the surrounding terrain. An F Company patrol made a search of hedgerows but did not encounter any Germans. An old man and a boy dressed in slave-labor garb were encountered. A Ranger officer yelled "Shoot the bastards." While the victims screamed in horror, the officer and a senior NCO killed them.

Other Rangers were filled with horror and disgust at this insanity, this murder.

Meanwhile back on Pointe du Hoc, a search of the observation post uncovered a copy of the German Naval Pennant Code, valuable naval intelligence. On the 2d Ranger periphery, patrols made contact with the 5th Rangers.

With reorganization complete, the 2d and 5th Rangers moved by stages to a bivouac area near the Grandcamp sluice gate. It was a time for recuperation. Battalion supply vehicles arrived, and hungry and tired men were provided with ammunition, food, water, and bedrolls.

On June 9, the 2d and 5th Ranger Battalions marched eight miles in light rain to a bivouac area near Osmansville. Patrolling began on the 10th. A French farmer came into the 2d Ranger Company F area, excitedly repeating what the Rangers interpreted as *"Le boche cinq, cinq!"* The Rangers thought the Frenchman knew of the location of five Germans, and some of the Rangers went after them.

When they reached the German position, the Rangers opened fire and captured a German headquarters unit, complete with payroll. Two Germans were killed and fifty-three taken prisoner. The Germans did not resist and may have sent the farmer to announce their desire to give up.

On the 11th, the 2d and 5th Battalions had their first mail call since departing England. Men of the 1st Platoon Company C, 2d Rangers, were attacked by a wounded cow, but the animal was not supported by its herd and lost the engagement. Once again the battalions moved, this time to an area near Bois de Molay, where they became part of V Corps reserve. Every night the German hit-and-run bombers came over. The exploding bombs and the hammer and crash of anti-aircraft guns made sleep difficult. Men rested during the daylight hours.

Replacements came in, were interviewed and assigned or rejected. Weapons and equipment were checked. On the 15th, a 2d Ranger sergeant saw three Germans sighting on a Ranger in the bivouac area. The Ranger sergeant shot first, wounded one, and captured all three of the Germans. On June 16, the 2d and 5th Ranger Battalions marched seven miles to Colombieres, where they bivouacked and became part of First U.S. Army reserve. Training of replacements continued. On the 19th, the 2d Rangers welcomed back Capt. Duke Slater, Lieutenant McBride, and nineteen other men who had been on the D Company LCA that sank on the way to Pointe du Hoc.

Col. Eugene Slappey had been commander of the 115th Infantry Regiment of the 29th Infantry Division. The division commander, General Gerhardt, wanted another officer in command of the 115th and relieved Colonel Slappey. Sent to First Army, Slappey was given command of the Ranger Group, and Lieutenant Colonel Rudder reverted to command of the 2d Battalion.

On June 20, the kitchens and hot food arrived. Awards came as well. Over the period June 21–23, officers and men of the 2d Ranger Battalion were awarded eight Distinguished Service Crosses and fourteen Silver Stars for their performance during the landings.

Also on June 20, the 5th Ranger Battalion moved from Colombieres to Foucarville, where they began POW guard duty.

From June 25 to July 2, the 2d Rangers served as guards

for German prisoners. Some ten thousand captured enemy were taken from prisoner cages of the 4th and 79th Infantry Divisions and escorted to the Utah Beach area for further processing.

On July 3, 1944, the 2d Rangers moved to a former German military post near Beaumont-Hague. Here, where once the men of a German flak battalion made residence, the 2d Rangers lived well with barracks, showers, and sports. All this was periphery to the training however. Day and night training was conducted, progressing from dry- to live-fire exercises and marches that increased to thirty miles.

On the 5th, the 5th Rangers moved some thirty-eight miles by motor convoy to Greville. On the 8th, they moved another twenty-two miles to Dialetto. On July 11, the 2d Rangers relieved the 24th Cavalry Reconnaissance Squadron of the defense of the Beaumont-Hague Peninsula. There was little German activity remaining, but the enemy held the Guernsey Islands which were off the coast. Patrols and observation-post duty fulfilled the mission. On July 19, the 15th Cavalry Reconnaissance Group relieved the Rangers.

Once again, training was resumed. Men wounded in D-day fighting began to return to the unit. Through July and into August, duties consisted of escorting prisoners and training. Twelve select men were sent to sniper school. On August 6, the 2d and 5th Rangers became part of a combat team that had a mix of infantry, artillery, and armor. Four days were spent in combined-arms training for a mission that was canceled. On August 12, the 2d Rangers closed on Buais.

The new mission was to secure the right flank of the First Army in the vicinity of Mortain. High command was trying to contain German forces in the area, so the mission included preventing a German withdrawal to the south. During this time, the battalion was attached to VII Corps and further attached to the 4th Infantry Division. On August 13, the 2d Rangers were moved to a defensive position east of Mayenne. Here, the Rangers relieved the 2d Battalion of the 16th Infantry. From August 13 to 17, the 2d Rangers occupied defensive positions guarding bridges across the Mayenne River and ran patrols. During this time, the battalion was attached for supply and administration to the 9th Infantry Division.

On the 17th, the 2d Rangers were attached to VIII Corps and alerted for movement to the area of Brest.

Brest was the second largest port in France and a city of some eighty thousand people. The deep-water port had excellent rail connections inland and had been a principal submarine base for the German Navy. The city had been bypassed in earlier attacks, and the German defenders were now isolated. But Brest was a fortress city, heavily defended against attack by land or sea. In time, the besieged German defenders could have been starved out. But in the opinion of senior logistical planners, there was no time to wait. The port facilities of Brest were urgently needed to carry the logistical flood of men and material that was pouring into Europe.

Gen. Troy Middleton's VIII Corps had the mission of capturing Brest. To accomplish this mission, Middleton's corps was given forces that included the 2d, 8th, and 29th Infantry Divisions, and the 2d and 5th Ranger Battalions.

The German defenses were formidable: a series of lines with strong points containing self-propelled guns and automatic weapons, protected by mines, wire, and antitank ditches. The ratio of attacker to defender was not favorable for the Americans. Intelligence thought there were twenty thousand Germans in Brest; the actual number was close to fifty thousand—about the same size as the attacking American force. The German units included the 2d Parachute Division, marines, and sailors. Commanding the German forces was Maj. Gen. Herman Ramcke. It was Ramcke and his 1st Parachute Division who fought with such determination at Monte Cassino in Italy.

Middleton's VIII Corps assumed an arclike position around the fortress city of Brest. The 29th Division was on the right, the 8th Division in the center, and the 2d Division on the left.

On August 19, after a harrowing night motor trip in rain and with exhausted, accident-prone drivers, the 2d Rangers arrived in a bivouac in the vicinity of Le Folgoët. The duty was corps reserve, with a liberal amount of combat patrolling thrown in.

Rumors that the Germans wanted to surrender were rampant and often false. A platoon from Company A, 2d Rangers, was sent to take a group of Germans that were said to be giving up. The Germans ambushed the Rangers and killed an officer and three men.

Individual company missions were the order of the day. Companies A, B, and C provided security for VIII Corps Headquarters, and D Company and elements of the 86th Mechanized Cavalry Reconnaissance Squadron went patrolling together. E and F Companies were on outpost duty near St. Renan and taking a pounding from German artillery.

While the 2d and 5th Rangers were moving on the forts of Brest, a significant Ranger event was taking shape on the other side of the world.

From his headquarters in Hollandia, New Guinea, Lt. Gen. Walter Krueger, commander of the United States Sixth Army, directed the formation of a Ranger battalion for the Pacific Theater. Krueger was an old soldier, a tough disciplinarian, and a wily fighter. He had kept informed of events in Europe and felt a Ranger battalion could perform useful missions against the Japanese.

Unlike Ranger Battalions 1–5, which were formed from volunteers organized into a unit, the 6th Ranger Battalion was formed from a unit that became volunteers. The 98th Field Artillery Battalion, armed with 75mm pack howitzers, had been in the Pacific since January 1943 and had fought in New Guinea.

The commander of the 6th Ranger Battalion would be Lt. Col. Henry "Hank" Mucci[1] from Bridgeport, Connecticut. While not physically large, Mucci had the reputation of being tough and capable. He had held the post of provost marshal of Honolulu.

Mucci called for volunteers from the 98th to become Rangers. Those who declined were transferred, and volunteers from other units were brought to the unit. The unit was organized as a Ranger battalion with six Ranger rifle companies and a headquarters company, and began training. They were not yet officially designated as "Ranger."

In Europe on August 22, D, E, and F Companies of the 2d Rangers were attached to the 29th Infantry Division for rations and supply in the St. Renan area. The Germans in this area were prone to operate patrols with as many as fifty men. These could be rifle companies that had seen prolonged action or sailors turned infantry, who lacked sufficient infantry-experienced leaders. Tipped off by the French Forces of the Interior (members of the civilian resistance) that a German patrol was coming, the Rangers set an ambush. Three Germans were killed and the remainder dispersed. Soon thereafter, the Germans attacked the positions of F Company, and were beaten off with losses. The Rangers remained unscathed, and this was due to some alert thinking: knowing their positions had been revealed, the Rangers withdrew several hundred yards to a new location. Intense German fire from 88mm guns fell on the area they had just left.

On the 23d, the 2d Rangers were attached to the 29th Infantry Division for the attack on Brest. Part of the Ranger duties were to work with the French to establish a location behind the German lines where Frenchmen within those lines could bring information about the German dispositions. At 0800 on the 25th, the 2d Ranger intelligence officer, Capt. Harvey J. Cook, and select men of his section began to infiltrate German lines to establish the intelligence gathering point.

The VIII Corps attack on Brest began at 1300 hours on August 25. The 29th Infantry Division attacked with the 115th and 116th Infantry Regiments and met heavy resistance.

Capt. Harold K. "Duke" Slater, 2d Battalion executive officer, led "Force Slater." This force consisted of B, D, E, and F Companies of the 2d Rangers, scout cars, and light tanks. Slater employed his men in an aggressive screening of the right flank of the 175th Infantry Regiment, 29th Division reserve force. Three Germans were killed by the Rangers on the 25th. On the 26th, the 175th Infantry was committed, and the Rangers roamed south and west, killing fifteen Germans. The terrain was open, and when nighttime positions were dug, the orders were "Stay in your hole. Anything moving gets shot."

On the 26th, 81mm mortars used by Company C supported a French attack on a German fort. Companies A and C moved on the 27th to join Force Slater which was at Kervaourn. Slater's group was attached to Task Force Sugar of the 29th Infantry Division.

Task Force Sugar began as a small force under the command of Lt. Col. Arthur Sheppe, executive officer of the 175th Infantry Regiment. Within a short time, the task force grew to include the 2d and 5th Ranger Battalions, a battalion from the 116th Infantry, the 224th Field Artillery Battalion, and elements of reconnaissance, engineer, 4.2-inch mortar, and antiaircraft artillery units.

Moving from a position near St. Renan on August 27, Task Force Sugar sent elements south and west. On the south shore of the Le Conquet Peninsula, near a town called Lochrist, was a German battery of powerful 280mm guns. Named the Batterie Graf Spee, these big guns threatened the 29th Division right flank. To the north of Batterie Graf Spee were other German positions.

Companies A and C (Force A under Capt. Edgar L. Arnold) of the 2d Rangers had the mission of clearing the enemy from the east coast south of Tresien. Accompanied by French Forces of the Interior (FFI), Force A moved to the attack on the afternoon of August 27. Fifteen Germans were soon captured.

The mission of Task Force Sugar was becoming increasingly important to the 29th Infantry Division. As of August 28, the task force came under the command of Col. Edward McDaniel, 29th Division chief of staff.

On the morning of the 28th, Force A, with attached tank destroyers of the 644th Tank Destroyer Battalion, came through morning fog to attack a German strongpoint. The Rangers pounded the Germans, killed nine, captured ninety-four, and eliminated the enemy position.

During the 2d Ranger attacks, Ranger Dominick Sparaco had been instructed to fire a rifle grenade into a German-held building. Sparaco fired accurately but forgot to remove the safety pin. The sight of the unexploded round bouncing around the interior of their building, however, was sufficient encouragement for over thirty Germans to surrender.

Also on the morning of the 28th, Force Slater began conducting aggressive reconnaissance to the west. Ranger observers located German positions and brought down artillery on them. The Germans responded in kind and five Rangers were wounded. At 1115 Companies E and F, accompanied by light tanks, moved west on a reconnaissance. Three Germans were killed and two captured. Reconnaissance continued, with Companies D and E working as a team and Companies B and F doing the same.

By noon, the men of Captain Arnold's Force A were in full stride. Among their prizes were 162 Russian soldiers that the Germans had been using as slave labor. The Russians were under effective leadership and quickly reorganized into a fighting force.

In the afternoon, Arnold's men attacked another strongpoint on Pointe de Corzen. This was a tough fight, and supporting artillery was requested but not received. With the tank destroyers giving covering fire, the Rangers advanced under a hail of enemy artillery, mortar, automatic-weapons, and small-arms fire. By nightfall, it appeared the Germans might be ready to surrender, but they hung on grimly. The Russians ambushed a German eight-man patrol and killed them all. The Russian commander sent a note of apology to Captain Arnold for not saving a German for interrogation.

Task Force Slater's D and E team, with elements of the 86th Cavalry Reconnaissance Squadron, continued west against light resistance to Kersturet. B and F Companies followed D and E Companies, then moved to Kervegnon, where Force Slater went into defensive positions for the night.

At 0730 on the 29th, Force A began pounding the Germans with tank-destroyer fire. The Rangers closed on the German position, holding their fire and sending a German prisoner forward to encourage his comrades to surrender. The tank destroyers had killed eight, and the remaining seventy-two Germans surrendered. Force A then continued south to the coast. As darkness fell on a rainy night, the Rangers were brought under German 20mm fire. Unable to locate the position of the guns, Force A went into night bivouac and awaited the dawn.

On August 29, the 5th Ranger Battalion entered the Brest campaign. Companies A and C, under the command of the battalion executive officer, Maj. Hugo Heffelfinger, were attached to the 2d Infantry Division for operations. This Ranger force provided flank security for the 23d Infantry Regiment. The action included employment in defensive positions and patrolling. Company E of the 5th Rangers was given the mission of maintaining contact patrols between the 2d and 8th U.S. Infantry Divisions. German forces attacked into the gap but were beaten off by the E Company Rangers.

On the morning of August 30, D and E Company, 2d Rangers, continued west to Hill 63. One Ranger was wounded, but fifteen of the enemy were killed and fourteen were wounded. B and F Companies also moved to Hill 63, and a perimeter defense was established. The Germans had accurately surveyed the area, and soon artillery and mortars began to beat on the Ranger position. A deep foxhole was necessary to survive, as Ranger casualties from this fire climbed.

On the morning of the 30th, Arnold's men found the German 20mm was part of the defense of a German strong-point. The Germans were occupying a hill flanked by two other hills. Without being detected by the enemy, Company A and several tank destroyers climbed to the top of a hill that overlooked the German position, and life became difficult for the defenders. The 20mm gun was in an open emplacement and was soon put out of action. Heavy supporting fire from other German positions held up the Rangers who dug in for the night.

On August 31, the nasty fight continued in earnest. Battling from fortified positions, the Germans hung on grimly. The 20mm gun was back in action, and mortar fire added to its punch. With A Company, 60mm and 81mm mortars, tank de-stroyers, and 105mm artillery in support, Company C man-aged to close by infiltration on the Germans. Now the Germans brought a rain of artillery fire on the attackers, forcing them to withdraw under the cover of smoke. The 2d Ranger Cannon Platoon moved to a hill-protected location close to the enemy and began firing 75mm artillery, knocking out the 20mm gun. The night closed a stalemate, but it was the Germans who had most to dread from the dawn.

Meanwhile, Force Slater was dug in on and patrolling from Hill 63. German artillery and mortars continued to work over the hill. One Ranger was killed and ten wounded on the 31st.

On September 1, Captain Arnold called on the 210mm howitzers of corps artillery to blast the Germans out of their holes. The big tubes could not find the mark, but the artillery officer directing the 105mm batteries was skilled and efficient. Using ammunition designed to penetrate concrete, he directed the 105mm howitzers[2] in accurate and deadly fire. Meanwhile, Companies A and C moved closer to the German positions. Two P-38 fighter aircraft were requested to bomb the Germans, but their bombs splashed harmlessly into the sea. Both sides continued to pour fire on each other. To the disgust of the Americans, the Germans had been able to put the pesky 20mm gun back in action.

Lieutenant Colonel Rudder had other priorities to attend to. As darkness fell, he sent Captain Arnold with Company A and the tank destroyers on another mission.

Captain Slater's force was still holding Hill 63. Ranger reconnaissance patrols reached the coast, while combat patrols rooted out German defensive positions. On September 1 two Germans were killed and over one hundred captured. German artillery continued to be the nemesis, playing over Hill 63 and wounding eleven Rangers.

Also on September 1, the remainder of the 5th Ranger Battalion was attached to the 29th Infantry Division. Moving into position, elements of the 5th had to drive off the Germans to get control of their assigned bivouac area. Companies A and C were active, running combat patrols to German-held hills: the Rangers killed three Germans and brought back three prisoners.

The 2d Battalion found itself facing a courageous German defense at the strongpoint in front of Force A. Rudder decided to hold the Germans in position while he attacked elsewhere. On September 2, twenty men of Company C were left in position, while the remainder of the force moved to a road junction 79. Company A was ordered to take Trebabu to the west, while the remaining men of Company C had the mission of seizing Tremail in the south.

Supported by tanks and accompanied by FFI, Company A occupied Trebabu and killed three Germans manning a machine gun beyond the town. Company C was also accompanied by FFI. Ranger patrols, leading the advance, destroyed two German machine guns, killing four and capturing one German. The Company C Rangers encountered a force of some 150 Germans, and the FFI broke and ran under fire, causing the forty Rangers difficulty. Under artillery fire and enemy counterattack, the Rangers withdrew from Tremail and set up a defense for the night.

The 116th Infantry Regiment was charged with attacking on the right of the 29th Infantry Division zone. To the right of the 116th, the 5th Ranger Battalion was assigned the critical mission of knocking out five German forts. The chain of these forts stretched westward from Recouvrance some seven miles to where the sea entered the Bay of Brest. Fort Tolbrouch was the largest of the forts, the first the Rangers were to encounter. A reconnaissance was in order to develop the situation. B and D Companies of the 5th Rangers led off. Lt. Stan Askin and his 1st Platoon of Company B moved south while Lt. Louis Gombosi led the 2d Platoon of Company B on a route that took them into the German fort. The Germans were inside in strength. Despite being reinforced by another platoon, the Rangers were forced to withdraw under heavy fire. The Germans now began a night of counterattack. Lieutenant Askin's 1st Platoon was pulled back, and Headquarters Company Rangers had to be brought forward and fight beside the Ranger rifle companies to help stop the German thrusts.

Maj. Richard Sullivan, commanding the 5th Rangers, knew that a head-on attack on Fort Tolbrouch, even with artillery preparation, could result in the loss of many lives, but as the war had progressed communication and cooperation between air and ground forces improved. The air support that could have saved the 1st and 3d Rangers at Cisterna was available, and Major Sullivan was determined to use it.

Sullivan planned to use P-47 fighter/bombers of the XIX Tactical Air Command to precede his attack. Company B would lead the ground force, followed by Company D. The remaining companies would be in support. Lieutenant Gombosi's 2d Platoon led off down a draw approach to the fort. The first air attack was four hundred yards off target. The Rangers held position and called for another air strike, but the second attempt was also wide of the mark. Patiently, the 5th Rangers tried again. Artillery, firing rounds of purple smoke, was used to mark the target. The smoke rounds did not detonate, and another attempt was made, this time using white phosphorus.

The marking rounds landed right on target, and the P-47s dived to attack. Sixteen five hundred–pound bombs tore into the German position. Now Capt. Bernard M. Pepper's Company B swept forward while overhead the thick-bodied fighters made three strafing passes, firing within twenty yards of the advancing Rangers. Pinned down by fire, the Germans found the Rangers on top of them before they could recover. In less than ten minutes, the 5th Rangers captured Fort Tolbrouch. Five officers and 242 enlisted men of the Third Reich raised their hands in surrender.

On September 3, Company C of the 2d Rangers, now reinforced with the Cannon Platoon and two tank destroyers, moved on Tremail. The Germans had departed, so Company C continued on. In late morning, Company C and a thirty-man German patrol encountered each other. The Ranger trigger fingers were faster, and five of the enemy were killed, six captured, and the rest scattered. Three Rangers were wounded, two lightly enough to remain in battle.

Later in the morning, heavy resistance was encountered. P-38 fighter aircraft were available for ground-support missions, and the Rangers took off their white undershirts and spread them on the ground to mark their position. The fighters strafed the Germans and, alternating with 105mm artillery fire, hit the Germans hard.

On the 3d, Company A continued its advance against light resistance, killing eleven Germans. As darkness fell, the two Ranger companies made contact with each other.

September 3 was not a good day for Force Slater. Still holding on to Hill 63, Slater's men came under fire from German 88mm guns and the big 280mm guns of the Batterie Graf Spee at Lochrist. Two Rangers were killed and twenty-one wounded.

The fort-busting 5th Rangers spent September 3 going after Fort de Mengant. In this attack, Major Sullivan used F Company to secure a high-ground position and supported while D and Headquarters Companies used the same air-support tactic that worked so well the day before. Three hundred badly battered Germans surrendered to the 5th Rangers. Company F moved at dark to seize the line of departure for the next attack.

By midnight, Company F was on the objective and had captured another twenty prisoners.

By September 4, Rudder and Slater decided that something had to be done to reduce the Hill 63 casualty list of the 2d Ranger Battalion. Companies D and F were moved off the hill to a rest area some five hundred yards away. The men of B and E Companies spread out and maintained a thinned-out defense. The German shelling continued, but with fewer Rangers to serve as a target, only three men were wounded for the day.

On the 4th, Captain Arnold held his positions, with A and C Companies contenting themselves with directing artillery on the Germans. This accurate fire did yeoman service in silencing an enemy battery and breaking up an enemy force moving as though it intended to attack Company C.

On September 5, D and F Companies moved back onto Hill 63, while B and E Companies went to the rest area. German positions to the front were identified in an area close to the French. American 4.2-inch mortars brought the Germans under the horror of white phosphorus. The terrified and burning Germans ran and, in doing so, came under the sights of French snipers who took a heavy toll. In their turn, the Germans fired their mighty 280mm guns at Hill 63. Rangers were buried alive by the heaving of the earth, and though rescued, they were in a state of shock. The German shelling caused the FFI to flee their positions, and 2d Ranger Battalion headquarters personnel had to fill the gap.

On the 5th, Arnold's Force A continued to work over German positions with supporting fire. One P-38 mistakenly dropped a bomb on Company A positions: no one was injured, and it did wonders for the chaplain's collection plate. The Rangers were preparing for the attack and all available men were needed, even though the tough German position at Kergolleau was still holding out. Fourteen more Rangers of Company A were taken from Kergolleau to strengthen Force A, leaving only one officer and five Rangers to hold the Germans in their Kergolleau dugouts. To give the appearance of strength, the Rangers dressed fourteen Russians in American uniforms.

The 5th Rangers spent September 5 going after Fort de

Dellec. Company B had the lead, with Company F and a platoon of tank destroyers in support. Preparatory fire was used, but the Germans were becoming attuned to the Ranger tactic. As Company B made their assault, they were struck in the flank by a German counterattack. B Company withdrew, and Company F, supported by the tank destroyers, fixed bayonets, charged, and captured the fort. The Germans again counterattacked, assisted by American fighter/bombers that mistakenly bombed the Rangers. With men thrown about like rag dolls from the bombing, Company F was in serious trouble. Sullivan sent both A and E Companies to their support, and the gains were held. The 5th Rangers had suffered eighteen casualties, while the Germans lost more than one hundred killed and seventy prisoners.

At 0830 on the morning of September 6, the 2d Ranger Battalion moved on the Germans at Hill 63. Behind heavy preparatory fire, Companies B, D, and E attacked abreast, with Company F in reserve while Arnold's A and C Companies launched a diversionary attack. This was a day of heavy fighting, under fire from German 75mm self-propelled and 88mm guns. By late afternoon Force Slater had gained a thousand yards. Germans fleeing shelter encountered Company A and Company C: Charlie Company killed five Germans, and together the two companies captured twenty-two more. The Germans said that American 4.2-inch mortars firing white phosphorus rounds had killed another twenty-six. At the close of day, the attack had killed sixty enemy and captured another forty. One Ranger was killed and nineteen wounded.

The 5th Rangers also continued in the attack on September 6, suffering one casualty. The Germans lost thirty-nine captured and approximately fifty killed.

At 0730 on the 7th, 2d Ranger Force Slater resumed the attack. By the close of day, the Rangers had reached their objective and were astride the Brest–Le Conquet road. The withdrawing Germans left eleven dead and twenty as prisoners. By midafternoon, the task forces of the 2d Ranger Battalion had merged. Patrols continued and 144 more of the enemy were captured and 30 killed without the loss of a Ranger.

The night of the 7th, the 2d Rangers were in position, with the 3d Battalion of the 116th Infantry on their left. The 5th Ranger Battalion had joined Task Force Sugar, moving by foot, motor, then foot again to take up position to the right of the 2d Rangers.

On September 8, Ranger Lukovsky, missing in action since September 3, was found dead. The bodies of seven dead Germans lay around him.

The German 280mm Graf Spee battery at Lochrist had left its mark upon the Rangers, and the hour of retribution was at hand. Despite intense efforts, the exact location of the battery of great guns had not been determined. The 2d Ranger plan of attack called for the companies to be widely spaced but move in converging directions. Rudder's orders were to move rapidly, allowing the enemy no time to establish a defense. The attack would begin at 0830 hours September 9. The 3d Battalion of the 116th Infantry was attacking on the left of the 2d Rangers to seize Plougenvelin, while the 5th Rangers were on the right, going after the town of Le Conquet.

The 2d Rangers would later observe that PT (prisoners and terrain) slowed the advance for some companies. The Germans knew the battle had been lost, and so many Germans surrendered that the battalion had to establish its own prisoner-of-war enclosure.

E and F Company were on the verge of attacking a town, when B Company came in from another direction. Company commander Sid Salomon had his men hold fire until they were close to the unsuspecting enemy. When Salomon opened fire, his men followed suit, and the Germans promptly surrendered.

Lieutenant Edlin and four men of A Company, 2d Rangers, were the first to enter the Graf Spee battery at Lochrist. Edlin and his men showed the German commander their credentials: a hand grenade with the safety pin pulled free. The German surrendered. The four 280mm guns were the heart of a powerful position that included 88mm and 20mm guns.

On the 9th, the 5th Rangers attacked the town of Le Conquet. Company E had the lead in vicious fighting against Germans in reinforced concrete emplacements. The 5th Rangers prevailed, and over one hundred of the Germans survived to become prisoners. Supported by tank destroyers and air strikes, Company C attacked the town from the east while A and E Companies came from the south. At the close of daylight Le Conquet fell. The 5th Rangers watched with humor and amazement as French Forces of the Interior, who had not been significantly involved in the capture of Le Conquet, sauntered into town accepting the townspeople's thanks for their liberation.

The Rangers were now fighting within sight of the English Channel. An inlet on the channel coast separated the captured town of Le Conquet and Le Mons Blanche, a town on a small spit of land. An attack by rubber boats was in the offing, but air and artillery pounded the area so badly that the mission became a comparative walkover. The Germans lost 5 killed and 130 taken prisoner. The 5th Rangers suffered five casualties.

Rudder's 2d Battalion kept pressing forward, and German fortifications tumbled, while the prisoner-of-war count continued to swell. At St. Matthieu, the last town on the Le Conquet Peninsula, Rudder accepted the surrender of the German Lieutenant Colonel Furst. Furst commanded all but a few die-hard Germans on the peninsula, so the prisoner count soared; 814 prisoners went into the 2d Ranger bag that day. The battalion diary notes with dry humor: "This night was extremely quiet."

With their zone of action cleared and mission accomplished, the 2d Battalion scattered to various blocking and security missions.

Now it was time to return to Kergolleau and its tough and determined German garrison, which had been softened up for several days by 155mm guns. At 1100 hours on September 10, Companies A and C moved to the attack behind the rolling thunder of 105mm howitzer preparatory fire; 155mm self-propelled guns added their power. Still the German garrison fought on, using mortars and machine guns. Captain Arnold gave orders to cease fire at 1509. His Rangers had followed the advancing artillery fire and were now almost on top of the objective. At 1515 the Germans surrendered. Seventy-four prisoners were taken.

While A and C Companies were attending to unfinished

business, the remainder of the 2d Ranger Battalion performed mop-up and guard duties. On the 10th, the Le Conquet Peninsula was turned over to the members of the French Forces of the Interior.

B and C Companies of the 5th Rangers were working with the 29th Division Reconnaissance Troop in mop-up operations that netted the Rangers some forty prisoners. Meanwhile, the rest of the 5th Battalion, led by Company D, attacked the town of Le Cosquer. The Rangers captured the town, took over two hundred prisoners, then came under American artillery fire that fell on the town.

On September 14, a motor convoy arrived to take the 2d Rangers to Landerneau, where the battalion began to refit and rejuvenate. New orders came on September 17, when the 2d Ranger Battalion was attached to the 8th Infantry Division to clear the Crozon Peninsula. The 2d Rangers relieved a task force of cavalry and infantry. Next came the mission of clearing the Le Fret Peninsula. The 2d Rangers accomplished that in short order. Some forty prisoners were taken, and four hundred American and Allied soldiers were freed from German captivity. One of those freed was a Ranger of the 2d Battalion.

Le Fret was secured by the 2d Rangers, including a large hospital complex with over one thousand German wounded.

The fort-busting 5th Rangers were called upon once more to display their talents. On September 17, Fort du Portzic became the objective, and the reinforced concrete fortifications of the Germans were tough to crack. A platoon of Company E led by Lieutenant Aust carried a forty-pound charge of explosive to one of the pillboxes and performed the dangerous task of placing the charge in the vision slit. Other Germans saw the Rangers at work and loosed a mortar barrage that killed two of the Rangers and wounded another. To add insult to injury, the explosive charge did no visible damage to the German fortification.

Sullivan's Rangers were determined to try again. Under cover of darkness and supporting fire, an eleven-man patrol carried ninety pounds of explosive and twenty gallons of mixed oil and gas to the pillbox. The explosive was positioned and the pillbox doused with the fuel. The night went silent then ripped apart when, at 2210 hours, the charge was detonated. Seventeen Germans were killed. German soldiers in other fortifications were justifiably terrified. When the Rangers went to attack the next fortifications, they found the Germans had them heavily outposted with machine guns that covered the fortifications with fire.

On September 18, the German garrison of Brest surrendered, and the German Gen. Herman Ramcke was a prisoner along with his men. The victorious Americans well knew that the German fortifications had been formidable but the degree of comfort in which the enemy lived, sometimes as deep as two hundred feet below the surface, was surprising: Recreation areas, mess halls, and showers had been at the disposal of the German soldiers.

Ironically, the port of Brest, so badly needed for the logistical effort when the operation began, was now of little value—the port facilities were destroyed, and the front had moved toward Germany at a much faster rate than Allied planners had envisioned. The expansion of the invasion had also been followed by the St. Lo breakout in late July and August. Exploitation became pursuit. The port of Antwerp, Belgium, was captured on 4 September, and though it would not be fully opened until late November 1944, Antwerp in conjunction with Cherbourg, Le Havre, and other French ports fulfilled the Allied need.

On September 20, the 2d Rangers were released from attachment to the 8th Infantry Division and moved to Kirbilben. Physical conditioning was needed, and sports were stressed. It is not usual for units to note the results of a softball game in their historical reports, but the 2d Rangers included the following: "The 2d and the 5th Ranger Battalions competed in a softball tournament, with the officers and the NCOs of the 2d Ranger Battalion each winning their respective games." Loaded with commendations for their fort busting, the 5th Rangers said: "Wait till next time."

On September 26, the 2d and 5th Ranger Battalions moved to Landerneau, France, where on September 28 they entrained on the notorious French boxcars known as 40 and 8 (for the number of men and horses the car was rated capable of carrying). Next stop—Belgium.

The German commander, Field Marshal Von Rundstedt, was fighting a desperate battle to establish a defensive line and stem the Allied advance. The once-famed German West Wall that ran from the vicinity of Arnhem in the north to Karlsruhe in the south was in a bad state of repair, and the Germans worked feverishly to repair it. The Americans and British saw the Rhine River draw ever closer and continued to work a logistical miracle as men and material poured into Europe.

Near Arlon, Belgium, the two Ranger battalions went into bivouac and began training and refitting. Arlon was a good leave town. The men of the 2d and 5th Rangers were welcomed into the homes of a grateful people. After the battles of the forts at Brest, the opportunity to have hot food, clean clothes, see a film, and drink a beer felt like a free pass to heaven.

On October 6, 2d Ranger Battalion Sgt. Maj. Leonard Lomell was discharged from the United States Army. His separation was brief. On the 7th of October, Len Lomell was appointed a 2d Lieutenant in his beloved Company D. (It was not unusual for an NCO to be discharged, then immediately commissioned. The 2d Ranger morning report reflects this, and it is shown on many such commissions.)

CHAPTER 11

THE PHILIPPINE INVASION

As the train carrying the men of the 2d and 5th Ranger Battalions rolled toward their bivouac in Belgium, the men of the 98th Field Artillery Battalion were nearing the end of their training in New Guinea in the South Pacific. Though they were not officially a Ranger unit yet, their hard work was paying off. The training in amphibious operations, speed marches, patrolling, and small-unit actions had built a force eager to close in battle with the Japanese. Finally, the men were given legitimacy when the 98th Field Artillery Battalion was officially redesignated as the 6th Ranger Infantry Battalion on September 26, 1944.

Gen. Douglas MacArthur, the American commander and the former field marshal of the Philippines, had vowed to the people of the Philippines that he would return. The Japanese were disturbed when over one hundred thousand other Americans came along.

The main objective for the invasion of the Philippine Islands was the island of Leyte. "A" day (the day of the assault) for the operation would be October 20, 1944. At the entrance to the Leyte Gulf were three small islands named Dinagat, Homonhon, and Suluan—that posed a threat to the invasion. The position of the islands made them likely locations for Japanese radar and coast artillery. Dinagat Island was the largest of the three; located off the northeast tip of Mindanao and just south of the entrance to Leyte Gulf, it had few people and hard terrain. The rugged hills and sharp peaks of the east coast moderated toward a more level ground on the west. Homonhon Island lay south of the Guiauan Peninsula of Samar Island, and featured thick woods, mountains, and beaches fringed with coral. Suluan Island was ten miles east and very much like Homonhon Island but smaller.

The Japanese were known to have their 16th, 30th, and 102d Divisions; five hundred aircraft, and a fleet that included three battleships, an escort carrier, seven cruisers, some fourteen destroyers, and two submarines in the Philippine Island area. Dinagat was believed to be occupied by about five hundred Japanese soldiers of the 30th Division. Homonhon and Suluan were thought to be unoccupied.

The mission of the 6th Ranger Battalion was to lead the invasion of the Philippine Islands by landing on the islands of Dinagat, Homonhon, and Suluan on October 17 (A day minus 3). The 6th Rangers were to clear the islands of enemy forces. The beaches they would land on carried the common designation of "Black." Black Beach 1 was on Dinagat and would be the site of the major landing, while Black Beach 2 was on Homonhon Island and Black Beach 3 on Suluan Island.

Company A would be transported on the APD *Schley*, Company B on the *Herbert*, Company C on the *Crosby*, Company D on the *Kilty*, and Companies E and F on the *Ward*. Headquarters and a supporting hospital and radio section would be on HMS *Ariadne*.

At 0805 hours, October 17, Company D of the 6th Ranger Battalion, under the command of Capt. Leslie Gray, landed at Black Beach 3 on Suluan Island. The mission of the company was to move to a lighthouse located on the southern end of the island, destroy any enemy installations there, and then return to Black Beach 3 where they would reembark.

Under heavy gray skies, strong winds, and a driving rain, D Company went ashore without opposition. With scouts leading off, the Rangers followed a coastal trail. Four unoccupied Japanese storehouses were located and set ablaze. Continuing the march, the Ranger scouts were taken under fire by Japanese defenders. Scout Darwin C. Zufall was killed and Donald J. Cannon wounded. The Rangers went into the assault, and the Japanese withdrew into dense jungle. The march continued toward the lighthouse as the weather continued to deteriorate.

Meanwhile Companies A and C made an unopposed landing on Dinagat and secured Black Beach 1. E and F

Ranger Companies came ashore, followed by Company B of the 21st Infantry. While Company A Rangers and B Company of the 21st Infantry remained on security, C, E, and F Companies of the 6th Rangers moved to clear "Desolation Point"—after accomplishing the mission, the Rangers were to return to the beachhead.

On the island of Suluan the Company D Rangers had arrived at their objective. The lighthouse was located on a sheer pinnacle of rock, jutting upward some three hundred feet, a single pair of steps leading to the top. Deploying, the D Company Rangers moved forward only to find that the Japanese occupants had fled. The on-site radar equipment was destroyed by the Rangers, who by 1200 hours had completed their mission and begun the withdrawal to Black Beach 3.

On Dinagat, C, E, and F Companies found Desolation Point an easy chore. E and F Companies returned to Black Beach 1, where B Company of the 21st Infantry went back aboard ship—C Company remained at the point and killed one of the enemy.

The storm had now grown to typhoon proportions. On arrival at the beach, the D Company Rangers found that the landing craft had been broached by the raging waters, and radio contact had been lost. The company established a perimeter defense and waited out the night. The next morning, under clearing skies, a combat patrol was dispatched in search of the Japanese. In an area of tall grass, the Rangers were fired on, and Ranger Roscoe Dick wounded. The Rangers could not determine the exact location of the enemy but sprayed the area with fire. Filipino reports were that five Japanese were killed. Ranger Roscoe Dick would later die of his wounds.

Contact was regained with the mother ship, the APD *Crosby*. Before the Rangers returned to the ship, they buried Pfc. Darwin Zufall in the center park of the village of Granadas.

On October 18, off Homonhon Island, Capt. Arthur D. "Bull" Simons[1] and his Rangers of B Company waited aboard the flush-decked destroyer *Herbert*. The landing was delayed a day by the fierce storm, but at 0900 came the call "first wave prepare to disembark." Riding in small, plywood Landing Craft Personnel (LCPR), the 1st Platoon led the way toward shore. The entrance to the landing beach was narrow, allowing only two of the craft entrance at a time. Once again, the landing was unopposed by the Japanese. As the beach-head was secured, natives came forward and reported there were no Japanese on the island. The Rangers preferred to make their own check, and patrols were dispatched. The mission was critical as the main invasion force was scheduled to pass through the channel between Homonhon and Dinagat Islands: Colasi Point on Homonhon overlooked the passage route and was secured by the Rangers. A party of amphibious scouts accompanied the Rangers, and they had the mission of setting up a three-hundred-pound light to aid navigation. A Ranger platoon provided security for this critical operation.

On the 18th, the Rangers reported the islands were secure for the passage of the invasion fleet.

On the 19th, B Company on Homonhon raised the American flag. Thus to the Rangers went the honor of being the first of the returning American forces to fly the Stars and Stripes over Philippine soil. As the flag was hoisted, the men stood at attention and saluted. A 6th Ranger Battalion report said of the pride of the men, "It was as if each man's heart reached out and pushed the flag a little higher."

A civilian came into Ranger camp with the information that with the departure of D Company, the Japanese on Suluan were murdering the Filipino civilians. B Company was itching for a fight, and the comment was made, "Here we are with all these goddamn bullets and no Japs." As the security of the navigational light was critical to the invasion, battalion denied approval for B Company to move to Suluan.

On October 20, 1944, the U.S. Army X and XXIV Corps landed abreast on the east coast of Leyte. General MacArthur had returned to the Philippines with his army, and once again the Rangers had led the way.

On Homonhon Island, B Company of the 6th Rangers had completed their island sweep without incident. On October 23, another request went forward to go after the Japanese on Suluan Island. This time the request was approved provided that B Company could find the boats to get them to Suluan.

On Dinagat on the 26th, a Ranger patrol to Tubujon, led by Staff Sergeant Kearns, killed seven Japanese naval personnel.

The cruelty the Japanese displayed toward the native population came back with a vengeance as the tide of the war turned. On the 26th, a ten-man patrol of Rangers was sent to Hiboson Island to pick up survivors from sunken Japanese destroyers—forty-two Japanese had survived the sinking, but only ten remained alive to be turned over to the Rangers by the natives. The Rangers on Dinagat continued to conduct extensive patrols to locate the enemy or check out reports of Japanese activity. Most of the Japanese they found were dead sailors from sunken ships. These Japanese had managed to get to shore, but many did not get beyond the beach before the natives killed them.

By October 27, Company B of the 6th Rangers had assembled three sailboats and eleven canoes for the eight-mile voyage between the islands. A security force was left with the navigational-light party. The remainder of the Rangers began boarding at 2400 hours. By 0150 hours on the 28th, the men of B Company of the 6th Rangers were in open water. By paddle and sail the Rangers headed for their objective, but a sudden storm played havoc with their plans. High winds and a heavy sea lashed the canoes, and seven were overturned, and though the men were saved, much equipment was lost.

Soaked and exhausted, the Rangers returned to Homonhon. The incident did not deter Simons and his men from their intent to get at the Japanese on Suluan. Weapons and equipment were gathered from the men of the navigational-light security force, and the men of Company B prepared for another attempt. At 0830 on the 29th, the 2d Platoon of B Company began the crossing in five sailboats. Japanese planes were in the area, so the men concealed their weapons and equipment in the bottom of the boats then used the ruse of appearing to be native fishermen. By 1100 hours, the Rangers were ashore and had established a defensive perimeter. Patrols were dispatched and a Japanese encampment located that contained considerable radio equipment. The Rangers destroyed the radios and poisoned the Japanese water supply. On the 30th at 0330 the remainder of the Rangers arrived after struggling for eleven hours against wind and current.

Patrols had determined that the main force of Japanese were located in the lighthouse on the south end of the island.

Anyone approaching the lighthouse up the narrow trail and high stairs was clearly visible. From this vantage point, a few men could hold off a large attacking force. The Japanese had also positioned a security and early-warning force on the trail that led to the steps.

Night reconnaissance revealed another alternative. On the west side of the lighthouse position was the coral-rock cliff: Though the cliff climb would be difficult, it was not impossible, and so it was selected as the approach. While Captain Simons and a small group of Rangers climbed the cliff under cover of darkness, the main force of Rangers would move into position to come from the flank and separate the Japanese security force from the lighthouse garrison. A red flare fired from the top would indicate the lighthouse was secured. A yellow flare would signal that the stairway was under control, and an orange flare would be the signal for the Rangers at the base of the cliff to attack. After the lighthouse was taken, any Japanese that survived the attack would be pushed toward the narrow tip of the island, where they would be destroyed.

Using Filipino guides, the attack force moved at 2115 hours under a bright moon. When nearing the Japanese positions, the Rangers removed their socks and put them on over their boots to help deaden the sound of footfalls. At 0100 hours the climb began. The coral rock tore at the men's hands, but they progressed, sometimes aided by vines that grew from the cliff face. By 0200 Captain Simons, guides, and the lead Rangers were on top.

The hunter's moon revealed that the flat at the top of the cliff was narrow and confined, giving little room to maneuver and offering scant cover and concealment. The sixty-foot-tall lighthouse was flanked by four white buildings, the closest of which was but eight yards from the Rangers, the farthest some twenty yards distant. Closer and easily identifiable by the stench was a Japanese latrine some five feet away from the point where the Rangers gained the top.

In the closest building unsuspecting Japanese soldiers were talking. Feeling the call of nature, a sleepy Japanese soldier made his way to the latrine. In the clear moonlit night, the approaching soldier moved close to one of the guides who, fearful of discovéry, raised his submachine gun and killed the man.

Many of the Rangers were still climbing, but there was no time to wait until they reached the top. The men on the cliff top opened fire on the buildings and began to shower the enemy with white phosphorous grenades. Private First Class Ortiz, a Ranger machine gunner, hurriedly brought his weapon up to the top and began firing, but on the coral surface, the gun could not get stable footing. Ortiz was forced to hold one leg of the tripod and pull the trigger while Captain Simons held another leg and the ammunition box.

The sudden onslaught took the Japanese by surprise. Confused, the enemy began running about and were shot down by the Rangers. Some Japanese jumped over the cliff edge. Shutting down the machine-gun fire, the Rangers moved against the building. In the rush, Ranger Couture of an assault squad was shot in the stomach. Staff Sergeant Potts was shot in the shoulder while in the act of throwing a grenade; Potts handed the grenade to another soldier, who threw it into the building under attack. The Rangers methodically cleared the building with small arms and grenades, killing the occupants. In twenty minutes, the only enemy action was a few shots from the lighthouse. The Ranger response was a fusillade of fire that quieted the Japanese.

On signal, the Rangers at the base of the lighthouse steps moved on the Japanese security force and began driving them into the narrow area at the southern end of the island. The retreating Japanese opened fire on the cliff top with an automatic rifle. Ranger Prokopovich was hit by two bullets and died from loss of blood; two other Rangers were slightly wounded. The Rangers at the base of the cliff killed or drove off the Japanese gunner.

The bodies of the Japanese lay sprawled about the cliff top, on the trail, and at the base of the cliff. Any surviving Japanese that were holed up in the lighthouse were soon accounted for when the Rangers brought up demolitions and destroyed the lighthouse and all the surrounding buildings.

While Company B was attending to the Japanese on Suluan, the remainder of the 6th Rangers were pushing patrols throughout the other islands. "Bortos," small native sailing craft, were often used to travel from island to island. Colonel Mucci, the battalion commander, and Major Garrett, the executive officer, set the example by personally participating in patrol actions.

A patrol led by Lt. Clifford Smith of Headquarters Company, 6th Ranger Battalion, exemplifies the type activity performed by the Rangers.

On October 29, Colonel Mucci, Lieutenant Smith, and a thirteen-man patrol with four native guides left Loreto for Mabini to check reported enemy movement. Natives there confirmed that the Japanese had passed through, and the patrol pursued the Japanese toward Dongoan. There, two natives reported that the Japanese had attempted to escape by boat, but the natives had killed four, and the remainder returned to shore. Reconnaissance indicated they were moving toward Sinongag on the island's other side. Moving cross-country, the Rangers arrived at Sinongag at 0700 hours on the 30th and began to search the area. The Japanese opened fire on the Rangers, who pinpointed the enemy position and went into the attack. The Japanese withdrew about one hundred yards and laid down a heavy volume of fire. The Rangers outgunned the Japanese and stayed after them. Fifteen Japanese soldiers were killed and one officer. The Rangers did not suffer loss.

The patrol then moved toward the village of Mabini. After moving about six hundred yards, more Japanese were encountered. Three of the enemy were killed here, but three of the native guides also died.

On October 31, another patrol killed seventeen Japanese enlisted men and one officer without Ranger casualties. Patrols continued, most without contact. The companies of the 6th Rangers with the exception of Company B were reassembled on Dinagat at Black Beach 1. Near Tubujon a patrol killed four more Japanese. Twenty-four days after the invasion of Leyte Island, the 6th Rangers, minus Company B, moved to rejoin the Sixth Army forces.

Over a period of several days, the Rangers of Company B, 6th Battalion, hunted the remaining Japanese on Suluan. On November 4 a patrol found two Japanese searching for food and killed them. On the 5th, two Japanese, who had just killed a Filipino, were spotted and killed. The hunt from this point on was without result.

On the 13th, the Rangers of Company B left the island of Suluan. The men who had been on navigational light security rejoined them. On November 14, 1944, the 6th Ranger Battalion was reunited on Leyte. Here, at Sixth Army Headquarters near Tolosa, they served as army security. Daily patrols were dispatched that traveled from six to fifteen miles. The 6th Rangers would remain at Tolosa until January 1945.

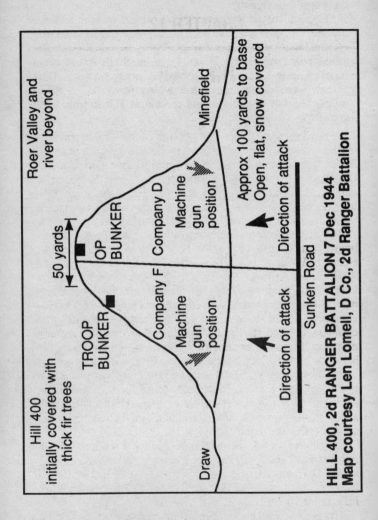

Hill 400
initially covered with
thick fir trees

Roer Valley and
river beyond

Draw

TROOP
BUNKER

50 yards

OP BUNKER

Company F

Company D

Machine gun position

Machine gun position

Sunken Road

Direction of attack

Direction of attack

Approx 100 yards to base
Open, flat, snow covered

Minefield

HILL 400, 2d RANGER BATTALION 7 Dec 1944
Map courtesy Len Lomell, D Co., 2d Ranger Battalion

CHAPTER 12

HILL 400

In Europe, on October 20, the men of the 2d Ranger Battalion moved by truck for the hour-and-one-half drive to Esch, Luxembourg, where they were attached to Combat Command A of the 5th Armored Division. Here the good life continued for the 2d Rangers. The weather was turning chill, but the companies were distributed among barracks and town buildings, and the men enjoyed some comfort.

The 2d Rangers moved on November 3, from Esch, Luxembourg, to the vicinity of Raeren, Belgium, where they were attached to V Corps and further attached to Combat Command A of the 5th Armored Division. Sid Salomon's wallet was a little heavier on this move—the dynamic commander of Company B had been promoted to captain on October 21. On November 4, the 2d Rangers were given an attack mission, and commanders and staff spent the day in reconnaissance and planning. The men continued a vigorous training program the battalion had in effect, but the attack was postponed.

On November 8, the 2d Ranger Battalion was placed on two-hour alert as a counterattack force for the Vossenack area, and planning began for the mission. On the 11th, still another mission was received, and planning began again, but neither operation came off.

On November 14, the 2d Rangers left Raeren and the 5th Armored at 1200 hours by motor convoy and moved to Germeter, Germany, arriving at 1700 hours. At Germeter the 2d Rangers relieved the 2d Battalion of the 112th Infantry, 28th Infantry Division.

The area was receiving light to moderate artillery fire but was otherwise quiet. On the 15th, contact patrols were maintained with adjacent units. The routine of defensive battle dragged on: Intermittent artillery and mortar fire fell on the Ranger positions daily, and field telephone wires that were cut by enemy shellfire had to be serviced. The Germans jammed the battalion radio frequency, causing a move to an alternate channel. For an hour, German artillery fired white phosphorus on the Company A area, but the Rangers escaped hurt. Ranger and German patrols were active at night. Flares would ignite, hiss, and pop, then oscillate to earth through the purple darkness. Men in foxholes leaned forward, straining their eyes to identify movement while other men froze in position to escape detection.

When daylight came, the game of cat and mouse continued. When German or American infantry became careless, the long arm of artillery or mortars would reach out to swipe at them.

On November 9 at 1430 hours, the 2d Ranger Battalion became attached to the 8th Infantry Division and were alerted for relief. Companies C, D, E, and F were relieved on the night of November 19 and moved to an assembly area about 2,000 yards west of Vossenack. Companies A and B remained in position on line. On the 21st, Company B was ordered to move forward to protect the flank of the 121st Infantry. A guide from the 121st led the Rangers through a mine field, and three Rangers became casualties. This mine field could have been the destruction of B Company, but Sid Salomon's Rangers kept their nerve and worked their way out of danger. Heavy artillery and mortar fire fell on B Company that night. On November 22, Company B found that its assigned positions were mined. Once again, the men kept discipline and survived.

A call was put in for engineers to clear the mines, but they did not arrive. The Germans plastered the area with artillery. On November 23, the ordeal of B Company continued. German patrols tried to flank the Rangers but were driven off, and German artillery and mortars were relentless. By this time the Company B position was carrying the name "Purple Heart Corner," and Company A was ordered to relieve Company B as soon as possible. While awaiting relief, Company B was hit once again, this time by American artillery that fell short.

On the 24th, Company B moved to the battalion assembly area. Company A remained on line until November 27, and on the 28th rejoined the battalion. On the 28th, the 2d Rangers received a mission to serve as a counterattack force. Planning and reconnaissance began. The men prepared covered foxholes and log shelters, and while they waited for the call to action, there was hot food for nourishment and dice games for relaxation.

Confusion reigned on November 30. The 8th Infantry Division ordered the Rangers to reconnoiter the Hurtgen-Kleinhau area while the commander of the 28th Infantry Regiment was ordering them to move on another mission. It was hurry up, wait, then just as the men were moving, all the missions were canceled. The end result was the 2d Ranger Battalion remained where it was.

December 1944 found the American and United Kingdom forces primarily along the German border. The British and Canadians were on the left (north), and on the right (south) were the American Seventh Army and the French First Army. In the center was the American 12th Army Group consisting of the First, Third, and Ninth Armies. The Allied armies were in an attack posture, driving for the Rhine River.

The Rhine represented more than just a body of water to both the Allies and the Germans. The Rhine River was steeped in legend and myth for the Germans, and militarily it was a psychological as well as a physical threshold: cross the Rhine and you are at the German throat. The Rhine was many things to many people. Adolph Hitler vowed it would not be crossed; the flamboyant Gen. George S. Patton vowed that he would piss in it.

As part of a general attack, the First Army mission was to seek a Rhine River crossing in the vicinity of Bonn and Cologne. If the crossing was not feasible, the First Army was to occupy itself clearing the near shore of any German resistance. The First Army had three corps: V, VII and VIII. V Corps was in the center of the First Army attack and consisted of the 4th, 9th, and 28th Infantry Divisions and the 5th Armored Division. The 28th Division had been on the attack since early November and was in need of rest and refit. The 8th Infantry Division had been borrowed from the VIII Corps as of November 19. Combat Command R of the 5th Armored Division and the 2d Ranger Battalion were attached to the 8th Infantry Division. The 2d Rangers were considerably under-strength, with companies more the size of rifle platoons, and the 8th Division staff primarily sought to use the Rangers as a rapid-reaction, counterattack force. The 8th Division began attacking on November 21 and seized the town of Hurtgen on November 28.

While the 2d Ranger Battalion became part of the U.S. First Army, the 5th Ranger Battalion joined George Patton's Third Army and was attached to the 6th Cavalry Group (Mechanized), commanded by Col. Edward Fickett. The Rangers and cavalry would serve as a screening force oper-ating to the front and flanks of the American divisions. The 5th Battalion headquarters moved on December 1, 1944, to Diesen, France, while Company A of the 5th Rangers joined Troop A of the 6th Cavalry Squadron, and Company D joined Troop D for combined operations, which included the 10th Infantry Regiment. The remainder of the 5th Battalion stayed intact.

On December 2, B and E Companies of the 5th Rangers at-tacked through heavy German artillery fire northeast across the Diesen–Carling road. D Company of the 5th, supported by Troop B and the Cannon Company of the 10th Infantry, at-tacked the town of L'Hopital. The attack developed into a slugging match, with the Rangers gaining the center of town, then being driven out by German counterattack. The Com-pany A attack did not materialize as the cavalry guides became disoriented. It was a day of hard fighting, with thirty-five Ranger casualties; German casualties were also heavy. B Company of the 5th Rangers came under heavy German counterattack the following day, but the attack was beaten off, and the Germans lost twenty-eight killed and a prisoner.

On December 4, Lieutenant Reveille's Company F, with fifty-five men, attacked the town of Lauterbach while the rest of the company supported by fire. The attack was made across five hundred yards of plowed furrows made wet and slippery from the rain. The German defenders were hitting the Rangers hard with mortars and small arms. The mission was to take the town, thus protecting the battalion right flank and preventing the Germans from using a critical highway. The Germans had two machine guns well positioned to provide a crossfire from the left and the right on the Rangers. When Company F was some two hundred yards into the plowed ground, the German machine guns opened fire, and men began to fall. An automatic rifleman, Ranger Leo G. Samborowski, did what had to be done to save his friends. Samborowski took both machine guns under alternating fire, then ran forward and killed the crew of the machine gun firing from the left. The German gunners on the right killed Ranger Samborowski, but his valor enabled his comrades to keep moving forward.

A German tank, supported by infantry, came after the Rangers, but the tank had trouble negotiating the deep mud of the fields. As the Rangers entered Lauterbach, Ranger Andrew "Pappy" Speir took shelter in a house and opened fire on the tank with a rocket launcher. The tank blew the house down around Speir, but he kept firing. Ranger mortars began to work over the German infantry, and when they retreated the tank did also.

F Company was badly shot up: 1st Sgt. John Hodgson was hit in the face, and the company had lost six killed and eighteen wounded out of fifty-five men.

Despite the loss, when darkness came, Company F Rangers succeeded in guiding A Company under the German weapons and into the town.

Company C of the 5th also attempted to come to the relief of Company F. Heavy German fire prevented the union, but the C Company Rangers took sixteen prisoners. Meanwhile, B Company surprised a German force trying to encircle it and took twenty-nine Germans prisoner.

In the First Army sector, a mission was assigned to 8th Division to seize several other towns, among which was the town of Bergstein and the adjoining high ground—a four-hundred-meter-high hill known as Hill 400 to the Americans and Castle Hill to the Germans. Civilians said a castle had stood upon its eminence in the twelfth century.

The approach to Bergstein was suitable for armor, and Combat Command R of the 5th Armored Division was given the mission of seizing the town. Supported by air and artillery, the 5th Armored succeeded in capturing the town on December 5 after a stiff fight. On the 6th, the Germans pushed home three counterattacks. In heavy fighting, the Germans gained a small portion of the east edge of town, but the Americans held the rest. Combat Command R was badly beaten up from a long stretch of commitment to battle. They had not taken Hill 400 and were scheduled for relief.

On the night of December 6, the 2d Ranger Battalion was given the mission of seizing Castle Hill and the Brandenberg–Bergstein ridges adjoining it. The hill was an eagle's perch: From its summit the Roer River dams could be seen, and the surrounding towns and countryside lay naked before an artillery observer's eyes. The Germans were involved in preparations for a major counterstroke in the Ardennes forest, and they could not comfortably allow the Americans to disrupt their positions or timetable.

For reasons unknown at the time, Lieutenant Colonel Rudder had been called to First Army Headquarters. The instructions for the mission thus were given to Maj. George S. Williams. Williams had been promoted on December 4 and with his promotion became executive officer to Rudder. Prior to promotion, Williams's primary duties had been those of a supply officer.

The 8th Division wanted a night attack; Williams preferred that but knew that a night attack made without time for reconnaissance was an invitation to disaster, so the time of 0700 was established for the attack on Hill 400 to begin.

Williams planned to use A, B, and C Companies to seize the ridges running south and east of Hill 400, establish defensive positions, and be prepared to serve as a counterattack force.

D, E, and F Companies would move through Bergstein to seize Hill 400 and defend it from anticipated German counterattack.

At 2330 hours on December 6, trucks bearing the 2d Ranger Battalion revved their motors and began a blackout trip toward Bergstein. The night was chill and filled with gloom and rain. At 0130 hours on December 7, the men detrucked near Hurtgen and began moving by foot toward Bergstein. The muddy road was flanked by water-filled ditches and was slippery with ice. Overhead, German buzz bombs (V-1 and V-2 rockets) sputtered on the way to their targets. The gloom was deepened by news that greatly disturbed the men: Lieutenant Colonel Rudder, the beloved commander of the 2d Rangers, was leaving them for a new command—the 109th Infantry Regiment of the 28th Division. As Rudder passed down the line saying farewell, the men felt the sense of affection and loss. Under Rudder, the 2d Battalion had flourished. Some men felt respect tarnished by anger. The battalion knew it was going into the attack in a few hours, and they knew they needed experienced leadership: The burden of command was not merely handed over but dropped on the shoulders of the newly promoted Major Williams.

The Rangers arrived at Bergstein at 0200 hours. Men of the 5th Armored were in the town, but the guides they were to provide did not appear and Ranger officers went forward to make a reconnaissance. Both sides were using interdictory and harassing fire with artillery and mortars. The *crump* and *crash* of high explosives muffled itself in the whiplash of a driving rain. Despite the rain, some houses were burning in Bergstein. Tired men, miserable with wet and cold, took what shelter they could find, some under the burned-out hulls of shot-up American armor.

About 0300 hours, A, B, and C Companies moved through the northwest edge of Bergstein and up the ridges that were their objectives. Some German artillery and mortar fire was received enroute, but there were no encounters with enemy soldiers. Company A found good fortune in the shape of positions prepared by the retreating Germans, Company B had to dig for shelter, and Company C had one platoon on a roadblock, while another manned 81mm mortars in Bergstein.

D, E, and F Companies of the 2d Rangers now moved through Bergstein enroute to the line of departure. D and F Companies sent reconnaissance patrols to check the approaches to Hill 400. D Company's patrol was led by the experienced Len Lomell and reconnoitered the right side of Hill 400. The six-man patrol of Company F was commanded by a new lieutenant but led by the under-ranked veteran Pvt. William Anderson.[1] The Company F patrol checked the left side of the hill. Anderson's patrol made a reconnaissance to and beyond what would become the line of departure. Going alone into the fog, Private Anderson scouted the location of German voices.

Some German soldiers still remained in the houses of Bergstein. For some two hours, while the Ranger patrol performed reconnaissance, the remaining Rangers occupied the cellars. During this time, E Company Rangers flushed out thirteen Germans and took them prisoner.

The reconnaissance patrols came back between 0500 and 0600, and no one was smiling. The mission looked bad. Capt. Duke Slater was in charge of D, E, and F Companies. Slater formed the men among the rubble. Crouching in the streets of Bergstein, the Rangers listened to Slater calling words of encouragement. Then D and F Companies moved toward Hill 400. Company E would remain in Bergstein.

With the coming of the cold, gray dawn, the men of D and F Companies approached the line of departure for the attack. The burned-out hulks of American armor littered the road. It was December 7, the third anniversary of "the day of infamy," when the Japanese attacked American forces at Pearl Harbor.

Meanwhile Companies A, B, and C had observed German vehicles moving to their front at a distance of several hundred yards, and the vehicles were believed to be self-propelled artillery. The Rangers and a 5th Division tank took the Germans under fire and drove them to cover.

At the eastern edge of Bergstein was a thick-walled church, with a cemetery to its right. About one hundred yards beyond the church was a road which would serve as the line of departure for the attacking Rangers. Hill 400 lay to the right front of the church and to the right of the sunken road. One side of the road was terraced, providing the Rangers with a protective embankment from frontal small-arms fire. This embankment was some two hundred yards long and approximately two-and-a-half-feet high.

D and F Companies of the 2d Rangers moved into position along the sunken road and faced Hill 400. Company F commanded by Capt. Otto Masny was on the left, and Company D commanded by Capt. Mort McBride was on the right. Though the embankment provided some protection from direct-fire weapons to the front, there was no protection from the rear and flanks, and the position was vulnerable to attack by mortars and artillery. This openness made some veteran Rangers edgy. The veterans knew it was a bad spot and wanted to get on with the attack.

Hill 400 was forested but in front of the Rangers' position was an open field about 75 yards wide sloping up somewhat toward high ground.

The German defenders were members of a task force from the 272d Volks Grenadier Division. The forward German defenses included several machine guns sited behind the tree line on Hill 400. Unknown to the Rangers, a well-concealed German fortification would be to their left as they crossed the field.

Captain Masny of F Company was tall and rangy. The men called him "Big Stoop," after a cartoon character of the time, though the nickname was not derogatory. Masny's men respected him; they could talk to him, and one noncommissioned officer remembers beginning a conversation with the words, "Goddammit, Big Stoop . . ."

In the D Company sector, Captain McBride led his men into position along the embankment.

Jump-off time for the attack was to be 0730, and the plan was that the attacking companies would be preceded by a rolling barrage of artillery. Moving closely behind these fires, the Rangers would keep the Germans pinned in position until they were upon them. As the Rangers bent low behind the embankment, a German soldier at the edge of the wood line leaped into the open and fired a flare, then began running toward his right in the direction of the unreported fortification. The flare was probably a signal for German supporting fires. Soon after its firing, German mortar rounds began to explode to the rear of the Rangers and march toward them. A few moments later American artillery began to fall on the Germans.

The distance between the exploding American artillery rounds and the crash of the German high explosive was some two hundred yards and shrinking fast. Caught in the center of the two fires, the Rangers were keenly aware that the German fire was closing on them and their position offered no protection from it. Tension built to anxiety—men knew it was only a matter of minutes before the shrapnel ripped them.

It was now approximately 0720, ten minutes remained before the American fire would shift to move farther up the hill. Along the line of departure, men began to dig in. Tension built to the boiling point. A replacement officer, new to battle, squatted beside Sgt. William "L-Rod" Petty, platoon sergeant of the 2d Platoon of F Company. "Send out a scout," ordered the officer. With the German position to their front and high explosive bursting around it, Petty knew the order was little short of murder. "Fuck you, no way!" Petty told the lieutenant. Angrily the officer then turned to Sergeant McHugh, 2d Platoon section sergeant, and repeated his order. McHugh's response was similar to that of Petty. The officer, then shouting loudly, ordered Ranger Private Bouchard to perform the mission.

Bouchard obeyed the order, went over the embankment, and had moved only a few feet when he was shot down. Petty and others crawled forward to drag Bouchard to safety.[2] The German mortar shells were bursting closer now, and the pent-up tension in the men was itself explosive. All that was needed was a spark and that spark was Sergeant McHugh. Leaping to his feet, the young Ranger brandished his submachine gun over his head and yelled, "Let's go get the bastards!" All the coiled-spring tension in the men suddenly released, and they leaped to their feet and swarmed over the embankment, snarling, cursing, yelling in blood lust. The line of Rangers swept up the hill.

Sergeant Petty's efforts to save Bouchard had left him a few paces behind. Seeing the assaulting line of Rangers going forward with fixed bayonets and firing from the hip was a memory he would never forget. "I know that I will never see a more brave and glorious sight," Petty recalled. "It was for me indeed a moment of being proud to be a Ranger."

D Company had moved on Captain McBride's shout of "GO!" and went into action, shouting and firing in marching fire. Captain McBride fell wounded and had to be evacuated from the hill.

At the sight of the oncoming Rangers, the German soldiers

left their positions. Some fled up the hill, others surrendered, and others died. Temporarily pinned down by German fire, Ranger Milt Moss followed after the initial Ranger assault. Moss saw a German gunner and his assistant slumped over their weapon. The remainder of the German machine-gun section had died trying to dig in or lay sprawled in a fruitless run for safety. The American artillery was still falling on the position: the earth heaved under the force of explosive and the air was filled with the sound of gunfire and the hoarse shouting of men.

The battle fever was upon the Rangers, yet almost without exception, they fell upon the enemy as men who retained decency in their souls. One, however, did not. A German soldier, who had surrendered, was coming down off the hill, being waved through the line of Rangers. F Company had an individual who on more than one occasion had shot down unarmed men who had surrendered. The German soldier had the misfortune to meet him. The German fell to his knees pleading for his life, but his pleas were to no avail. Though he was no longer a threat, the German soldier was shot through the head and killed. The Rangers who saw this reprehensible act were men who killed many of the enemy in battle. As they were good men, they were justifiably disgusted by this murder and the memory would never leave them. Whatever he felt he gained by killing prisoners, this individual lost the respect of his companions.

The forward impetus of the Rangers carried them into the wood line and into the fire of their own artillery. The 2d Platoon of F Company lost both its section sergeants, McHugh wounded and Winch killed. The Ranger charge had been born of emotion, and now the lack of control began to tell. Men moved forward toward the top of the hill at varying speeds. Platoon integrity had broken down, and men moved as individuals and small groups. As they closed toward the top of the hill, the Rangers moved from under the fire of the American artillery and into a quiet zone.

D Company Rangers crossed over the top of Hill 400 with some of the men getting close to the Roer River, when they were recalled with orders to dig in the forward crest of Hill 400. The frustration of Hill 400 was defined by the difficulty in digging in the rocky, root-filled soil of the hill. German artillery and mortars were pounding the hill with murderous precision. Trees shattered and splintered into deadly missiles. Men sought shelter in depressions and beneath tree trunks as the ground heaved and the air was ripped by jagged pieces of wood and stone. There was little or no protection. "It was a matter of luck," Len Lomell said.

In the F Company zone, the surviving Germans had fled. Bill Anderson, Manning, and Petty reached the top on the F Company side of the hill, and Manning led the charge over the top. Petty and Anderson saw a large bunker and went after it, but there was no return fire as they entered the main entrance. On the left was a hallway about eight feet long and a steel door. The door had a small opening in it covered by metal as though a place to pass messages through. The Rangers could hear the Germans inside.

Petty pushed the muzzle of his automatic rifle under the metal flap and fired a twenty round magazine. He then held the flap open while Anderson shoved two grenades through the opening.

Wanting to get clear of the exploding grenades, both men raced for the bunker doorway, with Anderson in the lead. As they stepped into the open, a German shell exploded in front of Anderson and blew his body back into Petty's arms. A large fragment had struck Anderson in the heart. Petty put his arms around his friend to support him, but the force of the geysering blood drove his hand from Anderson's body.

For a few moments, Petty was alone with his dead friend and his thoughts near the bunker; then other men came up. Captain Masny arrived, and D and F Company Rangers set about eliminating any other Germans that remained in the bunker. With the bunker cleared, the frustrating task of trying to dig in frozen, rocky soil began. Captain Masny, Lieutenant Rowland, Sergeant Petty, and another Ranger were standing by the bunker discussing the situation when four German artillery rounds hit the bunker. Though the explosive hurled them about and terrified them, they were not wounded, but one man became hysterical. Petty slapped him across the face, but the man was out of control and had to be placed inside the bunker. The German artillery was coming from south and east and German positions east of the Roer River. The shrapnel rain fell with ever-increasing intensity.

The bunker offered the only protection. Used to shelter the wounded, it was also a magnet for men who wanted to escape the German fire. It took considerable fortitude to remain outside in the face of the shrapnel, and unprotected men were hit repeatedly. Ranger wounded came down under their own power or were carried by litter and were then transferred to a battalion jeep in order to reach an ambulance for evacuation to a hospital. The trip to the hospital was a dangerous one—three of the Ranger litter vehicles were destroyed during the evacuations.

The capture of the hill was reported at 0830, but the Rangers were angry. Men were suffering and felt they were not getting assistance from battalion. Captain Masny knew the handful of Rangers on top of Hill 400 needed help and felt a messenger would not carry enough authority to get that help, so Masny decided to go back to battalion and personally get the assistance. Masny and Petty discussed the route Masny would have to take and disagreed. Petty had heard German voices and knew the enemy were about. Masny took a different route from that Petty recommended and disappeared from Petty's view. Within moments Petty heard Masny cry out *"Kamerad!"* and he knew the company commander had been trapped by the Germans. In a brew of sorrow, petulance, and apprehension, Petty cried out, "Goddammit, Otto, I told you not to go that way!"

The morning of battle was young: D and F Companies had Hill 400, but they had been shot up, the company commander of D Company was wounded and evacuated from the hill, and the company commander of F Company had been captured.

On the way up the hill, Sgt. Herm Stein, section sergeant of the 1st Platoon, F Company, led his men to the left in a half circle around the hill. On the forward slope, Stein decided to dig in and hold. The ground was frozen, rocky, and difficult to dig in, and the men were under fire from the Germans. As Stein and his Rangers dug, the Germans used variable-time fuses on their artillery and air bursts began to take their toll. Rangers Groenke, Biazo, and Ray were wounded, Biazo badly.

Ranger Bombardier, nicknamed "Bomber," went up to check the top of the hill. Stein and Ranger Moss were alone on the forward slope. Lt. Len Lomell of D Company came over to Company F to coordinate. Lomell was the only officer left in D Company. His hand was a bloody mess, with one finger hanging by a thread of flesh. Stein briefed Lomell, who suggested the two F Company men tie in with D Company just over the next plateau. Lomell continued on his duties. On the way down the wooded hillside, Stein and Moss met a D Company Ranger looking for his unit. The three men went down the hill a considerable distance, but they were going in the wrong direction and did not find Company D. Though exhausted, they breathed more easily in the absence of artillery and felt joy. They were near a gorge through which flowed the Roer River. Near a foot bridge, they could see a German soldier digging a foxhole some two hundred yards distant. The three Rangers found a position that overlooked a mountain trail and dug in. They could hear water rippling over a dam and saw what appeared to be a power station. German Volkswagen command cars were going to and from the power station, indicating that it was a command post.

Another car was visible, this one a four-door convertible Mercedes-Benz sedan of the type used by senior officers. Germans were gathered around this car and the group seemed to be in good spirits, laughing and gesturing.

A ten-man German patrol spread out and, moving like veterans, came along the trail. Prudently, the three Rangers let them pass. After a brief rest, the three men decided to go back to the crest of the hill. The climb was difficult, but a German artillery observer spotted them and gave them reason to move rapidly. Unable to locate Company D, Stein and his men dug in about forty yards from the top of the hill. The location picked was forward of the rest of the F Company positions but it offered the best field of fire. As Stein and Moss struggled to dig in, Carl Bombardier came down the hill and began to dig beside them.

The Germans wanted Hill 400 with a desperation that caused them to spend their men and material extravagantly. German artillery and mortars subjected the hill top to a constant and terrible pounding. Around 0930, a German attack swept in like the tide on the D Company positions. The Germans were coming from the southeast, their attack initiating in woods that offered concealment until they were close to the D Company Rangers. In this fight, Ranger Staff Sergeant Secor of Company D distinguished himself. Secor, who was normally a mild-mannered man, went after the Germans with fury and his section followed. They broke the attack and chased the Germans back down the hill. His own weapon destroyed by shrapnel, Secor was seen firing two captured machine pistols, blazing away with a gun in each hand. When the Germans were driven off, Secor and his men gathered up the German weapons and ammunition. When American ammunition became depleted, the D Company Rangers used the Germans' own weapons against them.

Across the hill, the few leaders were called from one location to the other, responding to cries for assistance, while the bunker filled with wounded. Underneath, a rage was building in some of the men, an internal rage generated by the feeling that some officers and senior noncommissioned officers were not on the hill. One of the badly wounded that Sergeant Petty carried to the bunker was Jack Anderson, the brother of Bill Anderson, who had died in Petty's arms. Petty could see Jack Anderson would not survive his wounds. Hill 400 claimed both the Anderson brothers.

Emotion, determination, fear, and frustration boiled in the men of D and F Company. Wounded men lay about the hill repeatedly hit by the constant pounding of the German guns, but there was nothing that could be done for the wounded. Seeing men bleeding to death and helpless to stop it, Lieutenant Lomell gathered his senior sergeants and, with tears of frustration pouring down his face, proposed they pull off the hill. The physically and emotionally wounded Lomell told his men, "We can let the Germans evacuate our wounded, then come back and take the hill again." The sergeants dissuaded him.

From the Company F left rear, in the vicinity of the flanking German fortification came two German probes, and each attack was repulsed without Ranger casualty. These were probably German reconnaissance patrols. Sergeant Petty and Whitey Barowski did a reconnaissance to pinpoint where the

Germans were coming from, and found the Germans organizing in preparation for the attack. Hurrying back up the hill, Petty went to the bunker and began to get F Company able-bodied men out and into a defensive posture. Lieutenant Rowland assisted him in this. There were no more than eight F Company Rangers involved in the action. By now the Germans were up the left side of the hill, and a hot firefight at close range had started. The Germans were prone or kneeling but the Rangers were seeking to close with them and most were standing, firing, and moving toward the Germans. Lieutenant Rowland charged forward and was shot in the chest. As Rowland fell there was a brief lull. Barowski went to Rowland, hoisted the officer on his shoulder and began moving up the hill. Another bullet hit Rowland, killing him. Barowski began yelling a warning, "They're firing from the tops of the trees." Herm Stein had come up and prepared to fire, but there were no Germans in the trees. The few trees left standing were bare sticks.

In command of F Company, Sergeant Petty had scarcely more than a squad of men fit to fight. Glancing to his left, Petty saw German soldiers moving to their left to flank the Rangers. Petty and Ranger Shannon moved toward the Germans and higher ground to spoil the German plan, but some of the Germans may have already gotten above the Rangers. As Petty was running, he saw a German soldier in the prone position taking aim at him. Petty fired but the German fired first. The bullet passed through Petty's shoulder and struck Ranger Shannon in the chest. Petty emptied his magazine into the German, killing him, but found he could not raise the weapon to reload.

Petty and Shannon retreated toward the bunker. The Germans were taken under fire by some men from D Company and withdrew.

Stein saw Petty coming up the hill. Petty had four men left in his platoon and had carried the burden of leadership for most of the F Company fight. Caught up in the intense emotion of battle, he was raging at the losses of his platoon, crying and worrying about his Browning Automatic Rifle. "Who's going to take my BAR?" Petty kept repeating. Sergeant Stein was Petty's close friend and, seeing Petty's emotional state, said, "I'll take it, L-Rod," and accepted the weapon. Stein later compared this to "passing on the baton in a mad relay race to nowhere."

Stein and the surviving Rangers pulled back, while the Germans did the same. For a brief period, while their men got clear, the Germans lifted their artillery fire. The Rangers felt like drowning men getting a last, clear, clean breath of air. Then the German artillery began to fall again.

After a brief period getting first aid in the bunker, Petty moved down the hill. He then went to battalion headquarters to get some help sent up to the men on the hilltop. As he entered the basement, Petty's first sight was of a senior noncommissioned officer Petty believed should have been on the hill. The man was relaxing against a wall smoking, and the sight infuriated Petty, who began kicking and cursing the man. When battalion officers intervened, Petty turned his ire on them.

Battalion was having problems keeping communications going with the companies. Wire lines were laid and immediately torn up by artillery. Radio was the primary means of communication, but it was not functioning well. Company A was moved into Bergstein to position it as a reserve or counterattack force. Companies B and C adjusted to include the gap left by Company A. Efforts were being made to get reinforcements for the men on Hill 400 from the 8th Infantry Division, but the hours of hell dragged on without relief.

At 1242, a report was made that only seventeen men of F and fifteen men of D Company were still in fighting condition. The evacuation of wounded continued. Corporal Korb of the medical detachment risked his life repeatedly to drive litter jeeps through shellfire to get men to medical assistance.

At 1450 another German attack came from the northeast. It was beaten off with the aid of artillery. Someone at battalion headquarters was counting the hits on the church—the thick-walled church had taken eighty-two hits by artillery and was still standing strong.

Sgt. Herm Stein was now senior man in the F Company sector. Stein organized his defense with Rangers Bombardier and Pischa on his right and Alvin White on his left. There were some six other men, but they were much farther down the line, and there was a wide and threatening gap.

As darkness fell on a cold and rainy night, Stein took the watch. Stein had found his men were exhausted, and he had to stay awake to be certain security was maintained. Alvin White was snoring while Herm Stein fidgeted. Stein had a need to defecate, but to leave the position meant the likelihood of being killed by foe or friend. Stein solved the problem by defecating in a K-ration box, then heaving it down the hill. White, waking with a start, blazed away with his rifle, and it took some time for Stein to convince White of the nature of the target.

At 1913 hours, six tank destroyers arrived in Bergstein. They were attached in pairs, two each to companies A and C, and three to D, E, and F.

In the darkness, some help came up the hill. Lt. Richard Wintz, executive officer and now commander of F Company, arrived with a section from Company E and moved to fill in the gap. Wintz did a superb job and brought an important addition: Lieutenant Kettlehut, an artillery forward observer from the 56th Armored Field Artillery Battalion of the 5th Armored Division.

Around 2100, more wounded men were evacuated from the hill. Lt. Len Lomell had been struck again and was evacuated. D Company was now led by its sergeants. At 2345, rations, water, ammunition, and additional weapons were brought in. Some resupply reached the hill while German artillery continued to pound Hill 400 and Bergstein. The explosions came with such rapidity that it was one continuous and horrifying sound.

At 0333, Company C of the 121st Infantry arrived and were sent to the right flank of Company D. A heavy-machine-gun team from this company was sent to assist Company D elements on Hill 400. A later German attack killed these machine gunners. Combat Command R of the 5th Armored was being withdrawn. 2d Ranger headquarters was setting up machine guns, expecting a last-ditch stand at the command post in the church.

About 0600, Herm Stein moved up toward the bunker. Stein and Ranger Moss were talking at the entrance to the bunker when German artillery hit with a fury. For nearly half an hour, an eternity to an infantryman, the German shells fell

like rain. When it ended, Stein could hear the cries of his men.
Pischa and White were badly wounded. The crackle of small-
arms fire spread across the hill. As the Germans tried to attack again, Herm Stein assisted his men. When Stein got
back to his position, he found his raincoat and canteen were
riddled with shrapnel. His trip to the top of the hill had saved
him from serious harm.

At 0700 another German attack began. Battalion estimated
each attack at about company strength. This one was supported by fire from armored cars and directed at Companies
B and C. German self-propelled guns tried to shoot their way
into town, but the Rangers, tank destroyers, and artillery beat
the Germans back.

German artillery continued to pound Hill 400. At 0850 on
December 8, the 2d Ranger Battalion received a report from
Company D, "Only ten men left."

In Company F zone, Herm Stein was occupied for some
time, caring for wounded and seeing to the evacuation of
those more seriously hurt. When the work was done, Ranger
Moss joined him and the two of them began to snipe at the
Germans in the valley. It was long-range shooting, but they
caught two unwary Germans walking along a railroad track
and shot them down. At 1036, artillery was used to break up a
German attack from the south.

In the afternoon, a flight of P-47 fighter bombers worked
over the German positions southeast of Bergstein. The Germans tried an attack on Company C which was now in Bergstein, but were driven off.

At 1330, officers of the 1st Battalion, 13th Infantry, arrived
to begin making arrangements to relieve the Rangers. The
popular Dr. Walter Block, 2d Ranger Battalion medical officer, left the command post to supervise medical evacuation.
He was killed by an artillery round as he stepped outside.

There were few men left to man the positions on the hill.
D Company had less than twelve men, F Company had about
five, and E Company had about a dozen. Herm Stein's foxhole resembled an arsenal. Spread out before him were two
Browning automatic rifles, an M-1 Rifle, and a .45 caliber
pistol, plus fragmentation grenades. Stein was cleaning his
weapons when the German artillery began another pounding.

Bending low in the foxhole, he waited until the shelling eased then looked over the edge of his hole. Two Germans were standing about twenty yards distant, talking with each other. Stein took aim, but the bolt of the automatic rifle slid forward with a dull thud. There is no more empty and lonely feeling in life than to be on a battlefield with a jammed weapon. Stein yanked back the bolt and squeezed the trigger again. This time the weapon fired true, and the two Germans died.

The Germans were pushing home a counterattack. As they came up the hill, the enemy were making whistling sounds and crying *"baa, baa"* like sheep. The Rangers felt the Germans were making the sounds as a control device and were grateful as the noise pinpointed the German location. Targets were plentiful, and the handful of Rangers fought furiously. Rangers Stein, Moss, Bombardier, Hanahan, and "The Mad Russian" Uhorczuk held what had been a company front. Uhorczuk was wounded and went back up the hill. The Germans kept coming into the Ranger cross-fire, and for three hours, the fight continued. Amid the clash of weapons, the crash of grenades, and the moans and screams of wounded, the whistles and sheep sounds of the German leaders sounded bizarre. The Germans obviously were using the bunker at the top of the hill as their objective. As the Germans pressed in closer to the top of the hill, Lieutenant Wintz used his forward observer to the maximum, and Lieutenant Kettlehut of the artillery was up to the task. Wintz called artillery on the Ranger position, and a hail of American shrapnel began to fall. The surviving Rangers had scratched out some depressions, though the experience was a thing of terror. The Germans, however, were exposed to the fires and paid the price. The *baa*s and whistles went back down the slopes of Hill 400.

Meanwhile the Germans had also been attacking Companies B, C, and E, and the artillery battle was terrifying. The Rangers were using the combined fire of eighteen American artillery battalions. The fire was so intense that the Germans were pinned between walls of falling shells which closed remorselessly upon them.

On the night of December 8, relief finally arrived. As the men of the 1st Battalion, 13th Infantry, 8th Division, came up the hill, Herm Stein of F Company; Sergeants Koenig, Secor, and Webb of D Company; and Sergeant Lare of E Company stayed behind to guide the newcomers into position. The new arrivals crowded into the bunker like sardines in a can. In disgust, the Ranger sergeants went down the hill. Between 2230 and 2400 hours, the relief was effected.

Twenty-two Rangers were all that remained to come down from Hill 400.

The German high command had wanted Hill 400 badly. General Model, chief of the German general staff, had offered the Iron Cross and a seven-day furlough to each member of the unit that succeeded in retaking the hill. A battalion of German paratroopers had been brought in to make another effort. The Germans fought with skill and courage, but they did not succeed. The American Rangers had bought Hill 400 with their blood, and they would not give it up.

As the Rangers came down from the grisly slopes of Hill 400, a thick snowfall began to lay a peaceful mantle of white over the torn and ruptured earth. Twenty-three Rangers were dead and 110 others were wounded or captured. At 0615, December 9, the remnants of the 2d Ranger Battalion closed into an assembly area and were attached to the 28th Infantry Regiment, 8th Infantry Division.

Now began a period of rest and refit. One hundred twenty men were given leave, sixty went to the V Corps rest center at Eupen, and sixty others were given leave to Paris. The city of light became a celebration of life for survivors. Women, wine, and, as an afterthought, song helped men cope with the reality of war.

On December 11, the 5th Rangers moved to Ziegelhutte, Germany, and then on deeper into the Third Reich. The screening mission was one of patrol versus patrol. The 5th Rangers had the front of a division to cover. When Company F relieved a large force of infantry, the infantry officers were showing the Rangers where the machine guns and mortars could go and all the positions that needed to be filled. When a handful of Rangers armed with M-1 rifles and a few Browning automatic rifles arrived as the relief force, the well-meaning officers were stunned.

* * *

Mid-December 1944 was an optimistic time for the Allies. Progress on the front was going well, the logistical system to support combat operations was in place and operating effectively, and General Eisenhower planned a major offensive in the beginning of 1945. The planned drive would finish the German Army.

But the German cause was not hopeless. German scientists had some impressive developments in the works. There were improved, long-range rockets that would punish England, and the ME-262, a jet-propelled fighter plane, had the capability of sweeping Allied aircraft from the sky. If a bold attack was successful, the Allies could be forced to the negotiating table.

Throughout his political career, Adolph Hitler showed himself to be a gambler. Against the advice of his generals, Hitler decided to commit two Panzer (armored) armies in the attack. Two additional German armies would support the flanks. The route of attack would be through the Ardennes forest. The American VIII Corps was in the Ardennes in a thin, defensive posture, and few intelligence officers thought the Germans could mount an armored attack through these forests in cold and snow. The Germans, however, had learned much about fighting winter war in Russia, and they knew what was possible. Hitler believed the audacity of the attack could bring it success. He hoped to attack over a direction of Bastogne, Brussels, and Antwerp—if successful, every Allied force to the north of that line would be cut off and destroyed.

At 0530 hours on December 16, 1944, the Germans attacked. The U.S. 28th and 106th Divisions were chewed up, and confusion reigned in the Allied ranks. At 0940 hours on the 16th, the 2d Ranger Battalion was alerted that it would be released from attachment to the 8th Infantry Division and attached to the 78th Infantry Division, where it was ordered to move to defensive positions in the vicinity of Simmerath. The battalion was woefully understrength: the men on leave in Paris could not be returned, and every other man that could carry a weapon was sought. By 2300 hours, the remnants of the 2d Rangers were closing into position. Four companies were on line, one in reserve, and Company D had been designated to serve as 81mm mortar crews. Company C of the

310th Infantry and Company K of the 309th Infantry were attached to the 2d Rangers.

Now began a period of reconnaissance and combat patrols. The German attack was not falling on the sector held by the Rangers, though there were frequent alarms and messages from higher and adjacent headquarters warning of impending German attacks. Work on defenses was feverish. On the 18th, fifty-three replacements were received and assigned to the companies, and concertina wire, mines, and booby traps were emplaced. Brief encounters with the enemy were the norm, with the Germans placing moderate artillery fire on the Ranger positions and getting back more and more than they gave.

Meanwhile the 5th Ranger Battalion was also finding itself with minimal involvement in the great battle. On December 21, a platoon each from C and D Companies distracted the enemy while a raiding party from Company B hit an enemy position in the Simmerath sector with an artillery barrage, then moved in for the assault. Twenty-eight Germans were killed, twenty-five wounded, and one prisoner secured. Only one Ranger was injured.

On December 24, the 5th Rangers moved to Metz, France, where they celebrated a memorable Christmas. On the 28th, the 5th Rangers were moved to St. Avold, France, where they were attached to the 95th Infantry Division. The mission was defense. Severely stung, Eisenhower and his generals were taking no chances, but the German offensive had run its course. At key points, American resistance broke the German timetable. German tanks ran out of gas and were sitting targets for American armor. Hitler meddled with his own successes, favoring commanders that were his political favorites over those that were having the most battlefield success. Also, winter storms had kept the Allied air forces from the skies, but on December 26, the sky cleared, and the Germans were shot up and bombed by a seemingly never-ending stream of fighters and bombers.

Though on line and ready, the 2d and 5th Rangers saw 1944 end on a relatively quiet note.

Properly chastened, the Allies closed out 1944, licking their wounds but also licking their chops. The Germans had paid a heavy price for their failed offensive, and had used up troops and equipment badly needed on both fronts. Eisenhower was determined to press the Allied advantage. The gambler, Adolph Hitler, was left with the old saying: "Gamblers die broke."

CHAPTER 13

CABANATUAN

Nineteen forty-five was the year of retribution. Adolph Hitler had boasted that his Third Reich would last a thousand years, but in the Third Reich's twelfth year of existence, the beleaguered Nazis saw their dreams of conquest becoming a nightmare.

In the Pacific, the Japanese were learning the sour taste of defeat. American naval power, on a scope the world had never seen, moved under air superiority to deliver combat-experienced ground forces to their targets. The liberation of the Philippines was proceeding.

January 1945 found the men of the 6th Ranger Battalion loading landing craft, then moving into the Leyte Gulf, destination Luzon. The 6th Rangers had held a rollicking New Year's celebration and needed time for some shipboard recuperation. The men of the 6th were so frequently on ships, they counseled the sailors on seamanship while they lounged, bare-chested, on the hatch covers under a hot Pacific sun.

In Europe, the cold winds of winter froze men to the marrow of their bones. January found the 5th Ranger Battalion still at St. Avold, France, where work on defensive positions continued. There were the usual false reports of enemy paratroopers to be checked out, and several suspicious-looking civilians were detained. Attached to the 95th Infantry Division, Sullivan's Rangers found their defensive mission an ideal time to bring in replacements, refit, and train.

The 2d Rangers were at Simmerath, manning and improving their defensive positions when orders came down from the 311th Infantry that "a prisoner must be taken by 2400 hours." A Ranger patrol left friendly lines at 1935 hours, made contact with the Germans at 2034, and were back with the prisoner at 2055 hours.

On January 2, the 311th Infantry of the 78th Division relieved the 2d Rangers, and the battalion moved to billets in Rotgen. The duty was as counterattack force, but the opportunity to rest, refit, and train was put to good use. Men experienced the joy of a trip to a shower point and the soothing beat of a hot spray of water. On January 8, the 2d Battalion moved to Schmidthof. Replacements arrived, and on the 15th, Maj. George Williams implemented an intensive training schedule.

Meanwhile in the Pacific, on January 4, the 6th Rangers joined a vast American convoy. The destination of the battalion was the Lingayen Gulf in northern Luzon. The shipboard days passed in briefings and preparation for battle, but there was plenty of time for sunbathing, card games, and watching Japanese planes make ineffective attempts to stop the huge convoy.

On the 9th, the convoy entered the Lingayen Gulf and commenced an awesome pounding of Japanese positions. The guns thundered throughout the day and night, and on the 10th, the 6th Rangers' landing craft moved to shore. A landing craft carrying Company A Rangers beached some fifty yards from shore in ten-foot surf. As the ramp dropped, Captain Lever and Pfc. Leon Bailey led the way. Both men promptly went down in deep water. Captain Lever resurfaced, then went down again. Lever was rescued, but Bailey was carrying a heavy flame thrower and did not reappear. T. Sgt. George Tainter leaped into the water and made a heroic attempt to find Bailey, but could not locate him. The remainder of the men were taken to shore by DUKW.

Moving inland about a thousand yards, the battalion set up a perimeter and proceeded to dig in. The officers were moving about checking on the positions, when they were called to a meeting at Colonel Mucci's command post. Close by where the meeting was held, Cpl. Louis Weiss was busily engaged in digging his foxhole. As the officers were in conversation, a Japanese fighter/bomber came to visit. The Japanese pilot had cleverly cut his engine and glided to the attack, strafing the Ranger positions and dropping a bomb. Caught in the open, the 6th Ranger officers made a dash for the closest fox-hole, the one owned and occupied by Lou Weiss.

In an every-man-for-himself charge, a number of the officers leaped into the hole and buried Corporal Weiss beneath them. Weiss no longer cared about the strafing or bombing. He was suffocating. When the Japanese plane passed on, Corporal Weiss's righteous anger was a sight to behold. He spoke to the officers of the need for them to have their own foxholes. Weiss exercised his freedom of speech in a marvelous manner, addressing the 6th Ranger officers individually and collectively with language of color and vigor.

January 11 found the 6th Rangers moving south near Dagupan barrio, where they began security duty for the Sixth Army headquarters.

On January 16, Capt. Arthur Simons of Company B, 6th Rangers, took a small patrol aboard two high-speed PT (patrol) boats and departed for Santiago Island. American commanders felt the small island was an ideal location for a radar site, and there were reports of thousands of Japanese there. The Ranger mission was to determine if the Japanese were really there and to learn if the site was feasible for radar.

Simons would control the operation from the PT boat while Lieutenant Elsworth of Company E; Sergeant Crocker of Company A; Sergeant Potts of Company B; and Technician Four Smith, Technician Five Betzner, and Private, First Class Straub of Headquarters Company made the landing. Others on the patrol included a Filipino guide and a radar technician.

The fast boats carried the Rangers to a debarkation point, where at 0200 hours on the 15th, the patrol used rubber boats and paddles to row to shore. As often happens in war, the men soon noticed they were heading for the wrong objective. For two and a half hours, Elsworth and his men rowed through the darkness to reach Santiago Island. All around them the sunken hulks of Japanese shipping rose above the hungry waters. The hulks were twisted and torn in their death agony.

With Private, First Class Straub serving as scout, Elsworth's patrol moved ashore and began to check out native houses nearby. The inhabitants thought the intruders were Japanese coming to kill them and the terrified screams of women and children filled the night. When the natives were finally calmed, the Rangers learned that thousands of Japanese had been on Santiago but had departed on the 14th for the mainland. When daylight came, the small group of Rangers split into two patrols and, with Lieutenant Elsworth and Sergeant Potts each leading a group, checked out the remainder of the island. They found it devoid of enemy.

Meanwhile back at the 6th Ranger Battalion base camp, the popular battalion surgeon Capt. James C. Fisher of Arlington, Vermont, was assisting a Filipino woman to give birth to a healthy boy. Fisher became the child's godfather.

On the afternoon of the 19th, Companies B and E of the 6th Rangers departed for Santiago. The Rangers were security for engineers and radar personnel. On Santiago Island and from the base perimeter on the mainland of Luzon, the Rangers sent forth numerous patrols, finding large quantities of Japanese equipment and liquor. The equipment was turned over to Filipino forces—the liquor was not.

At 1130 on the morning of January 27, 1945, Colonel Mucci was ordered to report to 6th Army G-3. A mission was being assigned the Rangers, a mission that would live in history and be a source of particular gratification to those who participated on the American side.

With considerable justification for their view, Americans had come to look upon the Japanese as vermin that should be exterminated. This was a deeply personal feeling. Though formal advance notice of war was as passé as the longbow, most Americans viewed the surprise attack by the Japanese at Pearl Harbor on December 7, 1941, as the work of cowardly, back-stabbing sneaks.

Japanese experience and culture was so alien to that of the Americans as to be considered savagery. The Japanese warrior code, known as Bushido, was more demanding than the western code of chivalry. A Japanese of senior rank was bound as much as his junior, and violating the code required the offender to take his own life. The Japanese were a dedicated, insular, racist society, with a pecking order that gave considerable latitude for cruelty to subordinates. In their days of victory, the Japanese visited great suffering on conquered people and, in particular, on white prisoners of war. Though many Japanese would surrender as the war progressed, a large number chose death. That men would surrender rather than die was an unworthy act in the view of the Japanese military. They felt prisoners deserved harsh treatment.

Some 72,000 Americans were captured when the Philippines fell to the Japanese on April 9, 1942. The horror of the Bataan death march was but a prelude to the inhuman, foul treatment that the Japanese subjected these prisoners to in barbed-wire hell holes. Thousands of Americans and a higher number of Filipino men died of starvation, disease, torture, and murder in death camps.

One such camp was in the Nueva Ecija province of eastern Luzon. The camp was near the village of Pangatian located by the Cabanatuan Cabu road some five miles east of the city of Cabanatuan and a mile west of Cabu. In a barbed-wire enclosure scarcely larger than six hundred by eight hundred yards, the Japanese had crammed nearly six thousand sick and emaciated men. Through death and transfer, this group had been reduced to some 511 by mid-January 1945.

As the American Sixth Army drove on Manila, it reached a line along the villages and cities of Aliaga, Quezon, Casanova, Manacsac, and Guimba. This placed the army less than forty miles from the prison camp near Cabanatuan. Concern for the safety of the captives had long been expressed by American guerrilla commanders. Now that the army was close, the need for action surfaced at General MacArthur's headquarters. As the Japanese were withdrawing, it was considered likely that the Japanese would kill these prisoners rather than let them be liberated. MacArthur ordered Sixth Army to rescue the unfortunate American, English, and Dutch captives, and the 6th Ranger Battalion was given the job.

Mucci received aerial photographs of the prison camp and a briefing on the plan of operation. The mission would involve moving behind enemy lines a distance of some thirty-five miles. The terrain was rugged and would require crossing many ravines and a river and working around the populated areas known as barrios. There were Communist guerrillas operating in the area who were opposed to both sides and could spoil the operation. To pass through the enemy lines undetected, move over difficult terrain through the vastly numerically superior enemy, surprise and kill the camp guards, and free the prisoners was only half of the mission. How to then get hundreds of emaciated, ill men back through the enemy to freedom was equally difficult.

One of the best of the ingredients for success was the degree of information and technology that was available to the Americans. The information came from daring groups of men, some American, some Filipino. The technology was American and came in the shape of a heavily armed, night-capable fighter aircraft made by Northrup and called the P-61 or Black Widow.

Some Americans had eluded the Japanese net in 1942 and became leaders of Filipino guerrilla bands. Maj. Robert Lapham and Capt. Harry McKenzie were among this group and distinguished themselves in surviving and providing vital information for the American return to the Philippines. Lapham's Filipino comrades were excellent fighters. The devotion of the Philippine people was a wondrous thing, and there was trust in the army and General MacArthur: this man with the crushed cap and long-stemmed corncob pipe, who had carried the gold Marshal's baton of the Philippine Army prior to the outbreak of World War II, had promised to return and the Filipinos had faith he would keep his promise.

Within Sixth Army headquarters was a small band of brothers known as the Alamo Scouts. The name "Alamo" came from the telephone designator of Texas-born Gen. Walter Krueger's Sixth Army. The scouts were the eyes and ears of U.S. Sixth Army. Usually working as small teams consisting of an officer and three to seven enlisted men, the Alamo Scouts performed vital reconnaissance missions. They were good soldiers. General Krueger said words to the effect that he would not take the whole damn Jap army for one Alamo Scout.

The last and certainly among the most critical men of the Cabanatuan operation were superb young Filipino officers named Juan Pajota and Eduardo Joson. These aggressive leaders commanded forces of Filipino guerrillas, anxious for the opportunity to kill Japanese. The Filipino knowledge of the terrain and people and their ability to get information from Japanese-held areas was vital to this operation. Their courage in battle was magnificent.

After discussion, a plan was worked out whereby the Alamo Scouts would move into Japanese territory on the 28th and, with the guerrillas, reconnoiter the area for twenty-four hours before the Rangers launched the attack on the night of January 29.

Colonel Mucci returned to base camp and selected Company C commanded by Capt. Robert Prince and the 2d Platoon of Company F led by 1st Lt. Frank J. Murphy for the operation. Mucci was besieged by volunteers and finally agreed to allow four other sergeants to participate. Total strength of the Rangers would be 107 men. Filipino units commanded by Captain Joson and Captain Pajota would add approximately 160 additional armed men to the rescue force.

The first stage of the operation began on January 28, with a briefing and departure at 0515 to move by truck seventy miles to the front-line town of Guimba. Units of the 6th Infantry Division were in position here. Arriving at Guimba at 1300 hours, the men off-loaded and began marching south. Mucci met with Major Lapham, who briefed him on the enemy situation. The area in the vicinity of the prison camp was an important and well-traveled enemy supply route. The Japanese had a battalion and four tanks close to the camp and were believed to have some seven thousand troops in Cabanatuan. Additional forces were using the campsite as they bivouaced, enroute to mountain defensive positions.

To deal with the tanks, Mucci borrowed several rocket launchers and some antitank grenades from the 6th Infantry Division. A Ranger communications team with an SCR-694 radio was left at Guimba, while the rescue force carried a similar radio with them. After eating, the Rangers departed Guimba, following a Filipino guide, who led them southeast to the guerrilla camp of Captain Joson. Movement was swift. The Rangers wore soft caps and carried only light infantry weapons and K rations. There were no packs. The carrying-load priority went to ammunition and some small packets of cigarettes and candy for the prisoners.

Joson moved with eighty of his men in support of the rescue, and other Filipinos were dispatched as flank security.

The Filipinos informed local inhabitants that dogs were to be tied and muzzled and chickens penned to prevent alerting the Japanese. Around 1830 hours on the 28th, the rescue force moved east into darkness and Japanese-held territory.

The passage into enemy-held lands demonstrated what is possible when well-trained men have accurate intelligence of enemy dispositions. The move called for Mucci and Joson to pass close to Japanese positions, crossing roads used by the Japanese and over open areas subject to enemy observation. At one point the rescue force moved on the run for some two miles to cross an exposed area. The route was well to the north of the prison camp, winding into a left hook to come on the camp from the north.

The terrain and enemy dispositions made the movement somewhat slower than had been anticipated, and dawn found the rescue force short of Plateros which had been designated the rendezvous point with Pajota. Near Balincarin, approximately five miles north of the prison camp, the rescue force put out security and went to ground for the daylight hours. Part of the force hid under some parked buses to avoid aerial observation. Alamo Scout lieutenants, William Nellist and Thomas Rounsaville, met the rescue force at Balincarin. Though getting ever closer to the objective, there was little reason to fear betrayal. The Japanese had but a few days earlier gunned down a large number of civilians in a reprisal for guerrilla actions—the locals hated the Japanese and wanted only vengeance.

Around 1600 hours, the rescue force moved in two elements to Plateros. Around 1900 hours, Captain Pajota with a force of 90 armed and 160 unarmed men joined Mucci and Joson. The unarmed men would serve as litter bearers. The Alamo Scouts and Filipino guerrillas agreed that there were many Japanese in the area but their number and location was sketchy. Colonel Mucci wisely wanted more detailed information. He postponed the attack for twenty-four hours and prepared a list of questions. The Alamo Scouts and guerrillas were dispatched to get the answers.

What then occurred was a masterpiece of information gathering. In the small hours of January 29, American and Filipino scouts returned with detailed descriptions of routes of approach to the camp. They also described the layout of the camp, its gates, the number and location of the enemy, and his equipment, including the location of the guards and prisoners.

The Japanese guard force consisted of some 90 men and a unit of about 150 Japanese that were passing through and stopping over. A detailed map of the prison camp was made. Mucci also made arrangements for some fifty carabao (ox) carts to be brought to the Pampanga River, which lay between the Rangers and the camp. The Pampanga River was some three hundred yards wide, swift but fordable, and the carts would be used to carry the weakened prisoners after they passed over the river.

Reconnaissance was continuous. In daylight, an Alamo Scout and a Filipino guerrilla moved close to the objective to keep watch for any last-minute changes in Japanese dispositions.

After a thorough briefing on the plan of attack, the rescue force set forth as darkness fell on the night of January 30. Much of the march was made in three columns with Captain Joson's men on the right, Captain Pajota's men on the left, and the Rangers in the center. Pajota marched with knowledge he did not share with Mucci—an additional four hundred men were available to him, their armament including four .30 caliber, water-cooled machine guns.

Mucci's plan sent Captain Joson and his force to establish a roadblock on the Cabanatuan–Cabu road some eight hundred yards southwest of the camp; six Rangers with the rocket launchers accompanied this group. Captain Pajota's men covered the other flank by setting up a blocking position three hundred yards on the northeast side of the road. Lieutenant Tombo, an excellent Filipino scout, moved to cut the Japanese telephone lines to Cabu while a Ranger cut the line running to Cabanatuan.

High grass allowed the Rangers to approach undetected, but beyond the grass, it was necessary to crawl for over a mile of open ground to within seven hundred yards of the Japanese positions. As twilight came, Mucci's Rangers began to separate to move in teams toward their objectives. This movement was covered by a simple but effective deception. The Japanese had been hit hard by American air power and were quickly distracted when a plane flew overhead. About forty-five minutes before Mucci was scheduled to attack, a lone P-61 Black Widow of the 547th Night Fighter Squadron made two low-level runs over the camp, which distracted the Japanese and kept them looking skyward.

Lieutenant Murphy and the 2d Platoon of Company F moved by culvert and ditch to their assault position. Six men were assigned the mission of eliminating a bunker at the northeast corner of the stockade, while other Rangers were designated to kill the sentries in the watchtowers at the east and southeast corners of the stockade. The remainder of Murphy's platoon were to kill the enemy guards at the rear entrance to the stockade and adjoining buildings and to prevent an aroused enemy from getting to that portion of the compound where the prisoners were located. Murphy had the most difficult job of getting into position, and his shot would signal the assault.

Lt. William O'Connell's 1st Platoon of Company C had the mission of attacking from the front of the camp. The first section was to break through the gate, killing the gate guards, and the weapons section would follow and destroy the Japanese tanks and trucks. Initially firing from outside through the wire, the second section of the platoon would cover the movement of the first two groups, then enter the camp and prevent any of the enemy from escaping to the west.

Lt. Melville Schmidt and his 2d Platoon of Company C had the task of supporting the remainder of the force by fire then following the 1st Platoon into the compound and freeing the prisoners. One half of the 2d Platoon would move to buildings occupied by the Japanese transient force and kill the enemy, and the second half would account for the Japanese officers and men in their sleeping quarters. The weapons section of the 2d Platoon and the Alamo Scouts served as a force reserve and had the mission of assembling the prisoners and using the sixty unarmed Filipinos to get the weakened men through the front gate.

At 1945 hours on January 30, Lt. John Murphy fired his M-1 rifle into the camp, and the gates of hell opened for the Japanese. Surprise was total. Guards were shot out of towers or dropped at their posts, and Japanese-occupied buildings were blasted with automatic fire and rifle grenades. Sgt. Theodore Richardson and Ranger Leland Provencher killed two enemy guards, and Richardson shot the lock off the front gate. The Rangers then attacked in a textbook execution of an operations plan.

Some eight hundred Japanese soldiers were bivouacked to the east, and a stream with a bridge lay between these Japanese and Captain Pajota's blocking force. Pajota placed explosive under the bridge and sited his machine guns well. When the sounds of firing came from the prison camp, Pajota's men opened fire on the Japanese and blew out much of the bridge. The Japanese elected to make repeated frontal attacks and were mowed down like wheat. Enemy vehicles, including tanks, were destroyed by Pajota's fighters, and over three hundred Japanese were killed, their blood coloring the stream red.

Back at the camp, the rescue effort was proceeding smoothly, and the newly freed men were being escorted toward the gate. Rangers took off their field jackets, placed rifles through the sleeves, and used the jackets as makeshift litters. Some of the prisoners were carried on the backs of their rescuers; others, so emaciated that they resembled wrinkled skin over bones, were carried like babies by the Rangers and Alamo Scouts. A Japanese mortar fired several rounds which landed near the front gate, and the 6th Ranger Battalion surgeon Capt. James C. Fisher, Sergeant Alfinzo, Corporal Estesen, and Private, First Class Peters of the Alamo Scouts were wounded.

The Japanese were being systematically hunted down and killed—within fifteen minutes of Lieutenant Murphy's opening shot, most of the Japanese garrison and transients were dead. Scattered fire continued to be received, however, as Capt. Robert Prince made a second check to ensure the prisoners' compound was empty.

Satisfied that all the prisoners were in American hands, Prince fired the red-flare signal that the liberation was complete. The operation had taken some thirty minutes from the first shot.

As the last men of Murphy's 2d Platoon of Company F

withdrew along the outside of the camp, some Japanese survivors took them under fire. Cpl. Roy Sweezy was shot through the body.

A Japanese column of trucks and tanks, traveling in the direction of Captain Joson's column, was intercepted by one of the ten Black Widow fighters patrolling the night sky. The fighter's cannon and machine guns left the convoy a blazing pile of wreckage and discouraged Japanese movement from that direction.

When the flare signal for withdrawal was given, Joson and Pajota disengaged, Pajota leaving a shattered Japanese battalion behind him.

Some three hundred of those freed could walk, and these men were promptly escorted to Balincarin. Fisher and Sweezy, who were badly wounded, and the liberated men who were too weak to support themselves were taken across the Pampanga River and placed in the carabao carts. The roads were muddy, and the carts, carrying over two hundred weak men, would become stuck or slip from the trail and spill. The Rangers had to manhandle the carts much of the way in an exhausting process.

At Plateros a prisoner who had been a doctor, a squad of Rangers, and the Alamo Scouts remained with Fisher and Sweezy. Both men were in serious condition. Fisher had been hit in the stomach and Sweezy in the chest. The detachment that remained with them attempted to build a landing strip for light aircraft, but the effort was to no avail—the aircraft did not arrive. Captain Fisher and Corporal Sweezy died. They were the only American fatalities in a brilliant operation that saved the lives of 511 prisoners.

Through the night of January 30–31, the prisoners continued to move toward safety. Between Balincarin and Guimba at a place called Sibul, Mucci was able to make early morning radio contact. Mucci reported the success of the mission and requested ambulances and medical assistance. Movement continued toward friendly lines. As noon of the 31st approached, the Rangers made contact with an American reconnaissance unit. The ambulances were close behind. By early afternoon of the 31st, the 511 former prisoners were hospitalized and enjoying the sweet air of freedom.

* * *

While the men of Companies C and F were carrying out the rescue mission, Captain Lever with Company A and Lieutenant Anderson's platoon from Company D were undertaking another mission. Intelligence had reported that a force of one thousand Japanese had infiltrated American lines and were planning to blow three critical bridges. Contact with the enemy was made by a patrol from Company A meeting a six-man Japanese patrol. Ranger patrol-leader Sergeant Rongstead killed the first of the enemy, shooting him through the forehead, and the other Rangers killed three and wounded two of the six-man patrol.

Captain Lever was given command of a task force that consisted of Rangers, a company of infantry, a company of tanks, and a reconnaissance troop. A platoon-size fight in a field of tall grass resulted in two Japanese killed and one wounded. There were no Ranger casualties.

On February 1, Captain Shearon loaded his men of Company E and departed base camp to patrol the Cabaruan Hills. Intelligence that Japanese forces were in the hills received unofficial confirmation when the Rangers saw civilians evacuating their homes in these hills. Scattered contact was made. A Ranger platoon-size patrol fought a stiff fight with a larger Japanese force. Sgt. William Harris used his automatic rifle with telling effect, earning the Silver Star for the action. Still, the Japanese held the field and Ranger Sergeants Toredel and Conners were missing. A concentrated search was made for the two men without result.

On the 3d Company A moved out to establish a security guard for the advanced echelon of Sixth Army Headquarters. Captain Simons's Company B was ordered to prepare to join Lever's Company A. D Company had success when one of their patrols killed three Japanese.

February 4 was Decoration Day for the 6th Rangers. General MacArthur called the Cabanatuan raid "magnificent," and Colonel Mucci was awarded the Distinguished Service Cross. Officers who participated in the raid received the Silver Star and all enlisted men the Bronze Star.

Meanwhile, the search parties located Sergeant Conner's

body, and the clothes of Sergeant Toredel were found scattered about. Men of Company C finally located Toredel, lying in a carabao hole, badly wounded. Taken to a hospital, Toredel told his comrades, "I guess I'm too tough to be killed."

Col. Henry Mucci left the 6th Ranger Battalion on February 10 to assume another command. Maj. Robert Garrett, the executive officer, assumed command. Capt. Arthur "Bull" Simons became battalion executive officer. The 6th Rangers were moved to San Fernando in the relative comfort of city homes. Men were beginning to earn rotation home. One group of two officers and eight enlisted men received twenty-one-day home leave and went on a forty-day tour to boost home-front morale.

CHAPTER 14

ACROSS THE SAAR—ZERF

In Europe, on January 23, the 5th Ranger Battalion entrucked and moved to Johannesbannberg, France. More training was in store for Sullivan's men. January 29 saw the 5th Rangers being attached to the 26th Infantry Division, where training continued, with emphasis on cold weather operations.

For a brief time on February 2, it appeared that the 5th Rangers would be moving to relieve the 2d Battalion of the 104th Infantry, but XX Corps had another mission in mind. While awaiting new orders, the Rangers began a three-day training program on compass, sketching, and reconnaissance.

XX Corps was commanded by Gen. Walton Walker. Small in stature but large in aggressiveness, Walker was a fit companion to his mentor George Patton. Walker knew his XX Corps had a difficult area of operations ahead of it. The area that glowered at Walker from his maps had received the military designation of the Saar–Moselle Triangle. The eastern boundary of the triangle was the Saar River, the western boundary the Moselle. In the south, the base of the triangle, through which the Americans would have to attack, was an east-west run of the Siegfried line. The triangle was heavily wooded, rugged terrain, with few roads that would support armor. In distance, the Saar–Moselle Triangle measured some ten miles wide at the base and nineteen miles from the base to the top.

The triangle was important because crossing the Rhine River to the heart of Germany was important. To open up the Moselle corridor and get to the Rhine, the fortress city of Trier at the top of the triangle needed to be taken. For XX Corps to get to Trier meant going through the Saar–Moselle Triangle. The Germans had built a powerful position along the base of the triangle called the Seigfried Switch Line. Two kilometers deep, the switch line had resisted American efforts of penetration since November 1944.

The Germans placed strong reliance on the vast defensive network of the Siegfried line, including concrete and steel pillboxes, backed up by tank traps, nicknamed for their appearance "dragon's teeth." Barbed wire, mines, and all the weapons that could be brought to bear were assembled in terrain that was itself naturally strong. Crossing a river in some areas of the triangle meant coming up against cliffs so steep that the German defenders often had to have supplies raised to them by rope and pulley. The concept of the German defense line was that the attacker would be so exhausted and beaten up by the time of penetration that aggressive counterattacks could easily destroy him.

The German defenders of the triangle included the 2d Mountain Division, an Austrian division recruited of men from the Alps; the 416th Infantry Division, a unit comprised of men in their late thirties; the 19th Volks-Grenadier; and 25th Panzer Grenadier Divisions. All the German divisions had been badly mauled in earlier fighting and some no longer functioned as divisions.

General Walker planned to use two divisions to fight through the Saar–Moselle Triangle, and the two divisions he chose were a study in contrast. The 94th Division was infantry. Relatively new to combat, the 94th had been bloodied in January attacks on the Siegfried Switch line and proved itself an aggressive fighting unit. The 10th Armored Division was a battle-hardened veteran division. Many of its replacements were combat-experienced paratroopers from the 82d Airborne Division. The 10th Armored was resting from heavy fighting in the Ardennes.

Walker planned to cross the Saar and break the Seigfried line with the 94th Infantry Division, then send the 10th Armored through the breach to exploit the success. He decided to begin his attack on February 19.

On the 4th, V Corps alerted the 2d Rangers for movement to join the 9th Infantry Division. The mission was to lead the way in a river crossing and establish a bridgehead. Several days of reconnaissance was performed.

The 5th Rangers were ordered on February 7 to establish liaison with the 94th Infantry Division and perform reconnaissance as directed by them. On February 9, the 5th Ranger Battalion was detached from the 26th Infantry Division and moved to Wehingen, Germany, and attachment to the 94th Infantry Division. Despite its smaller size, the 5th Ranger Battalion relieved both the 1st and 3d Battalions of the 302d Infantry. The battalion front was 11,000 yards long, and required constant patrolling.

The bridgehead mission of the 2nd Rangers was canceled on February 11, and the training schedule was resumed.

The sector of the 5th Rangers was relatively quiet. In quiet sectors of the battlefield, death becomes very much an individual experience: a man is killed in a minefield; another bleeds to death when hit on patrol. Each day the Rangers and the Germans harassed each other with mortars. Running as many as six eight- to twelve-man patrols a day, the Rangers kept up the pressure.

In the chill morning of February 19, General Walker's offensive began. The 5th Rangers launched an attack against German fortified positions of the Siegfried Switch line in the vicinity of Oberleuken, Germany. An antitank ditch, protecting the German positions, was crossed by Company F, who found themselves in an electronically controlled minefield. A properly established minefield is always covered by fire, and the defending German soldiers knew their trade: machine guns in well-concealed pillboxes at each end of the ditch ripped into the Rangers, and mortar fire began to explode about them. The Ranger attack was stopped cold, and casualties began to mount. Company A was following F Company and fared no better. A platoon of B Company tried to join the lead element and was stopped; a platoon from Company E met the same result.

In late afternoon, Company A was able to approach the German position from the flank and began to clean out the defenders. Twelve Germans were killed and forty taken prisoner but the price of the day's fighting had been high. The names of fifty-five Rangers were added to the casualty lists, and the German positions had not been seriously dented.

On February 20, ten additional prisoners were captured,

and the 94th Infantry Division attack was moving forward. On the 21st, the 5th Ranger Battalion moved to Weiten, Germany, and again was given a screening mission. The Rangers outposted the towns of Hamm, Orcholtz, Keuchingen, and Taben. Companies C and D were attached to the 3d Cavalry Squadron, Company C occupying pillboxes in the area south of Orcholtz, while Company D maintained patrols along the west bank of the Saar River.

The 2d Ranger Battalion was completing a three-day exercise on the 22d when Major Williams was informed that the 2d Rangers would be attached to the 102d Cavalry Group. On February 23, the 2d Ranger Battalion was attached to the 102d Cavalry Group and moved to Dedenborn where they went into V Corps reserve. The battalion was enjoying a period when its ranks were filled with replacements, bringing it to a strength of six hundred. A training program was started to prepare the Rangers and cavalry to work as a team.

Meanwhile on February 23, XX Corps G-3 issued orders relieving the 5th Rangers of their defensive mission without waiting until their place on line was taken by another unit. The 94th Infantry Division had pierced the Siegfried line, and General Walker was now ready to exploit the success with the 10th Armored Division.

There was a difficulty with the American plan. On the German side of the Saar was the town of Zerf, a railroad center and a base of operation for the German Ardennes offensive. Running east and south from Zerf was a high-ground road network that the Germans could use to strike the flank of the 10th Armored Division units that had crossed the river. The Germans could also use the road to strike at the bridgehead across the Saar, cutting off the 10th Armored units that had crossed. To prevent the Germans from using this road network was a critical part of one of the most important operations in the war in Europe.

The 5th Ranger Battalion was given the mission of blocking German usage of the road, and the entire operation would begin with the 5th Rangers passing through the 94th Division bridgehead in the vicinity of Taben Rodt to cross the Saar River. The Rangers were then to pass through the lines of the 302d Infantry and proceed north. When penetration of the enemy lines was accomplished, the Rangers would secure high ground to the rear of the Germans that would cut the Irsch–Zerf road. Two units were given linkup missions with the Rangers: An armor-heavy task force from the 10th Armored Division would come from the north, and the 301st Infantry Regiment would come from the west. It was estimated that the Ranger mission would take about forty-eight hours until linkup occurred.

By February 22, the incoming volunteer replacements had brought 5th Ranger Battalion strength to 378 enlisted men and 20 officers. The headquarters section of Companies A–F each included two light machine guns and two 60mm mortars. The battalion weapons pool included six 81mm mortars, twelve rocket launchers, and fifty Thompson submachine guns.

Preparations for the mission began immediately. Each of the men was instructed to take a K and a D ration, and each rifleman was to carry an antitank mine. Six extra boxes of machine-gun ammunition would be carried for each gun.

Lt. Col. Richard P. Sullivan,[1] 5th Ranger commander, believed in personnel reconnaissance. Sullivan took the S-3, Captain Luther, and Lieutenant Gambosi's platoon from B Company, and crossed the Saar River at about 1900 hours. As Sullivan made the effort to step from the footbridge to the bank, a hand of assistance came through some bushes to help him. As he was being pulled to the bank, a voice behind the hand said "For Christ's sake! I ought to drop you!" The voice was that of a Major McBride, an old friend, who had been a cadet company commander under Sullivan at the Massachusetts Military Academy. Capt. Ed Luther, Sullivan's S-3, was also from the same school, and the three men held an impromptu reunion. At an advance command post of the 302d Infantry, Sullivan was given current information of German activities. Sullivan had intended to use dry creek beds that ran north just short of the objective as his route of approach. The officers of the 302d Infantry informed him that the Germans were covering these creek beds. Sullivan sent Lieutenant Gambosi back across the river to bring the company commanders forward for new instructions. Sullivan then went forward to reconnoiter. The situation was unclear; the battalion that the Rangers were to pass through was not where it was reported to be, and the American attack was stalled—Sullivan had to revamp his plans.

Meanwhile, the various companies of the 5th Ranger Battalion had moved from defensive positions to Weiten. The companies, minus Company B, then moved to assemble at the town of Taben Rodt; Company B was already in the town. The route of movement to Taben Rodt was under enemy observation and artillery fire; at 1730, just before Company A reached the town, two rounds of artillery landed on the 1st Platoon of Company A. Capt. Charles Parker, commanding Company A, reported six Rangers killed and eighteen wounded.

At 2000 hours on February 23 the companies moved down a steep slope to the Saar River. Order of march was B, C, D, E, F, and A Companies. They crossed the Saar on a footbridge built by the 94th Infantry Division, and found a guide sent by Colonel Sullivan waiting for them. They were then taken up the steep slopes of Hocher Hill, where the company commanders were briefed by Colonel Sullivan. Sullivan directed a route of march that would follow a compass azimuth of ten degrees.

Two columns were formed, with the order in the left column being C, F, and A Companies, and the right column being D, E, and B. The two columns would move about fifty yards apart. Within the companies, the men would move one behind the other in a column of files. Leading the way on point were two men with Thompson submachine guns and two with Browning automatic rifles. Several men were hit as enemy artillery and mortar fire played about the assembling Rangers. Accompanying Sullivan was an artillery liaison section from the 284th Field Artillery Battalion. The 284th would be in direct support of the 5th Rangers. Commanded by Capt. Stephen McPortland, the liaison section consisted of three forward-observer teams, each of which was commanded by a lieutenant.

At 2345 hours on February 23, the 5th Ranger Battalion passed through friendly positions of the 302d Infantry and began to move into enemy territory. This was a difficult movement over rugged, densely wooded terrain. The route would have been hard travel by daylight; moving in the black of night made the effort an even greater challenge. The

Rangers were accustomed to moving as silently as possible, but there was a complication: the antitank mine each man carried had a spiderlike device on top that rattled with every step. The sound carried, and while the Germans could not pinpoint the precise location, it made them nervous and they fired at the noise. High-velocity tank or self-propelled artillery fire began to strike, and German infantry opened fire. From time to time, the point element and the Germans met and exchanged fire in the darkness until contact was broken. Several Rangers were wounded in these contacts, and a forward observation team had its lieutenant badly injured, his radio operator killed, and their radio destroyed.

The two columns had been maintaining contact, but the combination of German artillery fire, rough terrain, and the darkness among the trees began to cause breaks in contact. The first phase line was a creek bed north of Hocher Hill. The 2d Platoon of Company A lost contact, and some of its members became separated from the platoon. Capt. Bernard Pepper of Company B had a major problem: His company headquarters and 1st Platoon had become separated from Company E to their front, and to compound the difficulty, around 0145 Pepper's 2d Platoon, led by Lieutenant Gambosi, and the weapons section had become separated from the company. Using radio, Pepper and his 1st Platoon reestablished contact, but the 2d Platoon of Company B was not as fortunate and remained separated.

Knowing reorganization was necessary, Sullivan used radio to contact the companies and establish a phase line at a road. When the companies reached the road, contact patrols were sent to the flanks and regained contact with battalion headquarters. A patrol from Lt. James Greene's Company E fell on a German position and captured twenty Germans.

At 0630 hours on the 24th, the 5th Rangers arrived at a high-ground area that served as a rallying point. The battalion halted and established a perimeter defense of about two hundred yards in diameter. Sullivan needed to find his missing men and get more information as to the nature of the terrain and the enemy. Sullivan sent out two reconnaissance patrols to the north and to the east, each consisting of an officer and three Rangers. Stray Rangers, who had become separated during the night march, were filtering in, but Lieutenant Gambosi's group was still missing. D Company men had a brief fight with a German patrol and took several prisoners.

Lieutenant Gambosi had made several attempts to move on the ten degree azimuth but came under heavy artillery, mortar, and machine-gun fire. Radio contact was made with Sullivan, who could not afford to wait and ordered Gambosi back to Taben Rodt. Gambosi wanted to make every effort to rejoin the battalion; he heard that Zerrig had fallen and moved there to await his opportunity to rejoin his company.

About 0815 the recon patrols returned and reported route information to Colonel Sullivan. By 0900 the 5th Battalion was again on the march, with the companies arranged in a wide, arrowlike configuration:

```
                    E
    D              HQ              A
    F               B              C
```

The movement was easterly through thick woods, and while the terrain was ideal for concealment, the density of the trees made pinpointing the battalion location and that of the objective difficult. A halt was made and patrols dispatched without success. Sullivan had radio communication with 94th Division, and it was a godsend. He called for artillery to fire two rounds on the Ranger objective. The men listened as the rounds rumbled overhead and were able to pick up the general direction in which they had to travel.

The march of the 5th Rangers continued against light opposition from the enemy. At 0930 on February 24, the Rangers reached the edge of the thick woods, halted to check their position, then resumed march. Their objective, a wooded highpoint hard beside the Irsch–Zerf road, lay to the northeast.

The movement was now to the north. After about eight hundred yards of travel, three German pillboxes were encountered by D Company patrols, and the Rangers took the unwary Germans by surprise and captured another twenty to thirty prisoners. Capt. William D. Byrne, the battalion S-2, led a D Company patrol that captured another pillbox and fifteen more prisoners.

The prisoner count was mounting: some fifty Germans had been captured and were a burden to a unit operating behind enemy lines. As Captain Pepper's Company B only had about fifteen men remaining, they were given the job of guarding the prisoners.

The march continued north and was passing near some high ground, when the tail of the column came under attack by about fifty Germans. The Germans seeing a few Americans considerably behind their lines probably assumed the Rangers were a patrol. The Germans went into line formation and assaulted across an open field. The Ranger companies opened fire on them from the center, with Capt. George Miller's Company D hitting them from the flank. Twenty Germans were killed, and the survivors were captured. The Rangers were now about three thousand yards behind the German lines and had to contend with some 110 prisoners.

Meanwhile, Lieutenant Gambosi had taken his men to the newly captured town of Zerrig and made contact with an armor-heavy task force from the 10th Armored, Combat Command B under the command of Lieutenant Colonel Riley. Task Force Riley consisted of the 21st Tank Battalion, minus Company B; Company A of the 54th Armored Infantry; and a platoon of engineers. The infantry however was not with Lieutenant Colonel Riley when Lieutenant Gambosi met him. Riley had orders to attack through the 94th Division bridgehead and move on Irsch. There he would meet Lt. Col. Miles Standish (direct descendent of the colonial hero) who commanded the 61st Armored Infantry Battalion (AIB). The two units would then move east, contact the 5th Ranger Battalion, and take the high ground west of Zerf. As Riley had no infantry support and was going toward the main body of the 5th Battalion, the meeting was advantageous to both men.

Gambosi's twenty-four Rangers were put in six half-tracks, and the advance continued. When Task Force Riley arrived at Irsch, they thought it had been taken by the 61st AIB, but Colonel Standish and his men were still fighting their way toward the town. Riley's lead company went into the town and was ambushed by German tank-supported infantry. With a loss of five tanks, the American tankers withdrew and requested the Rangers clear the town. Gambosi and his men went from house to house, clearing out the German infantry and driving their *Panzerfaust* teams from the roadblocks. Three roadblocks were cleared. A German Tiger tank, deprived of its infantry support, withdrew, and the task force occupied Irsch. The Rangers found a second Tiger on the edge of town and reported its position. Gambosi's men took sixty Germans prisoner. As night fell, Task Force Riley was fighting around Irsch against elements of the German 416th Infantry Division. Additional companies of 10th Armored units arrived. During the night, the 10th Armored units were organized into "Temporary Team A" to complete the mission of reaching the 5th Ranger Battalion.

The German command did not seem aware of the 5th Ranger presence. The situation was fluid, with various columns of Americans making penetration. German unity of command had broken down, and while some units were fighting hard, others fled or surrendered. A Ranger described the German front as having the consistency of a sieve. "Movement is our greatest defense," Sullivan told his artillery liaison officer. When Sullivan encountered German resistance, he would make a definite change in direction, tacking back and forth toward the objective. This seems to have aided the Ranger movement by confusing the Germans. Unfortunately, the happy circumstance of being unlocated was about to come to an end.

Around 1600, the 5th Rangers halted and dug in. Sullivan had a choice of continuing through thick woods or waiting until dark and going over open fields toward the objective; Sullivan chose the latter course of action. Given the large number of prisoners that the Rangers were burdened with, it is not surprising that some got away. Four of the prisoners escaped and soon thereafter artillery and mortar fire began to strike the Ranger location. The German resistance was now beginning to take form. Small scattered counterattacks and artillery and mortar fire showed that the enemy was now aware of the American advance and was preparing to meet it.

Movement continued against light resistance. Around 1700, a platoon-size patrol from Company A checked out eight houses located on a crossroads in the center of an open area. Save for civilians in the basements, the houses were unoccupied.

At 2200 hours on the 24th, Sullivan moved the battalion through the woods and on the road toward these houses. Using infiltration by company, the 5th Rangers set off with the order of march A, E, C, F, D, and B Companies. Rangers of Company A were first on the road. A group of about ten Germans were fired upon and scattered. A white-painted German medical car came down the road and was halted by Company A. Captain Parker reported the capture of a German doctor and four medical aidmen. The German doctor was astounded. "This is four thousand yards behind the lines," he exclaimed. "No, no! You cannot be here." Despite his surprise, the German doctor adapted well and proved of good service in caring for both German and American wounded.

As they closed on the new position, Company B received automatic and small-arms fire from four buildings some two hundred yards east of the Ranger location. The *Kalferthaus* (Kalfert House) and a nearby pillbox were the source of most of the German fire.

Sullivan sent a patrol, led by Lt. Oscar A. Suchier, Jr., from Company F to the *Kalferthaus* area. The patrol came under direct fire from some pillboxes and attacked. Some thirty prisoners were taken; one Ranger was killed and one wounded.

Sullivan wanted artillery placed on the German positions, and it got there but only after considerable difficulty. One of the basic questions of the infantry is, "Where the hell are we?"—neither the Rangers nor their artillery liaison team knew their precise location. The artillery was being fired using grid coordinates, and the German countryside was sprayed with shrapnel until it got on target.

Daylight was coming, and Sullivan wanted to secure the higher ground to his front. He attacked with F Company followed by E Company, then brought up the rest of the battalion. The Germans made a brief fight of it, then jumped on trucks and fled. By 0500 on February 25, the Rangers had cleared out the *Kalferthaus* nest, and by 0900 they were occupying the area.

At 0600, Temporary Team A, with Lieutenant Gambosi and his twenty-four Rangers, again attacked on the road to Zerf.

The problem of 5th Ranger Battalion location was now clearing itself. The Rangers would have to move about one thousand yards north from the *Kalferthaus* to be in position to control movement on the Irsch–Zerf Road. The Rangers moved out with Jim Greene's[2] Company E in the lead, with the mission of cutting the Zerf road. Shortly after 0800, Company E reached their objective, and a defensive position was established on the high ground south of the road to cover the road by fire. Greene placed a rocket-launcher team on a road junction and sewed the road surface with antitank mines. The remainder of the battalion closed and occupied a perimeter defense about two hundred yards wide and one thousand yards long. Company C was to the left of Company E and Company D to the right. Company A remained south of the *Kalferthaus* to hold the pillboxes in that area.

Shortly after Company E was in position, a German self-propelled gun came from the west, heading toward the front. The crew saw the waiting Rangers, jumped from their vehicle and ran. The Rangers fired a rocket at the stranded vehicle without result, then poured gasoline on it and set it ablaze.

The Germans were now closing on the Rangers. In mid-afternoon, about two hundred heavily armed German infantry struck the 2d Platoon of Company A. Company A was somewhat isolated from the rest of the battalion, artillery support was not good, and the fight became hand-to-hand, with point-blank exchanges of automatic weapons fire. After about forty-five minutes of battle, the Germans withdrew. Company B, still with only a handful of men, was now guarding some 150 prisoners and trying to help Company A. Company A withdrew to *Kalferthaus* to come under the protective fire of the battalion. The German force which had previously attacked tried again, assaulting the gap in an effort to isolate Company A from the rest of the battalion. Parker's company killed a number of Germans and drove the rest off.

Ammunition resupply for the machine guns was critical. Word was passed back to 94th Division Artillery, and two of their light observation aircraft loaded up with boxes of machine-gun ammunition and prepared for a low-level drop. The Germans did not cooperate, and their heavy fire kept the aircraft from getting below fifteen hundred feet. The U.S. 3d Army after-action report waxes enthusiastic about this opera-

tion, claiming fifty-seven successful sorties flown with ammunition, food, and water delivered.

The Rangers took a different view. The first light aircraft
dropped its delivery to the Germans. The second trip was
more on target, but after putting up with the risk of being hit
with the falling boxes, the Rangers were disgusted to learn
that the ammunition dropped from fifteen hundred feet was
so beaten up that it could not be used. Later, the planes tried
dropping belted machine-gun ammunition. This worked better, though the ammunition was filthy and had to be cleaned
before use.

As darkness fell, German patrols were coming from all directions, attempting to pinpoint the Ranger location. In the
event it became necessary, the Rangers checked escape
routes, and it appeared that only to the southwest was there a
chance of a breakout. About 0300 on the morning of the 26th,
some six hundred Germans attacked from two directions.
The main attack was coming in on the northwest flank of
Company E. The left flank of Company A was being hit from
the southwest. The Germans came charging against Company E yelling "Surrender, *Amerikanische*!"

The fight was being waged in thick cedar forest in utter
blackness. Only the different sound of weapons could be used
to gauge the German and American positions. Company E
ripped the Germans with heavy fire, and the attack was contained until the Ranger machine guns ran out of ammunition.
As the Germans began to break through, positions were lost.
Sullivan shifted the bulk of his artillery support to the Company E sector. Sullivan also sent Captain Parker and the 1st
Platoon of Company A (thirteen men) to assist Company E,
but the reinforcements were not sure of Company E's location, and confusion resulted. The Company A platoon came
into the right of Company C and were immediately engaged
in fighting off a German attack. Companies A and C fell back
to a firebreak and established a defensive line, facing north.
The Rangers pulled artillery close in, hammering the area
just vacated. The Rangers were dug in and the Germans were
not, and for thirty minutes, high explosives tore at earth and
flesh.

When dawn came on the 26th, Sullivan sent the twenty-six

men of Company F in the attack to regain the lost positions. Live Germans were not to be found. The enemy had left and behind him was a woods littered with German corpses. Sullivan began to use artillery on likely areas where the Germans could form for an attack.

At 1155 hours on February 26 men of the 10th Armored Division, Temporary Team A came down the Irsch–Zerf road and made contact with a Ranger, who came forward to meet them. Five half-tracks were sent to take off Ranger wounded. The armor then continued attacking toward Zerf. Lieutenant Gambosi was unaware that contact had been made and returned to Irsch until he could get more information on the battalion location. At 1900 hours, another 10th Armored tank column brought much needed assistance, and more wounded were taken off. Ammunition, food, and water arrived and the burden of prisoner watch went to other shoulders.

A clearly defined front did not exist, and with the Americans exploiting the penetration, German and American units collided with each other and fought individual battles. The Germans came again against the 5th Rangers with a battalion-strength attack. But the Germans were confused about the Ranger location and seemed to be making an approach march to their line of departure. When the fight began, the Germans ran forward calling on the Rangers to surrender, but the 5th Rangers caught the attacking Germans in a cross fire that mowed them down in rows. Sullivan estimated 150 Germans were killed. Good fortune had smiled on the Rangers for the Germans were heavily armed—about every third man had an MG-42 machine gun.

Around 0900 on the 27th, American 94th Infantry Division units began to arrive close by. At 1155 Lieutenant Gambosi and his men rejoined the battalion, and five tanks and four half-tracks showed up. The Rangers hung out recognition panels and welcomed home their own. German artillery was steadily increasing, but their attention was now much more on trying to stem the advance of the 10th armored at Zerf. Still, German units that had been fighting to the west or had broken free tried to use the Irsch–Zerf road. A German half-track ambulance, trying to get to the rear, ran over a 5th Ranger mine and blew up.

The Rangers were now attached to the 301st Infantry. Colonel Haggerty, the commander of the 301st, ordered the Rangers to remain in position and informed Sullivan that he would reinforce the Rangers. The 94th Division had been ordered to continue to expand the bridgehead, and there was a series of eleven hilltops in the densely wooded terrain that were the 94th Division objectives. The 3d Battalion of the 301st was to take the hills designated 4, 5, and 6, near Zerf. Sullivan informed the 301st not to send men overland into the Ranger position at night as they might be fired upon mistakenly. The 10th Armored had road priority, with the result that the men of 3d Battalion of the 301st Infantry had to make a long approach march, staying clear, yet accomplishing their mission.

During daylight, four tank destroyers, four tanks, and two quad-.50-caliber machine-gun-mounted half-tracks came into the Ranger position, where preparations were being made for an attack to the south.

Meanwhile the weary infantrymen of K Company, 3d Battalion, 301st Infantry, were continuing forward, approaching a wooded area they believed had to be cleared before they could reach Hill 4. At 0300, they arrived just short of the woods held by the 5th Rangers. In the darkness, K Company came in echelon formation. The Rangers were not expecting a friendly force and challenged. The platoon leader of the lead right platoon gave the correct password, and his men were passed forward. At the other end of the line, no response was given to the challenge, and the Rangers opened fire. It was only a brief burst of fire, but three of the Company K men were killed and seven wounded. The Rangers had followed military procedure and were blameless, but that did not take away the hurt.

On the morning of the 28th, Lieutenant Harbin's 1st Platoon of Company C were fired on from a bunker short of *Kalferthaus*. The Rangers attacked and took the position and twelve prisoners. Continuing on to *Kalferthaus*, the platoon took fire from a house and woods to the southeast. The 1st Platoon moved close to the house and fired ten rockets into it; one hundred two enlisted men and four officers came out to surrender. The 1st Platoon, Company C, 5th Ranger Battalion, had captured what was left of a battalion of the German 416th Infantry Division.

At 1130 on the 28th, the 5th Rangers left their defensive positions and joined the 3d Battalion of the 301st in the attack. The objective was Hill 4, some five hundred yards south. The tanks and tank destroyers protected the right flank, sweeping across open fields to the right, while the Rangers moved on the left through a wooded area. The firepower of the tanks was much appreciated. Also appreciated was the distance between them and the Rangers. The tanks drew artillery fire to themselves, proving the old adage that "a moving target attracts the eye."

The fighting was heavy. D Company was hard hit, and German rockets fell on Company C, causing five casualties and leaving the company with twenty-five men. In Company B, ten casualties were sustained in the first fifteen minutes. In 2d Platoon, Company B, only Lieutenant Gambosi, his radio operator, and a rifleman remained. Despite these losses, the Rangers and tanks took their objective and repulsed several small counterattacks. The hill was the command post of the 136th Regiment of the German 2d Mountain Division. The commander of that unit was either killed or escaped, but the five officers and 105 enlisted men, who were the remnants of the 136th, were taken prisoner. As the 136th was a prime opponent of the Rangers throughout this mission, their destruction was particularly gratifying.

While the hill seemed to no longer hold tactical significance, the Germans fought hard to get it back. They pounded the thickly wooded hill with artillery and mortar fire, and a thirty-six-hour artillery battle ensued. German soldiers infiltrated the Ranger positions and in the darkness, American and German foxholes were intermingled. A German machine-gun section made considerable noise as they were setting up close to Lieutenant Gambosi's position. Gambosi, thinking they were American, yelled at them to be quiet.

Meanwhile, new instructions had been received by the 2d Ranger Battalion. D and E Companies of the 2d Rangers were

ordered to relieve elements of the 309th Infantry northeast of
Ruhrburg. Capt. Duke Slater was in charge of the operation,
and the relief was effected by 1200 on March 1. That evening,
patrols from Companies D and E waded the shallow Roer
River and determined that the Germans had evacuated the
area. At 0345 on March 2, Company F of the 2d Rangers
began to cross, and by 1215 hours, the remainder of the battalion began crossing. The 2d Rangers then began a road
movement along a series of objectives. Three roadblocks were
encountered, bypassed, and reported. Mines were the constant
threat, and Lt. Ed Kucinski and Sgt. Julius Belcher demonstrated raw courage in picking routes through the snow-
covered fields. The weather alternated between winter sun and
sudden snow flurries, and the only constant was the cold.
Lieutenant Kucinski, Sergeant Belcher, and six other Rangers
formed a patrol to establish contact with the 310th Infantry.
The patrol came under German mortar and machine-gun
fire from a German platoon-size force, and Cpl. Peter T.
Bubanovich was killed. Other men were wounded by mines.
Company C mortars and 105mm howitzer fire destroyed the
machine gun and dispersed the Germans. It was difficult to extract the wounded through the mine fields; vehicles could not
chance the uncleared roads, and wounded men had to be carried on litters for long distances. The 2d Battalion assumed
defensive positions and dispatched patrols.

The 5th Battalion had experienced another difficult night.
The Ranger strength was so depleted that headquarters per
sonnel, including drivers and cooks, were in the foxholes. On
the morning of March 2, the Germans were driven off and
Rangers were once again on the attack. This time on Hill 3,
Companies A and F led the assault in a well-conceived plan.
The German positions had been intermittently pounded by
heavy concentrations of artillery throughout the night. Under
the covering fire and darkness, the Rangers moved into position some three hundred yards short of the German-held hill.
Captain Miller and Lieutenant Smalling, the forward observer, began the attack with a rolling barrage that started on
the objective, rolled back toward the Rangers, then back
again on the objective. The Rangers followed close behind,

lifting and shifting their artillery. Company A Rangers shot down eight Germans outside of a pillbox, then kicked in the door. They found the exhausted Germans had been trying to sleep—four German officers and forty-seven men were taken prisoner here without casualty to Company A. Company F worked over the remainder of the objective with assault fire and grenades, killing some fifty Germans and taking another fifty prisoner.

Meanwhile, Company A had taken fifteen more prisoners and was coming under heavy artillery fire from the Germans. The German telephone lines were still operating, and Captain Parker moved the German prisoners into the open and had the senior officer telephone to lift the artillery fire before it killed the German prisoners. The German artillery held off, and that gave the Rangers time to dig in. The senior German prisoner was furious as he thought the purpose was to allow time for the Germans to be taken to the rear but only when the Rangers were satisfied with their positions, were the prisoners taken to safety. When it resumed, the German bombardment was heavy, but the Rangers were now under cover.

A defense line was organized with A and F Companies on the forward slope and D and the remnants of Company E on the rear slope. Two tanks were brought up. Company F Rangers were moving to position, when they came face-to-face with a German self-propelled gun. The Rangers captured three of the crew, but the gunner fired several rounds, stunning the Rangers, and the vehicle withdrew rapidly some 250 yards away where it kept up a petulant fire. As the afternoon wore on, B and C Companies came to the relief of A and F.

By March 3, it was over: The two-day mission had taken nine days, and the 5th Ranger Battalion was bled dry. Company A had one officer and twenty-four men remaining. Company B had begun the operation with a strength of three officers and fifty-nine men; thirty-seven of the fifty-nine men were casualties. Company F had two officers and eighteen men remaining, and so it went with the rest of the battalion. During February, the 5th Battalion had lost 34 Rangers killed, 140 wounded, and 12 missing.

In the Zerf operation, the 5th Ranger Battalion accomplished a classic Ranger mission. Penetrating enemy lines, the 378 men and 20 officers moved a distance of 5,200 yards (nearly three miles) into enemy territory, blocked a road that was critical to the enemy, then held the position until relieved. Colonel Sullivan reported that the battalion had captured some six hundred prisoners, killed an estimated three hundred, and wounded a large number.

The 5th Rangers were relieved by Company L of the 376th Infantry on March 4 and moved to Serrig where they became part of the 94th Infantry Division reserve. On the 6th, the battalion moved to Schwebsingen, Luxembourg, for R & R (rest and relaxation).

On March 3, the 2d Rangers moved to secure the high ground in the vicinity of Wolfgarten. The 2d Infantry Division was moving on Gemund, and the roads were clogged with their passing. The Rangers found themselves trying to move through a swarm of Indianhead Division soldiers. The marching was constant, and at midnight the battalion received orders to join the 102d Cavalry Group near Paulushof. Another march began, and at 0445 the footsore Rangers arrived in their assigned assembly area.

Rest was in store for the weary feet. Each of the companies of the 2d Ranger Battalion was now joined with a cavalry troop in task-force fashion. Companies A, B, and C joined with Troops A, B, and C of the 38th Cavalry Squadron, respectively, and Ranger Companies D, E, and F were with Troops A, B, and C of the 102d Cavalry Squadron. Each Ranger company had at least two quarter-ton trucks, two two-and-a-half-ton trucks, and two half-tracks.

The objective was to move from the Roer River to the Rhine to exploit the gap left by the rapidly withdrawing enemy. The terrain dictated road travel, and the Rangers had to move quickly against the enemy. When German resistance was encountered, the cavalry would try to pin the enemy in position by fire while the Rangers dismounted and moved to attack the German flank.

The method of operation worked well. On March 4, the task force which included A, B, and C Ranger Companies eliminated a German position near Hergarten, knocking out two machine guns and taking five prisoners. Meanwhile in early evening darkness, fog, and mist, Company D was fired upon by the 2d Division Reconnaissance Troop. A brief firefight ensued, but fortunately, there were no casualties.

CHAPTER 15

ACROSS THE RHINE—VE DAY

The Germans were hurrying to get across the Rhine in early March 1945, and many seemed to be throwing away their uniforms and changing to civilian clothes. Withdrawing German units were also destroying supplies and equipment. The German civilians seemed to be well informed on the progress of the American Army; few civilians attempted resistance; some waved and some gave useful information on roads and bridges. The pursuing 2d Ranger Battalion and cavalry passed through town after town, chasing the Germans. The mop-up was left to other units. The pursuing Rangers were finding their most difficult problem was to get resupplied.

On March 5, Company C, 2d Rangers, had cleared the town of Schwerfen and was moving on Gehn when the Rangers surprised a group of about one hundred Germans, who were laying a mine field. The Ranger attack dispersed the enemy, killing a number and resulting in sixty more German prisoners.

That night at Rissdorf, the Rangers found a German castle which captured their hearts. B and C Companies located and outposted the beautiful castle, admiring the hunting trophies and weapons, but the stay was short-lived, and men were soon back on the road.

The pursuit was so rapid that the Germans were kept in constant flight and unable to organize a defense. The American 62d Field Artillery was in direct support of the advance, and some guns would be kept in position while others displaced forward in a continual leapfrog manner. Rangers burst into buildings to find the German cooking fires still burning and hastily abandoned equipment scattered about. The Germans were kept on the run.

On March 7 near Vischel, Company A of the 2d Rangers caught up with the rear of the retreating 272d Volks-Grenadier Division. The Rangers killed eight Germans and captured nine without Ranger loss. At Kreuzberg, Company B observed a small horse-drawn supply train enroute toward Altenahr. Tank destroyers were brought forward and opened fire. The result was pandemonium as carts overturned and burned and horses and men fled.

The scene was repeated on a larger scale at Altenahr. A German column with about one hundred soldiers with over fifteen vehicles and horse-carts was dispersed. A firefight developed in the town. Receiving superb fire support from S. Sgt. Ray Alm's 81mm mortar section, the 2d Platoon of B Company carried the brunt of the fighting in Altenahr. Using assault fire, and terrifying the Germans with their constant shouting and yelling, the 2nd Platoon Rangers made a relentless attack under heavy fire. The Germans had numerous machine guns and automatic weapons in the houses and snipers firing from high ground, but the Rangers rooted them out. About a dozen Germans were killed and fifteen taken prisoner. The surviving Germans set up a machine gun on the opposite side of a stream and prevented the Rangers from crossing. Lt. Thomas Victor dashed across a fifty-foot bridge in an attempt to destroy the machine gun but was hit and lay wounded on the German side. Pfc. Paul H. Hickling crossed the bridge to assist his lieutenant, dragged him from the line of fire, and remained with him. That night, B Company commander, Capt. Sidney Salomon, and Ranger Kobylinski crossed the bridge and, with Hickling's help, brought the wounded Lieutenant Victor to safety.

Altenahr was the toughest fight of the operation. Sgt. William Thomas was killed at Altenahr, and seven additional men, besides Victor, were wounded. At daybreak, the 1st Platoon of Company B was ordered to cross the bridge. Captain Salomon led by example and was the first man to cross the bridge. Fortunately, the Germans had fled.

The winter cold seemed without end. Men shivered under the falling snow and the wet of chill rain. The skin itched and flaked. Men yearned for warmth, yet the slightest temperature increase brought thick, gluelike mud. The food was not to the liking of many of the Rangers. Men complained about the coffee being hot, colored water and the skimpy rations issued before an attack seemed designed to increase the fury of the Rangers. These were veterans and members of a conquering army, and as their ancestors did in previous wars, the Rangers made foraging an art. Many a German chicken went in the pot; milk, cheese, and bread were wolfed down; and some of the more enterprising got German women to cook a hot meal.[1]

"When you are carrying a rifle," one Ranger observed, "it doesn't take a lot of conversation to get what you need."

Writers who called the Rangers "spirited" seldom knew how well-founded their remarks were. The men had an infinite capacity for sniffing out any spirits that were in the area. Few connoisseurs knew more about German wines, cognac, and beer than those hardy Rangers who volunteered for reconnaissance patrols.

On March 8, Company A made a cross-country move to Mayschoss. There were about forty Germans in the town, and they were taken by surprise and captured. Twenty-one French prisoners were liberated.

At 1500 hours on the 8th, the 2d Rangers and 102d Cavalry Squadron closed on Ahrweiler. The Ranger/cavalry boundary was pinched out by larger American units, and for most of the men the operation was over. Company D of the 2d Rangers and Troop A of the 102d Cavalry were attached to the 38th Infantry and performed the screening missions to the front of the regiment and contacted with the 8th Infantry Division.

The 8th also brought time for the routine of army life to catch up to the 2d Rangers. The battalion was still divided into Force A/B/C and Force D/E/F, and local security, patrolling, and treating foot infections were the highlights of the period.

On the 9th, Force D/E/F divided to perform separate missions. Company D was attached to the 38th Infantry Regiment of the 2d Infantry Division as a screening force. Moving south on the Bad Neuenahr–Konigsfeld road, Company D reached Konigsfeld at 1745 hours and outposted the town during the night. Company E had moved to Dernau, while Company F occupied Ahrweiler—both companies set up defensive positions and outposts and dispatched patrols. The battalion command group, while displacing to Marienthal, discovered two large tunnels: One of the tunnels contained a power plant; the other was the hiding place for 3,500 German civilians and French, Russian, and Polish slave labor.

Task Force A/B/C, 2d Rangers, spent March 10 in security and patrol missions. Company D was attached to the 9th Infantry and given the mission of making contact with 3d Army forces to the south. The Rangers moved out aggressively, clearing towns along the way. At 1130 hours, the 2d Platoon of Company D made contact with elements of the 11th Armored Division. The remainder of the company flushed a German force, killed six and captured sixteen. At the close of the day, Company D of the 2d Rangers had captured four towns and sixty-nine prisoners and destroyed two German vehicles.

On March 11, the 2d Ranger Battalion was detached from the 38th and 102d Cavalry Squadrons, and Force A/B/C assembled in the Mayschoss area, while Force D/E/F moved to Ahrweiler. In adding up their accomplishments during the mission just completed, the 2d Ranger Battalion listed 24 towns captured, along with 467 German soldiers.

The 2d Rangers now began a period of light activity. Reconnaissance and patrolling of the battalion zone was interspersed with guarding tunnels, refit, and reorganization. With the war winding down, garrison life was coming back. Inspections, trips to quartermaster shower points, and training programs were the daily activities.

The 5th Rangers had used its rest to good advantage. One hundred ninety-one replacements had joined the battalion and were being trained. The veterans concentrated on building good memories in Arlon, Belgium, and Luxembourg City.

On March 19 the 5th Rangers were moved to Trier, then St. Wendel. D Company returned to Trier. The Germans had taken people from many European nations to concentration camps or to serve as their laborers; once liberated, these people were known as displaced persons. With the war winding down, D Company of the 5th Rangers was now guarding a camp for displaced persons.

On March 24, Companies D, E, and F of the 2d Ranger Battalion were alerted for movement on the 26th. The mission of the battalion was to rejoin the 102d Cavalry Group, cross the Rhine River, and move to the relief of the 27th Armored Infantry Battalion, 9th Armored Division, in the vicinity of Wallendar. Force D/E/F Companies were reattached to the cavalry companies they had previously worked with and crossed the Rhine at 0845 hours. Companies A/B/C crossed later and moved directly to Wallendar to effect the relief, accomplishing the mission at 1925 hours. The 2d Rangers were in hot pursuit of the Germans March 27, the mission to extend American control to the east of the Lahn River. A series of phase lines was established, and the companies moved on these. Company F, with Troop C of the 102d Cavalry Squadron, moved first on what turned out to be a mop-up operation. Ninety-seven prisoners were soon captured and six 88mm guns destroyed. Company D, with Troop A of the 102d Cavalry, passed through Company F, captured sixty-two Germans, and made contact with the 2d Battalion, 9th Infantry of the 2nd Infantry Division. Company E, with Troop B of the 102d Cavalry, passed through Company D and captured thirty-five more Germans, while linking up with the 9th Armored Division.

On March 28, the mop-up operations continued for the 2d Rangers. Force A/B/C Companies were moved to Dietz and relieved elements of the 9th Armored Division by 0815. During the day, Company B captured twelve Germans, and Company A added two more. At 1900 hours, the Rangers were relieved by the 346th Infantry Regiment. Force D/E/F spent the 28th conducting patrols and setting ambush positions to trap fleeing Germans. Company D captured eighty-six Germans, killed two of the enemy and captured thirty vehicles. On the 29th, Force D/E/F and the command group moved to Wolfenhausen, while Force A/B/C served as a mobile reserve for the 102d Cavalry.

In the fluid situation that existed, highly motivated German units continued to attempt to harass the advancing Americans. On the 30th, a German force ambushed a kitchen truck of Troop A of the 102d Cavalry, and D, E, and F Ranger Companies went after the Germans. A combat patrol from Company D established contact with the Germans, and Company F closed with the enemy driving them from positions. Pursuit continued through several towns until the Germans joined a larger force in prepared position. The Rangers, accompanied by cavalry, closed for a battle that was complicated because the Germans were located in the zone of another American unit that refused to give permission to fire artillery in its zone. Some of the Rangers were riding on the outside of light tanks, and three Rangers were killed when a *Panzerfaust* rocket launcher destroyed their tank.

The unsupported attack continued against heavy resistance. Though the Americans had tank support, the Germans were dug in, and the absence of American artillery hindered the operation. The Germans were well armed and were using machine guns, mortars, and antitank fire. The firefight lasted until late afternoon. Four Rangers were killed and seven wounded, while twenty Germans were killed and five taken prisoner.

On March 31, the 5th Battalion moved to Friedberg, Germany. The mission was that of maintaining law and order in a society that was in shambles. April 1 brought some action to the 5th Rangers. A platoon from Company F and two platoons from Company B were searching a woods near Ossenheim when they encountered some 150 German soldiers. The Rangers killed some thirty Germans and captured sixty-six. One Ranger officer was slightly wounded.

The 2d Ranger Battalion began the month of April 1945 still configured as two three-company teams and acting as a task force with cavalry units. Maj. George Williams commanded Force A/B/C while Capt. Duke Slater commanded D/E/F. On April 1, the battalion moved to Fritzlar and secured the airfield against light resistance. American cargo aircraft began to land in a constant stream on the airfield, and the Rangers found that the aircrews had a deep yearning for war trophies. The war in Europe had many drawbacks, but it was a trophy hunter's paradise, with German pistols and cameras high on the list. Men bragged that they could shoot an SS thug and have his camera and pistol before his body hit the ground. The Rangers supplied these trophies to the airmen, and as there was an element of risk involved in the trophy-collection business, prices were inflated.

Even though the trophy business was brisk, aggressive patrolling was conducted and outlying towns secured. Sixty-six prisoners were taken. The next day, Ralph Goranson's Company C captured sixteen Germans, while Slater's men also captured sixteen Germans and destroyed four 88mm guns. On the 3d, six Germans fired on a patrol from Company E. The Germans were hemmed in and captured. Heavy patrol activity netted light contact and four more prisoners on the 4th.

On April 4, the 5th Rangers moved to Melsungen. On the 5th, Company F captured seven Germans, and on the 7th, Company F brought in thirty-three more German prisoners. On April 11, the battalion moved to Heyerod.

The 5th Battalion began to dispatch elements to a wide variety of towns. The Rangers searched for German soldiers, guarded warehouses and supply points, and kept control of the population.

April 5 brought some excitement to the 2d Rangers. The Germans launched a balloon which traveled east at a high rate of speed, and while there was talk of a secret weapon, the purpose of the balloon could not be determined. The battalion executive officer, Capt. Edgar Arnold, returned from detached service and assumed command of the A/B/C force. Major Williams returned to his command post group. The feeling that the Rangers were merely touring Germany was temporarily dispelled on the 6th when two tanks and a self-propelled gun opened fire on a Ranger patrol. There were no casualties, and it was soon back to day after day of movement, patrols, and security, with the prisoner count growing.

On April 13, a car containing four Germans tried to force a checkpoint of Company A, 2d Rangers. The Rangers opened fire and killed all four of the Germans. One of the dead men was General Major Gustav Feller, commanding general Panzer Troops of Wehrkreis IX.

By the 15th, Company A of the 2d Rangers was clearing Darmstadt, and Company C had a fight with some two hundred Germans well equipped with antiaircraft weapons that were highly effective when the gun barrels were lowered. The 2d Battalion took over one hundred prisoners on this date.

April 15 was proof that the war was coming to a close: On the 15th, the 5th Rangers were ordered to guard a signal dump at Lehesten. Many Germans were denying the horrors of the concentration camps. To burn the memory of this evil into the German brain, General Patton directed that German civilians be given a tour of the camps. On the 16th of April, the 5th Rangers escorted one thousand German civilians to Buchenwald.

Each day brought more movement for the 2d Ranger Battalion as town by town, city by city, river by river, the advance continued. After the cold of winter, the warmth of spring was welcome. The heady taste of victory was in the mouths of men, and the prisoner count swelled daily. The worst of the war was over, but a man could still get killed. Those Germans that were still fighting had an arsenal of weapons to choose from, and they came to battle heavily armed.

On April 19, Rangers of Company E, 2d Battalion, captured a hospital that contained American and British wounded men that had been prisoners of the Germans.

On April 21, the 5th Ranger Battalion received orders attaching them to the 3d Cavalry Group. The battalion divided, with Colonel Sullivan and B, C, and E Companies further attached to the 3d Cavalry Squadron, and Companies A, D, and F, under Major Heffelfinger, the battalion executive officer, attached to the 43d Cavalry Squadron. The mission was to drive to the Danube River and secure bridges for the 71st Infantry Division. The movement was made against scattered machine-gun and small-arms fire. Some twenty rounds of artillery harassed the Rangers but did not deter them. When the Danube was reached on April 23, Colonel Sullivan, with B, C, and D Companies, captured a bridge near Burglengenfeld; the remainder of the bridges had already been blown. The 3d Cavalry Group secured the bank, and the 71st Infantry Division had a routine crossing.

As the month of April drew to a close, the Rangers of the 2d Battalion were operating in forests as did American Rangers of the colonial period. The German forests and their small towns were ideal hiding places for the small bands of sabotage groups that the Nazi leaders had hoped would carry on the fight. The Rangers and cavalry would surround a town, with the cavalry vehicles forming a circle. The Rangers would then search the town, round up the inhabitants in a central point and interrogate them. A typical action occurred on April 22 at Bachra when Company A of the 2d Rangers and their companion cavalry troop came through the forest after the Germans. Six of the enemy were killed and five captured in a firefight. After interrogation, thirteen suspects were arrested; two were shot trying to escape. Eleven of the thirteen men arrested proved to be soldiers who had taken off their uniforms.

On April 23, Company E of the 2d Rangers located a former Hitler *Jugend* (Hitler Youth) school at Naumburg. Twenty-two former instructors of differing nationalities were arrested. The captives protested their innocence but the German penchant for record keeping was their downfall, and documents found at the school proved their guilt.

As the Allies closed in on Berlin, Adolph Hitler designated Admiral Doenitz as his successor on April 29 and prepared to commit suicide.

On the 30th of April, the 2d Ranger Battalion was at Grafenwöhr. This was the great training ground for Hitler's legions where the Panzer divisions which terrorized Europe equipped, trained, and prepared for war. Erwin Rommel trained his Ghost Division at Grafenwöhr. But the thunder of German tank cannon was stilled, and the American Rangers ruled Grafenwöhr. In time, the area would become a significant training ground for American armor. American tank crews, not even born when the Rangers took "Graf," would hone their shooting skills on the firing ranges of this vast military base.

In the round-up of April 1945, the 2d Ranger Battalion had taken 1,426 German soldiers prisoner. The next move would be to the vicinity of Pilsen, Czechoslovakia, where they would remain until the close of the war.

May 1, 1945, saw the 5th Rangers move to Straubing to maintain law and order. Company D went to Traubling to guard a prisoner-of-war compound.

On May 3, Capt. Sid Salomon had a narrow escape. Fourteen SS men were reported hiding in a woods, and a Ranger patrol surprised the Germans and killed a sergeant; the rest of the Germans fled. Salomon was leading a seven-man patrol down a fire break, when two Germans stepped into the open and fired on him with automatic weapons. The Rangers dived to earth, and Salomon fired on the SS men with his submachine gun. The Germans ran into the woods.

May 3 and 4 saw various guard-type missions performed by the 2d and 5th Battalions. The 5th Battalion spent the 5th chasing down a fruitless rumor of German SS troops near Aufhausen.

On the 7th, the 5th Battalion moved to various communities in Austria. The battalion command post and Company F moved to Ried, Austria, while the remainder of the companies searched their assigned areas for several days. Four hundred prisoners were captured.

At 2301 hours on May 8, 1945, the war in Europe was pronounced officially ended.

With the fighting in Europe finished, the men of the 2d and 5th Rangers turned their thoughts to home. The sacrifice and service rendered by the 2d and 5th Ranger Battalions is a record of pride. As an example, in the 2d Ranger Battalion, eighteen men received the Distinguished Service Cross, seventy-seven the Silver Star, and sixty-seven the Bronze Star. Nearly one thousand Rangers who served in the 2d Ranger Battalion received the Purple Heart for wounds in action.

The 5th Rangers spent the remainder of May 1945 guarding prisoners of war and in garrison duties. The 5th Rangers had entered the continent of Europe on D-day, June 6, 1944, and from then until May 9, 1945, they captured 4,451 Germans and estimated they had killed 1,572. One hundred fifteen men of the 5th Rangers had been killed in action, 552 wounded, and 27 either missing in action or captured.

CHAPTER 16

THE PACIFIC—VJ DAY

While the 2d and 5th Rangers were mopping up the last German resistance and the war in Europe was winding down, the battles in the Pacific were still raging.

On March 9, 1945, the men of the 6th Ranger Battalion were performing reconnaissance patrols in mountainous jungle areas of the Philippines. Five patrols went out for three hot days and three cold nights. The area was polluted with the bodies of dead Japanese, and the large flies that were attracted to the dead were a constant nuisance to the living Rangers. A patrol led by Lieutenant Kruger located a Japanese artillery battery moving so close that Kruger could hear the Japanese officer giving commands. Kruger and his men plotted the position and returned to friendly lines. Later Lieutenant Kruger went aloft in a spotter aircraft and directed the artillery fire which destroyed the Japanese guns. One patrol reported moving through a Japanese bivouac area in which guards were awake and paid no attention to them. A patrol from Company A had a firefight with a group of Japanese in dress uniform as though they were preparing for a parade. Several Japanese were killed without loss to the Rangers. The Rangers changed their patrol camps frequently, and this practice paid off when a large Japanese force attacked a vacated camp. The Rangers sometimes passed the night sleeping in the open fields among the dead bodies of the Japanese.

On March 26, Companies D, E, and F were involved in the patrolling, while A, B, and C continued to guard Sixth Army headquarters and perform local patrols. A twenty-nine-man F Company patrol led by Lieutenant Kelley was moving at night when he met a force estimated at fifty-plus Japanese. The Japanese did not see the Rangers and were traveling close together. Kelley passed the order that, on signal, each man was to throw two fragmentation grenades. The forty-eight grenades ripped the Japanese force. Uncertain of the numbers of the enemy, Kelly withdrew one hundred yards and kept changing position to preclude enemy mortars from pinpointing him. The Rangers could hear the cacophony of squalling and screams of the wounded, the hoarse voices of Japanese leaders bawling orders, and the sounds of makeshift litters being constructed. In the darkness, the Japanese could not locate all their casualties. The next morning, the Rangers found eleven bodies that remained behind.

The 6th Rangers had a high respect for the ability of the enemy with a mortar, and the Japanese 155mm mortar was particularly deadly. These mortars wounded Sergeant White and Private, First Class Dykes and killed Sergeant Mortenson of Company F on the patrol.

As March turned into April, the men of the 6th Ranger Battalion were continuing their joint duties as reconnaissance experts in the mountains and jungles and palace guard for Sixth Army Headquarters. The battalion did not fight as a unit but operated tactically by company and smaller sized elements. Companies A, C, and F were hunting isolated Japanese units in the mountain rain forest of the Dingalan Bay, while F Company had the mission of working with guerrilla units, whose knowledge of local terrain and information gathering net made the hunting very good.

The 6th Rangers were also training several companies of Filipino guerrillas, and many of the patrol missions stemmed from reported sighting of Japanese by natives. The information often proved imaginative but sometimes paid dividends. On April 25, a guerrilla force reported they had surrounded a group of Japanese officers in a bunker, and the guerrillas wanted the Rangers to come and eliminate them.

This opportunity for combat was welcomed by the Rangers. Lieutenant Evans, a recent graduate of the United States Army Infantry School, had been with the battalion about a week, and the battalion officers wanted to see his fine training put to use. With the battalion commander, Maj. Robert "Woody" Garrett, and other officers tagging along to observe and enjoy the fun, Evans was given control of the attack.

In textbook fashion, Lieutenant Evans established a base of fire, then under the cover of this fire, led a maneuver element to close on the enemy. As they neared the objective, Major Garrett challenged Lieutenant Evans, betting him a beer that Garrett would kill a Japanese before Evans did. At that moment, a Japanese soldier rose from cover and took aim at the two officers. Evans killed the enemy soldier with a single shot; a second enemy soldier appeared, and Evans killed him, too. Garrett was down two beers, and the fight had not yet begun.

When it did begin, Ranger Stinson threw two grenades into the bunker, and the Rangers moved in shooting. Seventeen Japanese officers were in the bunker, and in less than five minutes, the Rangers killed them all.

The trophy-loving Americans could scarcely believe their good fortune. Each of the dead Japanese officers carried a bright and shining sword.

There were so many rumors of enemy to check out that Garrett established a roving patrol of one officer and twelve Rangers. Mounted in vehicles and radio equipped, this patrol could respond rapidly. In early May, B Company relieved Company F at Dingalan Bay, and the remainder of the Battalion continued to guard Sixth Army Headquarters. On May 19, the 6th Battalion finished training the Filipino guerrilla force, and on the 20th, Company D relieved Company B in the green hell of the insect-ridden, mountain rain forest of Dingalan Bay.

May 29 brought another company-size mission. Company B left base camp to join other American forces in the I Corps Section of northern Luzon at Laoag, Illocos Norte. Some nine thousand Japanese of the 80th Brigade and the 103d Division were believed holed up in an area where only Filipino troops were operating. From Laoag, Capt. Leo V. Strausbaugh's Company B moved to Ballesteros, established a command post, and commenced operations. The Rangers were part of an eight-hundred-man task force commanded by and named after Maj. Robert V. Connolly. Task Force Connolly was the left hook of a double envelopment. Connolly's men would move more than 450 miles along the northern Luzon coast with first the South China Sea, then the Babuyan Channel on their left flank. The mission was to deny the Japanese the use of the city of Aparri and its airfield. Plans were to drop an Airborne unit to seize the Aparri airfield.

The remainder of the battalion was busily engaged in operations at platoon level. Each day platoon-size combat patrols would be sent out to search for the Japanese. Traveling twelve to twenty miles a day, the Rangers hunted down and killed isolated Japanese. Three on one day, eight the next, the Japanese were systematically rooted out.

The army had developed a system of accumulating points to return home. The criteria were based upon who had been overseas and in combat the longest as well as who had children. A man earned a point for each month of service in the army and another point for each month of overseas service. Combat decorations earned five points each time they were awarded, and there was parenthood credit of twelve points for each child under age eighteen, with a limit of up to three children. In mid-May 1945, the magic number for departure to home was 85 points.

On June 4, 1945, Company A of the 6th Rangers moved under the control of I Corps near Camiling, Tarlac. Reconnaissance and combat patrols began. On the 7th, Company C joined the mission, establishing their command post at Tibag, Tarlac. The companies each had three half-tracks. Operations were very successful, and a profitable war-trophy business had been established, with the navy proving to be a superb market.

On June 10, 6th Ranger battalion commander Maj. Robert W. "Woody" Garrett[1] received the silver oak leaves of a lieutenant colonel.

On June 29, the mission of Company B ended. After thirty bone-weary days of tense jungle fighting, the Rangers returned to base camp. The men were tired but happy. Moving fast on the night of June 20–21, the Rangers had seized Aparri and the airstrip before the paratroopers of the 511th

Airborne could jump into action. The Rangers raised the American flag over the badly cratered airstrip and reported thirty unserviceable Japanese aircraft. The news of the capture was passed to army headquarters but General Krueger wanted more American forces in the area and gave orders that the drop would continue. When Lt. Col. Henry Burgess and the men of the 511th Parachute Regiment came in by parachute and glider on the 23d, they found the Rangers waiting to greet them. What would have been a humorous circumstance was marred by the difficulties of the jump. Some eighty American paratroopers were injured in high ground winds.

The Ranger operation at Aparri had been preceded by a hazardous four-man volunteer patrol. Lt. Lawrence Evans, Sgt. Delbert Griffith, Sgt. Oliver Williams, and Pfc. Eli LaLande crossed the Cagayen River at night and reconnoitered Japanese positions in the city of Aparri. The men then brought the company into action and led the assault. Each man received the Silver Star.

After the Aparri operation, the Rangers initially led the American attack, then moved to flank security until the campaign ended.

On return, the Rangers had an airborne experience of their own. Company B was flown home to the States by C-47 aircraft. On the way out, it had taken ten days to get to Northern Luzon; they were flown back in fifty-five minutes.

On July 1, Eighth Army replaced the famed Sixth Army, and the 6th Ranger Battalion changed character. Two-hundred forty-five veterans had sufficient points to return home, and 253 replacements had arrived, most of whom had not yet reached twenty years of age.

On August 15, 1945, the long, bloody ordeal of World War II ended with the unconditional surrender of Japan. While there were spontaneous outbursts of joy at home, the men of the 6th Rangers greeted the welcome news with the quiet satisfaction of having achieved victory and survived.

On August 20, 139 veterans, the bulk of the men who originally formed the 6th Rangers, departed for the United

States. On September 5, another contingent of fifty-eight men sailed for home.

With the end of the war, combat training ceased, and garrison duty began. The emphasis now became close-order drill—the 6th Ranger Battalion was called upon to provide an honor guard for General Krueger.

On September 15, the 6th Rangers boarded ship in a driving rain and sailed from Manila harbor. Passing the island of Corregidor, where Americans had fought so valiantly in defeat, the men bade farewell to the Philippine Islands: Their destination was the islands of Japan.

At 1715 hours on September 25, the 6th Rangers began to debark at Wakayama Beach on Honshu, the main island of Japan. The battalion then moved sixty-five miles by rail and two miles by truck. The destination of the Rangers was the ancient Japanese capital of Kyoto. Lieutenant Colonel Sullivan accepted the surrender of a Japanese infantry unit and their barracks from Colonel Itakura of the Imperial Japanese Army. The 6th Rangers moved into Fujinimori Barracks and changed the name to Camp Fisher.

The transition from fighting unit to garrison was now complete. Arrogant in victory, the Japanese people were docile in defeat, and the occupying army met no resistance. Men spent their days in cleaning, repairing, and improving their new home. Retreat parades were frequent. The strength of the battalion was in constant decline as men departed for the States.

Home was the thought uppermost in the minds of all of America's fighting men. The most terrible war in history was finished. It is seldom that evil is so clearly defined as it was in World War II: an international war with the solid support of American people and the American media. The men were welcomed home.

EPILOGUE

The contribution of the Ranger battalions of World War II far outweighed their numbers. From Dieppe in the dark days of 1942 to the invasion of the Philippines, in Africa, Sicily, Italy, and over bloody Omaha Beach on D-day, the Rangers led the way. They climbed the cliffs at Pointe du Hoc and cracked the Siegfried Line. Rangers were the first soldiers to kill the German foe, and the first to die in battle.

They were not supermen or demigods. They were well-trained and highly motivated volunteers, steeled in the cauldron of war. You cannot see what makes a Ranger different. The courage, the devotion, the willingness of sacrifice is contained within the man. They can achieve anything because Rangers know that it is all in the heart and in the mind.

APPENDIX A

TABLE OF ORGANIZATION AND EQUIPMENT

MHI
Copy 1

*T/O & E 7–87

TABLE OF ORGANIZATION
AND EQUIPMENT
No. 7–87

WAR DEPARTMENT,
WASHINGTON 25, D. C., 29 February 1944.

RANGER COMPANY, RANGER INFANTRY BATTALION

*This table supersedes all prior tables and equipment lists on the organization of this unit.

325

T/O & E 7–87

RANGER COMPANY, RANGER INFANTRY BATTALION

SECTION I
ORGANIZATION

Designation: Company †-.; ‡- - Ranger Infantry Battalion

	Unit	Specification serial No.	Technician grade	Company headquarters	Platoon headquarters	Section headquarters	Assault squad	Light machine gun squad	Total section	Special weapons section	Total platoon	Total company	Enlisted cadre
					2 platoons (each)	2 assault sections (each)							
2	Captain, including	1542		(ᵖ1)								(1)	
3	Company commander			1								(1)	
4	First lieutenant, including	1542			(ᵖ1)						(1)	(2)	
5	Platoon leader	1542			1						(1)	(2)	
6	Total commissioned			1	1						1	3	
7	First sergeant	585		ᵖ1								1	1
8	Technical sergeant, including	651										2	2
9	Platoon				(ᵖ1)						(1)	(2)	(2)
10	Staff sergeant, including	652									5	10	5
11	Section leader	652				(ᶜ1)				(1)	(3)	(6)	(3)
12	Squad leader	653					1	1	2			(6)	(2)
13	Sergeant, including	652									3	6	
14	Section leader, assistant	653				(ᶜ1)				(1)	(2)	(4)	
15	Squad leader									(ᵖ1)	(2)	(4)	
16	Corporal, including										2	6	
17	Corporal, company	405		(ᵖ1)								(1)	
18	Private, first class, including			2			4		8		(6)	45	
19	Ammunition carrier	504								(ᵖ2)	(12)	(12)	
20	Gunner, machine gun	604						(ᵖ1)	(1)		(2)	(4)	
21	Gunner, machine gun, assistant	604						(ᵖ1)	(1)		(2)	(4)	
22	Gunner, mortar	607								(ᵖ1)	(1)	(2)	
23	Gunner, mortar, assistant	607								(ᵖ1)	(1)	(2)	

Remarks

† Insert letter of company.
‡ Insert number of battalion.
ª Armed with rifle, antitank, cal. .55, if required.
ᵇ Armed with rifle, cal. .30, M1903A4.
ᶜ British equipment.
ᵖ Armed with pistol, automatic, cal. .45.
ᵈ Armed with gun, submachine, cal. .45.
ᵉ For specification serial numbers for enlisted men shown in column 2, see AR 615-26. For officers, see TM 12-406 and 12-407.

T/O & E 7–87

RANGER COMPANY, RANGER INFANTRY BATTALION

		(¹ 1ᵃ)	(ᵇ 1)	(¹ 1)	(¹ 4)		(4)		(1)(8)(1)	(3)(16)(2)	9
24		Messenger									
25		Rifleman									
26		Rifleman, sniper									
27		Total enlisted	3	3	1	5	5	11	6	31	65	9
28		Aggregate	4	4	1	5	5	11	6	32	68	9
29	O	Gun, machine, cal. .30, light, flexible								2	4	
30	O	Gun, submachine, cal. .45		2		1				2	6	
31	O	Launcher, rocket, at. 2.36-inch	2					1		1	2	
32	O	Mortar, 60-mm			1						2	
33	O	Pistol, automatic, cal. .45	2	1		2	2	2	3	8	17	
34	O	Rifle, antitank, cal. .55ᵃ									2	
35	O	Rifle, cal. .30, M1	2	1	5	3	3	9	3	22	46	
36	O	Rifle, cal. .30, M1903A4		1	1	5				1	2	

3

RANGER COMPANY, RANGER INFANTRY BATTALION

SECTION II

EQUIPMENT

GENERAL

1. This table is in accordance with AR 310-60, and it will be the authority for requisition in accordance with AR 35-6540, and for the issue of all items of equipment listed herein unless otherwise indicated. This table rescinds all Tables of Basic Allowances and Tables of Equipment heretofore published except T/E No. 21, Clothing and Individual Equipment, so far as they pertain to the allowances of equipment for the organization and individuals covered by this table.

2. When there appears a discrepancy between the allowances shown in column 2, "Allowances," and column 3, "Basis of distribution and remarks," the amount shown in column 2 will govern.

3. Items of clothing and individual equipement, components of sets and kits, spare parts, accessories, special equipment, special tools, and allowances of expendable items are contained in the following publications:

Army Air Forces.

 Air Corps Stock List.

 Technical Orders of the 00-30-series.

Chemical Warfare Service.

 Standard Nomenclature and Price List.

 Chemical Warfare Series, Army Service Forces Catalogs.

Corps of Engineers.

 Engineer Series, Army Service Forces Catalogs.

Medical Department.

 Medical Department Supply Catalog.

 Army Services Forces Catalog, Medical 4.

Ordnance Department.

 Standard Nomenclature Lists (SNL), index to which is the index to Ordnance Publications, Volume 1, OFSB 1-1.

 T/A for Cleaning, Preserving and Lubricating Materials, Recoil Fluids, Special Oils and Similar Items of Issue.

 T/A 23, Targets and Target Equipment.

Quartermaster Corps.

 Table of Clothing and Individual Equipment, T/E 21.

 Quartermaster Series, Army Service Forces Catalogs.

 AR 30-3010, Items and Price Lists of Regular Supplies Controlled by Budget Credits and Price List of Other Miscellaneous Supplies.

Signal Corps.

 Signal Corps Catalog (T/BA items).

 Signal Corps Series, Army Service Forces Catalogs.

AR 310-200, Military Publications, Allowance and Distribution.

AR 775-10, Qualification in Arms and Ammunition Training Allowances.

T/O & 7–87

RANGER COMPANY, RANGER INFANTRY BATTALION

ARMY AIR FORCES

1	2	3
Item	Allow-ances	Basis of distribution and remarks
Raft, Pneumatic life, A-2, complete w/CO₂ cylinders and hand pump.	6	
Vest, life, preserver, type B-4 - - - - - - - - -	68	1 per indiv (10 percent overage incl in and asgd to hq co).

CHEMICAL

Alarm, gas -	1	
Flame thrower, portable, M1A1 - - - - - - - - -	1	
Kit, chemical agent detector, M9 - - - - - - - -	1	In T of Opns.
Mask, gas, service, lightweight, M3-10A1-6.	68	1 per indiv (mask, gas, sv will be issued as directed by the WD until exhausted)

ENGINEER

Board, drawing, machine gun - - - - - - - - - -	2	1 per plat.
Compass:		
Lensatic, luminous dial, w/case - - - - - - - -	20	1 per off; 1st sgt; s sgt; sgt.
Wrist, liquid filled - - - - - - - - - - - - - - - -	48	1 per indiv not issued compass, lensatic. Pending availability substitute compass, watch.
Demolition equipment, Set No. 5, individual.	8	1 per sqd.
Protractor, plastic, semi-circular, MG, 10-inch graduated in mils.	4	1 per MG sqd.

ORDNANCE
Weapons and miscellaneous

Binocular, M13 - - - - - - - - - - - - - - - - - - -	22	1 per off; 1st sgt; t sgt; s sgt; sgt.
Gun:		
Machine, Browning, cal. .30, M1919A6, flexible.	4	1 per LMG sqd. See SNL A-6.
Submachine, cal. .45, M3 - - - - - - - - - - -	6	2 per co hq; 2 per plat hq. See SNL A 58.
Knife, trench, M3, w/scabbard, M8. - - - - - -	68	1 per indiv. See SNL B-37.
Launcher:		
Grenade, M7 - - - - - - - - - - - - - - - - - - -	46	1 per rifle, cal. .30, M1. See SNL B-39.
Rocket, 2.36-in, M9. - - - - - - - - - - - - - -	2	See SNL B-36.
Mortar, 60-mm, M2 w/mount M2. - - - - - - -	2	1 per sp wpns sec. See SNL A-43.
Mount, tripod, machine gun, cal. 30, M2.	2	1 per sp wpns sec. See SNL A-6.
Pistol, automatic, cal. .45, M1911A1 - - - - -	17	1 per indiv armed w/pistol as shown in sec I. See SNL B-6.

T/O & 7–87

RANGER COMPANY, RANGER INFANTRY BATTALION

1	2	3
Item	Allow-ances	Basis of distribution and remarks
Projector:		
Pyrotechnic, hand, M9	8	1 per sqd (see SNL B-38). (Pending availability of projector, pyrotechnic, hand, M9, issue pistol, pyrotechnic, AN-M8, see SNL B-33.)
Signal ground, M4	4	Limited standard item. (See SNL B-24.)
Rifle, U S cal. .30:		
Antitank, cal. .55, Boy's	2	1 per indiv armed w/rifle, anti-tank, cal. .55 as shown in sec I non-standard item).
M1	46	1 per indiv armed w/rifle ca. .30, M1 as shown in sec I (each rifle to be equipped w/bayonet, M1905 and scabbard bayonet, M3, see SNL B-21).
M1903A4, (Sniper's)	2	1 per indiv armed w/ rifle cal. .30, M1903A4 as shown in sec I. See SNL B-3.
Watch, wrist:		
7 jewel	65	1 per EM.
15 or more jewels	3	1 per off (in T of Opns outside continental limits of US).

Organizational clothing

Brassard, arm, gas	3	
Gloves, protective, impermeable	2	1 per 40 EM outside continental US (to be stored in nearest available dep for issue as determined by T of Opns comdr).
Mittens, asbestos, M1942	12	2 per MG; mort.
Suit, protective, one-piece impermeable . . .	2	1 per 40 EM outside continental US (to be stored in nearest available dep for issue as determined by T of Opns comdr).

Individual equipment

Bag, canvas, field, od, M1936	3	1 per off, except in Alaska.
Belt:		
Cartridge, cal. .30 dismounted, M1923.	48	1 per indiv armed w/rifle cal. .30 as shown as in sec. I.
Pistol or revolver, M1936	20	1 per indiv not atzd belt, cartridge, cal. .30, dismounted, M1923.
Carrier, pack, M1928	65	1 per EM, except in Alaska.
Cover, canteen, dismounted, M1910	68	1 per indiv.
Haversack, M1928	65	1 per EM, except in Alaska.
Pocket, magazine, double web, EM, M1923.	17	1 per indiv armed w/pistol, auto, cal. .45.

T/O & 7–87

RANGER COMPANY, RANGER INFANTRY BATTALION

1	2	3
Item	Allow-ances	Basis of distribution and remarks
Strap, carrying, general purpose	3	1 per bag, canvas, fld (strap, carrying, od, bag, canvas, fld, will be issued in lieu thereof until exhausted).
Suspenders, belt, M1936	3	1 per off.

Organizational equipment

Axe:		
Handled, chopping, single-bit, standard grade, weight 4-lb.	1	
Intrenching, M1910	7	1 per 10 EM.
Bag:		
Canvas, water, sterilizing, complete w/ cover and hanger.	1	
Carrying:		
Ammunition	86	
Rocket, M6	4	2 per launcher, rocket.
Delousing	2	1 per 35 indiv or maj fraction thereof in areas where louse-borne typhus is low when atzd by WD.
	or	
	3	1 per 20 indiv or maj fraction thereof in areas where louse-borne typhus is high when atzd by WD.
Bucket, canvas, water, 18-qt	10	1 per sec; 4 per co.
Can, water, 5 gal	14	1 per 5 indiv.
Carrier:		
Axe, intrenching, M1910	7	1 per axe, intrenching, M1910.
Cutter, wire, M1938	68	1 per cutter, wire, M1938.
Pickmattock, intrenching, M1910	14	1 per pickmattock, intrenching, M1910
Shovel, intrenching, M1943	47	1 per shovel, intrenching, M1943 (carr, shovel, intrenching, M1910 will be issued when shovel, intrenching, M1910 is issued).
Case, canvas, dispatch	6	1 per off; msgr.
Chest, record, fiber	1	
Clipper, hair	2	1 per 30 indiv or maj fraction thereof operating in extremely cold areas when atzd by army or T of Opns comdr.
Cutter, wire, M1938	68	1 per indiv.
Desk, field, empty, fiber, company	1	
Flag, guidon, bunting	1	
Kit:		
Barber, w/case	1	In T of Opns outside continental US.
Sewing	6	1 per 12 indiv or maj fraction thereof.
Lantern, gasoline, 2 mantle, commercial.	1	
Machete, 18-in blade, M1942	8	1 per sqd.
Pick, handled, railroad, 6–7 lbs	2	
Pickmattock, intrenching, M1910	14	2 per 10 EM.

T/O & 7–87

RANGER COMPANY, RANGER INFANTRY BATTALION

1	2	3
Item	Allowances	Basis of distribution and remarks
Ropes, climbing set. - - - - - - - - - - - - - -	12	6 per plat (non-standard item)
Screen, latrine, complete (with pins-and-poles).	1	
Sheath, machete, leather, 18-in blade, M1942.	8	1 per machete.
Shovel, intrenching, M1943 - - - - - - - - - - -	47	1 per off; 7 per 10 EM (shovel, intrenching, M1910 will be issued in lieu thereof until exhausted).
Typewriter, portable, w/carrying case.	1	Per desk, fld.
Whistle, thunderer - - - - - - - - - - - - - - -	22	1 per off; 1st sgt; t sgt; s sgt; sgt.

SIGNAL		
Chest BC-5 -	1	
Flag:		
Kit MC-44 -	2	
Set M-133 -	2	
Flashlight TL-122-( ) - - - - - - - - - - - - - -	22	1 per off; 1st sgt; t sgt; s sgt; sgt.
Lantern, electric, portable, hand- - - - - - - - -	2	
Reel Equipment CE-11 - - - - - - - - - - - - - -	4	
Telephone, EE-8-( ) - - - - - - - - - - - - - -	1	
Wire W-130-( ) on mile Spool DR-8. - - - - - -	1	For use w/reel equipment CE-11.

[A. G. 320.3 (11 Feb 44).]

By order of the Secretary of War:

G. C. MARSHALL,
Chief of Staff.

Official:
  J. A. ULIO,
    Major General,
      The Adjutant General.

APPENDIX B

LINEAGE, CAMPAIGNS, AND BATTLE HONORS OF THE RANGER BATTALIONS OF WORLD WAR II*

LINEAGE

1ST RANGER BATTALION: Constituted May 27, 1942, in the Army of the United States as the 1st Ranger Battalion. Activated June 19, 1942, at Carrickfergus, Northern Ireland. Redesignated August 1, 1943, at the 1st Ranger Infantry Battalion. Disbanded August 15, 1944, in the United States.

2D RANGER BATTALION: Constituted March 11, 1943, in the Army of the United States as the 2d Ranger Battalion. Activated April 1, 1943, at Camp Forrest, Tennessee. Redesignated August 1, 1943, as the 2d Ranger Infantry Battalion. Inactivated October 23, 1945, at Camp Patrick Henry, Virginia.

3D RANGER BATTALION: Organized May 21, 1943, in North Africa as the 3d Ranger Battalion (Provisional). Constituted July 21, 1943, in the Army of the United States as the 3d Ranger Battalion. Redesignated August 1, 1943, as the 3d Ranger Infantry Battalion. Disbanded August 15, 1944, in the United States.

4TH RANGER BATTALION: Organized May 20, 1943, in North Africa as the 4th Ranger Battalion (Provisional). Constituted July 21, 1943, in the Army of the United States as the 4th Ranger Battalion. Redesignated August 1, 1943, as the 4th Ranger Infantry Battalion. Disbanded October 24, 1944, at Camp Butner, North Carolina.

*Source for lineage and decorations: Army Lineage Series, Infantry Part I: Regular Army, Mahon and Danysh. Office of the Chief of Military History United States Army, Washington, DC, 1972.

5TH RANGER BATTALION: Constituted July 21, 1943, in the Army of the United States as the 5th Ranger Battalion. Redesignated August 1, 1943, as the 5th Ranger Infantry Battalion. Activated September 1, 1943, at Camp Forrest, Tennessee. Inactivated October 22, 1944, at Camp Myles Standish, Massachusetts.

6TH RANGER BATTALION: Constituted December 16, 1940, in the Regular Army as the 98th Field Artillery Battalion. Activated January 20, 1941, at Fort Lewis, Washington. Converted and redesignated September 25, 1944, as the 6th Ranger Infantry Battalion. Inactivated December 30, 1945, in Japan.

CAMPAIGNS

1st Ranger Battalion
  Algeria
  Tunisia
  Sicily
  Rome–Arno
  Anzio
2d Ranger Battalion
  Normandy
  Northern France
  Rhineland
  Central Europe
  Ardennes–Alsace
3d Ranger Battalion
  Sicily
  Naples–Foggia
  Rome–Arno
  Anzio

4th Ranger Battalion
  Sicily
  Naples–Foggia
  Rome–Arno
  Anzio
5th Ranger Battalion
  Normandy
  Northern France
  Rhineland
  Central Europe
  Ardennes–Alsace
6th Ranger Battalion
  New Guinea
  Leyte
  Luzon

DECORATIONS

Presidential Unit Citation (Army), streamer embroidered EL GUETTAR (1st Ranger Battalion cited; WD GO 56, 1944)

Presidential Unit Citation (Army), streamer embroidered SALERNO (1st and 3d Ranger Battalions cited; WD GO 41, 1947)

Presidential Unit Citation (Army), streamer embroidered POINTE DU HOC (2d and 5th Ranger Battalions cited; WD GO 73, 1944 and WD GO 10, 1945)

Presidential Unit Citation (Army), streamer embroidered SAAR RIVER AREA (5th Ranger Battalion cited; WD GO 23, 1947)

Presidential Unit Citation (Army), streamer embroidered CABU–LUZON (Company C, 6th Ranger Infantry Battalion cited; DA GO 26, 1945)

French Croix de Guerre with Silver-Gilt Star, World War II, streamer embroidered POINTE DU HOC (2d and 5th Ranger Infantry Battalions cited DA GO 43, 1950)

Philippine Presidential Unit Citation, streamer embroidered 17 OCTOBER 1944 TO 4 JULY 1945 (6th Ranger Infantry Battalion cited; DA GO 47, 1950)

APPENDIX C

INSIGNIA AND GUIDON

In 1942, fifty American Rangers participated in the raid on Dieppe. After the return of the survivors, American soldiers in the United Kingdom began to pretend they were Rangers in order to enhance their image, particularly with English females. Capt. Roy Murray, senior Ranger officer who participated in the raid, noted this phenomenon in his after-action report on Dieppe and recommended that the Rangers be permitted to wear a shoulder insignia.

The officers and men of the 1st Ranger Battalion began to discuss among themselves what their insignia should look like. Early on, it was decided that in order to reflect their close tie with the British Commandos, the American insignia would be in the shape of a scroll as was that of the British.

On August 28, 1942, Brig. Gen. Lucian Truscott, Jr. sent a memorandum to Major General Clark endorsing favorably Lieutenant Colonel Darby's request for authority for the Rangers to have their own insignia. The reasons given were:

1. Tremendous boost to morale.
2. Soldiers all over UK are spreading stories about the recent raid and pretending to be Rangers.

Truscott wrote that the insignia would only be on the service coat and would not be worn in battle. He also stated that Darby had the material and needed only permission to wear the new insignia. The patch would be similar in form to the Commando shoulder patch with a blue background and white lettering.

Though no documentation has been located, it is apparent that approval was granted. Darby announced a contest to see who could develop the best design. Some sources say the prize was a three-day pass, others that award for the best design was twenty-five dollars.

The prize was won by Sgt. Anthony Rada of Flint, Michigan, a member of Headquarters Company, 1st Ranger Battalion.

The patch was probably intended to be red, white, and blue. It is the recollection of Roy Murray that, due to wartime conditions, the color of dye needed was not available and the insignia became red, white, and black. Another source believes (without verification) that the colors were taken from the Nazi flag and were intended to indicate to the Germans that the Rangers were going to jam the colors red, white, and black down the German throats.

A United States Army signal corps photograph dated October 8, 1942, shows the completed Ranger insignia and indicates the beginning of its use.

The men were justifiably proud of their insignia, and, despite Truscott's letter, they wore it into battle. Some men wore the Ranger scroll on both shoulders. There were occasions when men would take off the Ranger insignia from their shoulder in order to give this precious gift to a badly wounded friend being evacuated to a hospital.

While this activity was going on in Europe, on April 16, 1943, the 2d Ranger Battalion came into being at Camp Forrest, Tennessee. On July 16, 1943, the Department of the Army approved a shoulder sleeve insignia for all Ranger battalions. This approved insignia was designed by a member of the 2d Ranger Battalion. In its final state, the insignia was diamond shaped with a blue background, yellow/gold letters and edging, and the word "RANGERS."

The men of the 2d Ranger Battalion received this insignia in September/October 1943 while at Fort Dix, New Jersey, preparing for overseas movement.

The Blue Diamond patch was not liked by the men. The Sun Oil Company (supplier of gasoline known as Sunoco) service station signs bore a close resemblance to the "authorized" Ranger insignia, and soldiers from other units on occasion mocked the Rangers with catcalls of "Blue Sunoco." Fights resulted.

On September 1, 1943, the 5th Ranger Battalion was activated at Camp Forrest and began to wear locally a patch based on the blue diamond.

When the 3d and 4th Battalions were activated, they adopted the red, white, and black scroll. The 2d wore the diamond during D-day (June 6, 1944), but when the 2d and 5th got deeper into Europe, they also began to wear the red, white, and black scroll.

The 5th Battalion forwarded a request to the War Department asking for official permission to wear the scroll. The request was denied. Ignoring the War Department response, the 5th Battalion pursued their intention of wearing the red, white, and black scroll. The 5th Battalion had their insignia made by nuns in a Bavarian convent and paid with German marks taken from a German Army paymaster.

In the Pacific with the 6th Battalion, there was a period when an insignia featuring a trench knife appeared on signboards. The 6th Ranger Battalion soon adopted the red, white, and black scroll.

After the war, the men of the Ranger battalions formed an association and used the red, white, and black scroll as the association insignia.

In 1947, the army abolished the "Blue Sunoco" insignia. For over thirty years, including the war years of Korea and Vietnam, men tried to get the red, white, and black scroll approved without success. In the early 1980s, Korean War Rangers with the strong support of the Rangers of World War II waged a fight to make the insignia official. With the birth of a Ranger regiment and the Ranger success in the Grenada operation, approval finally came.

Today, the red, white, and black scroll is the official insignia of United States Army Ranger units.

RANGER GUIDON

The guidon used by the Ranger companies during World War II was a standard infantry guidon, featuring white crossed muskets on a blue background with the company letter designation.

APPENDIX D

WEAPONS USED BY WORLD WAR II RANGERS

Automatic Pistol, .45 Caliber, M-1911 and M-1911 A1
(Ref. Field Manual 23-35)

Known as "The Equalizer" or simply "The 45," this weapon was a recoil-operated, magazine-fed, self-loading hand weapon. The overall length of the pistol was 8.593 inches. Weight of the pistol with magazine was 2.437 pounds. The approximate weight of the loaded magazine with 7 rounds was 0.481 pounds. At 25 yards, the velocity of the round was 788 feet per second with a striking energy of 317 foot-pounds. At 25 yards, the round would penetrate 6.0 inches of white pine.

Carbine, .30 Caliber, M-1 and M-2
(Ref. Field Manual 23-7)

The carbine was a magazine-fed, air-cooled, gas-operated shoulder weapon. Most Rangers carried the M-2 version, which could be fired automatically or semiautomatically and used the 30-round magazine. The weight of the weapon with 30-round magazine loaded was 6.60 pounds. Cyclic rate of fire on full automatic was 750–775 rounds per minute. The weapon had a muzzle velocity of 1,970 feet per second. Maximum effective range was listed as 300 yards, but few men would trust the carbine beyond 100 yards.

Rifle, .30 Caliber, M-1 (Ref. Field Manual 23-5)

The "M-1" was a gas-operated, semiautomatic (self-feeding) shoulder weapon weighing 9.5 pounds. A clip of ammunition contained eight rounds. Clips were carried in the cartridge belt and bandoleers. The bayonet weighed one pound. The M-1 had a reputation for reliability.

Browning Automatic Rifle, .30 Caliber, M-1918A2
(Ref. Field Manual 23-15)

The "BAR" was a gas-operated, air-cooled, magazine-fed shoulder weapon, weighing approximately 21 pounds without the sling. The magazine contained 20 rounds and weighed 1 pound 7 ounces when full. The weapon fired on a slow cyclic rate of approximately 350 rounds or a normal cyclic rate of 550 rounds per minute. The BAR was a heavy brute, subject to frequent jams, but when operating smoothly, it was devastating.

Thompson Submachine Gun, .45 Caliber, M-1928A1
(Ref. Field Manual 23-40)

Frequently referred to as the "Tommy gun," this weapon had been portrayed as the favorite weapon of gangsters in the days when Al Capone ruled south-side Chicago. The Thompson was an air-cooled, recoil-operated, magazine-fed weapon. It would accept a box magazine carrying 20 rounds or a drum carrying 50. Without magazine, the weapon weighed 10¾ pounds; with loaded 50-round magazine, it weighed about 15¾ pounds. Cyclic rate of fire was 600–700 rounds per minute. A selector switch allowed the weapon to be fired on semiautomatic or automatic. When fired on automatic, the muzzle of the weapon had a tendency to climb. The Thompson was at its best when used within 50 yards of the target.

Grenades (Ref. Field Manual 23-30)

A. *The Fragmentation Grenade*
The primary hand grenade of the Rangers was the grenade, hand, Mk-II. About the size of a large lemon, the grenade was made of cast iron. The outside surface was deeply serrated, both horizontally and vertically, to assist in the dispersal of

uniform-sized fragments on explosion. The filler of the grenade was EC blank fire powder or TNT. The weight of the grenade was 20 ounces, and its bursting radius was 30 yards.

B. *The sticky grenade or "Bomb"* (Ref. description contained in October 26, 1942, *Life* magazine and information from Ranger veterans)

The Sticky Bomb (as the Rangers called it) was promoted by those who did not have to use it as an antitank weapon. One form of this bomb was a soldier's white sock, fill the sock with TNT, attach a fuse, tie off the top, then cover the top in axle grease. The grenade would then be thrown against the side of a tank, where the axle grease could cause it to stick until exploding. From Africa to Italy, the men of the 1st, 3d, and 4th Ranger Battalions used a different kind of sticky bomb: glass containers with incendiary fillers.

CREW SERVED WEAPONS

The Boys Antitank Rifle, .55 Caliber (Ref. TM 30-40 Handbook on the British Army, 30 September 1942)

When the 1st Ranger Battalion was formed in 1942, this British weapon was included in the equipment tables to provide antitank defense. The weapon was a bolt-action, shoulder-fired, magazine-fed rifle. The Boys weighed 36 pounds and was five feet, four inches long. The maximum range was 500 yards and the effective range was 200 yards. The five-round magazine was loaded with a 930-grain armor-piercing bullet, fired at a muzzle velocity of some 3,000 feet per second. This weapon did not remain in the Ranger Tables of Equipment.

Rocket, AT HE, 2.36 Inch (Ref. Field Manual 23-30)

The antitank rocket launcher was a smooth-bore, breech-loading, electrically-operated shoulder weapon of the open-tube type. Depending on the model, the launcher weighed 13–15 pounds and was between 54.5 and 61 inches long. The launcher gave direction to the rocket. There was no recoil as the jet action of the propellent powder inside the stabilizer provided propulsion. The 2.36-inch rocket launcher had a maximum range for point targets of 300 yards but was most effective within 100 yards.

60mm Mortar M-19 (Ref. Field Manual 23-85)

A smooth-bore, muzzle-loaded, high-angle-of-fire weapon. The mortar (barrel) was normally used in conjunction with a bipod and baseplate and had an overall weight of 45.2 pounds. Maximum rate of fire was 30 rounds per minute, with a sustained rate of 18 rounds per minute. Maximum range with high-explosive ammunition was 2,000 yards.

81mm Mortar M-1 (Ref. Field Manual 23-90)

The 81mm mortar was a smooth-bore, muzzle-loading, high-angle-of-fire weapon. The 81mm mortar consisted of three units—mortar, baseplate, and bipod. Each unit was considered a separate carrying load. Forty-nine point five inches long, the mortar and mount weighed 136 pounds. The 81mm mortar would fire a 6.87-pound high-explosive shell at ranges from 100–3,290 yards. The normal rate of fire was 18 rounds per minute.

Browning Machine Gun .30 Caliber HB M-1919A4 (Ref. Field Manual 23-45)

This air-cooled, recoil-operated weapon was fed from woven fabric belts that would hold 150 rounds. The weapon was usually mounted on a light machine gun tripod (M-2). The weight of the gun with tripod was 42.25 pounds, and it fired an M-2 ball cartridge with a muzzle velocity of 2,700 feet per second. The cyclic rate of fire was 400–550 rounds per minute. The maximum usable rate of fire was 150 rounds per minute.

APPENDIX E

THOSE WHO SERVED*

The following are men known to have served with the Ranger Battalions of World War II.

FIRST RANGER INFANTRY BATTALION

Last Name	First Name	Initial	Last Name	First Name	Initial
Aasve	Kermit	E	Alsup	James	K
Abkill	John		Altieri	James	J
Ably	Chester	M	Altoonan	Paul	P
Achton	Robert	E	Alvarado	Mateo	P
Adamick	Raymond	F	Ananich, Jr.	John	
Adams	Bryan	L	Anctil	Roland	R
Adams	Harold	A	Anders	William	H
Adkins	Lewis		Anderson, Jr.	Oscar	
Aescback	Fred	G	Anderson	Axel	W
Agy	George	W	Anderson	Donald	E
Ahlers	Barney	B	Anderson	Ernest	N
Ahlgren	Frederic	F	Anderson	Forrest	C
Alabek	Joseph	F	Andes	Gordon	C
Alden	George	A	Andre	Howard	W
Alden	Paul	M	Andrutis	Alfred	A
Aldridge	Lindell	O	Anglin	Julius	D
Allen	Raymond	F	Aponik	Edmund	J
Allen	Robert	G	Archer	James	
Allen	Troy		Arimond	William	
Alleway	Norman	L	Armstrong	Eugene	D
Allgood	William	S	Armstrong	John	E
Allum	Albert	M	Arnbol	Andrew	K

*If there are any men who served in the Ranger Battalions of World War II whose names are not listed, they or their survivors may contact:
Ranger Jack McDevitt, President, the Ranger Battalions
Association of World War II
1322 Park Ave. E. Road
Mansfield, Ohio 44905
Telephone 419-589-7247
Proof of service is required

Arndt	Robert	G	Beauchamp	James	V
Arnett	George	W	Beauchard	Arthur	
Arnold	William	J	Beaver	Corwin	W
Ash	Randolph	I	Beckham	Robert	L
Atkins	Raymond	M	Beckhorn	Edward	W
Auger	Ulysses	G	Bednarski	Isadore	
Avigne	Mark	D	Bell	Warren	N
Ayers	Robert	H	Bellefleut	Wilfred	J
Ayres	Ames	A	Bellinger	Edward	F
Baccus	Edwin	V	Bennett	Richard	J
Back	Harley		Bens	David	L
Backes	George	C	Bensdiker	Rudolph	
Bacon	Robert	W	Benson	Olen	W
Bacus	Dean	A	Bergstrom	Dennis	A
Bailey	Charlie	E	Bernal	Felix	T
Bailey	Raymond	L	Bernardo	Armand	S
Baiscj	William		Bernier	Honorius	A
Baka	Raymond	F	Bero	Joseph	
Baker	Clarence	H	Bertholf	Merritt	M
Baker	Jack		Bevan	Robert	M
Baker	Ralph	A	Beverly	Carl	W
Ball	John	J	Bevil	Richard	H
Balsz	Joseph	B	Bierbaum	Kenneth	
Bane	David	D	Bietel	Clare	P
Banner	Charles	A	Bille	Nelson	V
Bannister	Floyd	R	Billheimer	Guy	
Barbarino	Edward	R	Billingsley	Maurice	
Barefoot	James	H	Bills	Perry	E
Barker	Walter	A	Billyard	Lyle	A
Barnes	William	B	Birchfield	Odis	L
Barnett	Charles	T	Bire	Imre	
Barringan	Leonard		Black	Edmund	
Barry	John	M	Blackburn	William	M
Bartkowiak	Richard	F	Blaisdell	Darius	O
Bartley	Charles	L	Blake	Fred	E
Barton	Joseph	J	Blakely	Howard	M
Bartow	Clifford	H	Blassingame	Earl	C
Basil	Albert	E	Bledoes	Robert	A
Batcher	Gerald	L	Blizniak	Edward	J
Bateman, Jr.	Charles	D	Bloom	Elmer	D
Baum	John	L	Bloyer	James	G
Bayardo	Refugie	G	Blum	Edward	
Beaman	Doyle	S	Blum	Gilbert	T
Beard	Joe	W	Bobanich	Joseph	A
Bearden	Otis	J	Bock	Woodrow	C
Beatty	Walter	C	Body	William	B

Bohn	Robert	E	Bruder	Robert	
Bolduc	Wallace	H	Bruun	Mervyn	P
Bolka	Joseph	S	Bryant	Robert	L
Bolton	Floyd	H	Buck	Paul	B
Bond	William	R	Buck	Peer	A
Bone	Fred		Buddinhagen	Russell	T
Bonislawski	Stephen		Buie	Alvin	R
Borg	Darrell	O	Bullington	Lee	M
Bortz, Jr.	Gerald	J	Bullock	Douglas	F
Boudreau	Burton		Bunde	Carl	R
Bowman	Jasper	J	Buona	Wayne	A
Boye	Edward	M	Burchfield, Jr.	Earl	E
Brackens	William	A	Burdine	Carl	C
Bradbury	Allen	G	Burgess	Clyde	R
Brady	Sherald	P	Burgess	Kenneth	B
Brake	Douglas	E	Burgess	Willis	C
Brassfield	John	S	Buringrud	Wendell	E
Brauer	Eldort	A	Burke	Herman	N
Breen	Junior	L	Burkett	Herman	N
Brennan, Jr.	James	F	Burkowski	Edward	J
Brennan	Newman	F	Burns	Philip	W
Brennan	Wallis	W	Burns	Richard	R
Bresnahan	Walter	A	Burton	Charles	L
Breuers	Jacob		Burton	Eldred	H
Brezzell	John	G	Burwell	George	L
Briggs	John	W	Bush	Stanley	
Bright	Ollie	P	Buss	LeRoy	L
Brinkley	William	L	Butler, Jr	Henry	T
Bristol	Jess	B	Butler	Grant	R
Brock	James	K	Butler	Jack	M
Brock	Vernon	L	Butler	Robert	A
Brode	Harry	F	Butler	Walter	H
Brodeur	John	A	Butts	Theodore	Q
Brown, Jr	George	D	Buzbee	Wilton	T
Brown	Delbert	E	Cabalcs	Robert	D
Brown	Floyd	H	Cain	Paul	W
Brown	George	D	Calahan	Rollie	F
Brown	John	E	Calfayon	Varton	
Brown	John	T	Calhoun	Edward	T
Brown	Lester	L	Calkins	Cyril	J
Brown	Paul	G	Callahan	Peter	E
Brown	Paul	P	Callivas	Gus	
Brown	Robert	L	Campbell	David	W
Brown	Roy	A	Campbell	Joseph	S
Brown	William	E	Canderelli	Salvatore	A
Browning	David	B	Canfield	Richard	H

Donato	Joseph	D	Eklund	Robert	D
Donley	Ralph	E	Elder	Jack	C
Donnelly	William		Elder	Garland	A
Doss	John	F	Elding	James	L
Dotson	Houston		Elias	Paul	
Dowd	Robert	J	Eline	Elray	A
Dowhunick	Tony		Elkins	Charles	L
Doyle	Samuel	F	Ellingson	William	C
Drost	Carl		Elliott	Clyde	W
Duarte	Daniel	F	Elliott	Richard	C
Dubbs	Fred	E	Elliott	William	J
Dubois	Robert	E	Ellis	Cecil	E
Duckworth	Glen	A	Elmo	Ernest	L
Dudley	Paul	E	Elwood	William	O
Dudrow	Douglas	S	Emerson	Irvin	F
Duffy	Frank	A	Emler	Delbert	E
Duffy	William	B	Emmons, Jr.	Oral	E
Dukes	George	E	Ernest	Roy	W
Dunn	Donald	E	Ervin	Bill	E
Dunn	Robert	C	Eskola	Elmer	I
Dunnagan			Estes	Calvin	H
Dunnaway	Floyd		Evans, Jr.	Charles	W
Durham, Jr.	Glenn		Evans	Warren	E
Dusseau	Robert	R	Evenson	Walter	P
Dye	Joe		Everingham	Millard	
Dye	Raymond	N	Ezzell	Alvin	D
Eagan	Vincent	K	Farioly	Vincent	
Eagle	Bear	R	Farley	Cammy	M
Eagles, Jr.	Arthur	C	Farwell	Stanely	T
Earhart	Thomas	A	Fassnacht	Clarence	M
Earl	Llewellyn	F	Fauber, Jr.	William	C
Earnest	Charles	A	Faulkner	Claude	J
Earwood	Don	A	Feasel	Merrit	H
East	John	A	Fedczysyn	Henry	A
Eastman	Earl	G	Feile	Ralph	J
Eastwood	Philip	H	Ferczek	John	
Eaton	William	A	Fergen	Thomas	B
Eaton	Richard	E	Fernandez	Adelfeo	
Eaves	Jerald		Ferrante	Leo	J
Edelman	Baron	R	Ferrier	Leslie	M
Edmundson	Raymond	B	Ferries	John	W
Edstrom	Robert	G	Ferrington	Roy	M
Edwards	James	O	Ferru	Edwin	R
Eger	William		Fey	Louis	J
Ehalt	Robert	E	Fields	Daniel	F
Eineicher	Clarence	W	Fields	Charles	L

Finn	John	N	Fusiara	John	F
Finn	William	J	Gabriel	Martin	J
Fischer	Reuben	D	Gabriel	Norman	O
Fisher	Chester		Gafferio	Walter	A
Fisher	George		Gagne	Vernon	F
Fitch	Bert	E	Galbraith	John	
Fitch	Henry	S	Galddrone	John	
Fitzgerald	James	W	Galgano	Raymond	J
Fitzhugh	Norman	R	Gallahan	John	A
Flanagan	Robert		Gallardo	Jesus	M
Flanagan	Martin	P	Gallup	Wilbur	L
Flood	Thomas	G	Galtier	Edwin	J
Foley	John	J	Gangath	Phillip	
Folsom	Harold		Gannon	George	J
Fontenot	Lee	J	Gannon	Ivan	J
Ford	Avery	J	Garcia, Jr.	Anastacio	
Ford	Richard		Garcia	Doningo	
Foreman	Elmer	P	Garmen	Howard	P
Forster	Frankie	S	Garrett	Dalmer	J
Fortenberry	Ike	S	Garrison	Elmer	W
Fortunato	Vito	P	Gasienica	John	
Fortunato	Vitto	P	Gaskill	Robert	K
Fouhse	Clifford	C	Gates	Doyle	D
Fowler	James	T	Gault	Floyd	K
Fowley	James	C	Gauvey	John	C
Fox	Arlo	G	Gavins	Raymond	
Frank	Martin	J	Geagan	James	V
Franz	George	J	Gearratano	Frank	
Frary	Clarence	J	Gee	Howard	C
Frederick	Donald	S	Geislet	Wilfred	G
Freeman	Roy		Gelchion	Robert	A
Freemire	George		Gemerchak	John	B
Frerichs	John	C	Generalski	Alex	P
Frey	Quentin	P	Gerard	James	D
Freyholtz	Vernon	F	Gerkins	Eugene	S
Friedman	Abraham		Gerski	John	E
Friedman	Murray		Giannopoulos	John	J
Frizzelle	D	W	Gibbons	Noble	
Frodermann	Robert	J	Gibson	Theodore	
Fronk	Junior		Gifford	Philip	
Frye, Jr.	Clarence	C	Gilardi	Americo	
Frye	Joseph		Gilbert	Lawrence	R
Fulks	Warren		Gilbert	Nolan	M
Fullerton	Edward		Gilbert	Roy	B
Fullerton	Edward	D	Giles	Ellery	J
Fultz	William	F	Gillespie	William	B

Gillette	Robert	L	Gritton	Joseph	E
Gipson	Frank	R	Grogg	Francis	J
Girdley	William	S	Grossman	John	C
Girdley	William	S	Groves	George	J
Glasgow	Herbert		Gryniuk	Joseph	J
Glass	Louis		Gummel	Kenneth	E
Glumac	Peter		Gust	Joe	V
Goddard	Jack		Gustafsen	Maurice	E
Godsey	Mack	A	Hafner	Edward	
Goins	Archie		Haines	James	
Goldstein, M.D.	Josef	J	Haines	Robert	W
Golembiewski	Stanley		Hall	Clarence	A
Gollinger	Bernard	H	Hall	Cornelius	
Gomez	Simon	R	Hall	Francis	M
Gonzales	Pete	C	Hall	Herbert	E
Gonzalez	Manuel	A	Hall	Wayne	
Gonzolas	Lalo		Hallczuk	Stephen	
Gordon	Craig		Halley	R	E
Gordon	Roy	V	Halliday	Robert	H
Gorman	John	E	Hambrick	Clifford	H
Gotay	Feinaldo		Hancock	Victor	
Gould	Oren	F	Hankins	Harold	W
Gover	Charles	L	Hanna	James	L
Gracan	Stephen	E	Hansen	Tage	
Grace	Joseph		Hanson	James	B
Grafton	Thomas	A	Harden	John	E
Gramke	Melvyn	P	Harley, Jr.	John	J
Grant	Charles	F	Harn	Lonnie	R
Grapel	Dale	D	Harper	Louis	M
Gray	Glenn	W	Harr	Gerald	J
Gray	James	E	Harrington	Lester	C
Gray	Lyman		Harris	James	F
Green	James	W	Harris	Lemuel	G
Greene	Leonard	L	Harris	Randall	
Greene	Othel		Harris	Thurman	E
Greene	Richard		Harris	Walter	L
Greenfeather	James	I	Harrison	Elby	W
Greenland	Dale	E	Harrison	James	P
Greenwood	John	R	Hart	Donald	W
Greer	Aggy	L	Hartin	Maurice	D
Gregg	Arlington	C	Harvey	Thomas	D
Griffin	John	H	Hathaway	Charles	A
Grimes	Charles	F	Hauck	Cecil	
Grimm	Robert	W	Haugh	Richard	F
Grindler	Joseph	E	Hawkins	George	
Grisamer	George	W	Hayatt	Wayne	E

Hayes	Charles	E	Hobday	Charles	W
Hayes	Donald	L	Hoctel	Lamont	
Hayles	Bobbie		Hoffiens	John	R
Haynes	John	A	Hoffman	George	C
Haywood, Jr.	Edward	H	Hogan	Robert	E
Heacock	Mervin	T	Hogue	Charles	N
Healy	James	E	Holbrooks	James	J
Hebert	Howard	J	Hollar	Charles	C
Heckert	John	E	Holliday	Bandall	T
Heddix	Richard	A	Hollingsworth	Earl	
Hedensted	Howard		Holtzman	Maurice	
Hedges	Richard		Holy	Norman	E
Hedgpath	John	W	Honig	Richard	P
Hedrick	Vernon		Hood	Charles	H
Heid	Ivan	R	Hooker	Dean	
Heiser	Robert	F	Hooker	John	F
Hendrickson	Robert	S	Hooks, Jr.	Alfonso	
Henggeler	Eugene	J	Hopkinson	James	F
Henry	Howard	M	Hornung	Phillip	F
Hensen	Albert	H	Hortado		
Hensley	James	W	Horton, Jr.	James	J
Henson	Trumand		Hotz	Robert	H
Hconer	William	R	Hough, Jr	Daniel	P
Herbst	William	C	Houseman	Robert	H
Hermsen	Paul	S	Huckle	WIlliam	J
Hern	Alfred	J	Hudak	Paul	
Herold	William	L	Hudson	Jack	
Herrick	Clarence	C	Hummer	John	F
Herron	Lester	L	Hunsaker	Lynn	M
Hester	Morris	E	Hunt	Russell	W
Hickey	Walter	J	Hunter	Lewis	E
Hicks	Amos	R	Hunter	James	C
Hicks	Robert	C	Huntington, Jr.	Lee	R
Higgins	John	J	Hurtado	Empemenio	L
Higgins	Michael	J	Hutton	Thomas	G
Hildebrandt	James	J	Hyatt	Lloyd	O
Hill	Earl	W	Iford	Herman	G
Hill	James	G	Iglesias	Gilberto	
Hill	John	E	Ingram	John	R
Hill	John	H	Innsford	Francis	G
Hill	Stanley	L	Iron Shell	Frank	
Hillier	William	D	Isola	Pasquale	
Himsl	George	J	Jackson	Cecil	H
Hines	Gerald	T	Jackson	Lester	E
Hirchert	Harold	C	Jackson	William	A
Hixenbaugh	Verl	V	Jacobs	Shirley	G

Jacobsen	Albert	T	Jones	Webb	J
Jacobson	Leonard		Joubert	Harry	E
Jalbert	Conrad	J	Judy	Donald	E
Jamson	William	J	Junge	Herman	R
Jantz	Irvin	W	Justice	Ashley	S
Jarrett	William	A	Kaiser	William	W
Jawor	John	W	Kallis	Milton	R
Jebs	Raymond	B	Karabinos	Leonard	G
Jech	Randolph		Karas	Edward	G
Jeffcoat	Tye		Karbel	Howard	W
Jenkins	Vernon	M	Karboski	Stanley	
Jenkins	Richard	E	Katona	William	G
Jennings	Roy	L	Katzen	Murray	A
Jensen	Ernest		Katzenberger	Harold	J
Jernberg	Innes	A	Kavanaugh	Marvin	L
Johnson	Charles		Kazura	Charles	
Johnson	Charles	R	Keberdle	Robert	C
Johnson	Donald	G	Keegan	John	E
Johnson	Eric	W	Keen	Leon	P
Johnson	Everett	L	Keener	Vance	
Johnson	Francis	K	Kegley	Green	W
Johnson	Gilmor	L	Kelley	John	P
Johnson	Howard		Kelly	Theodore	L
Johnson	Jack	W	Kendig	Bernard	F
Johnson	John	J	Kendrick, Jr.	Collins	W
Johnson	Lonnie	E	Kennedy	Winfred	W
Johnson	P	D	Kenney	James	H
Johnson	Robert	L	Kenyon	Kenneth	G
Johnson	Robert	O	Keough	Raymond	J
Johnson	Robert	W	Kerecman	Michael	
Johnson	Roy		Kerridge	Kenneth	
Johnson	Thomas	W	Kessler	Clair	B
Johnson	Warren	E	Ketzer	Steve	
Johnson	Warren	L	Key	James	N
Johnston	Bobby	J	Kidder	Wallace	E
Joiner	William		Kielman	Harold	O
Jondal	Ozoville		Kight	Calvin	D
Jones, Jr.	Hugh	J	Kimball	Harold	A
Jones	Claude	S	Kimball	Rollin	C
Jones	Dearl	D	Kimbro	Charles	R
Jones	Donald	L	King	Claiborne	R
Jones	James	A	King	James	E
Jones	James	B	King	Thomas	J
Jones	James	E	Kingsley	Anderson	B
Jones	Richard	A	Kinser	George	L
Jones	Robert	E	Kionne	Edwin	H

Kirby	Richard	W	Lafler	Julian	D
Kirkman	Edward		Laird	Robert	D R
Kissman	Albert	C	Lake	Curtiss	C
Kittle, Jr.	William		Lakowicz	Michael	
Kittleberger	Frederick	J	LaMandia	Anthony	
Klebanski	Walter		Lamandre	Dominick	
Klefman	Gordon	L	Lamar	Francis	E
Klein	Arthur	E	Lamarga	Samuel	
Klein	Peter	J	Lamb	Oliver	
Kliegel	Edward	J	Lambert	Daniel	
Kliest	Lloyd	E	Lambert	Harold	D
Kline	Ira	B	Lampo	Robert	
Klock	Donald	C	Lanctot, Jr.	Sidney	F
Kluczynski	Alphonse	S	Landis	William	J
Knapp	John	J	Lane, Jr.	Nathan	B
Kness	Lester	E	Lang	John	E
Kness	Marvin	E	Lange	Albert	L
Knight	Calvin	D	Langel	Kurt	A
Knoblock	Frank		Langley	Edward	
Knox	John	K	Langona	Paul	
Knudson	Dean	H	Lanning	William	B
Koetting	Harold	H	LaRocca	Joseph	D
Kolasinski	Stanley	G	LaRocque	David	E
Koons	Franklin	M	Larson	Kenneth	E
Koontz	Calvin	G	Laseter	Douglas	E
Kopanda	George		Lathrop	Donald	E
Kopetchny	Stanley	R	Latimer	Clarence	J
Kopp	William	G	Launer	Harvey	L
Kopveiler	Eugene	N	Laurent	Ferdinand	
Kosco	Mike		Lavoie	Roger	E
Kraft	Leroy	A	Lawhorne	James	C
Krall	John		Laxton	James	E
Kramer	Leonard	J	Laycoax	Russel	E
Krieger	Donald	H	Lazarski	Egnacy	J
Kriessel	Arthur	G	Leach	George	
Krise	Edward	F	Leach	Walter	Z
Kristinich	George	H	Leckliter	Edgar	E
Krzysztofiak	Walter	P	Lee	Leon	
Kubenick	John		Legas	John	
Kuhl	Howard	V	Legg	Sherman	L
Kunkle	Ronald		Lehman	Joe	C
Kutinsky	Ralph	E	Lehmann, Jr.	Carl	H
Kuzakiewziez	Stanley		Leibli	Larn	B
LaBonte	Romeo	A	Leighton	Charles	F
Lacosse	Frank		Leinhas	William	E
Ladd	Garland	S	Leithschuh	Joseph	F

Lenkowski	Walter	F	Lowell	Bob	L
Lenzen	Everett	W	Lowrey	William	M
Leonard	Albert	P	Lozeau	Richard	N
Leonard	Joe	E	Lucanio	Michael	N
Lerberg	Robert	H	Lucas	Joseph	P
Levai	Nicholas		Lucci	William	F
Leven	Gordon	A	Lucid	John	M
Lewallen	Everette	F	Luckhurst	Judson	B
Lewis	Carl	A	Ludwig	Alfred	L
Lewis	John	W	Luton, Jr.	James	E
Liddell	John	C	Lyle	James	B
Lidgett	Raymond		Lynch	William	J
Liebhaber	Frank	B	Lyons, Jr	Arthur	L
Liefer	Robert	M	Lyons	Fred	D
Lienhas	William	E	Mabe, Jr.	William	H
Lima	Daniel		Mackin	Robert	
Linde	George	R	MacLachlan	James	
Lindsay	William	G	Madson	Marvin	K
Lindsey	Leslie	R	Magee	Tom	R
Lingenfelter	Irving	H	Maginn	Francis	T
Lingle	Doyle	M	Mahoney	Edwin	
Lipan	Leon	J	Mahoney	James	
Lisky	John	A	Maier	Herman	
Litman	William	I	Maim	Robert	G
Livingston	Van		Makepeace	Ralph	L
Llunsford	Francis	G	Malisch	Robert	E
Lodge	Vernon	W	Malone	Bermon	D
Loebig	Neal		Mangum	Joseph	A
Logan	William	J	Manley	Floyd	J
Logsden	Chester		Manning	Jacob	
Loman	Robert	B	Manning	Robert	D
Lomos	F		Manoleas	James	P
Long	Leonard	H	Manska	Jack	H
Long	Victor	A	Manyak	Francis	P
Long	Harry	T	March	William	S
Longmire	Robert		Marchion	Vincent	P
Longona	Paul		Marchori	Mario	
Longton	Raymond		Mariani	Danto	
Lonnes	Edward	W	Marino	Frank	C
Loper	James	E	Markham	Kenneth	M
Lopresto	Victor	R	Markle, Jr.	Channey	
Lorion	Robert	V	Markoff	Marco	V
Loucks	Walter	J	Markovich	William	
Loucks	William	V	Marshall	John	L
Loustalot	Edward	V	Marszowski	Stephen	
Low	Austin	G	Martin	Edwin	R

Martin	Edwin	W	McGee	William	A
Martin	Grant	E	McGinley	William	F
Martin	Jack	P	McGowan	John	C
Martin	Marvin	H	McGraw	Elvis	G
Martin	William	E	McGuire	Jim	
Marty	Joseph		McHiernan	Leonard	J
Marty	Raymond	E	McHugh	Robert	
Masalonis	Edward	W	McKenna	James	F
Mascari, Jr.	Thomas	M	McKenna	Thomas	G
Mathias	Donald	W	McKinnon	Angus	G
Matta	Thomas	Z	McLain	Henry	P
Mattivi	Frank		McLaren	Walter	A
Maure	George	H	McLenson	Stanley	P
Maurisak	Harry	H	McLenson	Stanley	P
May	Joseph	C	McLeod	Arch	M
Mayberry	Howard	M	McLeod	William	Z
Maynard	James	W	McMahon	John	J
Mays	Ewing	W	McMahon	Regis	M
Mazzillo	John	F	McMahon	Thomas	J
McAllister	Harold		McNeely	James	O
McBride	Carl	W	McTague	Charles	P
McBride	James	D	McVay	James	O
McBride	Kenneth	G	McWilliams	Harold	L
McBryde	Charles	M	Mead	George	
McCabe	William	R	Meade	Stephen	J
McCaffrey	Cornelius	D	Mccccw	Arlo	
McCandless	Vern	F	Meehan	Francis	E
McCarthy	Eugene	S	Mellon	Robert	D
McCarthy	John	P	Melton	Austin	
McCarthy	Martin		Mercuriali	Gino	
McCauley	Frank	E	Merrill	Allen	E
McCauley	Robert		Merritt	James	M
McClain	LeRoy	J	Mette	Bernard	G
McCollam	Donald		Meyer	Howard	G
McCormick, Jr.	Robert	C	Meyers	Paul	
McCoy	Keith	M	Michalik	Edward	R
McCulley	Robert	C	Mickelson	Arthur	H
McCunniff	Francis	E	Mielcarski	Edwin	A
McDevitt	Francis	J	Mikel	John	W
McDonald	Forrest	H	Milewski	Teddy	P
McDonald	Harold	J	Miley	Eugene	D
McDonough	Patrick	J	Miller, Jr.	Thomas	E
McDoughall	Darrell	A	Miller	Albertus	H
McDowell	Robert	L	Miller	Alvah	N
McEllrath	Kenneth	E	Miller	Beverley	E
McFarland	Robert	K	Miller	Charles	L

Nochta	John	E	Paskavan	Jacob	J
Noel, Jr.	Grover	R	Passera	August	R
Nofzinger	Orison	J	Patrick, Jr.	James	E
Nordland	John	J	Patrinos	Paul	
Norman	John	R	Patterson	Archie	C
Northrup, Jr.	Jay	D	Patterson	Francis	B
Northrup	Arthur	J	Paxton	Leon	S
Novak	John	F	Payne	Gerald	M
Null	Francis	M	Pedigo	Paul	R
Nulph	Arthur	R	Peed	George	W
Nutt, Jr.	Grover	C	Peifer	Ellis	F
Nyarady	Eugene	J	Peltz	Harold	E
Nye	Walter	F	Perez	John	A
Nystrom	Alder		Perlmutter	Harold	
O'Connor	William	F	Perry	Emory	L
O'Dell	Ray	A	Perry	Lawrence	A
O'Rourke	Daniel	J	Perry	Paul	E
O'Sack	Frank		Pesserilo	Solomon	
Odom	Robbins	D	Peters	Dixon	A
Olesen	Robert	H	Peters	George	A
Olsen	Lynn	M	Petersen	Henry	
Oneskunk	Samson	P	Peterson	Ronald	I
Osborne	Charles	H	Petit	Alfred	R
Oslund	George	L	Pettit	Robert	E
Ott	Calvin	G	Petty	Clarence	A
Owen	Johnny	D	Pfann	William	
Owens	Robert	A	Pfrunder	David	L
Owens	Roy	E	Phelan	Frank	J
Padgett	Roy	L	Phelps	Thomas	E
Padilla	Elmer	J	Philippson	Hermann	E
Padrucco	Francis	P	Phillips	Charles	A
Pafundi	David	J	Phillips	Joe	
Pagunano	Charles	E	Pierce	Joseph	E
Palade	Weslie	W	Pierce	Raymond	
Palmer, Jr.	Frank	W	Pilgrim	Ray	C
Palmer	Merritt	M	Piontkowski	Robert	J
Pamer	Frank	W	Piscitello	Archie	R
Pandure	Ralph	A	Place	Kenneth	
Parachini	Mario	A	Plemmons	Clarence	T
Parish	Earl		Plovc	Thomas	W
Parker	Isaac	M	Polisenom	Americo	
Parker	Walter	A	Pollard	Paul	F
Parson	Perry	A	Pollock, Jr.	Paul	J
Parsons	Wiliam	T	Polubinski	Edward	K
Parton	Edward	M	Polus	Matthew	
Pascoe	Edward	A	Porter	Charles	T

Porter	Richard	W	Reed	Eugene	M
Posey	Richard	H	Reed	Ralph	D
Post	Arthur	C	Reed	Robert	
Powell	Phillip	J	Reeder	Eugene	F
Powell	Walter	R	Reevas	Donald	G
Powers	William	J	Reger	Robert	J
Prange	William	J	Reid	James	J
Preston	Joseph	A	Reid	Lawrence	
Preston	Pete	M	Reilly	Charles	
Price	James	E	Reine	Joseph	R
Pritchett	Floyd	C	Reiter	Alvin	F
Proefrock	Arthur	L	Reiter	Leonard	
Prokopowicz	Leonard	E	Rembecki	John	S
Prosise	Paul	L	Rensink	Gerrit	J
Provost	William	P	Retig	Roland	
Prudhomme	Thomas	H	Rettinghaus	Bernard	J
Pruit	Charles	R	Rexoat	Wilbert	M
Pruit	Thomas	J	Reyes	Fernando	A
Pruitt	Lloyd	S	Reynolds	Jack	
Prussia	Charles	J	Rhoades	Hugh	R
Przybylo	Joseph		Rice	Herbert	J
Puccio	Charles		Richard	Clarence	J
Pucheu, Jr.	Lucas	F	Richard	Jude	J
Puchinsky	Walter		Richards	Lloyd	D
Purcell	Charles	J	Richardson	Earl	E
Purvis	Ray	E	Richardson	George	J
Quinn	Leslie		Richman	Bernard	
Quirk	Robert	R	Ricklefs	Donald	R
Rada	Anthony		Riedel	William	
Rader	Sam	L	Riege	Kenneth	L
Raines	Thomas	G	Rieker	John	E
Rama	David		Riffle	Elmer	A
Rambis	Michael	J	Riggs	Everette	G
Ramey	Austin	M	Riley	Bernard	P
Ramos	Albert		Riley	William	H
Randall	Joseph	H	Rinard	Harold	L
Rao	Frankie	J	Riopel	Raymond	W
Rasch	Elmer		Riordan	James	F
Ratcil	Wendell	T	Rios	Donald	M
Ratliff	Roy		Risberg	Lawrence	A
Ratliff	Vinson		Ritchey	James	C
Rayhorn	Russell	E	Ritzert	William	E
Reagan	Harry	M	Roach	Calvin	C
Reams	Max	L	Roach	Thomas	P
Redman	James		Roach	Walter	H
Reed	Clyde	D	Roane	George	H

Schultz	John	W	Sichler	Edward	A
Schumacher	Dennis	L	Sidaway	Robert	W
Schunemann	Gustave	E	Sidora	Paul	
Schwartz	Joey	H	Sieg	Walter	R
Scioli	Achillo		Sikorski	Chester	
Scott	Clyde	H	Silkwood	Monzell	
Scott	Earl	J	Simmins	Lorin	
Scott	Ross	W	Simmons	John	M
Scrogtins	Alfred	L	Simmons	Perry	J
Searle	William	A	Simons	Donald	L
See	John	C	Simons	Gerald	C
Sellers	Richard		Simpson	Ernest	A
Semo	Paul	T	Simpson	James	V
Serksnis	Carl	A	Simpson	Richard	C
Serrano	Henry	W	Sischo	Glen	C
Sewell	Guy		Sitarchyk	Joseph	A
Sexton	Donald	R	Sittler	Alfred	
Shaffer	William	D	Sivil	Charles	
Shaffner	John	C	Sivil	Charlie	E
Shain	Edward		Six	Nelson	D
Shamitko	Steve		Skaggs	Robert	H
Shamonski	Edward	J	Skarberg	Charles	F
Shanahan	James	A	Skarie	Robert	W
Shaw	David	E	Skripac	Anthony	P
Shaw	Henry	W	Smith, Jr.	Ralph	E
Shaw	William	F	Smith	Clinton	
Shawiak	Benjamin		Smith	Daniel	S
Sheets	Harry		Smith	James	D
Sheffer	George	A	Smith	James	H
Sheldon	Ervin	L	Smith	John	H
Sherer	James	C	Smith	Richard	G
Sherman	Charles	H	Smith	Thomas	F
Shettelsworth	James		Smith	William	
Shields	William	O	Snarski	Richard	C
Shimer	Benjamin	J	Snow	George	L
Shippey	Henry	G	Snowden	Shelby	
Shippy	Zane	G	Soehl	John	W
Shirey	Ernest	L	Sole	Raymond	A
Shontz	Andrew	M	Sommers	Sheldon	C
Shramek	Walter	F	Sommers	Virgil	O
Shropshire	J	D	Somuk	John	A
Shuff	Joseph		Sorby	Tom	
Shumaker	Douglas	M	Sorenson	Vern	L
Shunstrom	Charles	M	Sorrell	Charles	A
Shuput	Michael	M	Sosh	James	
Shurmak	Sylvester		Southmayd	Gale	R

Spackman	Arthur	
Spangler	Theodore	
Sparks	Garrett	D
Sparks	Martin	E
Spirito	Jack	F
Sporman	Leonard	E
Stacy	Burkley	
Stafford	Jack	L
Stancil	John	
Stanton	John	J
Stapleton	James	H
Stark	Ernest	
Stealy	Richard	E
Steele	Frank	A
Steen	James	P
Steigler	Willis	E
Stein	Harold	
Stempson	Kenneth	D
Stenseng	Vernon	S
Stephens	Dale	G
Stephens	Eldon	R
Stern	Phil	
Stewart	Byron	T
Stewart	Estel	
Stewart	Roland	D
Stiles	George	J
Stillwagon	Robert	E
Stojak	Andrew	J
Stojewski	Raymond	A
Stoopes	Leslie	
Stovall	William	S
Strange	Lewis	A
Strauss, Jr.	Fred	
Strauss	George	
Street	Jack	B
Strehl	George	
Strickland	Woodrow	W
Stroka	Frank	
Stroud	Pressley	P
Stubblefield	Lee	J
Sudy	George	
Sugrue	John	E
Sullivan	Thomas	
Sumpter	Gerald	C
Sumpter	Gerald	C
Sunshine	George	P

Surrat	Robert	C
Sutton	Harold	W
Svaton	Arnold	E
Swain	Donald	J
Swank	Marcell	
Swankie	Thomas	C
Swanson	Allen	E
Swanson	Dick	W
Swanson	Robert	
Swavely	William	E
Sweany	Harry	W
Sweazy	Owen	
Sweltzer	John	J
Swicker	Howard	B
Swiderski	John	C
Swindle	Benjamin	T
Syring	Wallace	J
Syroid	Mitchell	
Szcesniak	Steven	S
Szima	Alex	I
Szlavick	Adam	
Tabor	Jack	W
Talbot	Warren	E
Tarlton	Alvin	S
Taylor	Willis	E
Taylor, Jr.	Alpha	O
Taylor	Clarence	A
Taylor	Robert	R
Teel	Patrick	A
Terrill	George	T
Teryek	Joseph	
Texter	Calvin	J
Thacker	Robert	N
Thiel	Robert	
Thivierge	Leo	P
Thomas	J	
Thomas	Lynn	D
Thomas	Wallace	B
Thompson	Charles	F
Thompson	Clarence	N
Thompson	Clyde	C
Thompson	Dula	C
Thompson	Ed	
Thompson	Evan	
Thompson	Herbert	R
Thompson	Howard	R

Thompson	Melvin	D	Vanskoy	John	R
Thompson	Richard	N	Vasquez	Leonard	B
Thompson	Robert	E	Vaughn	Edward	L
Thornbury	Arson		Vaughn	John	W
Thornton	Frank		Ventrone	John	M
Thurman	George	W	Vest	Chester	L
Tiberi	Michael		Vetcher	Peter	
Tickle	Hiram	W	Vickmark	Clayton	O
Tiggelaar	Samuel		Vieira	Edmond	T
Tigghon	Robert	M	Villareal	Reynoldo	J
Till	Paul	H	Vivrett	G	L
Tillman	Joseph	U	Vogt	Harry	F
Tittle	Dale		Volmar	William	C
Titus	John	O	Von Kamp	Fred	J
Tongate	Kenneth	C	Wachowicz	Julian	
Torbett	Donald	K	Wagner	Eugene	
Torneby	Samuel	C	Walker	James	F
Tourney	David	J	Walker	Ralph	
Trabu	Edward	W	Walker	Roy	T
Tracy	Robert	W	Walker	William	H
Traufler	Donald	A	Wallace	George	W
Travers	Joseph	A	Walliser	Samuel	R
Tremblay	Russell	R	Wallsmith	Clotis	
Trent	Nelson		Walsh	Robert	J
Treumer	Clarence		Walters	Charles	
Trijillo	Bernie	R	Walton	Harold	B
Trowbridge	Warfield	E	Walton	Herbert	R
Troxell	Lawrence	E	Wandolowski	John	G
Trynoski	Joseph	R	Warekois	Eugene	A
Tryon	William	S	Warner	Harvey	L
Trzeciak	Edward	J	Warren	Richard	H
Tucker	Louis	O	Warriner	Guy	F
Tucker	Samuel		Wary	Charles	R
Turner	Robert	E	Waterman	Charles	J
Tweit	Fuller	A	Watson	James	M
Twigg	Roger	M	Watson	John	C
Twilley	Jack		Watson	John	R
Tyner	George	D	Watson	Martin	R
Upton	William	B	Watt, Jr.	Robert	M
Urban	Henry	A	Watts	Benjamin	R
Urbealis	Ralph	W	Weber	Eldred	E
Vallery	Gordon		Weiboldt	Rudolph	B
Van Alstine	Earl	W	Weich	Kenneth	L
Van Schriver	Harry	A	Weichmann	Jack	E
Vanderpool	Robert	L	Wellborn	Carl	H
Vanhorn	Roy	A	Wells	Royal	H

SECOND RANGER INFANTRY BATTALION

Last Name	First Name	Initial	Last Name	First Name	Initial
Adams, Jr.	Bernie	W	Biesterfelt	Herbert	
Adams	Clark		Bikner	James	W
Adams	Herbert	H	Bisek	Louis	J
Adams	LeRoy	G	Bladorn	Kenneth	K
Adkins	Sammie		Blum	James	L
Aguzzi	Victor	J	Bodnar	John	A
Ahart	John	R	Bogetto	Domenick	B
Akrdige	Walter	O	Bolin	Brownie	L
Alexander	James	R	Bollia	Charles	E
Alm	Raymond	F	Bombardier	Walter	T
Anderson	Christopher	M	Borowski	Walter	J
Anderson	William	E	Bouchard	Gerald	A
Andrusz	Edward	A	Bowens	Howard	
Angyal	Joseph		Bragg	Keith	
Antio	Richard	E	Bramkamp	Charles	J
Arman	Robert	C	Branley	Michael	J
Armbruster	Thomas	J	Brewster	Harry	E
Arnold	Edgar	L	Brice	Robert	M
Arthur	Lester	G	Brown	Owen	
Ashline	Donald	L	Browning	Maurice	R
Austin	Robert	L	Bruce	Guy	W
Bachleda	Anton		Bungard	Henry	
Bachman, Jr.	Clarence	E	Bullard	Gerald	D
Bacho	John		Burnett	John	S
Bakalar	John		Burns	Lloyd	C
Bake	Eugene	B	Butzke	Elmer	W
Bare	Sheldon		Byzon	Paul	B
Bargmann	Kenneth	H	Caler	Francis	M
Bass	William		Caperton	Willis	C
Baugh	Gilbert	C	Caringola	Ernest	J
Bayer	Otto	C	Carmen	William	
Beech	Cecil	E	Carpenter	Ledford	L
Beedle	Frederick	A	Carr	Elmer	C
Beekler	Volney	E	Carty	Robert	C
Behrent	Oscar	E	Casino	John	
Belcher	Julius	W	Catelani	Anthony	P
Bell	William	D	Cerwin	Carl	C
Bellows, Jr.	Charles	H	Clark	George	M
Belmont	Gail	H	Clark	Rex	D
Berg	Charles	T	Clark	William	C
Berke	Neal	B	Cleaves	Joseph	J
Bialkowski	Walter	T	Clendenin	Harold	E
Biddle	John	C	Clifton	John	M

Cobb	Madison	B	Doughty	Eugene	C
Colden	Garness	L	Dreher, Jr.	William	
Coldsmith	William	H	Drobick	Mike	
Cole	Raymond	A	Duenkel, Jr.	Arthur	J
Coley	Leonard	E	Duffy	Joseph	J
Colvard, Jr.	E	G	Dugas	William	F
Conaboy	John	F	Duncan	Delmas	O
Connolly	Francis	J	Dunlap	Charles	M
Cook	Harvey	J	Dycus, Jr.	Elijah	D
Cook	William	I	Earle	John	W
Cooley	Robert		Eason	Wilbur	L
Cooper	Robert	J	East	Archie	D
Cooper	Thorpe	T	Eberle	Gerald	A
Corder	Frank	H	Edlin	Robert	T
Corona	John	J	Elder	Eugene	E
Cournoyer	Joseph	R	Elsie	Alfred	F
Courtney	William	J	Elzy	Clarence	L
Crego, Jr.	Floyd	H	Engle	Albert	L
Cripps	John	I	Epperson	Conway	E
Crisp	Ketchell		Erdely	John	
Crook	George	H	Farrar	Henry	S
Crull	Edison	W	Farver	Richard	D
Cruz	William		Fate	Harry	J
Culbreath	Fred		Fendley	Donald	E
Dailey	Robert	L	Ferguson	Delbert	
Daniels	Joseph	V	Ferguson	Eugene	T
Daugherty	Duncan	N	Ferris	Wilfred	E
Davidson	Elmer		Ferry	Harry	J
Davis	Charles	L	Filzen	Paul	R
Davis	Kenneth	W	Findish	Henry	J
Davis	Ralph	E	Flanagan	Charles	C
Davis	Raymond	G	Fitzsimmons	Robert	C
Davis	Robert	G	Flanagan	Charles	C
DeCapp	Donald	D	Flanagan	Joseph	L
Denbo	Charles	H	Franklin	Earl	D
Depottey	Walter	A	Franklin	John	W
Detweiler	Billie	M	Frazier	Ottis	
Devoli	Joseph	R	Frechette	George	J
Dillard	John	T	Frederick	Charles	E
Dix	Frederick	A	French	Paul	W
Doinoff	William	K	Fritchman, Jr.	Harry	G
Dolinsky	John		Fronczek	Louis	J
Donahue	James	E	Fruhling	Robert	A
Donlin	Paul	J	Fulford	Charles	E
Donovan	John	F	Fulton	James	E
Dorchak	Joseph	J	Fyda	Walter	A

Gallo	Dominick	F	Hellers, Jr.	George	H
Galloway	Paul		Hendrickson	Kenneth	A
Garfield	Ray		Hensley	Clinton	M
Gargas	Michael		Henwood	John	R
Garrett	Richard	G	Herlihy	Robert	D
Gary	Robert	P	Herman	Louis	
Gavan	William	H	Hickling	Paul	
Gaydos	Joseph	P	Hicks	James	O
Geitz	William	A	Hill	Jacob	J
Geldon	Walter	B	Hillis	Virgil	A
Genther	Henry	W	Hinch	Milton	B
Gervais	William	A	Hinman, Jr.	Robert	P
Gilhooly	John	J	Hoffman	Wilbur	K
Gillespie	Robert	E	Holland	Richard	L
Gleckl	Gilbert	N	Holliday	James	H
Goad	Wayne	D	Honhart	Robert	A
Golas	Henry	S	Hooks	Tasker	L
Goranson	Ralph	E	Hoover	Irving	J
Gottel, Jr.	William	J	Horvath	William	J
Goudey	David	L	Houchens	Barkley	C
Gould	Charles	E	Hower, Jr.	Percy	C
Gourley	John	S	Hoyt, Jr.	Ralph	W
Gower	William	E	Hubbard	Richard	
Graham	Henry	N	Hubert	Raymond	N
Graham	Will	H	Hudnell	James	H
Graham	William	L	Huff	Harley	R
Graziose	Eugene	H	Huth	James	L
Gross	Charles	C	Irvin	Leslie	M
Gunther	Harold	W	Isaacson	Sidney	L
Gurney	Edward		Jackson	Maurice	W
Guthle	Bernard		Jackson	Orley	R
Gutowski	George	L	James	Theodore	A
Hall	George	A	Jimenez	Ernest	J
Hamilton	Richard	D	Johnson	Edward	A
Hanlon	John	M	Johnson	Lawrence	M
Harding	Eddie	W	Jones	Edward	J
Hareff	Norman	J	Jones	Emory	B
Harris	Lester	W	Jones	Ivor	R
Harrison	Granville	P	Jones	James	E
Hart	Garland	V	Jones	Paul	M
Harwood	Jonathan	H	Kane	James	A
Hastings	Jack	W	Kassmeier	Leonard	P
Hayden	Millard	W	Keating	John	V
Heaney	William	G	Keefer, Jr.	Mark	A
Hebbeler	Elmer	F	Kennard	Frank	L
Heffelbower, Jr.	Melvin	C	Kennedy	Charles	F

Kerchner	George	F	Lomasky	Irving	
Kerr	James	P	Lomell	Leonard	G
Kettering	Charles	E	Long	Clarence	J
Kiihnl	Herman	W	Longest	Vergil	L
Kimble	Dennis	F	Lorence	Richard	D
King	Herbert	A	Lorett	James	A
Kirk	Marvin	D	Lowe	Colin	J
Klaus	William	V	Luning	Gordon	C
Knor	Paul	P	Lutz	Marvin	O
Kobylinski	Edward	J	Lynch, Jr.	William	W
Koenig	Harvey	W	Lyons, Jr.	G	E
Koepfer	John	V	Machan	James	A
Kohl	James	E	Mackey	George	W
Kolodziejczak	Francis	J	Magee	Carl	R
Korb	Charles	W	Maimone	Salva	P
Korpalo, Jr.	Peter		Main	Harold	D
Kosina	Frank	J	Mains	Clifford	F
Kuhn	Jack	E	Majane	Wilfred	C
Kulp	Roy	G	Malaney	James	A
Kwasnicki	William	H	Malburg, Jr.	Theodore	A
LaBlanc	Wilfred		Malisa	Vincent	W
LaBrandt	Frank	J	Manifold	Max	D
Ladidess	Jack		Manning	Oloise	A
Lambert	Robert	C	Masny	Otto	
LaMero	Jack	W	Massuto	Daniel	J
Landin	Robert	G	Mathews	Marvin	E
Lang	Robert	W	McBride	Morton	L
Lapham	James	R	McCalvin	Charles	G
Lapres, Jr.	Theodore	E	McCann	Charlie	V
Lare	Lawrence		McCloskey	Regis	F
Latham	Roy	L	McCorckle	Andrew	P
Lavandoski	Leonard	L	McCreery	Donald	L
Lawrence	George	F	McCrone	Patrick	F
Lawlor	Lawrence	J	McCue	Harry	C
Lawson, Jr.	Jack		McCullagh	Robert	F
Leagans	Joseph	E	McCullers	James	R
Lefferts	Howard	J	McDonough	Michael	J
Lemin	Robert	N	McFadden	Albert	A
Lengyel, Jr.	George		McHugh	William	M
Lester	Harold	E	McKitrick	William	B
Lick	Ira	E	McKittrick	Robert	E
Lindheim	Donald	R	McLaughlin	Richard	E
Lindsay, Jr.	William	R	McWhirter	Wililam	H
Liscinsky	Stephen	A	Meccia	Alban	
Lisko	Louis	F	Medeiros	Paul	
Lock	Joseph	J	Mendenhall	Thomas	D

Mentzer	Donald	F	Parker	Charles	S
Merrill	Richard	P	Passetto	Geno	L
Middleton	Raymond	L	Patrick, Jr.	James	K
Miles	Roy	M	Pattison	Clyde	S
Miljavac	John	J	Peterson	Frank	H
Milkovich, Jr.	Mike		Petty	William	L
Miller	James	R	Pfeiffer	Clifford	F
Miller	Marcel		Pilalas	Theodore	M
Miller	Norma	G	Plumlee	Fred	W
Miller	Vayle		Poynter	Morris	D
Miller	William	J	Preston	Lawrence	W
Mitchum	Dalphus	G	Priesman	Maynard	J
Mlay	Andrew		Prince	Morris	
Moak	Stanley	F	Putzek	George	J
Mohr	Christian	J	Pyles	Robert	S
Mollohan	William	L	Rafferty	Joseph	A
Montgomery	Francis	E	Rankin	Richard	E
Moody	William	D	Raymond	Robert	J
Mooneyham	Bill	M	Reed	Nathan	C
Moore	Burl	C	Reed	Oliver	E
Moore	Jack	B	Reider	Donald	
Morrow	George	W	Rembert	Raymond	D
Mull	Everett	R	Remmers, Jr.	Julius	
Myers	William	D	Revels	Rolland	F
Nance	Alvin	H	Rich	Charles	E
Nelson	Roger	L	Richards	Jacob	H
Nezozon	Stephen	J	Richardson	Ollie	D
Nigohosian	Kegham		Ricketts	Henry	
Nosal	Aloysius	S	Riddle	Buford	L
Noyes	Nelson	W	Riendeau	Raymond	J
O'Connor	Edward	J	Riley	John	J
O'Keefe	William	F	Rinker	Randall	R
O'Leary	James	W	Roach	Francis	J
O'Neal	Frederick	A	Roberts	Harry	W
Oehlberg	John	D	Robertson	Harvey	E
Ogle	Roy	H	Robertson	Innes	R
Olander	Elmer	P	Robertson	Robert	L
Oropello	Frank	J	Robey	Hayward	A
Otto	Leon	H	Robida	Philip	G
Oudibert	Bertrand	J	Robinson	Frank	B
Pachacek	Donald	C	Robison	James	K
Pacyga	Francis	J	Rocquemore	Frank	
Painkin	Martin	H	Roe	Robert	K
Palmer	Roy	L	Rogers	Richard	A
Paniaha	George		Roken	Francis	J
Paradis	Roland	J	Roman	Victor	B

Roosa	Robert	G	Slager	Fred	
Rotthoff	Gerard	C	Slagle	James	W
Roush	James	L	Slater	Harold	K
Rubenstein	Manning	I	Sluss	William	E
Rubin	Leonard		Smith	Claude	A
Rubio	Robert		Smith	Clifford	T
Rudder	James	E	Smith	Edward	P
Ruggiero	Antonio		Smith	Frederick	D
Runyan	Jesse	J	Smith	Simon	
Rupinski	Frank	A	Smith	Winfred	P
Rustebakke	Alvin	S	Snedeker	James	B
Ruta	Peter	A	Snipes	Edward	W
Ryan	Thomas	F	Snyder	James	W
Sachnowski	Stanley	P	Sobal	Henry	
Salesky	Arthur	A	Sooy	Ralph	B
Salomon	Sidney	A	Sorger	Earl	W
Sampson	Harley	R	Sorvisto	Edwin	W
Schauer	Charles	F	South	Frank	E
Schmitt	Robert	G	Sowa	Edward	L
Schneller	George	O	Sparaco	Dominick	J
Schouw	Alfred		Spellman	Earl	W
Schribner	Donald	L	Spleen	Richard	J
Schroeder	Gerald	H	Stanley	Coy	N
Sczepanski	Stephen	J	Stecki	Henry	S
Seamans	Charles	F	Stefik	Rudolph	
Secor	Edwin	J	Stein	Herman	E
Sehorn	Harold	W	Stepancevich	Steve	
Selepec	George	L	Stephens	Otto	K
Semchuck	Charles	J	Stevens	Joseph	L
Shalala	James	R	Stinnette	Murrell	F
Shanahan	John	C	Stivison	William	J
Sharp	William	L	Stojkov	Alexander	M
Shave	Paul	L	Strassburger	Helmuth	M
Shedaker	Joseph	W	Styles	Mack	C
Sherertz	William	D	Sundby	Sigurd	
Shireman	Earl	W	Swafford	Glen	J
Shirey	Robert	F	Swanson	Ronald	E
Shoaf	Guy	C	Sweany	Melvin	W
Shock	Dorsey	L	Swedo, Jr.	Peter	
Sikes, Jr.	Henry	B	Sworsky	Edmond	A
Sillmon	John	J	Talkington	Woodrow	
Simkins	Floyd	H	Taylor	Bonnie	M
Simko	Marvin	A	Tennyson	John	
Simmons	Curtis	A	Theobald	Earl	A
Simons	William	H	Thomas	Jack	T
Sinbine	George	H	Thomas	William	J

Thompson	Bill	L	Whicker	Floyd	D
Thompson	Leroy	J	White	Alvin	E
Tibbets	Billy		White	George	A
Tindell	John	W	White	John	W
Tolias	Charles	S	White	Stanley	E
Tollefson	Raymond	R	White	Virgil	
Torbett	Harold	L	Whitehead	Robert	R
Trainor	Joseph	R	Wieburg	George	A
Trenkle	Fred		Wilde	Robert	E
Trombowicz	Edward	J	Wilder	Harry	
Turner	Ramsey	A	Wilkin	Frederick	G
Tutt	William	R	Williams, Jr.	Newton	R
Uhorczuk	William	J	Williams	George	S
Urban	Walter	R	Williamson	Charles	W
Uronis	Albert	J	Williamson	Robert	O
Van Hassel	Joseph		Willis	James	W
Vaughan	William	D	Wilson	Clarence	A
Vella	Charles	J	Wilson	Roy	M
Vermeer	Elmer	H	Wilson	Thomas	
VerSchave	Jean	N	Winsch	Carl	
Vetovich	Michael		Witt	Carl	R
Wadsworth	Loring	L	Wintz	Richard	A
Wagner	George	U	Wirtz	Benjamin	H
Walker	William	A	Wood	George	R
Walsh	William	D	Wood	Henry	A
Wardell	John	M	Worman	Russell	G
Ware	Harry		Wright	Orville	E
Watkins	Elmer	P	Wyder	Matthew	J
Watson	Floyd	L	Yadlosky	John	
Webb	Morris	N	Yardley	Andrew	J
Weber	William	F	Yater	James	C
Webster	Glenn	L	Yates	Leo	D
Wedding	John	H	Young	Kenneth	N
Weilage	Charles	F	Young	Wallace	W
Weimer	Martin	R	Youso	Robert	G
Wells	Robert	M	Zajas	Leonard	F
Welsch	Paul	P	Zarka	Stanley	A
Wetzel	Joseph	A	Ziekle	Eugene	J
Whaley	Clifton	F	Zimkus	Joseph	J
Wharff	Kenneth	L	Zuravel	John	

THIRD RANGER INFANTRY BATTALION

Last Name	First Name	Initial	Last Name	First Name	Initial
Abdill	John		Baumgart	William	R
Adams	Adam	R	Bayles	James	C
Adams	Calvin	J	Bearpaw	Tom	
Adams	Harold	R	Beauchart	Arthur	
Adams	Lee	R	Becker	Walter	H
Adamson	James		Begin	Richard	A
Adkins	Harris		Belcher	Virgil	M
Aiken	John	M	Belk	McDowd	
Alabek	Joseph	F	Benediktor	Rudolph	
Aleman	Gumesindo		Benedix	Francis	J
Allsbrook	John	A	Bennet	David	L
Almond	Francis	E	Bennett	David	S
Amtonucci	Ciro		Benoit	Arthur	J
Amundson	Walter		Berg	Bernard	S
Anderson	John	W	Bertholf	Merrit	
Andrieu	Robert	J	Betters	Clarence	
Anesgart	Harry	H	Biere	William	F
Applin	Raymond	A	Bigley	Goerge	C
Archer	James	P	Billingsley	Maurice	E
Arimond	William	E	Bills	Perry	E
Armstron	John	E	Bischoff	Harold	E
Arnbal	Anders	K	Blair	Richard	W
Arnold	William	H	Blake, Jr.	O	R
Ashton	Robert	E	Blanch	Gordon	H
Aunchman	Walter	W	Blanchard	Joseph	C
Back	Harley	B	Blauscr	Raymond	A
Backes	George	C	Bliss	James	F
Bacus	Dean	D	Block	Joseph	E
Badder	Carl	E	Bode	Ivan	M
Bader	Robert	D	Bodnar	Stephan	
Badgerow	Roy	M	Bogar	Nelson	M
Baker	Jesse	S	Bohannon	Roy	
Baldrey	Raymond	J	Bond	Fred	C
Bancker	Harold	F	Booker	Ralph	C
Barber	Edward	R	Boone	Winton	E
Bard	Carl	E	Booth	Frederick	H
Barnes	Charles	F	Borobowski	Chester	B
Barnes	Earnest	J	Bottitta	Joseph	F
Barnes	Russell	W	Boudreau	Maurice	J
Barnes	William	B	Bough	Eugene	V
Barnett	Charles	T	Bouley	Roland	R
Bartolino, Jr.	Nichols	J	Boullion	John	
Baum	John	L	Bowen	Phillip	

Bowman	Jasper	J	Callicut	Ed	
Boykin	Bufford	L	Calvin	Armand	A
Boyle	Raymond	V	Campbell	Joseph	S
Brady	John	C	Campbell	Raymond	E
Brake	Douglas	E	Campbell	Robert	M
Brandon	James	T	Cannon	Charles	E
Brazzell	John	F	Care	Charles	L
Brennan	Newman	F	Carlson	Douglas	H
Brest	John	A	Carmichael	John	R
Breuers	Jacob		Carr	Omer	B
Brewer	Cratham	E	Case	Howard	T
Brewer	Melvin	R	Case	William	E
Briner	Burdette		Cashner	Martin	D
Brinkley	Calvin	O	Cathcart	Addison	W
Brown	Max		Causey, Jr.	Charles	M
Brown	Melvin	D	Cavaner	Reed	
Brown	Willice	E	Cavazos	Julian	
Bruder	Robert		Cawthon	Virgil	A
Brunell	Joseph	C	Caydos	Albert	L
Bruno	Dominick	A	Ceja	Louis	S
Bubrowski	Julian	P	Chabre	Edmond	
Buchanan	Lawrence	W	Charles	Dale	
Buere	Robert	A	Chase	Edward	R
Bullington	Lee	M	Chavez	Senon	S
Bullock	Douglas	R	Chestnut	J	T
Burke	Donald	A	Chmura	Edwin	
Burke	John	J	Cialeo	Benjamin	
Burke	Parris		Ciesielski	Casimer	J
Burlin	Harry	M	Cinelli	John	
Burnette	George	L	Clark	Eugene	
Burns	James	W	Cleveland	Dale	L
Burse	James	M	Cline	Walter	T
Burton	Joseph	W	Cobb	Walter	
Burton	Wilard		Coddington	John	B
Butler, Jr.	Luther	W	Coggin	Otis	W
Butler	Grant	R	Cole	James	A
Byerk	Edward	J	Collins	Charles	
Byrne	Howard		Comes	Anthony	J
Caddigan	Walter	A	Connell	Richard	J
Cain	Leo	T	Connolly	Edmund	B
Cain	Paul	W	Contreas, Jr.	John	
Calderone	John		Conway	Frank	M
Cale	Charles	W	Conway	James	D
Callahan	Arthur	B	Cook	Ross	M
Callahan	Earnest	F	Coons	Carlos	B
Callaway	Marion	J	Cooper	Burnie	B

Cooper	Ralph	B	Decker	Lawrence	E
Coppa	Joseph		Deckman	Fred	
Corbin	Frank	H	Deckrow	Orville	L
Corbin	Kenneth	B	DeCoveny	Emanuel	
Cordaway	August	F	Defoe	Lavern	A
Cordle	Henry	C	Defranco	Phillip	
Corliss	Edward	N	Degia	Joseph	F
Costa	Dominic		Degrego	Salvatore	L
Cote	Jules	E	Delio	Rocco	P
Coucher	Jack	W	Demar	William	M
Covey	Russell	F	Dettrich	Ferdinand	J
Coville	Ralph	R	Dewbre	Milton	D
Cox	Albert	M	Dickey, Jr.	Edward	A
Cox	Donald	E	Didget	Leslie	L
Coy	Fernando	S	Dillion	Daniel	J
Coyle	William	F	Dirks	Leonard	F
Crawford	Franklin	A	Dittmar	William	J
Creighton	John	M	Dix	Cecil	D
Crnkovich	Charles	J	Dixon	William	C
Crotzer	William	D	Dodge	Melvin	V
Crown	Kenneth	F	Donahue	James	F
Crum	Arlie	B	Donahue	Raymond	P
Culler	Ansel		Donmoyer	James	C
Cummins	Clifford	P	Donnelly	William	H
Cunningham	Robert	L	Douglas	Andrew	W
Curtis	Clayton	B	Downey	John	T
Curvin	Fred	L	Draeger	Marvin	R
Custer	Theadore	E	Dragoo	Verne	E
Czajkowski	Edward	L	Drais	Donald	G
Dagesse	Herven		Drake	Wilson	K
Dahlgren	Carl	E	DuBois	Robert	E
Dahlquist	Clyde	A	Dubose	John	W
Damato	Pasquale	J	Duffy	Frank	A
Damico	Anthony	J	Dugay, Jr.	George	A
Dammer	Herman	W	Dulle	Vincent	S
Daniels	Aubra	D	Duva	Orlando	J
Dastugue	Hilaire		Dzinkowski	Albert	W
Daugherty	Vernon	E	Earl	Llewellyn	F
Davey	Otis	W	Eaton	Sheldon	E
Davies	Robert	C	Eaton	William	A
Davis	Edward	L	Edstrom	Robert	G
Davis	Fred	E	Edwards	Earnest	D
Davis	Harold	C	Edwards	Jasper	W
Dawlorn	Carl	W	Edwards	Lloyd	B
Dawsey	Herman		Eineichner	Clarence	W
DeAguero	John		Elkins	Charles	L

Ellingson	William	C	Flanagan	Patrick	J
Ellingsworth	James	R	Flinn	Lester	D
Elliot, Jr.	Richard	C	Folster	Charles	W
Elliot	Clyde	C	Foore	Acie	F
Ellwood	William	O	Ford	Avery	J
Emerick	Harold	L	Ford	Kendrick	B
Emerick	Robert	A	Forshaw	Dwight	
Engel	Walter	L	Fortenberry	Ike	S
Ernest	Charles	A	Fowler	William	P
Eumpula	Clayton	V	Fox	Arlo	G
Evans	Warren	E	Fox	William	H
Eyler	John	R	Fox	William	J
Ezzell	Alvin	D	Frado, Jr.	Anthony	E
Fahey	James	E	Frankford	Robert	L
Fahy	John	V	Frasier	Lawerence	A
Fair	Jack	C	Frederman	Robert	H
Fairburn	Harold	H	Freeman	James	M
Farr	Wesley	L	French	Albert	E
Fawver	Emory	A	Friel	Francis	P
Feathers	Earnest	E	Frierson	Herman	E
Fedczysyn	Henry	A	Fries, Jr.	John	
Fedorka	George	J	Froderman	Robert	H
Fedors	John		Fronczak	Edwin	A
Feigenbaum	Edward	P	Fulkerson	Wilbur	E
Feinberg	William	V	Fuqua	Q	
Ferrell	Dossie	J	Furey	John	F
Ferrier	Edgar	A	Gabriel	Norman	O
Ferrington	Roy	M	Galbraith	John	A
Ferris	Harold	B	Gambrell	James	W
Ferris	John	W	Gangnath	Phillip	H
Fidago	John	F	Gann	Arvel	D
Fiege	Charles	E	Gaskill	Robert	K
Fields, Jr.	Charles	L	Gathright, Jr.	Wilburne	M
Fields	Richard	B	Gauther	Howard	G
Fields	William	O	Gavins	Raymond	G
Fillmore	Floyd	B	Gawrys	Edward	T
Finch	Manford	F	Gaydos	Albert	L
Finley	James	T	Gee	Lem	A
Finn	John	N	Gerhart	Elmer	L
Finn	Thomas	E	Geuder	Herbert	M
Fishel	Alfred	S	Gibbons	Noble	
Fisher	Chester	E	Gibson	Clarence	
Fitzgerald	Edgar	C	Gibson	Marvin	G
Fitzgerald	James	B	Gideon	Gerald	P
Fitzpatrick	Donald	L	Giffin	Grant	M
Fix	Paul	A	Gilardi	Americo	

Gilliland	Edmond	T	Halliday	Robert	H
Gillis	John	D	Hancock	James	T
Gillmore	Comer	R	Hancock	Victor	S
Gipson	Marvin	C	Hand	James	L
Glasscock	Richard		Hans	Herbert	N
Glaze	Ray	J	Hardesty	Delbert	W
Goad	Clarence	G	Harford	Walter	L
Godsey	Paul	J	Harlow	Robert	M
Goins	Archie		Harper	Louis	M
Golde	Donald	G	Harris	George	A
Golie	Alvin		Harris	Jack	L
Gollinger	Bernard	H	Harrison	James	P
Gomez, Jr.	Joe	P	Hart	Donald	W
Gonci	Ladislaw	L	Hartley	G	O
Gonzales	Lalo		Hashem	Thomas	J
Goodheart, Jr.	Lester	E	Hauck	Cecil	E
Goodrum	Donald	E	Havard	Marion	
Goodsheller	George	J	Hayes, Jr.	Charles	E
Goodspeed	Rudolph	W	Hayes	Donald	L
Goodwin	Forest	I	Hayles	Bobbie	L
Gordon	George	W	Heaven	James	W
Gorski	Joseph	J	Hedden	Albert	B
Gorsline	Robert	V	Hedenstad	Howard	T
Gottfried	Francis	J	Hedges	Richard	T
Goucher	Jack	W	Hedrick	Vernon	B
Gowen	Otto		Hensley	Andrew	
Grant	Julius		Hensley	James	W
Gray, Jr.	Lyman	F	Hershberg	Meyer	
Gray	Justin		Hill	Denis	W
Greene	Donald	S	Hitchen	Robert	H
Greene	Richard	M	Hodal	Charles	J
Gremler	John	H	Hogue	Preston	B
Grimes	Edward	J	Holifield	Loyse	
Grover	Paul	A	Holt	Raymond	J
Gummel	Kenneth	E	Hooker	John	F
Gurnow, Jr.	George	E	Hope	Robert	P
Gust	Joe	V	Houdeshel	Robert	R
Gustafson	Maurice	E	House	Robert	S
Guteski	Edward	A	Houseman	Richard	J
Gutierrez	Hector	M	Houseman	Robert	H
Guynes	G	W	Houseman	Roy	K
Haas	Herbert	N	Houston	David	D
Haines	James	R	Houtz	Robert	F
Haines	Robert	W	Howard	Theron	E
Hall	George	W	Hudson	Jack	
Hall	William	L	Huelf	James	M

Huey	Winfred	F	Kayanek, Jr.	Frank	
Hughes	Anthony	R	Kazura	Charles	H
Hughes	Charles	E	Keberdle	Robert	C
Hulme	Donald	D	Keegan	John	E
Hunter	Robert	G	Keener, Jr.	Vance	W
Hurlbert	Kenneth	H	Keeth	Austin	R
Hurst	Lawrence	F	Keppel	Gordon	
Huss	John	M	Kerklin	Lawrence	V
Hutcheson	Clifford	S	Kerlcy	Herman	L
Hutchinson	William	R	Kerridge	Kenneth	G
Indehar	Rudolph	J	Kessler	Harold	
Ingram	Dannie		Kessler	Robert	W
Insleep	Lyle	N	Key	Carl	Q
Ireland	Virgil	R	Kiernan	Joseph	P
Ishee	B	F	Kimbler	Clifford	J
Isola	Pasquale		Kindle	Jack	W
Jablonski	Walter	A	King	Bernard	J
Jackson	Jimmie	M	Kingrea	Coy	C
Jackson	Lester	E	Kingston	Aurthur	J
Jackson	William	A	Kirkpatrick	Charles	C
Jacobs	Charles	R	Kirkpatrick	Emmet	E
Jacobson	Richard	E	Kirner	Robert	E
Jaep	Robert	P	Kiser	Johnny	
Jansen	Jan		Kitchens, Jr.	Edward	B
Janssen	Elmer	B	Kittley	Floyd	E
Jebs	Raymond	B	Kitziner	Earnest	L
Jensen	Earnest	R	Knee	Francis	D
Johnson	Charles	M	Knox	John	K
Johnson	Ernest	T	Koczot	Joseph	B
Johnson	Freddie	J	Kohnke	Wilburt	V
Johnson	George	C	Kopanda	George	C
Johnson	Lyman	G	Koster	Gerald	R
Johnson	P	D	Kot	Charles	
Johnson	Paul	W	Kowalski	Edward	M
Johnson	Russell	W	Krise	Edward	F
Johnson	Warren	L	Krusinsky	Edward	W
Johnston	Ronald	C	Kuhl	Howard	V
Joiner	Hobart		Kumpula	Clayton	V
Joiner	William	E	Kunkle	Ronald	L
Jondal	Orville	O	Kushner	Larry	S
Jones	Donald	L	Kwasek	Edward	L
Junge	Harold	E	Kwiatek, Jr.	Walter	W
Jury	Bennie	E	LaCrosse	Frank	H
Kalakewich	John		Ladd	Thomas	E
Kasoff	Herman	V	Lamadue	Harold	N
Katzen	Murray	A	Lamb	Percy	R

Lamont	Donald	E	Markle, Jr.	Chauncey	
Lanctot, Jr.	Sidney	F	Markston	Jordan	
Lanning	William	B	Marlow	James	M
Larkin	James	J	Marshall	Tom	
Larosa	Anthony	A	Martin	Charles	S
Larson	Roy	E	Martin	George	S
Lasobyk	Alex		Martin	Lewis	H
Latas	Edward	L	Martin	Paul	G
Launer	Harvey	L	Martin	Robert	L
Leach	Robert	W	Martinke	Mike	M
LeBlanc	Clenis	J	Mascak	George	J
Ledford	Walter	E	Massaro	Paul	
Lee	Archie	F	Massey	Kenneth	P
Leefman	Bert	M	Mastrangelo	John	
Leffingwell	Karl	R	Matay	Louis	J
Lefler	Mark	J	Matheny	Harry	A
Lehmann, Jr.	Carl	H	Matthews	Raymond	
Leinhas	William	E	Mayberry	Howland	M
Lemay	Normand	R	Mays	Ewing	M
Lemmon	Donald	F	McCall	Daniel	W
Lendach	Peter		McClees	Alvin	
Lenord	Joe		McCollam	Donald	G
Lentz	Carl	F	McConnell	James	W
Leven	Gordon	A	McCord	Don	L
Levesque	Gilman	H	McCormick	Donald	A
Lewallen	Everett	F	McCoy	Charles	A
Lewis	Jack	M	McCurdy	Fay	
Lindsay	Charles	M	McDaniel	Walter	E
Lingenfelter	Irvin	I	McGaffick	Wallis	A
Long	Joseph	E	McGowan	Ovid	D
Long	Victor	A	McGrath	Richard	E
Lowe	Field	S	McIsaac, Jr.	James	A
Lowery, Jr.	Raymond	M	McKnight	John	J
Lucas	Joseph	P	McLaughlin	Wilton	H
Luoma	Rudolph	A	McMahon	Regis	
Lyons	Fred	D	McNamara	Raymond	B
Mabry	Emery	G	McNeilly	William	C
Maclin	William	C	McPhee	James	E
Mader	Harry	J	McTeague	Patrick	
Mahoney	Jimmie		Meade	George	P
Maietta	Frank	M	Meade	John	W
Majewski	Lambert	F	Meester	Jacob	F
Malgady	William	J	Meltesen	Clarence	R
Maltais	Alfred	F	Mentz	John	E
Manyak	Francis	P	Meoli	Nick	J
Marinare	Raymond	M	Merryman	James	E

Metro	Joseph		Neal	Charles	
Metzger	James	R	Neff	Elmer	J
Meyer	John	W	Nelson	Walter	A
Michael	Milo	E	Newman	William	L
Miele	Hugo	J	Newrall	Nells	E
Mikula	Albert	A	Nichols	Joseph	X
Milak	Julius	S	Nixon	George	
Miller	Alvah	M	Nobles	James	E
Miller	Dean		Nofzinger	Orison	J
Miller	Edward	S	Northrup	. . . . .	
Miller	James	F	Nutt, Jr.	Grover	C
Miller	Seymour		O'Brien, Jr.	Thomas	F
Mirabella	Lewis	A	O'Brien	Michael	W
Mitchell	Dancil	E	O'Hare	Robert	J
Mitchell	Peronneau		O'Leary	Norman	L
Mitchell	Walter	R	O'Neill	John	P
Monroe	Harris	E	O'Neille	Eugene	F
Montgee	Elmer	J	O'Reilly	James	P
Montgomery	George	C	Oakes	George	R
Moore	Edwin		Odom	Robbins	D
Moore	George	B	Oerter	Herbert	L
Moore	Richard	W	Olenik	Joseph	
Moore	Robert	J	Ostlund	George	L
Morasco	Joseph	S	Pagotto	Luigi	
Morchesky	Stanley	J	Paich	Nick	
Morgan	Beryl	E	Palade	Wesley	W
Morits	Gordon	L	Palmer	Thomas	J
Morse	Russell	E	Palumbo	Charles	L
Moryl	Adam	J	Palumbo	Frank	A
Mosley	James		Pannone	William	T
Moyer	Adam	R	Pape	Roy	L
Mozzetti	Eric	C	Parish	Earl	O
Mulkey	Lamar	A	Parnell	James	R
Mullins	Charley	A	Partridge	Richard	C
Munkacy	George	G	Patania	William	
Munro	Kenneth	J	Pattan	Edwin	T
Murch	William	S	Patterson	Edwin	H
Murphy	Robert	F	Pearce	Kenneth	S
Musegades	William	M	Peltz	Harold	E
Myers	Ray	E	Perchinsky	Stephen	
Nabors	William	F	Peretich	Thomas	J
Nadeau	Gerard		Perez	John	A
Nahodil	Donald	A	Perryman	Robert	E
Nall	Howard	W	Peskoff	Herbert	
Nangle	William	L	Pestotnick	Charles	A
Nanny	James	S	Peterman	Henry	L

Sabine	George	G	Simpson	Edward	E
Safranski	William	P	Siorek	Leonard	J
Sander	Richard	D	Sipes	Edwin	W
Sandmayr	William	J	Siroid	Mitchell	
Sanger	Curtis		Sisson	Calvin	W
Sarver	Danna	E	Skaggs	Frank	A
Saskowski	Francis	D	Skidmore	Arthur	
Saum	Russell	D	Skrit	Thomas	S
Sausen	William	L	Smalley	Frank	S
Savage	Richard	N	Smith	Clyde	E
Schade	Fred	H	Smith	Earl	E
Schenavr	John	J	Smith	James	H
Schmitt	George	W	Smith	Russell	A
Schoebel	Sylvester	R	Smith	Thomas	F
Schooley, Jr.	Clayton	M	Snider	Michael	J
Schott	Clyde	H	Sobuta	Edward	A
Schultz	Edward	A	Sosh	James	C
Schumacher	Dennis	L	Spaller	Donald	R
Schuster	Emil	G	Spangler	Theodore	F
Schwab	Edward	J	Sparks	Martin	E
Schwartz	Joey	H	Spikes	Charles	
Schwatken	Chester	L	St. Germaine	Charles	
Scott	Lloyd	W	St. John	John	
Seaton	Don	R	Stancil	John	E
Seibeneicher	Walter	F	Stanton	John	J
Seigfreid	Miles	G	Staples	Frederick	W
Septoff	Jack	P	Stark	Earnest	E
Sewell	Ralph	E	Stealy	Richard	E
Sexton	Roy	S	Steen	Floyd	E
Seymour	William	H	Steffensen	Alfred	
Shakarian	Garabed		Stella	Michael	J
Sharp	Charles	V	Stendel	Harvey	W
Shaughnessy	Richard	G	Stevens, Jr.	Elton	A
Shaw	Dean		Stevens	Aldrich	J
Shawiak	Benjamin		Stewart	Donald	D
Sheets	Harry	L	Stewart	Max	C
Sheffield	Arnold		Stewart	Robert	
Sherril	Worth	L	Stoneking	Cecil	J
Shields	Berlin	G	Stoops	Leslie	I
Shuder	Raymond		Stovall	William	S
Shuff	Joseph		Stripling	Henry	H
Siebold	William	I	Stroka	Frank	
Sigel	Frank		Stroup	Forest	E
Silkwood	Monzel		Sullivan	Thomas	S
Sills	Johnny	W	Sunshine	George	P

Supthin	Olney	J	Waggett	Robert	F
Sutherland	Albert	S	Wagner	Christian	
Swain	Donald	J	Walliser	Samuel	R
Swanner	Olin	J	Walsh	Everett	L
Swart	Henry		Warner	Charles	O
Swindle	Benjamin	T	Warnock	Roy	S
Sylvain	Fernand	R	Warren	Richard	H
Sylvester, Jr.	Thomas		WasDyke	James	F
Tardio	Frank	J	Wasylecki	Joseph	W
Taylor	Edmund	S	Watkins, Jr.	Clark	E
Taylor	George	M	Watson	Albert	P
Taylor	Herbert	F	Watson	Emory	O
Taylor	Robert	J	Watts	Preston	L
Taylor	William	E	Webster	William	J
Teague	Morris	M	Weinzettel	Roy	J
Thibodeaux	Joe	E	Weissler	Benjamin	
Thoman	Charles	H	Wenzle	Charles	L
Thompson	Evan	J	Werts	Alvin	J
Thompson	Richard	L	Westerman	Frank	C
Thompson	Richard	N	Whited	Murel	C
Thompson	Thomas	H	Whitt	Franzier	
Thompson	Clyde	C	Wiggins	Odell	E
Tiggelaar	Samuel		Wigington	John	H
Tilford	Walter	B	Wilkerson	Edward	N
Tillman	Joseph	H	Wilkins	James	F
Tipton	Douglas	S	William	Ernest	M
Tomasewski	Edward	J	William	Howard	L
Tornecal	John		Williams	Malcom	J
Toomey	Martin	P	Wilson	Earland	F
Torche	Charles	B	Wilson	James	L
Traufler	Donald	A	Wilsoxen	James	P
Travers	Francis	J	Wing	Donald	L
Travers	Urban	W	Winsor	Ralph	S
Treworgy	William	S	Woloch	John	
Turner	Robert	E	Wood	Chester	L
Tuthill	H	L	Wood	William	A
Varga	Louis		Woodbury	Frederick	A E
Vaughn	Aubry	D	Woundy	George	T
Veenstra	Albert	W	Wright	George	L
Veneziano	Carmen	N	Wright	Syil	
Vetcher	Peter	A	Wynegar	John	W
Vieths	Willard	D	Yandell	Ray	C
Villedrrun	Edward	C	Yarlett	Joseph	C
Villereal	Jesus		Yates	Silas	I
Vitto	Daniel	J	Young	James	C

Zaccardi	Domenico		Zidel	Louis	J
Zaffino	Louis		Ziola	Frank	A
Zamora	Joe	E	Zisk	Charles	
Zanta	George	J			

FOURTH RANGER INFANTRY BATTALION

Last Name	First Name	Initial	Last Name	First Name	Initial
Aadland	Orville		Bartnikowski	Stanley	P
Aasve	Kermit	E	Barton	Joseph	H
Adams	John	P	Bartow	Clifford	H
Adkins	Lewis	E	Bates	Thomas	B
Adock	Range	J	Baun	Charles	W
Aeschback	Fred		Bayles	James	C
Agy	George	W	Bean	Robert	J
Albert	Elliott		Beard	Joe	W
Aldridge	Lindell		Beck	Howard	E
Allen	Gunesindo	A	Bednarek	Albin	J
Allgood	William	S	Bell	Thomas	
Allum	Albert	M	Benardo	Armand	
Alsup	James	K	Bennett	Richard	J
Altieri	James	J	Benson	Alen	W
Anderson	Ernest	N	Berkholz	James	A
Anderson	William	H	Bernier	Honorius	A
Andrew	Howard	W	Bertelsmeyer	Joseph	J
Antonucci	Ciro		Bertera	Mario	
Aponik	Edmund	J	Bethell	Paul	E
Arbergast	Paul	S	Bevan	Robert	M
Armbuster	George	E	Bigl	John	A
Ashton	Robert	E	Biglow	Donald	L
Auger	Ullyes		Billes	Robert	H
Avery	Stewart	W	Billiard	Lyle	A
Bacus	Edwin	W	Billingsley	Maurice	E
Bailey	Cecil	R	Birgman	Joseh	H
Bailey	Emmitt	J	Bishop	William	H
Bair, Jr.	Meral		Bivins	Merton	
Baker	Clarence		Black	Edmund	
Baker	Jay	L	Blade	Roy	E
Balcom	Charles	I	Bladsoe	Robert	
Barnes	Russell	W	Blake	Fred	E
Baron	Raymond	J	Blanton	Boyd	L
Barrigan	Lenard		Blassingame	Earl	C
Barry	John	M	Blodgett	Howard	A
Bartley	Charles	L	Blum	Edward	
Bartnikowski	Richard		Bolson	Marvin	H

Bonkowski	Frank	J	Butterworth	Dewey	F
Bordash	Andra	A	Butts	Theodore	Q
Bordenwich	John	P	Buxton, Jr.	Linwood	T
Boschet	Lloyd	V	Byrd	Donald	D
Bostwich	Chester	C	Caddy	John	R
Botts	Charles	E	Caffrey	Francis	W
Boucher	Joseph	P	Cain	Joseph	J
Boudreau	Burton		Calardo	Joseph	
Bowman	Edward	R	Calhan	John	A
Brackens	William	A	Calhoun	Edward	T
Bradford	Rafford	F	Calkins	Cyril	J
Brady	Gerald		Callayon	Barton	
Brady	Michael	H	Callis	George	L
Branson	William	A	Calvey	Herbert	W
Bray	Hoyt	V	Cann	William	G
Brazier	Olice	C	Card	Earl	E
Break	Robert	W	Cardwell	Cary	L
Breazier	Alfred	J	Carel	Robert	G
Brensinger	John	F	Carfield	Richard	H
Brigati	George	J	Carley	Leroy	A
Briggs	Harold	D	Carney	William	S
Bright	Ollie	V	Carpenter	Harold	
Brown	Charlie	A	Carr	William	K
Brown	Clyde	U	Carres	John	
Brown	George	D	Carroll	John	J
Brown	Paul	G	Carter	Ernest	A
Brown	Vester		Carter	Floyd	D
Brown	William	H	Carter	William	
Brown	William	S	Cary	Franklin	K
Bruce	Lonzo		Case, Jr.	Lewis	B
Brunn	Mervyn		Cashen	Louis	R
Bruno	Dominick	A	Caskey	Walter	F
Bryan	Robert	L	Catthon	Vergil	A
Buchanan	Dayton		Cauti	Camillo	
Buchanon	Carol	E	Chase	Harland	C
Buck	Paul	H	Cheramie	Edward	
Buff	Lloyd	H	Chester	Robert	T
Bunn	Radie	H	Christensen	Alfred	E
Burdick	Paul	W	Christy	William	R
Burke	Parris		Chromezak	Joseph	A
Burwell	George	L	Cioch	Alvin	A
Bush	Samuel	B	Clark	David	F
Bush	Stanley		Clark	Walter	I
Bush	William		Clarke	Joseph	L
Busha	Robert	L	Cleaver	Harold	J
Buss	LeRoy	L	Cleseland	Thomas	

Hamilton	William	S	Huckabey	Leonard	B
Hammer	Milton		Hudelt	Kenneth	H
Hanson	Albert	H	Hudson	Allen	L
Hanson	Tage		Hugh	Daniel	P
Hardenbrook	Richard	G	Hughes	Kevin	F
Hardman	Marion	D	Hughes	Russell	
Hardy	Edward	W	Hutchinson	Walter	H
Harger	Edwin	S	Idol	Billy	R
Harman	Richard	D	Ingram	Ralph	S
Harman	William	G	Jabs	Raymond	B
Harr	Gerald	J	Jackson	Glen	E
Harris	Edward	G	Jalbert	Conrad	J
Harris	Randall		Jameson	William	A
Harrison	Elby		Jantz	Ervin	
Harshaw	Robert	E	Jech	Randolph	L
Haverlick	Steve		Johnson	Charles	M
Hawkins	George		Johnson	Elwood	E
Hayes	Jack	C	Johnson	Howard	W
Hayward	Wendell	A	Johnson	Robert	O
Heinz	Louis	J	Johnson	Robert	W
Helnick	John	W	Johnson	Roy	E
Henselman	Chester	K	Johnson	Willie	P
Hepher	William	R	Johnston	Thomas	W
Hertel	Richard	J	Jolliff	Leo	E
Hicks	Amos	R	Jones	Claude	S
Higgins	John	J	Jones	Kenneth	R
Hildebrant	James	J	Jones	Lorin	W
Hill	John	H	Jones	Thomas	E
Hill	L		Kandziorski	Harry	A
Hintz	John	J	Katzenberger	Harold	J
Hix	Robert	H	Kautz, Jr.	Frank	A
Hobday	Charles	W	Keech	Raymond	P
Hoffmann	George	C	Keeler	Lester	C
Hofmeister	William		Kelly	Kenneth	W
Hogue	Charles	M	Kempson	R	P
Holey	Norman	E	Kennedy	Harold	L
Holt	William	C	Kennedy	Winfred	W
Honig	Richard	P	Kenny	James	P
Hood	Carl	R	Kerber	Leo	D
Hooker	Dean	W	Kersteter	Alfred	H
Hooker	John	F	Kidwell	Averiel	E
Horvat	Joseph		Kies	Paul	E
Houd	Charles		Kight	Calvin	D
House	Raymond	W	Kimbro	Charles	R
Houston	William		Kimmball	Rollins	
Howard	John		King	Thomas	J

Kingsley	Anderson	B	Leighton	William	H
Kingston, Jr.	Arthur	J	Leitschuh	Joseph	F
Kinzler	Earl	F	Lella	Antonio	S
Kipetzhny	Stanley	R	LePresto	Victor	R
Kirby	Richard	W	Levan	Walton	G
Kirk	Leonard	C	Lewis	Carl	
Kitzhell	James	E	Lewis	Henry	O
Klein	Arthur	E	Lewis	Thomas	G
Klim	George		Lindell	John	C
Kline	Jack	D	Lines	William	D
Kness	Lester	E	Lodge	Vernon	W
Kness	Marvin	E	Logan	William	
Knox	Billy	M	Loman	Robert	B
Knox	Louis	R	Long	George	W
Kocen	John	J	Long	James	L
Kolodziey	Walter	E	Long	Patrick	J
Komiski	Paul	M	Low	Austin	
Kopp	William	G	Lowry	William	W
Kopveiler	Eugene	N	Lucas, Jr.	Harvey	D
Kosciuszko	John		Lumnah	Oscar	E
Kozakiewicz	Stanley		Lunsford	Francis	G
Krajnik	Paul		Luzzi	Joseph	M
Kravitz	Martin		Lynch	Joseph	D
Kulas	Frank	J	Mabry	Emery	G
Kupczyk, Jr.	Joseph		Macin	Robert	R
Kutinski	Ralph	B	MacLacklan	James	
Kutnock	William	E	Macudcinski	Walter	
Kwiatkowski	Julius	G	Maddock	Richard	A
LaBarbara	Joseph	M	Malone	John	J
LaBonte	Remeo	A	Maloney	Ralph	A
Lafave	Maurice	F	Manderson	Jesse	
Lamandre	Dominic		Manska	Jack	
Lambert	Doniel	E	Marchiona	Vincent	
Lambert	John	C	Marchorio	Mario	
Lambert	Walter	E	Margolis	Reuben	
Langley	Edward	A	Marino	Frank	
Laramore	Edward	T	Marks	L	W
LaRoque	David	E	Markson	Jordan	Q
Lasarski	Egnacy	J	Marshall	Edward	
Lavin	James	J	Martin	Edwin	I
Leech	Charles	W	Martin	Grant	
Leefer	Robert	M	Marty	Joseph	M
Legas	John	L	Mascarenas	Isaias	
LeGrand	Albert	E	Massey	Asa	J
Lehman	Guenther	L	Matney	Johnnie	W
Lehman	Joseph	C	Matta	Thomas	A

Mauro	George	J	Mitchell	John	H
McBride	Kenneth	G	Mitrick	Stephen	G
McBride	Victor	H	Mixon	Joeque	
McCalligan	Edwin	T	Monash	Harold	
McCarthy	John	C	Moore	George	M
McCauley	Robert		Morris	Earl	C
McClain	Henry	P	Morris	Francis	J
McClennon	Earl	R	Morris	Fred	
McCreery	Paul	G	Morrison	Clifton	W
McCuniff	Francis	E	Morton	John	F
McCurdy	Fay		Moyer	George	R
McDevitt, Jr.	John	P	Moyer	Howard	G
McDevitt	Francis	J	Moyer	Wilber	M
McDugley	Daryll		Mulling	Julian	L
McGuigan	George	H	Munro	Finley	
McHugh	Robert	R	Muro	Michael	C
McKiernan	Leonard	J	Murphy	William	E
McNary	Phil	G	Murray, Jr.	Roy	A
McNeeley	Kenneth	A	Muth	William	L
McNulty	Francis		Nagle	Clifford	
McNutt	William	E	Nagle	William	S
McTeague	Charles	P	Neal	Robert	W
McVay	Harold		Nelson	Lewis	L
McVay	James	O	Nelson	Robert	L
Mead	William	A	Nelson	William	L
Medoires	Bernard		Nero	Verny	D
Merrill	Allen	E	Newman	Thomas	E
Metzgar	Raymond	J	Nicola	Herbert	L
Metzger	James	R	Nix	Jack	
Meunier	Gerald	R	Nochta	John	W
Meyer	Albert	L	Northrup	Lawrence	E
Mezza	Ernest		Novak	John	F
Mickelson	Arthur	H	Nunnally	George	B
Mikula	Albert	A	Nutt	Robert	W
Miley	Eugene	D	Nye	Walter	F
Miller, Jr.	Bert		O'Neil	James	F
Miller, Jr.	George	R	Oaks	George	R
Miller	Earl	I	Ocheske	William	G
Miller	Earnest	L	Odds	Gordon	R
Miller	Henry	F	Ohman	Richard	M
Miller	Junio	F	Oleiniczak	Arthur	
Miller	Robert	H	Olsen	Jorman	A
Millner	Gerard	J	Olsen	Len	
Minor	Allen	D	Oroszko, Jr.	Joseph	
Mirabella	Louis	A	Orzexhowski	Theodore	S
Mitchell	Eddie	T	Ott	Arthur	E

Ott	Charles	R	Rambis	Mitchell	J
Owens	Chester	H	Raponi	Dante	A
Owens	Robert	A	Rappi	Joseph	P
Paden	Saturina		Ratliff	Roy	
Padgett	Donald	L	Rayl	James	C
Palmer	Thomas	J	Reasland	Joseph	C
Panzarino	Vito	M	Reece	J	A
Patenaude	Eugene	F	Reed	Frank	A
Patterson	Francis	B	Reeves	Limuel	L
Patterson	Roger	L	Reilly	Charles	
Paxton	Raymond		Renecker	Ross	C
Peak	David	W	Rensink	Gerrit	J
Pearce	Richard	R	Revin	Bill	E
Peceora	Dominic	A	Rew	Donald	B
Peet	John	P	Richard	Jude	J
Perry	Leon	F	Richards	Lloyd	D
Perry	Paul	E	Richie	Lawrence	E
Peters	George	A	Richmond	Edward	C
Phillips	Thomas		Ridgeley	Lawrence	I
Phipin	Mike		Ridgely	Frederick	O
Phoenix	Maurice	R	Riley	Bernard	T
Pierce	Ira		Rinsmith	Herold	E
Pierce	James	W	Riopel	Raymond	
Pierce	Joseph	E	Ritter	Edwin	L
Plemmons	Clarence	T	Ritzert	William	E
Polich	Joseph		Rivas	Joe	
Pollard	Floyd	C	Rivera	Michael	E
Pollock	Paul	J	Rizzo	Joseph	S
Polumbo, Jr.	John	J	Roberson	Refford	
Polus	Mathew		Roberts	James	C
Popovich	Joseph	B	Robey	Charles	D
Porter	Richard	W	Robinson	LeRoy	
Powell	Hubbard	C	Robinson	Robert	B
Poznecki	Howard	C	Robinson	Thomas	M
Pratt	Harold	J	Rodriquez	Raymond	
Preuitt	Lloyd		Rollinsq	Robert	L
Prine	Frank	P	Rosak	Michael	
Pruitt	Charles	R	Rosenberg	Alex	L
Prussia	Charles	J	Ross	Carl	E
Pryor	James	A	Rothacher	Oscar	
Puccio	Charles	T	Rounsville	Donald	K
Purvis	Ray	E	Ruark	Walter	D
Puskar	Edward	J	Running	William	D
Rabchinsky	Stanley		Rushatz	Steve	J
Rac	Frankie	J	Ryan	Thomas	L
Rada	Anthony		Salinas, Jr.	Lee	

Saltman	Robert	W	Siracusa	Anthony	
Sampsell	Robert	L	Sirkin	Louis	J
Sanders	Albert		Sittler	Alfred	
Sanders	Owen	B	Skaggs	Robert	H
Sarb	Wiliam	E	Skidmore	Howard	S
Sarver	Dana	E	Sly	Ernest	D
Saylor	Benjamin	E	Smiley	Archie	F
Schank, Jr.	William	A	Smith	Charles	J
Schronce	Richard	P	Smith	Clinton	
Schwager	Owen		Smith	Donald	H
Schwantes	Don	L	Smith	Edward	C
Sciola	Archillio	A	Smith	Harold	J
Scott	Earl	J	Smith	Henry	D
Scott	John		Smith	Henry	O
Scully	Richard	F	Smith	Richard	P
Seaver	John	C	Smith	Russell	E
Sellers	Dick		Sniffin	Maurice	A
Sewalish	Nick		Snow	Arnold	F
Sewell	Guy	L	Snowden	Shelby	
Shabatka	Joseph	A	Snyder	Charles	W
Shabeck	Stephen	A	Snyder	William	H
Shadle	Wilbert	I	Socci	Mike	
Sharp	David	B	Somuk	John	A
Shaw	Joseph	J	Sowards	Henry	E
Shawoll	William	F	Sramkoski	Leo	F
Shealy	Robert	N	Stabler	Hollis	D
Shields	Berlin	G	Stapleton	James	
Shippey	Zane	G	Steele	Frank	H
Shives	Otis	E	Steppe	Paul	
Shoefler	Robert	R	Stewart	Bryan	T
Shoehl	John	W	Stewart	Estel	
Shor	Norman	N	Stewart	Paul	M
Shows	Arthur	H	Stitt	Hugh	
Shrewsberry	Archie	D	Stojake	Andrew	J
Shults	Donald		Stokes	Oliver	W
Shultz	William	A	Stone	John	W
Shur	Harry	H	Stornello	Dominic	
Shurmak	Sylvester		Strange	Lewis	
Sieg	Walter	R	Straub, Jr.	Henry	J
Sienkowski	Walter	A	Stroup	Forrest	E
Silverstein	Isaac		Stulhman	Fred	F
Simmons	John	M	Sugrue	John	E
Simmons	Perry	J	Sullivan	Roger	J
Simmons	Wayne		Sullivan	William	E
Simpson	James	V	Summerix	James	I
Sims	Paul	R	Swank	Marcell	G

Swankie	Thomas	C	VanArtsdalen	Donald	
Sweazy	Owen	E	Vance	Junior	
Swiderski	John	E	Vandergrift, Jr.	Philip	R
Swiker	Harold	B	Vasqueze	Leonard	B
Szczesniak	Steven		Vaughn	Edward	L
Szczurek	Anthony	J	Vickers	Charles	E
Szlavik	Adam		Vieira	Edmound	T
Tabor	Jack		Villebunn	Edwin	C
Tasso	Anthony	F	Volkman	Erwin	L
Taylor	Clare	H	Volman	William	
Taylor	Orin	E	Vosika	John	J
Taylor	Willise		Voytovich	Carl	
Teela	Robert	A	Vucinovich	Emmitt	L
Templin	Thomas	M	Wachowicz	Julian	J
Texter	Calvin		Wacstarf	Talmage	W
Thiel	Frank	N	Wagner	Eugene	C
Thompson	Charles	S	Wagner	Ralph	E
Thompson	Clarence	N	Walczak	Albin	A
Thompson	Edger	L	Walkanis	Anthony	
Thompson	Edwin	C	Walker	Charles	
Thompson	Lum	J	Walker	Ralph	
Thompson	Norman		Wall	Edward	J
Thompson	Richard	N	Wallace	Clay	J
Thompson	Robert		Wallis	Vernon	W
Thorn	Richard	O	Wallsmith	Clotis	R
Tillman	Joseph	H	Walters	Fredrick	
Timmons	Robert	E	Walton	Harold	B
Todd	Michael	W	Warekois	Eugene	A
Todro	Stanley		Warhatch	Walter	
Tomory	Andrew		Warren, Jr.	L	A
Tongate	Kenneth		Warren	Buford	O
Tornehy	Samuel	C	Watson	John	O
Treumer	Clarence		Watson	John	R
Trimblie	Dominic		Watts	Benjamin	
Trowbridge	Warfield		Wayryhen	Wayne	M
Trujillo	Bernie	R	Weaver	Tommy	F
Turner	Quitman	H	Webb	Warren	A
Tursins	Bruno	A	Webster	Roy	M
Tuttle	Vernon	L	Welsh	William	J
Twigg	Roger	M	Wentworth	Philip	A
Twilley	Jack		Wenzel	Raymond	
Ulatowski	Raymond		Wesman	Lawrence	
Upton	Albert		Whalen	Raymond	F
Upton	Alfred	J	White	Albert	M
Urbealis	Ralph	W	Whitten	Amel	L
Ustupski	George	J	Wihbey	Joseph	A

Last Name	First Name	Initial
Wilhelm	John	D
Wilkerson	Kimbrell	M
Williams, Jr.	Melcombe	J
Williams	Glen	A
Williams	Joe	
Williams	Joe	O
Williams	Riley	N
Williams	Robert	M
Williams	Thomas	L
Williams	Thomas	R
Williams	William	H
Williamson	Vincent	R
Willking	Robert	G
Willman	Joseph	L
Wilson	Charles	R
Wiltzenski	Henry	J
Winchell	Richard	W
Winchester	Everett	
Winewica	Albert	J
Winkompleck	Robert	W
Winner	Edward	N
Wipperman	William	H
Wisher	Bernard	A
Witmer	Eugene	J
Wojciak	Bernard	F
Wolf	Edward	J
Wood	James	G
Woodcock	Johnathon	
Woodhall	John	B
Wright	John	R
Yanishak	Nicholas	
Yeager	Henry	S
Yoder	William	H
Young	William	S
Yuyyle	Vernon	L
Zaffino	Louis	
Zaslaw	Stanford	G
Zidell	Louis	J
Zielinski	Herman	A
Ziemann	Donald	L
Ziola	Frank	A
Zitrin	Sidney	I

FIFTH RANGER INFANTRY BATTALION

Last Name	First Name	Initial	Last Name	First Name	Initial
Abraham	Edward	N	Antrim	Lawrence	S
Adams	Ralph	C	Antwine	John	
Adams	Warren	M	Archie	Samuel	D
Adams	Thomas	W	Arnett	Willis	L
Addy	Elmer	L	Askin	Stanley	L
Adkins	John	F	Augustyn	Edward	H
Adkins	Thomas	J	Aust	Richard	H
Akers, Jr.	Bernard	C	Austin	Arthur	R
Akin, Jr.	James	H	Backus	Wilbur	H
Aksten	Frank	M	Bactis	Edward	C
Alday	Hewy		Baggett	George	F
Alexander	Harold	L	Baker	Elmer	P
Allred	Bennie	L	Baker	Jerre	A
Amador	John	P	Baker	Charles	M
Andersen	Philipp	C	Baker	Hubert	A
Anderson	Richard	A	Baker	Nolan	D
Anderson	Dee	C	Baker	Clark	L
Anderson	Leohard	O	Bakos	Paul	A
Angement	Thomas	A	Baktis	Edward	C

Baldwin, Jr.	Leon	B	Blunt, Jr.	Thomas	R
Ballard	Eula	C	Boggs	Lawrencw	R
Banks, Jr.	Louis		Bojara	Stanlay	B
Banning	Elmo	E	Bojok	Albert	J
Barber	Alexander	W	Boles	George	W
Barriault	Richard	H	Bolinger	Richard	F
Barrows	Richard	H	Bolinger	Paul	M
Barry	Gerald	T	Bolmer	Charles	W
Bartkiewiez	Edward	T	Bolton	Harry	I
Bartlet	William	B	Borek	Roger	B
Bartlett, Jr.	Frank	R	Boudreaux	Dalton	L
Bartling	Howard	J	Boutilier	Howard	L
Barton	Harold	E	Boutin	Adelore	R
Bateman	William	T	Bowden	Thomas	
Bates, Jr.	Harold	J	Bowen	Zach	W
Battice	Robert	D	Bowen	Howard	C
Bazley	Lawrence	F	Bowser	Macey	
Beas	David	W	Boyd	William	E
Beattie, Jr.	Edward	P	Boyer, Jr.	Ralph	C
Beccuc	Galc	B	Boyington	Archie	A
Beck	Stephen	J	Brable	Joseph	F
Bellacome	Angelo		Bradford	Stewart	F
Bellis	Edward	F	Brady	Robert	W
Bellows	John	P	Brakhage	Rement	W
Bender	James	B	Braswell	Loren	D
Bendix	Richard	E	Brehm	Charles	F
Benevides	Joseph	M	Brennan	William	A
Bennett	Garett		Bridger	Ernest	S
Berger	George	G	Bridges	Robert	A
Berger	Stanley	P	Brinkman	Victor	
Bergstrom	Lloyd	V	Briscoe	Lawrence	L
Berkowitz	Bernard		Brisendine	Noah	L
Berry	Oscar	L	Brown	Lee	
Biava	Louis	A	Bruens	Weston	L
Bickford	Ralph	A	Brunelle	Rene	R
Biddle	Clyde	H	Bryant	Thomas	E
Bidwell	John	L	Bryne, Jr.	William	P
Bishop	Earl	E	Bugnacki	Jerome	V
Bixler	Johnnie	E	Bunker	Malcolm	L
Black	William	C	Burek	Zigmund	A
Black	Henry	R	Burgeen	James	R
Blair	William	V	Burke	John	L
Blakemore	Wallace	B	Burns	Edward	J
Blandford	Herbert	L	Burns	Emerson	A
Blauser	Joseph	L	Burns	James	T
Blowers	Adrian	M	Burns	Robert	P

Bursch	Floyd	A	Clopton	Lacy	W
Bush	Mack	E	Cloud	Robert	S
Butler	Edmund	J	Cohen	Martin	O
Butler	Warren	G	Colbath	Joh	E
Butrico	Nicholas	F	Cole	Robert	E
Butterfield, Jr.	Victor	J	Coleman	Max	D
Button	LeRoy	T	Comstock	Gardner	T
Caiati	Frank	A	Conboy, Jr.	Peter	J
Cail	John	E	Cone, Jr.	Melvin	M
Cain	Weyma	T	Confer	Robert	F
Cala	Joseph	J	Connelly	Thomas	D
Calabresi	Zordo	J	Constable	Grant	W
Calonti	Carmine	J	Cook	James	A
Campbell	William	H	Cooley	Vincent	W
Campbell	Douglas	C	Copeland	James	R
Campos	Joseph		Corbett	Ernest	T
Caraber	Andrew	J	Cordell	Marshall	T
Carawan	James	C	Cordes	Henry	J
Cardinali	Peter	L	Cotten	James	E
Caroll	Edmund	L	Coughlin	Francis	T
Carpenter	Earl	A	Cox	Alfred	T
Carroll	Arthur	J	Cox	Loy	L
Carter	Owen	H	Cox	James	R
Carter	Stanley	C	Craig	Thomas	F
Carter	Joe	D	Craig	Henry	
Carter	Roy	E	Crandell, Jr.	Moses	H
Caswell	Ales	E	Crawford	Edgar	R
Catron	William		Creason	William	E
Ceccanti	Albert	C	Creque	Charlie	E
Cesaretti	Edward	R	Crisafi	Frederick	F
Chance	Donald	L	Crouchman	Lavern	A
Charboneau	Carl	R	Crowder	Isaac	D
Chauncey	George	E	Crowley	John	F
Chavis	Aubrey	E	Crusing	William	F
Chiatello	George	F	Cunnally	Robert	J
Chin	Ying	S	Cunningham	Wayne	E
Ching	Randell		Curley	William	P
Christian	James	D	Curran	George	
Ciarmello	Frank		Daly	Timothy	C
Cioffi	Joseph	L	Damerau	James	B
Clarey	John	C	Darnell	Richard	L
Clark	George	E	Davis	Robert	P
Clawson	David	L	Davis	John	L
Clemento	John	A	Davis	Harry	
Clements	Gus	A	Davis	Powell	R
Cliff	Albert	O	Davis	William	F

Davis, Jr.	Everet	B	Edwards	Novis	C
Dawson	Francis	W	Eichner	John	T
Dean	Minor	C	Eilenberger	Mose	
Deck	Henry	C	Ekern	Howard	D
DeClue	Harold	J	Ellis	Carl	O
Dees	Dewey	C	Ellis	David	W
Dellinger	Hugh	A	Ensley	Glover	C
Dendy	Rayford	E	Epstein	Herbert	
Derby	Hugh	C	Erickson	Roy	
Derone	Joseph		Everett, Jr.	Davis	B
Detlefsen	Vern	L	Farley, Jr.	Daniel	D
DeTore	Roger	F	Farmer	Ray	
Deuvall	James	A	Farrell	Clyde	T
Devlin	Thomas	G	Fast	Victor	H
Dickman	Edward	W	Feagan	Raymond	D
Diehl	Ralph	R	Feather	Ralph	P
Dieterich	William	T	Fejes	Joseph	B
DiFilippo	Frank	J	Felix	Richard	
DiMarsico	Frank	F	Feltenberger	Francis	L
Dobeck	Henry	J	Fennhahn	William	P
Dorman	Elwood	L	Fereday	Charles	A
Dorsey	James	E	Ferrara	Patrick	J
Douglas	Paul	C	Fessler	Charles	E
Douglas	William	H	Feuerstein	Leonard	
Douglas	Robert		Fewell	Wiliam	H
Dowd	Theodore		Fields	Guy	E
Doyle	Morris	V	Fillingame	Charles	L
Drodwill	Joseph	J	Filmer	Thomas	X
Drozdowski	Edward	F	Filson	Clifford	C
Drumheller	Clarence	E	Fineran	George	T
Dufour	Francis	D	Fioretti	Joseph	
Duggar	Harold	D	Fishman	Edward	
Dukat	Chester	J	Fitzgerald	James	V
Duncan	James	H	Flaherty	John	P
Dunegan	Francis	E	Floyd	Clifford	L
Dunfee	Robert	E	Fogel	Clinton	L
Dunham	Harry	R	Folsom	Leroi	A
Dunkle	Harry	J	Fontana	Sebastian	L
Dunlap	Harold	E	Ford	Henry	M
Dutcher	Donald	H	Forrest, Jr.	Bruce	L
Dwyer	Thomas	M	Forrey	Donald	C
Eaton	Edwin	H	Forte	John	T
Eaton	Richard	F	Foster	Paul	J
Eck	William		Fowler	Robert	J
Edison	Alonzo	F	Fox	William	J
Edmonds	Leonard	L	Franks	Jack	T

Frazier	Joe	R	Gray	Roland	D
Frazier	Herman	E	Gray	Cecil	E
Freites	Frank	J	Greene, Jr.	James	F
Frink	Eugene	F	Greenwalt	Richard	D
Fruhn	Herman		Gregory	Matthew	
Futrell	Jack	C	Grenda	Bernard	A
Gabaree	James	W	Griffin	James	F
Gallaher	Wilburn	S	Grigsby	Harry	L
Garcia	Rudolph	A	Grimsley	Jack	N
Gardner	William	M	Griswold	Carl	K
Gardner	Clayton	E	Grondalski	Wladislaw	J
Gardner	Howard	T	Grove	George	N
Gardner, Jr.	Dean		Grubanowitch	Martin	R
Garfield	Jerome	J	Guentner	Richard	J
Garland	Albert	J	Gunnoe	Pierre	D
Garrison	Paul	R	Guthartz	Harry	
Garten	Emmett	L	Gwiazdowski	Leon	
Garvik	John		Hagen	Marlyn	W
Gates	Orval	D	Haggard	Paul	D
Gawler	John	M	Haight	Lewis	J
Gentry	Charles	E	Haines	Howard	E
George	Donald	L	Halacy, Jr.	Thomas	E
George, Jr.	Roy	E	Hale	Clarence	G
Germain	Irvin	L	Haley	Francis	G
Gezymalla	Sylvester		Haley	George	R
Gibbons	John	B	Hall	Harry	C
Gilbert	John	R	Hamilton	Ozley	K
Gill	Stanley	A	Hamrick	Verne	J
Gillem	Delmus	J	Hancock	Darrell	M
Gilley	Raymond	J	Handschin	Warren	H
Gillson	Howard	A	Haniebnik	Stanley	M
Gilmore	Richard	J	Haniebnik	Stanley	M
Gipson	Albert	P	Hanlon	Richard	J
Glassman	Henry	S	Hanny	Winfield	F
Gleason	William	E	Harbin	Darwin	D
Goforth	Clifford	S	Hare	Robert	R
Goldacker	Robert	M	Harman	Francis	R
Goldstein	Sherman	J	Harms	Donald	J
Gombosi	Louis	J	Harper	Paul	A
Goodwin	Robert	S	Harrington	Packard	K
Gordon, Jr.	James	S	Harrington	Charles	L
Gorzynski	Robert	W	Harris	Franklin	M
Grandchamp	Gilbert	O	Harris	Donald	E
Gratwohl, Jr.	Henry	L	Harrison	Ruben	W
Graves	Raymond	C	Harshbarger	Paul	E
Graves, Jr.	James	W	Hart	Henry	C

Hart	William	H	Hoover	Bill	G
Hartzell	William	M	Houghton	Cecil	E
Harvey	John	R	Howard	Robert	J
Harvey	William		Hoyt	Harry	R
Harward	Alton	L	Hruzdowski	Daniel	P
Hasselback	Harold	L	Hudson	Neal	E
Hathaway, Jr.	Richard	N	Huebner	Edward	W
Haugh	Darrell	D	Huereque	Rudolph	S
Haun	Charles	L	Huff	William	H
Haun	Raymond	H	Huffman	Paul	T
Haus	Anthony	P	Hughey	Rollie	L
Hayhurst	Leonard	L	Hunter	Kenneth	W
Hayslip	Cecil	M	Hurd	Windle	W
Healy	Francis	J	Huther	Theodore	W
Heatley	Robert	L	Hutnick	Joseph	
Hedrick	Richard	H	Hyman	Needham	I
Heffelfinger	Hugo	W	Ignatowicz	Joseph	W
Heflin	Jack	E	Ingalls	Wilbur	L
Heinz	Melvin	C	Ingham	Donald	E
Helfrich	Harold	A	Ingram	Jesse	L
Henderson	Lewis	H	Irvine	Joe	S
Hendricks	Francis	J	Ivey	Robert	C
Hensell	William	H	Jackson	James	V
Herder	Harry	J	Jackson	James	L
Herlihy	Rayond	M	Jagosh	John	
Herrero	Henry	P	Jakubowski	Stanley	T
Herring	Thomas	F	James	William	H
Hershkoff	Abrahm	L	Jarrell	Edward	R
Hiffner	Keith	E	Jeanes	John	D
Hildreth, Jr.	Lester	R	Jeffers	Christopher	
Hill	Johnnie	M	Jeffires	Jack	W
Hilsman	Joe	H	Jenner	William	H
Hinkle	Robert	F	Jensen	Lawrence	A
Hinson	Forrest	G	Johns	Herman	W
Hirth	Charles		Johnson	Jessic	W
Hite	Paul		Johnson	Denzil	R
Hobbs	George	T	Johnson	Willie	
Hodges	Arthur	J	Johnson	Wilbur	H
Hodgson	John	C	Johnston	Richard	H
Hoffmann	Thomas	V	Jones	R	D
Hohman	Paul	W	Jones	Harole	W
Holbrook	Jay	C	Jones	Carl	
Holder	James	E	Jones	Chester	C
Holloway	Eugene		Jones	James	W
Holmes	Rawlin	G	Jordan	Leon	L
Hoopes	Norman	E	Justus	William	G

Kachursky	Ernest	J	Kramlich, Jr.	Samuel	E
Kalar	William	R	Kreider	Aldus	P
Kaln	Chester	M	Kreitzer, Jr.	William	C
Kanatzer	Richard	L	Krumenacker	Edward	C
Kane	William	L	Kubie	Robert	H
Kapteyn	James	A	Kus	Emil	J
Karl	Louis	A	Kuzelka	Francis	J
Karla	Robert	G	Labhart	Hoesli	F
Kaufman	Ezra	A	Laboda	Bernard	J
Kaval	Stanley	W	Lacy	Joseph	R
Kay	George	A	Lake	Leroy	P
Keeble	George	J	Lake, Sr.	Kenneth	L
Keefe	Georg	L	Lambert	Lawrence	D
Kegley	Earl	T	Lamons	Jack	E
Keiber	Albert	G	LaMont	Frank	E
Keiser, Jr.	John	A	Landers	Lonnie	H
Kennedy	Joseph	A	Lanham	Thomas	E
Kepperling	Rene	G	Lantz	James	C
Keylor	Hildreth		Larson	William	E
Kidwell	James	E	Larson	Robert	B
Kiernan	John	D	Larson	Verl	K
Kijanka	Stanley	J	Laskowski	Andrew	L
Killion	William	J	Laughlin	Harry	D
Kimball	Ashley	R	Lavoie	Leonard	D
Kimbell	Oscar	L	Lawhon	Odis	L
Kimble	Melvin	H	Lawrence	Charles	A
King	Harold	L	Lawton	George	C
King	Harold	R	Le Blanc	Arthur	L
King	Norman	W	Lee	Earl	H
King	Gregor	W	Lemnitzer	Richard	C
Kinne	Milton	F	Lemon	Charles	C
Kinney	George	E	Lemons	Edwin	L
Kiser	Hubert	L	Lemperis	Harry	G
Klein	Charles	F	Lenell	Nils	H
Klett	Henry	M	Lenz	Robert	A
Kluesner	Edward	L	Lesko	Milan	
Knajdek	Raymond	G	Levers	Richard	C
Knew	Estle	W	Levesque	Joseph	W
Knight	Elwood		Levesque	Joseph	W
Knollenberg	Quentin	L	Levi	Walter	
Knox	Arthur	R	Lewis	Raymond	
Knutson	Emmet	E	Lewis	Harold	A
Koebbe	Ellsworth	L	Lewis	Ivan	G
Koon	Eddie	A	Lex	Ludwig	R
Koszlowski	Edward	P	Liebherr	Robert	J
Krakowski	Frank	E	Lineburg	Lous	F

Litrenta	Thomas		Mathias	John	R
Livingston	Herbert	D	Matie, Jr.	John	
Lockwood	Frank	E	Matte	John	R
Lodge	Russell	S	Matteson	William	L
Loe	Rex	V	Matthews	Archie	A
Loesch	Simon	A	Matthews	Floyd	E
Logan	Andrew	J	Maxfield	Delmore	A
Loltin	Leon	H	May	Joseph	C
Lombel	Arthur	O	Mazzullo	Michael	
Longpre	Arthur	L	McBee	Cleveland	R
Loschiavo	John	B	McCabe	John	F
Love	Homer	L	McCafferty	Frederick	E
Lowe	Joseph	T	McCauley	Lyle	S
Lucca	Anthony	J	McCausland	William	
Lunsford	Elmer	L	McCluskey	Frank	
Luther	Edward	S	McCool, Jr.	Lloyd	S
Lutick	Paul	J	McCoubrey	Robert	H
Lynch	Virgil		McCullough	Artur	J
Lynn, Jr.	Oliver	V	McDaniel	James	G
Lyons	Olen	L	McDaniel	Richard	A
Lyons	Raymond	C	McDaniel	Veiel	J
Macauley	Donald	M	McDannel	Melvin	I
Madden	Merle	L	McDonald	Howard	A
Madden	Jerry	II	McDonough	Vincent	D
Madore	Lawrence	R	McEleney	Edward	J
Malaney	John	F	McGaughey	Russell	A
Malavolta	Dominick	J	McGee	John	P
Malloy	Paul	F	McGuire	Wilfred	F
Maner	Archie	C	McGuire	Frank	W
Manifold	John	W	McGuire	Ernest	S
Manning	George	E	McGuire	Philiph	E
Manning	Robert	J	McIlwain	Walter	N
Mapes	Edward	I	McKissick	Howard	D
Marissal	Albert	A	McMahon	Lawrence	S
Markham	Patrick	E	McNeal	Glenn	H
Markoff	Howard	D	McPherson	James	W
Markowitz	Joseph	J	McPherson	Gilbert	
Marks	Bernard	F	Meadus	Carl	W
Marks	Robert	E	Mehaffay	Jay	H
Marmo	John	C	Melton	Leamon	S
Marquaz	Jeaquin	E	Melvin, Jr.	Thomas	H
Marshall	Edmund	A	Mercer	James	D
Martell	Richard	P	Merritt	Earl	R
Martin, Jr.	Sandy		Meshew	Wayne	B
Mason	Harold	F	Messuri	Joe	N
Masters	Kenneth	F	Metcalf	Ralph	L

Metcalf	Charles		Munro	Emmerson W
Metcalf, Jr.	Glenn W		Munroe	William E
Meyer	Lawrence E		Murray	William E
Meyers	Maurice L		Muscatello	Anthony F
Miela	Joseph J		Myers	Clair J
Miller	Richard J		Myers	Paul E
Miller	George		Nahass	Tofie J
Miller	Roger R		Nance	Troy L
Miller	Victor J		Nard	Roy F
Miller	Robert T		Nee	Richard J
Million	Harry J		Neighborgall	Roger B
Mills	Gardon E		Nelson	Floyd R
Minor	Stephen W		Nelson	David
Minor, Jr.	Charles F		Nelson	Vernon R
Mischke	Arden V		Nelson	Donald T
Mitchell	Richard F		Nelson	Donold R
Mitchell	Dennis P		Nelson	Emil H
Modjeski	Walter S		Nelson	James A
Molenda	Peter V		Nelson	Raymond G
Monahan	Raphael A		Nenna	John M
Mongeon	Hervey		Neuman	Edward J
Monihan	Earl R		Neumiller	Rinold
Monks, Jr.	George W		Niblach	Jesse M
Monroe	William B		Nicholson	Richard L
Montean	Theodore		Nielsen	Melvin C
Montgomery	Harvey M		Niemeth	Robert J
Mooberry	Morris E		Nixon	Elmer V
Moody	Willie W		Norman	Raymond B
Moore	Alfred E		Nunley	Robert A
Moore	Woodford O		Nutkins	William E
Moore	William L		Nyland	Albert
Morales	Jose H		O'Briant	William M
Moran	Harold F		O'Brien	James P
Morgan	Robert W		O'Brien	John K
Morgan	Carl W		O'Hare	James J
Morris	George L		O'Neil	John P
Morris, Jr.	George C		Oaks	Ernest Y
Morrison	A D		Oberholzer	Cecil M
Morse	Mathew E		Oblander	Fred C
Motos	Melvin D		Oboryshko	Steven
Moughton	Herbert J		Ogrosky	William J
Moyer	Harry L		Olcott	Ray E
Mulligan	William J		Olive	Wallace M
Mullin	Peter V		Olson	Walter W
Munley	John V		Onstott	Carl F
Munoz	Alegrando		Osborne	Perry D

Ovington	Robert		Ploeckelman	Leonard	A
Owen, Jr.	David	E	Podkowka	Edward	L
Owens	Richard	H	Poggie	Philiph	J
Papas	Charles	N	Poland	James	J
Para	Ferdinand		Pollard	Ernest	M
Paramo	Theodore	T	Pollier	Joseph	R
Parker	Charles	H	Polychronopoulos	Pete	
Parn	Orville	E	Popovics	Charles	
Parrot	J	B	Portell	Charles	A
Pascoe	Howard	W	Porter	Richard	J
Paskill	Daniel	G	Posey	Lloyd	F
Pasuk	Nickolas		Potter	Bernard	J
Pavey	Paul	H	Powell	Francis	D
Pavlicek	Eugene	F	Powell	Gordon	R
Pecker	Jack		Powell	Talmadge	W
Peddicord	William	R	Powell	Harvie	C
Peek	Hugh	D	Preston	Lewis	W
Pelkey	Paul	E	Presutti	Robert	J
Pendley	Raymond	W	Provost	Marshall	L
Pepper	Bernard	M	Pryor	Charles	G
Perich	John	P	Pugh	Alvie	A
Perkins	Kenneth	W	Puglise	George	J
Perry	John	J	Purchase	Francis	A
Peseroff	Roy	I	Puskas	Louis	Z
Peters	Gerald	W	Putney	Hubert	A
Petersohn	George	J	Pyles	Charles	R
Peterson	William	J	Pyrtle, Jr.	William	C
Peterson	Andrew	C	Quinones	Samuel	
Petit	Leo	H	Raaen, Jr.	John	C
Petranek	John	J	Racette	Hubert	H
Petrich	Thomas	G	Rackley	Raymond	
Peyton	Walter	R	Ragsdale	Ralph	W
Phelps	Donald	H	Rahme	Eugene	D
Phillips	Duane		Rahmlow	John	L
Pickens, Jr.	Thomas	C	Rakofsky	William	C
Piekarz	Henry	P	Ranney	Burton	E
Pierard	Philipp	J	Ravitz	Adolph	D
Pierson	Albert	L	Raymond	Harlyn	D
Piette	Francis	J	Raymond, Jr.	Frank	H
Pinder	Joseph	E	Read	Clinton	O
Pirigyri	John	A	Recher	Otto	F
Piston	Joseph		Red	Doy	W
Pitts	Arthur	H	Reed, Jr.	Ellias	E
Piwko	Stanley	T	Reeves	Albert	E
Plaskon	Peter	J	Reeves	Jack	C
Pletka	Robert	A	Rehm	Michael	J

Reilley	William	F	Saum	Jack	H
Reiter	Leonard		Saxon	George	W
Remes	Joe	E	Scarbrough	John	J
Reville	John	J	Scerbo	Frank	F
Rich	Melvin	B	Schaeffer	Donald	R
Ritchie	Balis	L	Schan	Anton	J
Rivas	Steve	D	Schappert	Joseph	A
Robbins	Charles	L	Schele	John	E
Roberts	Ted	O	Schneider	Max	F
Roberts	Alan		Schopp	Dan	D
Robinson	John	N	Schroh	Walter	D
Robinson	Abe	W	Schwendner	William	J
Rock	Louis		Scott	William	
Rogers	Fredie	E	Scoville	Montgomery	C
Rogers	Samuel	E	Seaman	Henry	R
Rogers	Bernard	C	Sebloski	Andrew	J
Rogers	John	H	Seeley	Norman	C
Rogers	Lysle	L	Seidel	Gerald	E
Rohlin	David	W	Shafer	James	F
Roller	Nathan	H	Sharp	Jack	L
Ronan	John	M	Shaw, Jr.	William	J
Rooney	James	B	Sheotes	William	G
Rose	Andrew	J	Sheron	Edward	A
Rose, Jr.	Manuel	R	Sherrill	James	R
Rosenblad	Orvylle	A	Shilling	Elmer	P
Ross	Stanley	T	Shingleton	Thurman	W
Roy	Bertrand	J	Shultz	John	N
Royle	James	E	Siatkowski	Francis	A
Rozakis	Peter		Sichak	Nick	
Rubin	Paul	F	Siegel	Samuel	
Rucker	Lewis	W	Sievers	Rowland	E
Rumfelt	Paul	J	Sigler	Gerald	H
Runge	William	M	Simmons	Aubrey	L
Rupczyk	Frederick		Simonette	Nicholas	J
Rush	Winfred	D	Simonowicz	Frank	S
Rutkowski	Edward	H	Skrba	Martin	J
Ryals	Ralph	A	Sloboda	Thomas	T
Ryan	Lawrence	H	Slowik	Theodore	
Ryan	Wilsie	A	Smart	Donald	C
Sack	Herman	F	Smitch	Jordan	D
Saffert	Edward	L	Smith	Woodrow	W
Salvaggi	Philip		Smith	Harold	I
Samborowski	Leo	G	Smith	Erton	
Sanford	Joseph	W	Smith	Russell	L
Santes	Henry		Smith	Lawrence	E

Smith	Sherby	L	Sullivan, Jr.	James	L
Smith	Glen	V	Summers, Jr.	Leon	
Smith	Ellwood		Surowitz	Joseph	J
Smith, Jr.	Noel	C	Sutton	Edward	E
Smolarek	John	C	Swartmiller	Leo	F
Smolich	Louis		Swazey	Vaughn	R
Sneed, Jr.	James	W	Sweeney	Albert	F
Snook	Harold	R	Swiader	Henry	
Snyder	Jack	A	Switay	Albin	F
Snyder	Emmet	W	Switch	Steve	
Soper	James	F	Szerecz	Stephen	
Sorensen	Swen		Table	Loza	W
Sorenson	Richard	T	Tagge	Roy	A
Sorkin	Leonard		Talley	Clyde	W
Soyars, Jr.	James	E	Tarlano	Chester	A
Spero	Allen	W	Tayler	Jesse	J
Spier	Andrew	L	Taylor	William	G
Spring	Bernard	V	Taylor	Oscar	L
Springer	Frederick	R	Taylor	Daniel	R
Spurlock	John	B	Taylor	William	G
Stahl	Louis	N	Templeton	Calvin	O
Stanfield	Gilbert	G	Terruso	Joseph	R
Steffen	William	E	Tervo	John	H
Stein	Robert	F	Thibodeau	Maurice	V
Stienen	Robert	C	Thigpen, Jr.	Elbert	
Stemmler	Robert	E	Thomas	Philipp	V
Stephens	Gaylord	M	Thomas	William	P
Sterling	Earle	S	Thomas	Joseph	C
Stevenson	James	R	Thompson	William	R
Stine	Donald	E	Thompson	Lawrence	O
Stockmaster	Andrew	L	Thornhill	Avery	J
Stofega	Edward	P	Tice	William	C
Stone	Henry	O	Tilley	Patrick	D
Stone	Dwight	H	Tobin, Jr.	John	J
Stone	Arthur	H	Toler	Billy	G
Stoneburg	Ernest	N	Tomainolo	Anthony	J
Stover	Harold	W	Tomaso	John	
Stowe	Oscar	R	Tomlinson	Clifford	M
Striker	Herbert	L	Toth	John	J
Stucker	Robert	E	Totin	Nick	
Stump	William	A	Townsend	Marvin	H
Stuyvesant	Herman	W	Trahan	Wilfred	J
Styles	Clarence	A	Trainor	Richard	J
Suchier, Jr.	Oscar	A	Travers	John	J
Sullivan	Richard	P	Traxler	Albert	D

Zelepsky	Stanley	D	Ziemsky	Leopold	
Zidjunas	Frank	E	Zifcak	Michael	G
Ziehme	Harold	H	Zima	Albin	J

SIXTH RANGER INFANTRY BATTALION

Last Name	First Name	Initial	Last Name	First Name	Initial
Aagaard	Kenneth	M	Biggs	Edward	L
Ablott	Vernon		Bishop	Lyle	C
Adams	Donald	A	Blandford	Robert	L
Adams	William	B	Blannett	John	D
Allen	Harvey	C	Bleak	Newton	
Allen	James	C	Boles	Ernest	T
Allen	Narvel		Boman	Joe	A
Allen	Rex	W	Bosard	Charles	H
Allen	Virgil	V	Bowen	Vancil	
Almjeld	Clayton	I	Boyd	Ulis	L
Anderson	Dustin	S	Brady	Eldridge	
Anderson	Floyd	L	Brewer	Leroy	
Anderson	Floyd	S	Britzius	Homer	E
Anderson	Keith	S	Britzman	Lee	W
Anderson	Robert	G	Brown	Charles	W
Anderson	Wallace	L	Brown	Jacob	B
Anyan	George	S	Brown	William	C
Arata	John	B	Bryant	William	X
Argubright	Joseph	L	Buckingham	Eldon	R
Arntsen	Arnold		Buckridge	Chester	W
Asche	Ferdinand	W	Burkhalter	James	A
Bagby	Austin	W	Burns	Frank	H
Ball	Warren	M	Butler	William	R
Barfield	Edward	L	Camp	Robert	L
Barnhart	Virgil		Cannon	Donald	J
Beane	Francis	P	Carbaugh	Alfred	H
Beckley	Glenn	L	Carter	Willard	L
Bell	Alfred		Castellaw	Harry	C
Bell	Edward	L	Champe	Atlee	B
Bell	Warren	M	Chaney	A	J
Bellinski	Robert	A	Chartrand	Francis	X
Benavidez	Cecillio		Christensen	Gerald	E
Benson	Jack	R	Clowes	William	J
Berg	Elmer	E	Conley	James	W
Bergum	Harold	J	Connor	Thomas	H
Bern	Leslie	S	Copenhaver	Lauren	W
Bernatz	Alfred	J	Crocker	Edward	
Berry, Jr.	William		Crumpton	William	F

Hey	David	M	Lemerond	LeRoy	J
Higgins	Norman	F	Lever	Norman	J
Hoffman	Gilbert	A	Lilipop	Ralph	T
Hogan	William	J	Littleton	Edward	
Holden	Palmer		Lombardo	Joseph	
Holmes	Eugene		Looney	Oral	E
Howell	Claude	R	Lopata	Chester	A
Howell	James		Lopianetzky	Steve	
Hudoba	Frank	C	Love	Lee	R
Hughes	F	J	Lowe	Boyd	E
Hummermeir	Karl	E	Lpanowski	Frank	
Hunter	Ivan	D	Lyman	Thomas	J
Hyde	Russell	O	Mace	George	E
Irvine, Jr.	James	M	Malone	Lester	L
Jackson	George	B	Marquis	Patrick	F
James	Boyce	O	Martin	Alfred	A
Jannicke	Herman	F	Mattson	Donald	E
Jensen	Preston	N	Mattson	Edmund	G
Jinkins	Alymer	C	Maxwell	Fred	J
Jochims	Arlo	T	McAllister	Richard	B
Karolchik	Stephen		McCormick	Alfred	D
Keith	Charles	E	McCue	Lloyd	E
Killough	Harry	G	McElroy	Billy	
Kinder	Marvin	W	McGinnis	Alfred	J
King	Charles	M	McGuire	James	B
King	Glenn	M	McHoes	Robert	C
Kiser	Vance	O	McIntire	Lester	H
Kluever	Henry		Meacham	Gerald	
Kluver	Elmer		Meany	Owen	M
Knarr	Glenn	A	Melendez	Ralph	C
Knowles	Edward	N	Mendenhall	Wilkins	S
Kocsis	Eugene	J	Michaelson	Harold	W
Kohout, Jr.	Edward	W	Millican	James	V
Koren	Mike		Minor	Elmer	P
Kosmicki	Alphonse		Mitties	Maynard	W
Kozacik, Jr.	Nicholas	S	Mohr	Charles	E
Kragness	Oliver	A	Moles	Clarence	
Kuchenbecker	Walter	O	Mollenkamp	Herbert	C
Kutac, Jr.	Ludwig	J	Moore	Richard	A
Kuykendall	Marioni		Morre	David	T
Lacasse	Lawrence	J	Mortensen	Milo	C
LaLande	Eli	T	Most	Norton	S
Lander	Edwin	H	Motley	Olen	H
Larson	Alfred	N	Mucci	Henry	A
Lawyer	William	A	Mueggenberg	Paul	B
Ledbetter	Mack		Murphy	John	F

Myerhoff	Leroy	B	Reynolds	James	M
Needing	Robert	E	Rhodes	Clarence	C
Nelson	John	W	Richardson	John	B
Nelson	Ward	L	Richardson	Johnnie	U
Neubauer	Paul	L	Richardson	Theodore	R
Neville	James	W	Riedinger	Lawrence	
Nicholsen	Wayne	O	Riesen	Paul	F
Norris	William	J	Rising	Harold	H
Norton	Cleatus	G	Roades	Jack	
Nundahl	Orville	E	Robbins	Alvie	E
O'Connell	William	J	Robbins	James	R
Olen	Glen	W	Robbins	William	A
Outwater, Jr.	Albert	F	Roberts	Hollis	H
Ozbold	Joseph	F	Roberts	Orvil	R
Palmatier	Alfred	A	Robeson	Henry	A
Palomares	John	G	Rongstad	Reuben	V
Paluck	Edward		Rowzee	Homer	H
Parker	James	W	Rubie	Edgar	L
Patterson	Albert	F	Ruehle	Math	E
Pearson	John	V	Rutledge	Arthur	C
Peters	Jack	A	Sales	Edward	N
Peters	Roy	B	Sandusky	Chester	H
Pfeifer	Albert	J	Schemmel, Jr.	Andrew	M
Phillips	Victor	H	Schilli	Francis	R
Picotte	Thomas	E	Schmidt	Ervin	I
Pinkston	Sydney		Schmidt	Louis	H
Pirkle	J	A	Schmidt	Melville	R
Pledger	Clifford	F	Schroer	Carl	B
Polzine	Alva	A	Sebeck	Roy	D
Popenhagen	Henry	E	Sharp	Rex	
Pospishil	Joseph	M	Shearer	Melvin	P
Prince	Robert	W	Shearon	Joe	J
Priphard	Paul	L	Shears	Vance	R
Propes	Grady	E	Shew	James	H
Proudfit	William	H	Smith	Clifford	K
Provencher	Leland	A	Smith	Elton	R
Prunelle	Arthur	L	Smith	Jack	A
Purtell	Merrie	K	Smith	Loyd	R
Purvis	Leslie	W	Smith	Walter	W
Ramsey	Robert	L	Smith	William	J
Randall	George	H	Snow	Alvie	
Reed	Berkley	A	Snyder	Charles	Q
Reese	Verle	D	Solf	Conrad	J
Reidinger	Lawrence		Southworth	Kenneth	J
Rennerfeldt	Stanley		Spencer	Burnam	
Renteria	Joseph		Spicer	Buford	K

Last Name	First Name	Initial	Last Name	First Name	Initial
Sritzius	Homer	E	Vavak	Franklin	J
St. John	Frank	F	Vincent	Louis	D
Staples	Wayne		Vrbancic	Walter	W
Staton	Mack		Wagner	Albert	M
Steele	Willard	G	Walczak	Frank	
Stern, Jr.	August	T	Watson	Clarence	
Stevens	Robert	H	Watson	Daniel	H
Stewart	Manton	P	Watson	Ralph	
Stinson	Norman	E	Way	Richard	E
Stoner	Donald	E	Webb	Leon	E
Strandfeldt	Robert	E	Webster	Virgil	E
Straube	Robert	C	Wellenbrock	Lester	H
Stryeski	Henry	M	Wentland	Leo	M
Sturges	Donald	C	Westmoreland	Jasper	T
Superak	Peter	P	Whisenhunt	Paul	C
Swain	Charles	S	White	James	O
Swank	Russell	J	White	Robert	W
Sweezy	Roy	W	Wiessbeck	John	
Thomas	Ronald	R	Wilcmen	Floyd	T
Thompson	Curtis	O	Will	Raymond	
Thompson	Dewey	M	Willenbring	Richard	V
Thompson	Guy		William	Robert	E
Threlkeld	Estel	L	Williams	Arthur	T
Tiede	Gerhard	J	Williams	John	T
Tilley	Marvin	K	Williams	Oliver	G
Toredel	Leslie	R	Williams	Ray	E
Tracz	Stanley	W	Williams	Robert	E
Trombetti	Gino		Willis	John	T
Trujillo	Edumenio	A	Wilson	James	H
Truskowski	Alexander	H	Wilson	Roy	D
Tucker	James	M	Workman	Marvin	R
Twiss	Cort	A	Youngblood	Carroll	E
Urban	Edwin	R	Youngblood	Joseph	O
Valentine, Jr.	Robert		Zufall	Darwin	
Van Sambeck	Henry	L	Zvacek	Rynold	

RANGER FORCE HEADQUARTERS

Last Name	First Name	Initial	Last Name	First Name	Initial
Avedon	Herbert		Blodgett	Howard	A
Bailey	Emmett	J	Cain	Joseph	J
Balcom	Charles	I	Cain	William	J
Barry	Lawrence	W	Cashman	Neil	S
Bigelow	Donald	L	Charlton, Jr.	Thomas	M

Contrera	Carlo		
Creed	George	H	
Dammer	Herman	W	
Darby	William	O	
Darbyshire	Charles	R	
Davey	Otis	W	
DiSantis	Anthony	V	
Farrell	Charles	S	
Fernandez	Adelfio		
Fitzhugh	Norman	R	
Franzinger	Robert	F	
Gonzalez	Charles	P	
Gray	James	E	
Guertin	Paul	E	
Haines	Owen	R	
Hall, Jr.	Harry	E	
Hoffhines	John	R	
Huckle	William	J	
Jackson	Gordon Mr. (Red Cross)		
Jett	Roger	W	
Johnson	Lester	R	
Jordan	Harold	B	
Karbel	Howard	W	
Kerecman	Michael		
Ketchens	William		E
Legg	Sherman		L
Luthe	William		F
Maginn	Francis		T
Mahoney	Edwin		
Martin	William		E
McCormic	Paul		D
McLain	LeRoy		J
Merrill	Von		D
Mossberg	Stanley		
Murphy	William		E
Pierce	Raymond		B
Pohopin	Mike		
Rapp	Joseph		P
Reasland	Joseph		C
Reeve	James		O
Roach	George		M
Roberts	Lewis		
Schwager	Owen		
Scoville	John		H
Shain	Edward	W	W
Stroud	Pressley	W	P
Swanson	Robert	P	E
Van Skoy	John	E	R

ENDNOTES

Space limits the number of Rangers whose service and life after World War II can be summarized. Those that follow are intended to represent the totality of this brave band of brothers.

CHAPTER 1

1. William O. Darby. As the first leader of the Rangers of World War II, Darby set the standard and the example. He was the right man for the job. After leaving the Rangers, Darby commanded the 179th Infantry, then was assigned to the operations division of the general staff in Washington, DC. He became assistant division commander of the 10th Mountain Division and was killed by German artillery in Italy on April 5, 1945. He was posthumously promoted to brigadier general. Bill Darby has become a Ranger legend, an almost godlike figure to many. This does a disservice to the struggle of this man who was a hard-nosed commander, dedicated and inspired. Rangers remember that, even in the presence of senior officers, it was Darby's personality that dominated.

2. Herman Dammer. After fighting in the Korean War, Herman Dammer retired as a colonel. Dammer deserves considerable credit for the success of Darby's Rangers. He served in the critical positions of executive officer and operations officer of the 1st Ranger Battalion, commander of the 3d Ranger Battalion, and as executive officer and operations officer of the Ranger Force. Long after Bill Darby's death, Herm Dammer remained a loyal friend. Dammer always praises others, never himself. I have never known Dammer to extol his own considerable talent. Robert E. Lee

said that "Duty is the sublimest word in the English language." Herm Dammer's service defines the word duty.

CHAPTER 2

1. According to Jim Altieri and other Rangers, the speed march was the heart of World War II Ranger training.

2. Most of the Rangers interviewed preferred fighting Germans to eating English food. Food was the major complaint of the Achnacarry phase of the Ranger experience.

CHAPTER 3

1. Recommended in-depth reading about the Dieppe raid is *Dieppe: The Shame and the Glory* by Terance Robertson, Little Brown Co., Boston, 1962.

2. Bill Brady retired from the army as a colonel, settled in Texas and was involved in civil defense. Brady was the nineteenth president of the Ranger Battalions Association.

3. Marcell Swank retired from the army as a colonel, settled in Texas and became an educator. Swank's research on American participation in the Dieppe raid was of significant help in this work. Among the Dieppe questions that remain are:

A. When the initial operation (code name RUTTER) was reinstated (as Operation JUBILEE), why were none of the nineteen Rangers (seven officers and twelve enlisted men) who had trained with the Canadians from June 19 until July 11 included in the Rangers who were sent?

Marcell Swank believes it was "a matter of readiness." The men who were sent on June 19 to the Canadians had not yet received Commando training. By the time the raid became reality, the Rangers who participated had received their Achnacarry training. The men who went with the Canadians on June 19 missed several weeks of training under the Commandos. It is possible that they were not sent for this reason.

B. Why did Lieutenant Flanagan's group not receive orders until August 15, leaving them no time to become part of the Canadian units to which they were attached?

Marcell Swank believes that the six Americans who went with the Canadians were "an afterthought token force" based on "a political decision." "The role of the Rangers with the Canadians," wrote Swank, "was one of tag-along observer with no purposeful mission."

CHAPTER 4

1. The great shortcoming of the Ranger experience has been the lack of public awareness. Throughout history, this has hurt the Rangers during times of military cutback. The writings of Robert Rogers and Jim Altieri, the photographs of Phil Stern, and the tapes of Lou Lisko have done much to fill this void of knowledge.

2. The soft-spoken Ed Dean rose from the ranks to command a company. He settled on a farm in Missouri.

3. A provisional unit is a temporary unit in the eyes of the army. Men serve, fight, and die in these units yet their battle honors, their lineage, is not continued. Much progress has been made, but the American Army still has a long road to travel in understanding the importance of tradition to the soldier.

4. Decorated Rangers included Leslie M. Ferrier, Austin W. Low, Gerrit J. Resink, Donald G. McCollam, Edwin L. Dean, Joseph Dye, Jacques M. Nixon, Leonard F. Dirks, Mervin T. Heacock, Max F. Schneider, Roy A. Murray, Herman Dammer, and William Darby.

5. After the war, Joe Fineberg turned his knowledge of acquiring things to a profitable war-surplus business. He also collects and repairs art, is involved in charitable activities and dancing, and divides his time between Philadelphia and Palm Beach.

CHAPTER 5

1. The 83d Chemical Mortar Battalion. The 4.2-inch mortar was designed to fire white phosphorous, high-explosive, and smoke rounds, all of which were considered toxic chemical rounds. The 4.2-inch mortar was most effective— and famous—for its deadly high-explosive rounds.

2. James Earl Rudder and the 2d Ranger Battalion were made for each other. Born in Texas, he achieved fame in

World War II. He retired from the army as a major general and became president of Texas A & M University.

3. A bivouac area is a place of rest in the field for military units. It is normally away from the battlefield.

4. The Truscott trot was a long, sustained, ground-eating stride that Ranger Jim Altieri called "our secret weapon."

CHAPTER 6

1. Interdictory and harassing fire is designed to keep the enemy off balance. The enemy never knows when a trail or crossroad will be fired upon just because it is there.

2. The collection and registration and, where possible, identification of dead bodies from a battlefield is the mission of graves registration units.

3. Roy Murray retired from a distinguished army career as a colonel. Murray did much to shape the Rangers of World War II. He was intellectually, physically, and morally courageous. His recommendations have proven valid over decades.

CHAPTER 7

1. The diary of Maj. Gen. John Lucas is a fascinating study of a senior officer's innermost thoughts while under great stress. It may be found at the United States Army Military History Institute, Carlisle Barracks, Pennsylvania.

2. The main line of resistance was the line of battle between the two ground armies in opposition to each other.

3. James Altieri rose through the ranks to become company commander of F Company, 4th Ranger Battalion. He has devoted his life to the Rangers. Author of *Darby's Rangers* and *The Spearheaders*, Altieri wrote the screenplay for the film *Darby's Rangers*. He has written numerous magazine and newspaper articles about the Rangers and was the ninth president of the Ranger Battalions Association. He resides in Southern California.

CHAPTER 8

1. Concertina wire is a form of barbed wire that comes in large, easily extended coils. It is an obstacle that is relatively easy for infantry to install.

2. Enfilade fire is fire that is coming from the flank, firing along the line of the enemy.

3. Max Schneider. One of the bright stars of the Rangers, Max rose from lieutenant to battalion commander with the Rangers. His D-day decision while commanding the 5th Rangers was critical to success. He died during the Korean War.

4. Ralph Goranson was company commander of Charlie Company, 2d Battalion, and his inspirational leadership carried over to a successful peacetime business career in motivating businessmen. He served as twelfth president of the Ranger Battalions Association.

5. Oerlikon machine guns. The Rangers were trained in the use of British landing craft and weapons.

6. Thermite grenades are incendiary. The heat they generate melts metal and will fuse moving parts of an artillery breechblock, rendering the gun useless.

CHAPTER 9

1. Sidney Salomon. My first meeting with Sid was at the WW II Ranger reunion in Washington. There was a stir in the lobby, and men began to call out his name. A slender, well-dressed, distinguished-looking man of approximately seventy years of age approached. It was Sid Salomon, and he was carrying several world-class medals he had just won for rowing. That's Sid Salomon. He served as sixteenth president of the Ranger Battalions Association.

2. James Eikner. Ike was the communicator of Rudder's Rangers. After the war, he returned to a successful career as a communications engineer with Southwest Bell Telephone Company.

3. Len Lomell, Distinguished Service Cross winner, was a fighter and a leader, who exemplified the can-do spirit of the Rangers. Lomell became a very successful lawyer in Toms River, New Jersey. He served as tenth president of the Ranger Battalions Association.

4. Lou Lisko of Brackenridge, Pennsylvania, became the historian of the World War II Rangers. Always seen with a tape recorder and more recently a video camera, Lou Lisko has performed a valuable service in the recording of Ranger history.

5. William "L-Rod" Petty. Some of the great moments in researching this book were spent with this combat soldier and his buddy Herm Stein. They keep a wary eye on a historian for what they term "bullshit." Bill Petty lives in New York State, where he ran a camp for underprivileged children.

6. Joseph Lacy. The gallant Ranger chaplain won the Distinguished Service Cross. After the war, he returned to Hartford, Connecticut, where he rose to monsignor in the Roman Catholic Church. He died May 18, 1990, at age 77.

7. Signal Operating Instructions include the assigned primary and alternate radio frequencies to be used by units and the call designators or signs they are to use. They are changed frequently. If a unit does not have the proper SOI, the result can be disaster.

8. Herman Stein went back to Fort Pierce, Florida, and became a roofer. Stein, who is known affectionately by Bill Petty as "my pet ape," was one of the best climbers in the Rangers. Forty years after D-day, Herm Stein proved he could climb Pointe du Hoc faster than young Rangers.

CHAPTER 10

1. Henry "Hank" Mucci. The man who turned a 75mm pack howitzer artillery unit into a Ranger battalion retired from the army as a colonel. For some time, Mucci had an automobile agency. He is now reported to be retired and living in Florida.

2. A howitzer is an artillery piece with a trajectory that is midrange between the flat-fire of a gun and the high-angle-fire of a mortar.

CHAPTER 11

1. Arthur D. "Bull" Simons. This 6th Ranger Battalion officer became a colonel and a special operations legend. During the war in Vietnam, he led a valiant attempt to rescue American prisoners, and he was later involved in operations to free hostages in the Middle East. Before his death, he became a farmer involved in raising livestock.

CHAPTER 12

1. William Anderson. Bill Anderson represents all the brave Rangers that space has not permitted me to record. Anderson was a private, busted from sergeant. He had a quick mind, was fast with his fists, and could not resist tweaking authority whenever and wherever a mistake was made. Bill Anderson was a leader, a fighter, a private who understood how to use terrain and supporting fire. He died in battle—up front.

2. Private Bouchard survived his wound.

CHAPTER 14

1. Richard P. Sullivan was a top-notch commander of the 5th Ranger Battalion through most of its combat experience. Sullivan had served as executive officer of the 5th Rangers and executive officer of the D-day Ranger group. He retired from the army as a colonel and settled in Massachusetts.

2. Jim Greene retired from the army as a colonel and settled in central Pennsylvania. He is a leading authority on military insignia and has done valuable work in cataloging and preserving insignia at the U.S. Army Military History Institute.

CHAPTER 15

1. The Rangers saw themselves as liberators, and at times, this meant liberating a chicken or a bottle of cognac. Herm Stein told of freeing up two suitcases filled with preserves from a German farm, only to have them confiscated by a non-Ranger colonel.

CHAPTER 16

1. Robert "Woody" Garrett, executive officer and commander of the 6th Ranger Battalion, retired from the army as a colonel and lives in the Washington, D.C., area.

BIBLIOGRAPHY

Altieri, James. *Darby's Rangers*. Durham, North Carolina: Seaman Printery Inc., 1945.

Altieri, James. *The Spearheaders*. New York: Bobbs-Merrill Co., 1960.

Bingham, J.K.W. and Warner Haupt. *North African Campaign 1940–1943*. English version, London: Macdonald and Co., 1969.

Bradley, Omar. *A Soldier's Story*. New York: Holt, 1951.

Churchill, Winston S. *Their Finest Hour*. Boston: Houghton Mifflin Co., 1949.

Combined Operations, The Official Story of the Commandos. n.a. New York: The Macmillan Co., 1943.

Cook, Graeme. *Commandos in Action*. London, Hart-David, MacGibbon, 1973.

Darby, William and O'Baumer, William H. *Darby's Rangers, We Led the Way*. San Rafael, CA: Presidio Press, 1980.

Department of the Army Historical Division. *Anzio Beachhead*. Nashville: The Battery Press, 1986.

Deposition of Hugh Cole at Plymouth Court, A.D. 1670, Collection of the Massachusetts Historical Society of the Year 1799. Series 1 VI of the First Series 2nd Ed. Boston: Freeman and Bolles 1800. Reprinted C. Little and James Brown, 1846.

Eisenhower, Dwight D. *Crusade in Europe*. New York: Doubleday and Co., Inc., 1952.

Haggerty, Jerome. *History of the Ranger Battalions of World War II,* Doctoral Dissertation Fordham University, 1981.

Ingersoll, Ralph. *The Battle is the Pay-Off*. London: John Lane, The Bodley Head, 1943.

Jackson, W.G.F. *The Battle for Italy*. New York and Evanston: Harper and Rowe, 1967.

Johnson, Forrest Bryant. *Hour of Redemption, The Ranger Raid on Cabanatuan*, New York: Manor Books Inc., 1978.

Journals of Major Robert Rogers. New York: Corinth Books, 1961.

King, Michael J. *Leavenworth Papers, Rangers: Selected Combat Operations in World War II*. Fort Leavenworth, Kansas Combat Studies Institute, June 1985.

King, Michael J. *William Orlando Darby, a Military Biography*. Archon Books, Hamden, Connecticut, 1981.

Robertson, Terence. *Dieppe, The Shame and The Glory*. Little, Brown and Company, Boston, Toronto, 1962.

Thompson, R. W. *At Whatever Cost, The Story of the Dieppe Raid*. Coward-McCann Inc. New York, 1956.

Truscott, Lt. Gen. Lucian King, Jr. *Command Missions: A Personal Story*. New York: E. P. Dutton and Co., 1954.

Vaughn-Thomas, Wynfordd. *Anzio*. Lowe and Brydone (Printers) Ltd., London, 1961.

UNIT HISTORIES

Danger Forward. The Story of the First Division in World War II. Albert Love Enterprises. Atlanta, 1947.

History of the Third Infantry Division in World War II. Washington, Infantry Journal Press, 1947.

29 Let's Go! A History of the 29th Infantry Division in World War II by Joseph Ewing, Washington Infantry Journal Press, 1948.

History of the 94th Infantry Division in World War II, Edited by Lieutenant Laurence G. Byrnes. Nashville. The Battery Press, 1949.

LETTERS

From Gen. Theodore J. Conway.

From Col. Herman Dammer

From Col. Roy Murray

From Col. Richard Sullivan

From Rangers Altieri, Petty, Stein, Lomell, Lisko, Sharp, Evans, Swank, Sommers.

MISCELLANEOUS SOURCES

Tapes of interviews conducted by Ranger Lou Lisko, Historian, Ranger Battalions of World War II Association.

Video cassette tapes provided by Rangers Lisko, Lomell, and Swank.

Personnel interviews with over forty Rangers who served in World War II.

Combat notes, after-action reports, messages, training guides, diaries, morning reports, narratives, and lectures obtained from the files of the National Archives in Suitland, MD; The U.S. Military History Institute, Carlisle Barracks, PA; The Infantry Center Library, Fort Benning, GA; and The Military Personnel Center, St. Louis, MO.

INDEX